1995

DALTONS DIRECTORY
of
BRITISH HOLIDAYS

Daltons Weekly

Published by
Daltons Weekly plc
C.I. Tower, St. George's Square, New Malden, Surrey, KT3 4JA
Tel: 0181-949-6199

A member of the United Newspapers Group

ISBN 0 903361 04 3   © Daltons Weekly plc

Cover pictures: Front – Gunnerside, Swaledale, N. Yorkshire.
Back – Harbour, Mevagissey, Cornwall.
Book Sales: John Wilson Booksales. Tel: (01884) 275927

un A United Newspapers publication

INTRODUCTION

"It's oh-so nice to go travelling – but it's so much nicer to come home." So sang Frank Sinatra.

But why not combine the two? After all, you can go travelling without having to stray too far from home because – no matter how often you've trekked round the world – you should still find time to discover what's on your own doorstep.

Most regions in the British Isles can boast sights and sounds, food and character, to match many a more exotic location – and you don't have to pay the price of jet-lag! Not that I escape that much. Little did I know that working on the Holiday Programme and breakfast television would have so much in common – one gives you jet-lag, the other just makes you 'feel' as if you have jet-lag!

To guide you through the riches that are available, this Daltons Directory of British Holidays is essential.

It's compiled by Daltons Weekly, the UK's leading holiday paper, so you can be sure it's packed with useful tips on where to go and what to do; as well as the latest information on all kinds of holiday accommodation, including hotels, guesthouses, self-catering, holiday parks, caravans, chalets and holidays afloat.

It couldn't be easier to hone in on a holiday that suits you. The classifications are clear and simple and divided into nine geographical areas.

To each of these areas I've written a short introduction to give you its profile in a nutshell. This is to remind you of what the territory covers; mountains, moors, lakes, rivers or seaside, as well as its history, towns and special attractions.

As you may know, Daltons Weekly is an established household name with over 120 years publishing experience and a reputation for offering the biggest selection of holidays in Britain – more than any other publication.

With that heritage, Daltons Directory of British Holidays is surely the most comprehensive you'll come across. So read it before you book – and have a wonderful holiday!

HOW TO USE THE DIRECTORY

Daltons Directory of British Holidays is simple to use with different types of accommodation clearly listed in alphabetical order by town name under county, Scotland or Wales headings.

Hotels and Guest Houses – includes farmhouses and all catered accommodation.

Self-Catering – a wide selection of all types of properties from Houses, Cottages and Bungalows to Flats, Flatlets and Apartments.

Caravans, Chalets and Holiday Parks – offers accommodation ranging from lively holiday parks often with full entertainment and facilities, to individual caravans in more secluded 'away from it all' locations.

Holidays Afloat – for those who seek the freedom of the waterways, whether by barge or cruiser, these can be found at the end of appropriate counties.

What's On – at the end of each county section includes just a small selection of the many places of interest you may wish to visit when taking that well deserved break.

Remember Phoneday – Sunday, 16th April, 1995 is Phoneday, every UK area code starting with 0 will start 01. When dialling outside your local area you will need to add the digit 1 after the 0. For instance 071 becomes 0171. Some of our advertisers have given new codes in their advertisements and these can be used prior to 16th April.

Five Cities receive an entirely new code, and digit followed by the existing local number:

Leeds	0532	>	(0113) 2
Sheffield	0742	>	(0114) 2
Nottingham	0602	>	(0115) 9
Leicester	0533	>	(0116) 2
Bristol	0272	>	(0117) 9

The choice is yours, we wish you a very happy holiday.

CONTENTS

SOUTH WEST ENGLAND

AVON • CORNWALL • DEVON • DORSET
SCILLY ISLES • SOMERSET • WILTSHIRE

The South West is the land of the famed "Six Counties" as well as the charming Scilly Isles!

The Scilly Isles themselves attract holidaymakers, who delight in a mild climate, palm trees and tropical plants. But, of course, the South West has many other, contrasting pleasures to offer. The county of Avon boasts two great cities: Bristol, with its exciting nightlife, and Bath, scene of Roman ruins and Georgian splendours, or if you do like to be beside the seaside there's Weston-super-Mare which is, for many, *the* resort when it comes to fun family holidays.

Cornwall's rugged north coast, with its exhilarating view of the Atlantic Ocean crashing against the shore, is a sight of natural beauty matched only by the windswept moors of the South West region – Dartmoor, Exmoor and Salisbury Plain. If bracing walks through lovely locations give you a healthy appetite, remember this isn't just the home of the Cheddar Gorge it's also the home of Cheddar cheese! And let's not forget – I know I won't – cider, cream, lamb, beef, seafood and other culinary delights...

This is a realm steeped in literary history. Where else can you read so many classics while savouring the atmosphere that inspired them? In Dorset alone, you can experience the old Wessex country that Thomas Hardy captured timelessly, and walk along the same dramatic Cob at Lyme Regis that was haunted by "The French Lieutenant's Woman". In addition, Cornwall boasts the brooding Bodmin Moor home of Daphne Du Maurier's "Jamaica Inn" and plentiful King Arthur legends. Indeed, Arthurian legends cast their magic spell over the entire region. For instance, Glastonbury, in Somerset, is reputed to be the final resting place of King Arthur and Lady Guinivere.

Add to this the sheer majesty of Stonehenge (the prime attraction of Salisbury Plain) and the charismatic Cerne Abbas giant (etched in chalk on the Dorset hills) and you can see that this is one of the most mystical and romantic corners of England.

My own family summer holiday of 1994 brought me to the edge of Salisbury Plain where it meets the charming whilst bustling town of Warminster. Warminster is the nearest large town to Longleat – home of the very adventurous, forward thinking if somewhat eccentric Marquess of Bath. Up until now his magnificent grounds, landscaped by Capability Brown, have been best known for the Safari park, and imposing Elizabethan mansion lying therein. But a new and futuristic leisure facility – the latest 'Center Parc' holiday village to open in Britain will prove to be an excellent hideaway nestling amongst the trees skirting one of the grandest estates to be seen in England.

The South West is equally noted for its naval history. Great ports like Bristol and Plymouth are memorably linked to the careers of Drake, Raleigh and Chichester; while Dartmouth features the grand Royal Naval College.

So, whether you want to ride the beaches of Newquay (the best surfing breaks in Britain, dude!) or trace the footsteps of Drake (without getting your feet wet) South West England has it all. And then some...

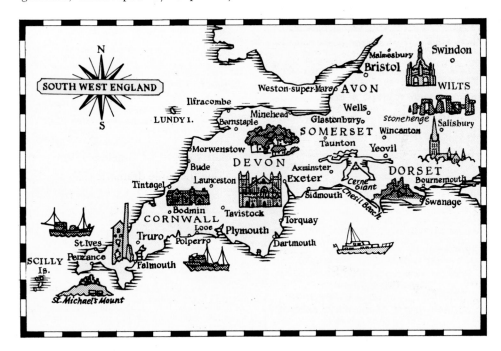

AVON

HOTELS & GUEST HOUSES

BATH (5 miles south). Green Lane House, Hinton Charterhouse. Originally three terraced 18th century stone cottages. Tastefully renovated and comfortably furnished bed and breakfast, combining traditional features with modern amenities. Rural setting in conservation village. Phone: (0225) 723631.

ASTOR HOUSE
14 Oldfield Road, Bath BA2 3ND
Elegant, comfortable and friendly guest house with good views, non-smoking, ¼ mile from Roman Baths and station. Colour TV, tea/coffee all rooms. Some en-suites, ample private parking, home produce. Superb varied breakfasts. Reasonable prices from £16.
Phone/Fax: Kathy and Rick Beech 01225 429134
RAC AA QQ ETB 2 Crown commended

BATH 10 miles. Longhope Guest House, Melksham. Large detached Victorian house. Private parking. Colour television. Tea makers in centrally heated double en-suite rooms. £58 2 persons for 2 nights bed and breakfast. No pets. Brochure Phone: (01225) 706737.

SANDBAY. 2 miles Weston super Mare. Friendly family run bungalow. Quiet, seafront position overlooking beautiful scenery. Lounge, tea making facilities. Television. Bed and breakfast from £12. Evening meal optional. Bookings from April 1st. Phone: (0934) 416994.

WESTON SUPER MARE. May Villa Guest House. Just off the seafront. No hills. Close to shops and all amenities. Home from home accommodation. Long or short stay. Phone: Violet Farmer on 621722.

WESTON-SUPER-MARE. Small guest house. Good home cooking. Colour television, tea and coffee facilities. Access all times. Bed and breakfast from £10.50 daily, half board from £70 weekly. Phone: (0934) 633114 (after April 16th (01934) 633114).

SELF-CATERING

BATH. Small terrace cottage for summer holiday rental. Situated close to city centre and near the river. Easy access from bus and rail terminals. Sleeping arranged in four bedrooms, one double, three singles. Phone: (01225) 316578.

BRISTOL, Bath 8 miles. 3 bedroomed self-catering oak beamed cottage with storage heating. Also terraced bungalows. One or two bedroomed, sleeping 2/4. Quiet, peaceful rural setting. Fishing inclusive. No pets. Phone: (01761) 490281.

TOGHILL HOUSE FARM
BATH 5 MINUTES
Warm and cosy barn conversions sleeping 2-4 on working farm. Just 4 miles from the historic city of Bath. Each cottage is equipped to a high standard. With every modern convenience. The lovely garden is surrounded by farm land where you are welcome to walk amongst the animals.

Price per week from £120-£300 including bed linen and towels.

CONTACT: DAVID OR JACKIE BISHOP

TOGHILL HOUSE FARM, WICK, BRISTOL
TEL: 01225 891261

COMPTON MARTIN, near Bristol. Quiet two double bedroom country cottage overlooking Chew Valley Lake. All inclusive. Linen provided. Oil fired Aga cooker, television. Trout fishing, good touring base or relaxing. Mrs Dury Phone: (0761) 221424.

UBLEY. Two comfortable cottages on dairy farm. Beautiful Mendip countryside, close Wells, Cheddar, Bath, Weston. Ideal walking, fishing, bird-watching. Fully equipped except linen. Personal supervision. Sae Perry, Cleve Hill Farm, Ubley near Bristol, Avon. Phone: (0761) 462410.

WESTON-SUPER-MARE. Kenwood House. Self-contained holiday flats. Close to seafront and town centre. Fully furnished, colour television. Suitable for 2-6 persons. £80-£150 per week. Chambers, Upper Church Road, Weston-super-Mare BS23 2HY. Phone: (0934) 621286.

WESTON-SUPER-MARE. Harbour holiday flats. Ideally situated on seafront overlooking harbour. 1 or 2 bedrooms, fully equipped and en-suite. For details and brochure write Woodbridge, 10 Stafford Road, Weston-Super-Mare, Avon BS23 3BW. Phone: (0934) 621122.

CARAVANS, CHALETS & HOLIDAY PARKS

WESTON SUPER MARE two miles. Privately owned, 3 bedroom, self-contained caravan on ETB registered site. Licensed club, heated pool, children's pool, play area, launderette, shop. Live entertainment in high season. Dogs welcome. Phone: (0249) 656468.

WESTON-SUPER-MARE. Ardnave Holiday Park, Kewstoke, Weston-super-Mare BS22 9XJ. For hire, deluxe caravans with shower, toilet. Colour television. 2/3 bedrooms. For sale, deluxe second hand caravans. Pets, Touring caravans welcome. British Graded 4 ticks. Phone: Mr & Mrs C.G. Thomas (0934) 622319.

WHERE TO GO

Bristol Zoo
Clifton, Bristol.
Tel: (0272) 738951
Attractions include, tigers, lions, reptiles, monkeys, polar bears, elephants, aviaries, childrens corner. New aquarium, shops and cafeteria. Disabled visitors welcome.

The Exploratory Hands-on Science Centre
Bristol Old Station, Clock Tower Yard, Temple Gate, Bristol.
Tel: (0272) 252008
Exhibition of lights, lenses, lasers bubbles, bridges, illusions, gyroscopes and much more, all housed in Brunel's original engine shed and drawing office.

SS Great Britain
Great Western Dock, Gas Ferry Road, Bristol.
Tel: (0272) 260680
Now being restored in her original dock, SS Great Britain was the first ocean-going, screw-propelled iron ship in history. Designed by Brunel and launched 1843.

Roman Baths Museum
Pump Room, Abbey Church Yard, Bath.
Tel: (0225) 461111
Roman baths and temple precinct, hot springs and Roman monuments. Jewellery, coins, curses and votive offerings from the sacred spring.

Victoria Art Gallery
Bridge Street, Bath.
Tel: (0225) 461111 ext 2775
Bath's city art gallery houses collections of eighteenth to twentieth century British and European paintings, prints and watercolours. It runs a programme of high quality temporary exhibitions in the recently refurbished exhibitions gallery on the ground floor. Admission free.

CORNWALL

HOTELS & GUEST HOUSES

CHRISMAR

Situated near centre of the village yet in a quiet road over-looking countryside. Hot and cold, one with private shower. TV, tea and coffee facilities, central heating all rooms. Central to coast and moors.

Wadebridge Road, St. Mabyn, Bodmin, Cornwall PL30 3BH
Tel: Mrs. Ruth Francis, 0208 841518
B.&B. from £10.50. D.B.&B. from £17.50

BODMIN. Come and visit us. Good food. A relaxing and friendly atmosphere, in beautiful countryside. Bed/breakfast, evening meal optional. Also self-catering annexe. Suitable 2 people. Central to coasts and Moors. Phone: (0208) 73747.

LANARTH

SMALL COUNTRY HOTEL ST. KEN HIGHWAY, BODMIN, CORNWALL PL30 3EE

Full licensed hotel set in 10 acres beautiful grounds with swimming pool. Rooms warm and comfortable, most facing south. TV, tea/coffee facilities etc. Ideal touring Cornwall and Devon nearby facilities including magnificent beaches, walks, golf, horse riding, surfing. Central heating. Open fire. Home cooking. Open all year.

B&B from £15
Evening Meal if required

01208 841215

BODMIN MOOR. Mill Park House. Bed and breakfast £10. Hot and cold, television lounge, bathroom, shower cubicle. Children half price, pets free. Woodland setting. Great for wildlife, bike and horse riding, also walking. Phone: (0208) 821397.

BODMIN
DENBY RIDING HOLIDAYS

In beautiful Camel Valley. Excellent facilities. Hacking, instruction on good horses to suit all abilities. Friendly atmosphere. Farmhouse accommodation or self catering cottage.

Mrs. D. Moore BHSAI,
Denby Farm, Nanstallon, Bodmin, Cornwall.
Tel: (01208) 72013

'ORANA' GUEST HOUSE

Lamorick, Lanivet, Bodmin, Cornwall PL30 5HB
Tel: Lanivet (01208) 831070
Bed & Breakfast Accommodation

Friendly family guest house set in large gardens, situated in **quiet** Cornish hamlet.

Plenty of off road parking, hot and cold in all rooms, free tea & coffee facilities. TV in lounge. Facilities for disabled.

A warm welcome and a good hearty breakfast is our speciality.

Lanivet is the centre of Cornwall,
$13^1/_2$ *miles from both South and North coasts.*
an ideal touring base.

FARMHOUSE ACCOMMODATION
HIGH CROSS FARM
LANIVET, BODMIN, CORNWALL PL30 5JR

 91-acre dairy farm, situated in the geographical centre of Cornwall. Three bedrooms with vanity units, separate dining room and TV lounge. Traditional farmhouse breakfast. Friendly atmosphere.

Optional evening meal. Approved by C.T.B.

Bed and Breakfast £13 nightly
Tel: 01208 831341
Mrs. Joy Rackham

BOSCASTLE. Relax in beautiful 300 year old former coach-house. All rooms en-suite. Colour televisions, clock radios, tea makers. Private car park and magnificent scenery. Warm and welcoming with friendly helpful owners. Disabled facilities. Phone: (01840) 250398.

BOSCASTLE. St. Christopher's Hotel, North Cornwall. Overlooking beautiful unspoilt National Trust harbour village of Boscastle. Comfortable, small Georgian hotel offers stepping stone to Cornwall's most picturesque beauty spots. Home cooking. Clifftop and valley walks. Phone: (01840) 250412.

BOSCASTLE. Pencarmol Guest House. Uninterrupted views of National Trust harbour. Ideal base for walkers, art enthusiasts, surfers, bird watchers. High standard bed/breakfast accommodation in restored Georgian Grade II listed house. En-suite available. Phone: (0840) 250435.

BUCKLAWREN FARMHOUSE
Bucklawren is situated in the countryside by the sea. Excellent B&B accommodation with sea views, en-suites plus colour TV. Evening dinner. Weekly rates.
Bucklawren Farmhouse, St. Martin by Looe, Cornwall PL13 1NZ.
Tel: Mrs. Jean Henly (01503) 240738

If you would like to find out how
Daltons Directory
could work for you simply telephone
0181-949 6199
for advertising rates and information

BUDE. Travellers friend. En-suite rooms over-looking golf course. All rooms colour television, tea and coffee making facilities. Bed and breakfast. Reasonable rates. Reduced for 3 days or more. Open all year. Phone: (0288) 355059.

BUDE. Friendly, family run guest house. Beautiful views. Gardens. Plenty of good food. Colour television in rooms. Free parking. Very reasonable rates. Children welcome. Ground floor bedrooms. For brochure, Marham Rise, 50 Kings Hill. Phone: (0288) 354713.

CAMBORNE near. Vellynsaundry. Comfortable country house with pleasant views. Guest sitting room and kitchen. Tea making facilities etc. Easy access north and south coast, beaches. Ideal centre for touring/walking. Very reasonable rates. Phone: Ellis (0209) 712983.

CAMELFORD. Countryman Hotel. Friendly, fam-ily run licensed hotel. All rooms with colour television and tea making facilities. En-suite accommodation available. Bowood Golf Course, Bodmin Moor, coastal footpath nearby. Open all year. Home cooking. Phone: (0840) 212250.

BUDE, Crackington Haven. Superb en-suite bed and breakfast accommodation on National Trust coast farm. Quiet position, wonderful views. Beaches and coast path within easy walking distance. Prices £13.50 - £16.50. Brochure Mrs. Crocker, Tregather Farm. Phone: (01840) 230667.

BUDE, Ciyth. Cottage. Four poster. Bed, break-fast. En-suite facilities. Self-catering cottage and caravan. Ideal for those seeking peace and quiet. Close to coast path, sandy beaches. Joyner, Penrose Dizzard, St. Gennys, Bude, Cornwall. Phone: (01840) 230318.

BUDE. Holiday with us. Enjoy the friendly atmosphere. Lovely situation, few minutes walk town centre, beaches. Hot, cold, tea making facilities, television lounge. Garden. Private parking. Bed and breakfast £16.00. Seaview, Killerton Road. Phone: (0288) 352665.

CARBIS BAY, St. Ives. Endsleigh. Family run Guest House. Offering comfort, cleanliness, warm welcome. Large car park. Close buses, shops, local beach. For a holiday at a price you can afford. Phone: Stella Noon, (01736) 795777.

CRACKINGTON HAVEN. Bed, breakfast in fifteenth century farmhouse, one mile from Atlantic coast. North of Boscastle, Tintagel. All rooms with private facilities. ETB 2 crown commended. For details phone Pat Anthony, (01840) 230276.

CRANTOCK. Licensed hotel. Uninterrupted sea views, quaint village location. Four posters available. Superb a-la-carte menu. Bed and breakfast from £12.95. National Trust walks, horse riding nearby. Dogs welcome. Phone: (0637) 830424.

CRANTOCK, Cornwall. Glynn Heath. Quiet, licensed hotel. Glorious sea and country views. All rooms en-suite. Television/tea making facilities. Golf and horse riding nearby. Open from Easter. Bed and breakfast from £13.50. Phone: (0637) 830314.

EAST LOOE. Edwardian licensed family hotel overlooking harbour. Panoramic views. En-suite rooms. All facilities. Superb food, residents bar. Vegetarians welcome. Daily, weekly terms. Reductions children, senior citizens. Special breaks brochure available. Killarney Hotel. Phone: (0503) 262307.

FALMOUTH. Ivanhoe Guest House. An immaculate Edwardian House near beaches and centre. Warm comfortable en-suite rooms with television and all facilities. Parking. Pleasant lounge. Tempting choice for breakfast. Bed/breakfast from £16. Phone: (0326) 319083.

FALMOUTH. Comfortable bed and breakfast accommodation. Television, tea making facilities in bedrooms, some en-suite. Separate dining tables. Excellent cuisine. Prices from £13 per person per night. Mrs June Leggett, 11 Dracaema Avenue. Phone: (0326) 314521

HELSTON. Farmhouse. Bed and breakfast. Friendly, relaxed atmosphere on our working dairy farm. Picturesque Helford River just 2 miles. Lovely walks. Comfort and cleanliness assured. Visitors lounge with television. Mrs Jane Blee. Details Phone: (0326) 231292.

HELSTON near. Warwick House bed and breakfast. 4 miles Helston, 12 miles Penzance. Near beaches and coastal walks. Bed and breakfast £13 weekly, £85 optional evening meal. Phone: (0736) 763544.

LAUNCESTON. Between Dartmoor and the sea. Olde worlde cottage with beamed ceilings, open fireplaces, on two acre smallholding. Golf, fishing, horse riding, surfing etc. all close by. Bed and breakfast £12, evening meal optional. Phone: (0566) 785369.

LAUNCESTON. Bed and breakfast, full board. Near moors and sea. Ideal for walking and sight-seeing. En-suite, tea making facilities. Home from home. A welcome awaits you. Phone: (0566) 86426. Mary Rich, 'Nathania', Altarnun, Launceston, Cornwall PL15 7SL.

LIZARD PENINSULA. Mounts Bay House. Own grounds with view across Kynance Cove. Licensed. ETB 2 crown commended. Bed and breakfast from £18. Short break/weekly reductions. Access/Visa. Dogs welcome. Penmenner Road, The Lizard. Phone: (01326) 290305.

LOOE. ETB 2 crowns. Spacious character farmhouse in the beautiful West Looe Valley. Twin, double and family en-suite rooms with colour television, tea making facilities and comfy armchairs. Little Larnick Farm, Pelynt, Looe. Phone: (0503) 262837.

LOOE 4 miles. Bed and breakfast. Attractive 16th century farmhouse in peaceful, picturesque countryside. Guest television lounge. Bedrooms include hot and cold, tea making facilities. Beaches, golf, riding, fishing locally. Wills, Polgover Farm. Phone: (0503) 240248.

LOOE, Schooner Point. Family Guest House overlooking river. Most rooms offering splendid river and woodland views. Some en-suite, all with colour television. Close to town, beach and coastal paths. Limited parking. For brochure Phone: (01503) 262670.

LOOE. Duchy, licensed, friendly family guest house. Children welcome, some free. Open all year. Special breaks. Disabled facilities. Ample parking. Colour televisions, videos, tea making. Special diets. Laundry service. Robinson, West Looe Hill. Phone: (0503) 262664.

LOOE 6 miles. 200 acre working farm. Cattle, sheep, pony, play area for children. Bed and breakfast. En-suite rooms with tea/coffee facilities in room. Ideal for touring Devon/Cornwall. Brochure. Phone: (0579) 347155 or 62237.

LOOE. Stonerock Cottage Guest House. Bed and breakfast, hot and cold, television, hospitality trays. En-suite available. Parking. Clean and comfortable. Quiet location. 2 minutes beach, tennis, bowling. Coastal paths. From £15 per person. Phone: (0503) 263651.

LOOE. Fieldhead Hotel. Turn of the century house in 1.5 acres, overlooking the sea. 14 bedrooms, all en-suite with panoramic views. Intimate candlelit restaurant. Heated outdoor pool. Car park. Special breaks. Relax and enjoy yourselves. AA 2 star. Phone: (01503) 262689.

LOOE, near. 300 year old riverside mill. Most rooms overlooking river. Licensed bar and restaurant. Ideally situated for touring Devon and Cornwall. AA/RAC listed. Highly recommended. 'Old Mill House', Polbathic, Torpoint, Cornwall PL11 3HA. Phone: (0503) 30596.

LOOE. 'Kantara' Guest House. Friendly, relaxed atmosphere. Convenient for all amenities. All rooms satellite television, beverages, washbasin, unrestricted access. Ideal touring, walking, fishing, birdwatching base. Children and pets welcome. ETB approved. AA 'Q' recommended. Phone: (01503) 262093.

LOOE. Sundown. Comfortable bed and breakfast accommodation. All rooms en-suite. Colour television, tea and coffee making facilities. Ample parking. Access/Visa accepted. Also holiday apartments available (self-catering). 34 Goonwartha Road, West Looe, Cornwall. Phone: (0503) 263359.

MARAZION. 'Old Eastcliffe House'. Magnificent historic Georgian country house set in an acre of walled gardens, enjoying spectacular views of St. Michael's Mount and bay. Country Livings' 'highly recommended' award. Brochure Phone: Rosalie Havery (01736) 710298.

MEVAGISSEY, Lavorrick. Orchard Hotel. Friendly family run licensed hotel with private gardens and parking. Excellent home cooking. Mostly en-suite rooms with colour television and tea making facilities. Children and pets welcome. Colour brochure Phone: (0726) 842265.

MEVAGISSEY. Tregorran Guest House. An attractive detached house, overlooking village with extensive views. Three minutes from harbour, cliff top walks and beach. Comfortable rooms. Parking. Excellent food. Friendly atmosphere. Mrs Avril Lawrence, Cliff Street. Phone: (01726) 842319.

MEVAGISSEY. 17th century inn, situated on the beach at Portmellon Cove. All bedrooms en-suite, colour television, tea making facilities. English breakfast. Car park. Evening A la carte menu. Brochure - Rising Sun Inn, Portmellon, Mevagissey. Phone: (0726) 843235.

MOUSEHOLE. Carn-Du Hotel. Elegant Victorian house in an elevated position above Mousehole. Cosy lounge, delightful cocktail bar and licensed restaurant specialising in seafood and vegetables. Terraced gardens. Private car park. AA 2 stars. Phone: (0736) 731233.

MULLION. Alma House Hotel. Close to beaches and shops. Our superbly appointed accommodation with sea views, candlelit restaurant and bar are probably among the finest in the area. Bed and breakfast from £16.50. Phone: (0326) 240509.

MULLION. Parc Cres. Bed and breakfast. Cornish owned guest house with beautiful sea views. 3 rooms (1 en-suite). Television, tea making facilities all rooms. Ideally situated for touring Lizard Peninsula. 15 Laflouder Fields. Phone: (0326) 240653.

MULLION, Campden House, The Commons, Cornwall TR12 7HZ. Family guest house. Home cooking. Most vegetables home grown. Tea, coffee making facilities. Large garden. Licensed. Ample parking. Golf course 1 mile. Phone: (01326) 240365.

NEWQUAY, near. Cornwall. Seavista Hotel. Short and long breaks. Golfing and fishing holidays. 3 or 4 days. Special details on request. Only fresh food used where possible. Phone: Carl or Hazel on (0637) 860276 for colour brochure.

NEWQUAY. Aloha Licensed Hotel. Personal, friendly service with home comforts. All bedrooms have colour television, tea and coffee, clock radio, central heating. 6 en-suites, 3 ground floor. Parking. Credit cards. Games rooms. 124 Henver Road. Phone: (01637) 878366.

NEWQUAY. Gwel-An-Mor Guest House, Trevarrian. Twixt Watergate, Mawgan Porth. Licensed bar. All rooms colour television, tea making, wash basins. Bed and breakfast, optional evening meal. Close to beaches. We specialise in fishing holidays. Phone: Terry, Gerry (0637) 860437 anytime.

NEWQUAY. Sherwood Lodge Licensed Hotel. Family run, 12 bedrooms, all with colour televisions, tea, coffee facilities. En-suites. Excellent home cooking. Games room. 4 minutes town/beaches. Car park and full central heating. Brochure from Terry/Jackie. Phone: (01637) 874651.

NEWQUAY. Belair Guest House, 28 Edgcumbe Avenue. Ideally situated. Close to beaches, railway station and town centre. Central heating. Comfortable bedrooms have colour television and tea making facilities. En-suite and showers available. Phone: (0637) 87 6503. S.a.e.

YONDER TOWAN HOTEL
Bed and breakfast, double, twin and family rooms available. Most en-suite. All have TVs, teamaking facilities. Very close to beaches and town centre. Child-free offers. Cots and high chairs available. Baby listening.
Tel: and Fax: (01637) 872756 for brochure
Beachfield Avenue, Newquay, Cornwall TR7 1DR

KENDRA
20 Arundel Way, Newquay TR7 3BB
Tel: 01637 871340
A detached dormer bungalow, situated in a quiet residential area close to Lusty Glaze Beach and only a short stroll to Newquay town centre. 5 bedrooms with colour TV, tea making facilities and central heating.
Terms £83 to £90 Bed and Breakfast (Dinner optional).

NEWQUAY. Henver Lodge. Bed and breakfast. All rooms have shower, colour television, tea making facilities. Separate tables in no smoking, dining room. Parking. Central heating. Open all year. Phone: Mrs Hipkiss (01637) 876446.

MARYLAND HOTEL
Comfortable, licensed guest house situated near Lusty Glaze and Tolcarne Beaches, Trenance Gardens. Zoo and golf courses are close by. En-suites available, optional evening meal. From £12.00 per person B.&B. One child under 5 years free. Ample car parking and colour TVs.
Stamp please to Maryland Hotel, 43 Henver Road, Newquay, Cornwall TR7 3DQ. Tel: 01637 874556.

NEWQUAY. Alicia. Small friendly guest house. All rooms colour television, tea making facilities. Some rooms en-suite. Special offers early and late season. Bed and breakfast from £12, evening meal optional. 136 Henver Road, TR7 3EQ. Phone: (01637) 874328.

ROMA
GUEST HOUSE
1 ATLANTIC ROAD, NEWQUAY TR7 1QJ
Telephone: (0637) 875085
Roma is a six bedroomed, family run guest house overlooking Fistral Beach and the golf course, a few minutes walk from all amenities, beaches and shops.
★ Private car park at rear of premises
★ All rooms have tea making facilities
★ Colour TV in all rooms,
★ Residential Licence.
Brochure with pleasure from:
Pauline Bevan
B&B from £77 per week.
Evening meal £6.00.

NEWQUAY. No smoking. Quality en-suite accommodation. Lovely detached Guest House. Just yards from lusty glaze beach and coastal footpath. Superb food and service. Parking. Ground floor rooms available. Quiet level position. Highly commended. Phone: (01637) 874521.

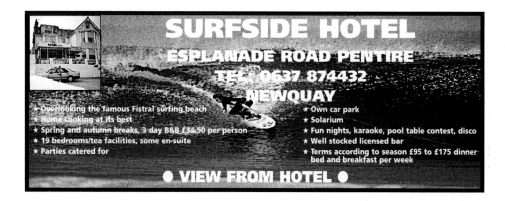

SURFSIDE HOTEL
ESPLANADE ROAD PENTIRE
TEL: 0637 874432
NEWQUAY

★ Overlooking the famous Fistral surfing beach
★ Home cooking at its best
★ Spring and autumn breaks, 3 day B&B £34.50 per person
★ 19 bedrooms/tea facilities, some en-suite
★ Parties catered for

★ Own car park
★ Solarium
★ Fun nights, karaoke, pool table contest, disco
★ Well stocked licensed bar
★ Terms according to season £95 to £175 dinner bed and breakfast per week

● **VIEW FROM HOTEL** ●

Castaways Beach Hotel
PORTH, NEWQUAY CORNWALL TR7 3NA
TELEPHONE: (01637) 876619

Proprietors: Nita and Paul Burns

A modern licensed family hotel, overlooking Whipsiderry Beach, where you and your children are made to feel really welcome.

- ★ 31 bedrooms ★ Tea/Coffee making facilities in all rooms
- ★ Heated indoor swimming pool
- ★ Colour TVs and telephones in all rooms
- ★ Entertainment ★ Children's Play area
- ★ Sauna and Solarium ★ Full Fire Certificate
- ★ Short Breaks early and late season
- ★ Central heating ★ Pool Table
- ★ Large Car Park ★ Baby Listening
- ★ Laundry service available
- ★ Bar snacks available lunchtimes
- ★ Open for Christmas
- ★ Access/Visa

Competitive Rates Available on Request
Free Child Offer All Year
Coach Parties welcome at Very Special Terms

NEWQUAY, Cornwall. 114 Henver Road. Bed and breakfast. 5 minutes from beach. Colour television, tea making facilities. Licensed bar. Free car parking. Come and enjoy a good holiday. Hope to see you. For booking form please Phone: (0637) 872576.

BERRICK LODGE
Atlantic Road, Newquay, Cornwall TR7 1QJ. Tel: (01637) 874462
A detached ten-bedroom family hotel, overlooking golf course and Fistral Beach. Only 5 minutes away from beach and town centre.
★ Tea/coffee making facilities in all rooms. ★ En-suite rooms available at an extra charge. ★ Ground floor en-suite family bedroom. ★ TV lounge. ★ Residential licence. ★ Private car parking. ★ Keys and access at all times. ★ Parties of single males/females welcome.
TERMS: Room & breakfast from £14 daily, £90 to £120 weekly. Evening meals available at an extra charge of £6 daily.

NEWQUAY. Smugglers Rest. Licensed guest house. Some rooms fully en-suite. Most with own showers. Colour televisions, tea making facilities in all rooms. Fine home cooking. Near to town centre and beaches. 1 Seymour Avenue. Phone: (01637) 874334.

PLEASE MENTION
DALTONS DIRECTORY
WHEN BOOKING YOUR HOLIDAY

NEWQUAY
INVERNOOK HOTEL
Small licensed hotel, centrally situated, all on the flat. E.T.B. 2 Crown. All rooms en-suite with heating, colour television, video player, fridge, hairdryer and drink facilities. Pool table. Reduced rates for children. Open all year.
Berry Road. Phone: 01637 872436

NEWQUAY. Pippin Guest House. Close to Porth and Lusty Glaze beaches. Colour television, tea and coffee making facilities. Most rooms with shower. Large car park. Plenty of good home cooked four course meals. Phone: (01637) 873979.

CHYNOWETH LODGE
1 ELIOT GARDENS, NEWQUAY
E.T.B. Three Crowns – Accessibility Three
Superior small hotel. All en-suite rooms including single and ground floor, colour televisions, tea makers, hair dryers, large car park, excellent cuisine, varied menu. Tariff £120-£160.
Ph.: Denyse (01637) 876684

NEWQUAY. Stratford House. Guest house. Close to amenities including bus and rail stations. Most rooms en-suite with colour television and tea making facilities. Reductions early and late for OAP's. Clark, 31 Berry Road. Phone: (01637) 875603.

NEWQUAY'S Fistral Beach Hotel. Licensed seafront bar and tea terrace. Heated swimming pool. Four poster, all en-suite. Satellite, video, beverage makers, radio, intercom. Surfing, golf, horse riding nearby. From £15 nightly. For brochure Phone: (0637) 850626.

PENZANCE. A small family hotel, the Blue Dolphin offers a warm welcome. Good food and clean accommodation. Close to all amenities. All rooms with television, tea making, en-suite available. Phone: (0736) 63836 for brochure.

Tremearne Farmhouse
In a wooded valley near Penzance, a 300-year old farmhouse offering bed and breakfast or self catering cottages.

Mrs. Sally Adams
"Tremearne," Bone Valley, Heamoor, Penzance, Cornwall TR20 8UG.
Tel: 01736 64576

PENZANCE. Pendennis Hotel, Alexandra Road, Penzance, Cornwall TR18 4LZ. Small licensed hotel. Close to sea and town centre. All rooms have central heating, satellite television, tea - coffee facilities. Most are en-suite. From £10 day. Dinner £6. Phone: (01736) 63823.

HOTEL MINALTO, PENZANCE
Short Breaks available, en-suite rooms, licensed bar and car park. Near seafront. Dinners available.
Also available: The Old Manor of Alverton self catering apartments and cottages.
Phone: 0736 62923
Alexandra Road, Penzance, Cornwall TR18 4LZ

EDNOVEAN HOUSE

Perranuthnoe, nr. Penzance, Cornwall TR20 9LZ
AA **Tel: (01736) 711071**
ETB

A beautifully situated, family run, 160 year old Victorian House, offering 9 delightful, comfortable rooms, most having en-suite facilities and panoramic sea views. Situated in one acre of gardens, and overlooking St. Michael's Mount and the whole of Mounts Bay, it has one of the finest views in the whole of Cornwall. Relax in an extremely comfortable lounge, library or informal bar. Enjoy a wide selection of fine food and wines in the candlelit dining room, which also caters for vegetarians. Ideal for coastal walks and exploring from the Lizard to Land's End. **For brochure phone or write to Arthur & Val Compton**

PENZANCE. Comfortable Guest House. Some rooms en-suite with colour television radio and tea/coffee making facilities. ETB 2 crown. RAC. WWBBA. Hopkins, Woodstock, 29 Morrab Road. Phone: (01736) 69049.

PENZANCE

Between Lands End and St. Ives

Small family guest house, offers Bed and Breakfast, optional Evening Meal. Ideal for beaches, walking, horse riding and golf. Family room, twin and double room available. Reductions for 2 nights or more.

Telephone (01736) 788814

PENZANCE. Keigwin Hotel. ETB 3 crown approved. Family run. Close all amenities. Excellent cooking, smoke free bedrooms. On street parking. Colour television, hot drink facility. Emons, Keigwin Hotel, Alexandra Road, Penzance, Cornwall TR18 4LZ. Phone: (01736) 63930.

TORWOOD HOUSE HOTEL
Alexandra Road, Penzance, Cornwall

Our hotel is situated in a beautiful tree-lined avenue, minutes from the seafront. Most rooms are en-suite. All rooms have colour TV, Satellite and video link. Tea/coffee facilities. Terms: Bed and Breakfast from £14 per person. Dinner, Bed and Breakfast from £24.50 per person per night.
For brochure and more information, write or phone

TEL: (01736) 60063

PENZANCE. Ideally situated. Long established Victorian guest house. Internationally recommended for its cleanliness and willing friendly service. All bedrooms have colour televisions and tea making facilities. Key access at all times. Major credit cards accepted. Phone: (01736) 65871.

PENZANCE. Sea and Horses Hotel. Small Small licensed Hotel on seafront. Overlooking Mounts Bay. Most rooms en-suite with tea/coffee facilities. Television, telephone. Free parking. AA 2 stars/ETB 3 crown commended. Alexandra Terrace. Phone: (01736) 61961.

PENZANCE. Homely, comfortable bed and breakfast accommodation. Private bungalow. Central position St. Ives, Marazion, Lands End. 3 double bedded rooms available. £10 per person, per night. Also parking space. Phone: Mrs Muriel Laity, Penzance (0736) 740875.

PENZANCE. Delightful Regency Hotel In Quiet terrace overlooking seafront and promenade. Close town centre, station, harbour, departure for Scilly Isles. All modern facilities. Private parking. A.A. listed. Annette Gooding, Camilla Hotel, Regent Terrace. Phone: (01736) 63771.

PERRANPORTH'S only ETB 3 crown guest house. Overlooking North Cornish coast. En-suite rooms all with television, tea machines, central heating. Excellent reputation. Central for touring Cornwall. Brochure: The Morgans' of Perranporth, Granny's Lane, Perranporth, TR6 0HB. Phone: (01872) 573904. Fax: (01872) 572425.

PERRANPORTH. Perranova Guest House, Cliff Road TR6 0DR. Family Guest House situated in an elevated position enjoying fine views. Ideal for touring. Coastal path. Colour television, tea makers. Comfortable rooms. Reduction children sharing parents rooms. Phone: (0872) 573440.

PERRANPORTH, Mansar. Comfortable holiday flats with extensive sea views. ETB 3 keys. 2 bedrooms, lounge, bathroom with shower, kitchen with full size oven, fridge, microwave. Bed linen provided. Green, St. Michael's Road. Phone: (0872) 573313.

PERRANPORTH, Poldark Country, bed and gourmet breakfast. All rooms en-suite with outstanding sea, beach and country views. Tea making, colour televisions. Children welcome. Ideal surfing. Adjacent golf course, for relaxation and private parking. Phone: (0872) 573425.

PERRANPORTH. Modern country home in idyl-lic surroundings. We aim to ensure you have a memorable holiday in a warm friendly atmosphere. We offer the following amenities: large swimming pool, sauna, solarium, jacuzzi. For details Phone: (0872) 571260.

PLYMOUTH near, Whitsand Bay. Dairy Farm, bed and breakfast. 600 yards sandy beach. En-suites, television, tea/coffee, television lounge. Large garden, croquet lawn, pool table, children's pony rides. Also self-catering. Ideal touring Cornwall - Devon. Phone: (0752) 822267.

POLPERRO, Looe. 400 year old farmhouse. Bed and breakfast. En-suite rooms. Evening meal optional. Glorious peaceful countryside, close coast and moors. Ideal base to explore both Devon and Cornwall. Open all year. Non-smoking. Phone: (0503) 220252.

POLPERRO. Crumplehorn Mill. 14th century Inn. Bed and breakfast, self-catering. Good food. Local fish, fine ales, farm scrumpy. Children, pets welcome. All rooms en-suite, colour television, film channel. Quaint fishing village. Lots to do nearby. Brochure. Phone: (0503) 72348.

CORNERWAYS

Bed & Breakfast: comfortable and friendly quiet location, easy reach of harbour. Some sea views. Family, double and twin rooms. H&C, colour TV, tea/coffee making facilities. Parking. **Holiday Bungalow:** sleeps 2 to 6. Comfortably furnished/equipped. 400 yards from beach/shops. Parking space. **Holiday Cottage:** fantastic harbour and sea views. Few mins' walk from shops, harbour. Sleeps 2 to 7. Garden. Parking. **Open all year**

Cornerways, Landaviddy Lane, Polperro,
Cornwall PL13 2RT. Tel: (0503) 72324
B&B from £13.50 Self-catering p.w. from £95-£300

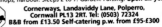

PORT ISAAC. Lovely 19th century stone house offering bed and breakfast in superb peaceful position overlooking harbour, coastline and picturesque fishing village. Ideal base for walking, touring. Close to sandy beaches. Dogs accepted. Parking. Phone: (0208) 880416.

PORT ISAAC near. Hendra is a small Georgian manor house incorporating all the elegance and charm of that era. For your comfort, we have installed all the comforts of today with food and wine. Phone: (01208) 841343.

PORTHALLOW, Gallentreath. Guest House situated in a pretty fishing village. Quiet and peaceful, lovely coastal walks, panoramic views. Bedrooms en-suite, colour television. Coffee and tea making facilities. P. Peters, Gallentreath, Porthallow, St. Keverne, Helston, Cornwall TR12 6PL. Phone: (0326) 280400.

PORTHLEVEN. Guest house. Magnificent sea views from well appointed rooms. Beaches, harbour and coastal walks close by. Excellent cuisine. Local fish, home baked bread. Recommended. Mrs. Cookson, Pentre, Peverell Terrace, Porthleven, Cornwall TR13 0DZ. Phone: (0326) 574493.

ROCK. Overlooking Camel Estuary. Silvermead. Licensed hotel. Abuts St. Enodoc golf course. Spacious rooms. Most en-suite with colour television and tea making facilities. Accommodation from £15. En-suite from £20. Half board available. Phone: Barbara Martin (01208) 862425.

SENNEN. Sunnybank Hotel, Seaview Hill.
Comfortable detached house with large gardens. Five minutes from Sennen Cove beach. Near Land's End and Minack Theatre. Tea-coffee making facilities, home cooked food. AA, RAC listed. Phone: (01736) 871278.

ST. AUSTELL. 2 cottages, 4 caravans. Set amongst lawns and mature trees. Secluded but not isolated. Access private beach. Walking distance Charlestown. 18th century harbour and Porthbean beach. B.A. Hill, Duporth Farm Cottage, Duporth Bay, St. Austell PL26 6AJ. Phone: (0726) 63929.

ST. EWE, Cornwall. Ewe. Bed and breakfast accommodation. Small quiet village 2 miles sea. Pub serves good food. Lounge, television, tea and coffee making facilities, electric blankets. Parking. Collins, Rose Cottage, St. Ewe, St. Austell, Cornwall. Phone: (0726) 842797.

ST. IVES, Cornwall. Dunmar, Pednolver Terrace. En-suite, licensed, television, AA, RAC, OAP, ETB. Car parking. From £90 weekly. Family run hotel, spectacular views. Arrive a stranger, leave a friend. Phone: (0736) 796117.

ST IVES, Woodlow. Small family guest house where a warm welcome awaits you. Central heating, vanitory units. Good food and personal attention. Separate tables. Comfortable television lounge. No restrictions. Phone: (0736) 797241 or (0203) 452572.

ST IVES, Derwent Guest House. Near town, beaches, seaviews. Parking, televisions, tea making. Child and OAP reductions, special short breaks. Renowned for good home cooking. Phone: Mrs S. Davies (01736) 797505. 6 Seaview Terrace, St Ives, Cornwall TR26 2DH.

ST. IVES. Surfside Guest House. Excellent sea views, standard or en-suite rooms. Full English breakfast. All rooms colour television, hairdryers, alarm clocks, tea and coffee facilities. Nearest accommodation to Tate Gallery. Alan and Freda, Phone: (0736) 793825.

ST IVES, 'Ormonde'. Licensed. Superb views. Few minutes town, beaches. Colour television, tea-coffee all rooms, private showers, A warm welcome and relaxed atmosphere awaits you. Highly recommended. Brochure 9 Park Avenue. Phone: (01736) 797131.

ST. IVES. Harbour view. Family run guest house, friendly atmosphere. Few minutes town, beaches. Limited parking. All rooms colour televisions, tea making. Super views. Selection of rooms with private shower. Clayden, 6 Park Avenue. Phone: (01736) 796102.

ST. IVES, Carbis Bay. Guest House. Large garden with putting green. All rooms en-suite or with private showers. Most with sea views. Television lounge. Large private car park. Brochure Phone: Sue or Tony (01736) 795677.

ST. IVES, Cornwall. Lovely, fully en-suite private hotel. Good bar, lounges, hot wholesome food. Ample 'safe' parking in grounds. Ideally situated for four lovely beaches. Brian, Lynne Crowston, 'Chy-an-Creet' Hotel. Phone: (01736) 796559.

ST. IVES. Comfortable bed and breakfast in Downalong quarter of harbour. Warm, friendly atmosphere. Tastefully decorated all rooms. Colour televisions and tea making facilities all rooms. Some with super sea view's. Contact Mrs Bishop, Phone: (01736) 794268.

ST. IVES, Cornwall. Guest house accommoda-tion. ETB registered. Personal supervision. Free parking on premises. Excellent food. Fresh farm produce. Highly recommended. Radio intercom and baby listening all rooms. Sae, 'Bella-Vista', St. Ives Road, Carbis-Bay, St. Ives TR26 2SF. Phone: (01736) 796063.

ST. JUST. Wellington Hotel. Licensed, family hotel. Ideal beaches, golf, climbing, walking, water sports, touring. Basic and luxury en-suite accommodation. £10 - £17.50 per person. Hot and cold. Bar food, local crab, fish, steaks etc. Phone: (0736) 787319.

TINTAGEL. Fully licensed hotel, occupying one of the most spectacular locations with panoramic coastal views and overlooking Tintagel Castle. Holiday apartments also available. Write colour brochure King Arthur's Castle Hotel, Tintagel, Cornwall PL34 0DQ. Phone: (0840) 770202.

TINTAGEL–CORNWALL

Small family run licensed hotel, magnificent cliff top position. All rooms with TV, tea and coffee facilities. Most en-suite. Sea views. Excellent home cooking. Nice dogs very welcome and free.

We regret no children under 12 years.

Open all year ring for our special Bargain Breaks.

Christmas Breaks also available.

PHONE EDNA ON
(0840) 770296
THE PENALLICK HOTEL

TINTAGEL. Willapark Manor Hotel. Bossiney. One of the most beautifully situated hotels in England. Excellent cuisine. Lovely accommodation. All facilities. Friendly informal atmosphere. Memorable holiday assured. Pets welcome. 14 acres garden - woodland. Overlooking bay. Phone: (01840) 770782.

Castle Villa
Guest House

Tintagel
North Cornwall
Tel. 0840-770373

TRURO. Lambourne Castle Farm. Near Perranporth. Non smokers. Home comfortable accommodation on working beef and sheep farm. Bedrooms with washbasins and tea making facilities. Hearty breakfast assured. Two miles from golden sands. Hawkey, Penhallow. Phone: (0872) 572365.

TRURO
PENHALE FARM
Come and relax on our working farm, set in peaceful countryside. Central for touring/beaches/National Trust properties. Warm welcome, comfort, cleanliness and excellent food guaranteed. Bed & breakfast, optional evening meal, child reductions.
Phone: (01726) 882324

TRURO. Marcorrie Hotel. Licensed Victorian family house. 5 minutes walk city centre. En-suite rooms. Television, telephone, tea making facilities. Credit cards. Parking. 3 crown ETB. Centrally situated for touring Cornwall. Phone: (01872) 77374. Sae 20 Falmouth Road, Truro TR1 2HX.

TRURO, Cornwall. Blue Haze. Delightful Regency bed and breakfast. Comfortable rooms with colour televisions, handbasins, tea making. Short level walk to city and cathedral. Ideally suited for touring Cornwall. £17 - £21 daily inclusive. Parking. Phone: (0872) 223553.

Daltons Directory and Daltons Weekly
The winning combination for all your holiday needs

SELF-CATERING

BODMIN MOOR. Mennabroom farm cottages, converted from granite barns in secluded rural setting, close Colliford Lake. Tastefully furnished, high standards. Washing machines, colour television, bed linen included. Ideal touring north, south coasts. For brochure Phone: (0208) 821272.

BODMIN MOOR. Traditional cottage on peaceful farm in an area of outstanding natural beauty. Just 6 miles from the coast, Port Isaac and rock. Superb walking, cycling and horse riding. From £100 per week. Phone: (0208) 850439.

BODMIN MOOR. Close seaside. Secluded natural beauty Nature Reserve, complex on River Camel. Quality cottages or cabins set in 4 1/2 acres. Trout fishing, cycling, walking, sports, games room. Book early for discounts. Colour brochure Phone: (0208) 74408.

BODMIN MOOR
Near famous Jamaica Inn, well kept self contained flat on farm in a beautiful setting, sleeps 4, washing machine, tumble dryer, microwave, colour TV, well equipped. From £80 per week. Sheets/pillowcases extra if required. Available all year. No pets.
Phone: (0579) 20587

BODMIN near. Luxury riverside bungalow over- looking river Camel in area of outstanding beauty with nature trail. Adjoining fishing, cycling. Easy reach both coasts and other sporting facilities. Sleeps 4. Reasonable terms. For brochure Phone: Mrs Lock (0208) 841222.

BODMIN/WADEBRIDGE. Character cottage. Situated in the quiet and pretty village of Nanstallon. On route of camel trail, ideal for walking and cycling, with use of bikes included. ETB 4 keys commended. £120 - £280. Phone: (0208) 831885.

BODMIN. Luxury, spacious house on farm. Sleeps 2/9. Equipped to high standard. 5 miles west of Bodmin, 2 miles from A30. Ideal base for coast/touring. Privacy ensured. Large gardens, barbecue. Open fire. Pets welcome. Phone: (0726) 890214.

BODMIN. North coast manor house apart- ments. Quiet setting, superb woodland gardens. 200 yards from village pub. Spectacular coastline; surfing, sailing, cycling, walking, riding. Brochure Phone: (01208) 841372. Tom Chadwick, Skisdon St. Kew PL30 3HB.

BOJEWYAN, far West Cornwall. Traditional family holidays in spectacular coastal scenery, secluded beach, moorland walks. Charming 200 year old 'listed' granite cottage, sleeps 7. Large peaceful garden. Central heating. Pets welcome. 17 foot fishing boat available. Brochure, Phone: (0492) 640667.

BOSCASTLE. Modern semi-detached bungalow, sleeps four. Panoramic views. Excellent walking area. Sandy beaches, golf, fishing, swimming pool, all within easy reach. Colour television, microwave. Garden. Parking off road. No pets. Phone: (0840) 250632.

BOSCASTLE. Peaceful farm cottage, edge of harbour village. ETB 4 keys commended. Sleeps 4/5. Open all year. Weekend breaks. Log fires. Friendly farmyard animals, pony rides. Also idyllic cottage for two. Gardens, barbecue. £90 - £330. Phone: (0840) 250528.

BOSCASTLE. Beautiful spacious Victorian villa. Overlooking village. Lovely views. 4 large bedrooms, two bathrooms. Sleeps 9. Fully equipped. Tastefully furnished. ETB commended. National Trust area. Near coastal walks, beaches. Phone for brochure: 081 878 4475/081 348 2165.

BOSCASTLE, near. Courtyard Farm, Lesnewth. Delightful, fully furnished 17th century cottages. Secluded area. Lovely walks, beautiful beaches within easy reach. Good touring centre. From £90 to £495 per week. Short breaks available. Brochure Phone: (0840) 261256.

BOSCASTLE. Stone cottage, sleeps 6-8. Colour television. Middle of village. Pets welcome. Hill, 16 Ilex Way, Middleton on Sea PO22 6PQ. Phone: (0243) 584062.

BOSCASTLE, Crackington Haven area. Modern bungalow, sleeping 2-8. ETB approved. Near sandy beaches and moors, cliff and valley walks. Heating, colour television. Beautiful scenery, rugged coastline. Available now onwards. Spring and Autumn £80 - £180. Phone: (0840) 250289.

BOSCASTLE. Self-catering cottage in unrivalled position overlooking National Trust harbour. Ideal base for walkers, art enthusiasts, surfers, bird watchers. Well equipped, sleeps 3/5. Private patio with furniture. Parking. Regret no pets. Phone: (0840) 250435.

BOSCASTLE. Luxury traditional cottage apart-ment. Close harbour. Sleeps four/six. Beautifully equipped with colour television, washing machine, tumble dryer, fridge/freezer, microwave. All linen provided. Spectacular scenery and coastal walks. Available all year. Phone: (0840) 250378.

BOSCASTLE, North Cornwall. Luxury 3 and 4 bedroom holiday cottages in pretty coastline village. Sleeps 5-8. Sorry no pets. Short breaks available. Phone: 081 337 0850 anytime.

BUDE, Cornwall. Alongside canal and beach. Luxury flat sleeps four. Family house next door sleeps five. Each has private garden and parking. Two minutes walk from sea, five minutes to town. Phone for details (01233) 850412.

BUDE. Comfortable character cottage. Beautifully positioned, close beaches, canal. Spacious interior with stripped pine and stained glass. Three bedrooms, sleeps six. Also gardens, parking. Linen, cot, television and washing machine included. Well behaved pet welcome. Phone: (0840) 230656.

BUDE. Comfortable 'olde-worlde' farmhouse, sleeps nine. Also immaculate luxury two bedroomed bungalow, sleeps 4. Close sandy beaches, surfing, golf, riding, fishing. Terms from £120-£270. Special rates May, June, September. Fox, Pollards Way, Stratton, Bude. Phone: (01288) 352559.

BUDE, Stratton. Extremely comfortable beauti-fully furnished cottage in picturesque village. All amenities. Sleeps 4, cot, highchair available. Babysitting service. Lovely enclosed garden with barbecue. Private parking. Close beaches, riding, golfing. Full brochure Phone: (0288) 353159.

BUDE, near. Devon/Cornwall border. Period cottage standing in 12 acres of farm and woodland. Secluded and peaceful. Coast 9 miles. Sleeps 6 plus cot. All modern conveniences. Central heating and open inglenook fire. Duvets, linen inclusive. Phone: (0409) 253311.

BUDE near, Morwenstow, North Cornwall. Quiet hamlet. Ideal for walking, touring local beaches. Two double bedrooms bungalow. Kitchen, diner, microwave, electric cooker, storage heaters, lounge, open fire, colour television. Large conservatory, enclosed garden, parking. Washing machine. Phone: (0288) 331559.

BUDE. Large luxury family home. Lovely set-ting in country by sea. 5 double bedrooms, 3 en-suite. Games room. Every modern appliance and convenience. Premium Sky television. Phone: (0288) 354427.

BUDE. Comfortable well equipped farm cottages with real fires. Beautiful countryside and beaches. Horse riding, golf, fishing, country walks etc. Weekends out of season. Colour brochure available. Goosenam Barton Stables, Morwenstow, Bude, Cornwall. Phone: (0288) 331204.

BUDE one mile. Secluded modern bungalow. Central heating, double glazed, fully equipped. Sleeps four. Set in own grounds, close all amenities. Beaches, golf, riding, fishing, bird watching. From £150 - £275 weekly. Phone: (0288) 353510.

BUDE. Trevose, Crooklets, Bude EX23 8NE. Well appointed furnished flat. Seconds walk from beach, minutes' walk from town centre, supermarket. Golf, tennis. Uninterrupted views over Bude Bay and Cornish coast. Phone: Fred Lester (0288) 353036.

BUDE near. Cucumber Cottage, Peter's patch and Wendy's cottage in tranquil unspoilt river valley. Sleeping 1 to 6. Comfortably furnished. Colour television. Phone: Austin (01409) 271298.

CALLINGTON. Two berth, balcony, bedroom, self-contained farmhouse annexe. Bathroom with shower. Smallholding location, beautiful countryside. Picturesque walks through Lynher Valley and Bodmin Moor. Easy access North and South coasts. Stabling available. Phone: Liskeard (0579) 63316.

CAMBORNE. Detached house, three bedrooms, sleeps six. Colour television. Large secluded garden. Situated in quiet cul-de-sac. Five minutes walk from town centre. Ideal centre for touring west Cornwall. Phone: Williams (0272) 696874.

CAMEL VALLEY. Luxury self-catering cottages. Sleep 6 and 4. Walking distance, river, camel trail. Excellent cycling, walking, fishing, riding. Ten miles beaches, four miles Bodmin. Moore, Denby Farm, Nanstallon, Bodmin. Phone: (0208) 72013.

CAMELFORD. Converted barns, farm cottages, listed historic houses. We can offer holidays for groups of 4 to 20 persons. Convenient for North coast or Bodmin Moor. Available all year round. Phone for brochure, (0840) 212526.

CAPE CORNWALL. Used in television's 'The Men's Room'. Simply the best coastal located cottage and studio in Cornwall. Set in National Trust land in panoramic settings. See sunsets and dolphins at your door. Phone: (0253) 771863.

Crylla Valley
Cottages & Bungalows
**Between
Plymouth and Looe**

Fourteen attractive cottages and bungalows set in 18 acres of beautiful grounds in the picturesque River Lynher valley at Notter Bridge. Ideal for fishing, golf, riding, town and coast and exploring Cornwall and Devon. Local Inn for good food. Short breaks and Daily rates.
For brochure:
Write or telephone:
Crylla Valley, Notter Bridge,
Nr. Saltash, Cornwall PL12 4RN.
Tel: (01752) 842187/843407

OPEN ALL YEAR

CARBIS BAY. Quiet, seclusion, just minutes from beach and picturesque St. Ives. Art galleries, ancient sites. Golden sands and glorious countryside all inclusive. Comfort. Sleeps 6. For details Phone: (0736) 793285.

MELVILLE APARTMENTS
2 DOWNS VIEW, BUDE, CORNWALL EX23 8RF

Excellent location overlooking the Bude Golf Course. Few minutes walk beach/town. Fully equipped to sleep 2/6. Heating/linen inclusive. Sorry no pets.
PHONE/FAX: 01288 354840

CORNISH COAST
BETWEEN NEWQUAY & ST IVES

2 adjacent semi detached houses sleeping 6-12 each at Perranporth from £175-£325 per week, per house. Wooden chalet at Porthtowan, sleep 2-6 from £99-£175 per week. All near glorious sandy beach.
**CONTACT GILL CAREY
PENWINNICK ROAD, ST AGNES, CORNWALL
PH.: (01872) 552262**

COVERACK. 'One of Cornwall's gems'. Delight-ful picturesque seafront cottages, including smugglers 17th century thatched. Spectacular sea views. Log fires for those chillier romantic evenings. Personally supervised to high standard. Open all year. Phone: (0736) 850649.

CORNWALL

Newlyn fisherman's cottage built 1790, renovated all modern conveniences, set in quiet, cobbled cul-de-sac. Amenities, harbour one minute, gas fire, hot water, bedding, car park included. Central holiday location, ideal for walking, beaches available all year. Sleeps six.

**Contact: Sue Strick on
Tel/Fax: (01736) 64679**

CRACKINGTON HAVEN. Peaceful wooded val-ley, sandy beach, rock pools, surfing. Traditional Cornish cottages and bungalows for 4/8. Unspoilt, uncommercialised. Coastal footpath, valley walks. Children and pets welcome. Tourist Board approved/commended. Colour brochure Phone: (01840) 230338.

CRACKINGTON HAVEN. Delightfully furnished, equipped bungalows. Sleep 6. Near sea. Colour television. Spacious lawns, excellent walks. Also two unique cottages for two people. One at Crackington Haven, the other on harbour at Boscastle. Dogs free. Phone: (0840) 230340.

CRACKINGTON HAVEN. 1 hour from Exeter. Cottages with fantastic views. Sleeps up to 6. Linen provided. Facilities include laundry room, games rooms, tennis court. Storage for bikes and boards. Dogs welcome. Brochure Phone: (01840) 230261.

Cornish Traditional Cottages

Self-catering cottages on both coasts of Cornwall and on Scilly

Send for your FREE brochure today or
telephone 0208 872559
LOSTWITHIEL, CORNWALL PL22 0HT
7 day Personal Service 9am-9pm

CRACKINGTON, Near. Haven. Delightful coun-try cottage off beaten track, down quiet country lane on working farm, only 10-15 minutes' drive to spectacular north coast. Absolute comfort. Chintzy sofas, log fires. Animals, pony rides, play area for children. Phone: (0566) 781232.

CRACKINGTON HAVEN HOLIDAY COTTAGES

Our cottages are carefully modernised and very well equipped, all with their own individual fenced gardens, patios & picnic tables; peacefully situated in quiet hamlets, some with spectacular sea views, and near to the sandy beach. All have colour televisions, open fires for burning logs and coal, central heating. Home-cooked takeaway meals, linen hire and maid service available. Colour brochure from Mrs. P. Preller, Broomhill, Rosecare, St Gennys, Bude, EX23 0BE. St Gennys
(0840) 230310 Fax: 230612

CRACKINGTON HAVEN, North Cornwall. 2 Cornish stone barn conversions, sleeping 2 or 4. Well equipped and comfortably furnished. Two miles from beach and coastal footpath. Open all year. Short breaks available. Phone: (0840) 230444.

CRACKINGTON HAVEN. Three character farm cottages and studio flat. Idyllic secluded setting, 300 yards coastal footpath. Sleep 2-9. Main farmhouse available August only. Sleeps 10. Swimming pool. Cleave, St. Gennys, Bude, Cornwall EX23 0NQ. Phone: (0840) 230426.

CRACKINGTON HAVEN. 16th century stone-beamed wagonhouse. Sleeps 2/7 plus cot. Linen, television, microwave, heating. Parking. Secluded, private lane. Excellent birdwatching, wildlife, cliff walking. Peaceful panoramic sea/valley views. £100-£280 weekly. Phone: (0840) 230371.

CRANTOCK. Newquay 4 miles. Cottage, sleeps 6. Bungalow, sleeps 5. Idyllic National Trust coastal setting. Land adjoins Polly Joke Beach. Safe bathing, surfing. Village 1 mile. Close other beaches, riding, golf, fishing. Colour brochure Phone: (0637) 830213.

FALMOUTH, Truro area. Small bungalow in creekside village. Recently modernised and refurbished. Sleeps 2/4. Good touring, bird watching and walking centre. £100 to £170 weekly. Phone: Mrs Charlton (0872) 864188.

FALMOUTH. Detached bungalow. Mylor Bridge. Country village. Two double, 1 single bedrooms. Shower over bath. Separate cloakroom. Linen optional. Washing machine, freezer, fridge, colour television. Parking. Near boating facilities. Phone: (0326) 315579 business, (0209) 861042 home.

FALMOUTH. Victorian style house, sleeps 9. Suitable for two families. Five bedrooms, two bathrooms. Fully equipped kitchen, dining room, lounge. Colour television. Close to beaches and town centre. Available July, August and early September. Phone: (0326) 374726.

FALMOUTH, outskirts. Tremorvah. Apart-ments. Superior 2 and 3 bedroom apartments with glorious sea views. 400 yards from beach and golf course. Ideal centre for Falmouth. Excellent for walking. Swanpool, Falmouth TR11 5BE. Phone: (0326) 312103.

FALMOUTH. Well appointed spacious Victor-ian house. Sleeps 6. En-suites. Handbasins in all bedrooms. Colour television, microwave. Convenient for harbour, beaches, pier, town. Leisure pool, golf course. Quiet road. Unrestricted parking. For brochure please Phone: (0326) 317247.

FALMOUTH. Quiet back cottage to 1830's sea captains terrace. Two bedrooms, sleeps four. Attractive, well equipped. Near lovely natural harbour and town centre. Convenient for all Cornwall. Vacant July, August, September. From £180. Phone: (0326) 315043.

FALMOUTH, Flushing. Charming waterside vil-lage. Delightful, tastefully furnished 2 bedroomed cottage. Sleeps 4. Colour television. Sunny garden. Peaceful location. Walks, sailing, beach nearby. Well situated for touring Devon, Cornwall. Phone: (0326) 374308 or (0326) 376002.

FALMOUTH area. Picturesque barns grouped around farmyard in quiet countryside with animals. 'Sage's', sleeps 6. Kitchen, lounge/diner, showers, toilets, central heating. Garage. Garden. Coast/town 20 minutes. From Easter £150. August £260. Phone: (0209) 860075.

FALMOUTH area. Three storey period house in quiet village of Flushing with harbour frontage. Comfortably furnished, sleeps 8. Dishwasher, microwave, washing machine, colour television, garage. Top floor can be completely independent. Details, colour leaflet Phone: (0483) 773576.

FALMOUTH, near. Pleasant flat, fully equipped Colour television, sleep two, three. Parking. Enquiries Phone: (0326) 373045..

FLUSHING. Modern cottage, newly fitted with everything for a family of 4. Microwave, dishwasher, washer-dryer, television, video. Free guide to waterside walks. Electricity and linen included. From £125 per week. Phone: (0737) 813116.

FLUSHING, near Falmouth. 3 rural apartments in quiet countryside, close to the estuary. Sleeps 2/4. Nicely decorated. Colour television. Parking adjacent. Cornish Tourist Board recognised. Brochure. £80-£180 per week. Phone: (0243) 372843.

FOWEY. Harbour cottages. Individual cottages and flats situated around the beautiful Fowey harbour. Many with harbour views, all ETB approved. Sleep 2-6. Fully equipped including linen (available on hire). Brochure: 3 Fore Street, Fowey PL23 1AH. Phone: (01726) 832211.

FOWEY. Comfortable, well equipped three bedroomed house for six with balcony. Close shops, beach. Cot, video, microwave, dishwasher. Washer/drier. Undercover parking in local garage. Sailing, fishing, touring, golf nearby. No pets. Phone: (01344) 26677 or (01726) 833354.

FOWEY. 1.5 miles. Traditional Cornish cottage, inexpensive, sleeps maximum 6. Picturesque coastal - rural area. Wide country views. Parking. Garden. Children, dogs welcome. Unspoilt beaches, coastal walking, horse riding, fishing, golf. Also family sailing school. Phone: (0208) 872470.

FOWEY, Cornwall. Comfortable holiday cottage to let. 2 bedrooms, sleeps 4. Fully equipped, modern kitchen. Close to town centre, shops and beaches. Privately owned. Reasonable rates. Car parking on site. Phone: (01299) 851669.

FOWEY 4 miles. Luxury bungalow attached to farm cottage. One double bedroom. En-suite shower room, toilet, lounge, kitchen - diner. Garden parking. Central heating. Ideal base for touring, fishing, walking. Electricity and bed linen included. Phone: (0726) 813765.

GILLAN. Overlooking Helford River. House, sleeps 8-9, cot. Television, washing machine, Aga, double garage, log fires, linen. Services included. Shops, pubs, sailing, golf. Open all year or long weekends. Phone: (0872) 864380 after 6 pm.

GORRAN HAVEN. Delightful beachside cottage with extensive sea views. Fully equipped. 2 people. All amenities. Beautiful coastal walks. Central heating, colour television, payphone. No pets, no meters. Ideal for relaxing holiday in small Cornish village. Phone: (0452) 760470.

GORRAN HAVEN, near Mevagissey. Spacious two bedroomed, self-contained flat in modern bungalow. All conveniences. Linen provided. Cleanliness assured. Village shops, sandy beaches, harbour and coastal walks. Parking. £110 - £240 per week. Also bed and breakfast. Phone: (0726) 843934.

GORRAN, South coast village. Traditional cottage on market garden. In area of outstanding natural beauty. Sleeps five. Linen, towels, electricity supplied. Beaches one mile. Ideal for walks - touring. Enquiries, Bulled, Mevagissey. Phone: (0726) 843517.

GORRAN HAVEN. Comfortable, modern flat. Sea views. Sitting room, 2 bedrooms. All conveniences. Sleeps 4/5. Beach 5 minutes. Car space. Hodges, Kerensa Chute Lane, Gorran Haven, St Austell PL26 6NU. Phone: (0726) 843734.

GORRAN HAVEN. Converted coastguard watch house. Unrestricted sea views prevented smuggling, and traditional modernised cottages within 100 yards, safe sandy beach. Comfortably furnished, well equipped. Night storage heaters. Sleep 2/4/6. Local caretaker. Phone: (01703) 775917/776928.

GORRAN HAVEN (South Cornish Coast). Cottages for 2/4/5 in seaside village. Vacancies all year. Beautifully modernised. Bed linen, spotlessly clean. 100 yards level walk beach. Tourist Board. All 4 key commended. Magnificent scenery. Phone: Mevagissey (0726) 842977.

GRIGGS QUAY, Hayle. Two new apartments, 1 three yards from quay. Second thirty yards from quay. Bird lovers paradise. Not suitable for young children or pets. Short breaks available. Central heating. Safe car parking. Phone: (0736) 757840.

GUNWALLOE, Helston. Trelawney House self-catering holidays. Outstanding position with magnificent sea views across Mount's Bay. Ideally situated for exploring the Lizard's secrets. Colour television. Parking. Bed linen (duvets) supplied. Brochure Phone: (0326) 240260, mobile (0860) 159400.

GWITHIAN, Cornwall. Fully equipped 4 bed-room bungalow. Sleeps eleven. Large lounge, kitchen, bath and shower. Extensive sea views. 3 mile sandy beach. Private site. Centrally situated for local attractions. Phone: Rice (0822) 613606.

HARLYN BAY. Area of outstanding beauty, near Padstow. Deluxe Georgian house. Sleep 6. 3 minutes beach. Phone: (01841) 521190, (01840) 212072.

HAYLE TOWANS. Holiday bungalow, sleeps 6 in comfort. Fully equipped. Bathroom, kitchen. Access for wheelchair. Three miles of golden sands. Close to many tourist attractions. Availability April to October. Phone: (0209) 211205.

HAYLE (near). Spacious, well equipped country cottage with own garden and parking. Sleeping 7. Linen, colour television and washer dryer provided. Situated within easy reach of North and South coasts. Tourist Board registered. Phone: (0736) 762407.

HAYLE. Three bedroom house with garden and parking. Colour television, microwave etc. Close all local amenities. Short breaks. Low season. Sleeps 5 plus cot. Pets welcome. For further information Phone: (0736) 62418, 24 hour answerphone.

HAYLE, Riviere Towans. 4 and 6 berth self-con- tained chalets. Near beach, sea views. Colour television, shower. Parking. Shops. Personally supervised by owner. Ideal touring centre. Terms: from £65 weekly. Phone: Mrs Rogers (0209) 714916.

HAYLE, Cornwall. Situated in the Towans. Three bedroom bungalow, near beach with three miles of golden sands. Also close to place of interest. For more details Phone: (0392) 424268.

HAYLE. Holiday bungalow within leisure com- plex. Sleeps 6. In/outdoor pools, sauna, solarium, bar, restaurant, entertainment etc. Beginning October to end May. £65 per week. For further details Phone: (0117) 9501406 (day), (0117) 9834504 (evenings).

HELFORD RIVER area. 3 homely cottages on small working farm. Sleep 4/6. Fully equipped. Linen provided. Ideal summer and winter breaks. Magnificent views across valley and woodlands. Area outstanding natural beauty. Children - pets welcome. Phone: (0326) 231341.

HELFORD RIVER. Area of outstanding beauty. Bargain autumn and winter breaks. Beautiful centrally heated bungalow. Riverside. All amenities. No extras. Bed linen provided. Phone: (0886) 884748.

HELFORD RIVER. Cosy Cottage, woodland set- ting overlooking Gillan Creek. Sleeps 2 to 4, fully equipped, central heating. Private slipway. Well behaved pets welcome. Available all year. Wonderful area for sailing, walking, birdwatching. Phone: (0326) 231310.

HELSTON, Gunwalloe. Holiday bungalow. Spacious, comfortable. Overlooks farmland. 3 double bedrooms, fully equipped. Central heating. 2 miles beach. Lovely coastal walks. Local pub. Many places of interest nearby. Garden. Ample parking. Phone: Helston (0326) 572050.

HOLYWELL BAY. Self contained ground floor holiday flat, rural setting with all facilities, close to surfing, beaches, pleasure park, golf, horse riding etc. Please send for brochure to Glenburn Cottage, Cubert, Cornwall. Phone: (0637) 830780.

HOLYWELL BAY. Bungalow on the beach. 2 apartments. 1 bedroom, sleeps 2/4. 2 bedroom, sleeps 4/5. Fully equipped. Right out of garden onto large sandy beach. Many local attractions. Phone: Poullouras (0208) 872982.

HOLYWELL BAY. Comfortable brightly fur- nished modern two bedroom bungalow (sleeps 5). Close to sandy beach. Sunny terrace. Enclosed garden. Dogs welcome. Parking two cars. Ideal swimming, surfing, building sand castles and walking. Phone: (0637) 830717.

HOLYWELL BAY. Well furnished bungalows in quiet cul-de-sac. Close to superb surfing beach. Patio doors open onto terraced lawns. Colour television. Sleep six. Parking. Also 3 bedroomed bungalow. Secluded garden at Porth Newquay. Phone: (0637) 830031.

HOLYWELL BAY, near Newquay. Delightful Cornish barn, tastefully converted into four spacious 2 bedroom apartments. Fully equipped. Colour television. Gardens, car park. 250 yards magnificent beach. Near leisure park and golf courses. Phone: (0277) 659156 for brochure.

LAMORNA. Post Office cottage. Unspoilt cove and wooded valley. Ideal bird watching, walking, fishing, painting, relaxing. Easy reach Penzance, St. Ives, Minack Theatre, Land's End. Pets welcome. Maximum three people. Owners personal attention. Margaret Dodd. Phone: (0736) 731210.

LAND'S END, Porthcurno. Delightful cottages in peaceful setting. Close to Land's End, Sennen Beach, Porthcurno and the Minack Theatre. Sleeps 4 and 5. Fully modernised and equipped. Personally supervised. Phone: Richard Jeffery (01736) 871263.

LAUNCESTON. Nestled in the peace and tran- quility of the North Cornwall countryside is our cosy well equipped farmhouse. Ideally situated for coast, moors and all leisure pursuits. Sleeps 6. Cleanliness is assured. Phone: (0566) 781372.

LAUNCESTON. Well equipped accommodation in 17th century farmhouse. Central touring centre. Carp lake and salmon fishing on farm. Riding stables, golf nearby. Bed and breakfast available. Mrs F.E. Broad, Lower Dutson Farm, Launceston, Cornwall PL15 9SP Phone: (01566) 776456.

LERRYN, near Fowey. Old lime kiln! Riverside. Sleeps 4/6. Set in one of the most beautiful villages in Cornwall. Children welcome. Regret no pets. Phone: (0208) 872695.

LERRYN, near Fowey. Lovely riverside house sleeps six. Mooring rights. For full details and photographs send sae to Mrs B. K. Harris, 41 Kirkway, Broadstone, Dorset BH18 8ED or Phone: (0202) 693661.

LISKEARD, Cornwall. Holiday bungalow. Quiet woodland site with bar/restaurant. Sleeps 4/5. Well equipped. Colour television, radio, duvets and pillows. March to December. Storage heating. Ideal coast, walking, fishing, touring Devon and Cornwall. Phone: (0724) 848401.

LISKEARD

Traditional self-catering bungalows in country garden setting at foot of Bodmin Moor. Well furnished and equipped. Ideal walking, fishing, golf, touring Devon and Cornwall. North and South coast beaches within easy reach. E.T.B. inspected. Children, pets and disabled welcome.

Brochure:

𝕽osecraddoc 𝕳olidays

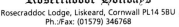

Rosecraddoc Lodge, Liskeard, Cornwall PL14 5BU
Ph.:/Fax: (01579) 346768

LIZARD PENINSULA. Comfortable rural 2 bed- roomed cottages on arable farm, 1 mile St. Keverne. Colour television, auto-washers, barbecues. Safe play area. No pets. Attractive early/late prices. Cornish Tourist Board approved. Trenoweth Valley Farm Cottages. Phone: Rosemary Peters (01326) 280910.

LOOE, Cornwall. Eastley, Little Larnick. Two cottages, sleeps 6 in each. Storage heater, electric fires. One cottage has a log fire. Cleanliness assured. Tourist Board approved. From £95 weekly. Riding stables near. Phone: (0503) 220205 evenings.

LOOE, Plaidy. Fully equipped, two bedroom bungalow, sleeps 4. Sea view. 700 yards beach. Patio, garden. Television. Own parking. Central heating. Ideally situated for coastal, country walks. Within easy reach of golf courses. Phone: (0503) 263122.

LOOE, Shallowpool. Secluded riverside bunga- low, sleeps 4-6. Patio overlooking river bank. Ideal walking and fishing. Looe 2 miles. Phone: (0503) 263775.

LOOE near. New quality apartment, sleeps three to five. Close to golf course. Superb views over rolling Cornish countryside. Colour television, microwave. £85 to £195 including electricity and linen. Phone: (0503) 240358.

LOOE. Two bedroomed flat, overlooking sea at Hannafore. Panoramic views. Lounge/diner/kitchen. Fully equipped with television, video, microwave. One dog welcome. Parking, one garden. Electricity, linen included in terms. Phone: (0503) 265177.

LOOE, Cornwall. 3 bedroom furnished bunga- low. Situated in an area of outstanding natural beauty. Minutes from Looe. Sea views, sandy beaches, golf, riding, water sports, fishing. Central for touring both coasts and Dartmoor. Phone: (0503) 240314.

LOOE, Polperro. Spotlessly clean, extremely comfortable and well equipped ground or first floor flat. Perfect accommodation for 2 but will sleep 4. One bedroom, large lounge/diner, kitchen and shower room. Private parking. No pets. Phone: (0503) 72664.

LOOE. Bryn Hyfryd is a large detached bunga- low situated in a beautiful valley near Looe. Fully equipped, sleeps six. Enclosed garden. Linen inclusive. For details and brochure Phone: (0579) 344014. Ideal centre for exploring Cornwall.

LOOE. Millendreath holiday village. Bungalow, 100 yards sands, sea view. Sleeps 4/6. Sky television, hard tennis court, watersports, restaurant, shop, launderette, takeaway, club bar, heated indoor pool. Parking outside villa. Children's activities. Pets accepted. Phone: 021 355 2292.

LOOE. Millendreath Holiday Village. Bungalow, sleeps 6. 200 yards beach. Colour television. Indoor pool, club house. Good choice of water sports available. Phone: (0202) 875158.

LOOE (near). Fully furnished apartments in spacious gardens, overlooking beach and sea. Beach 200 yards. Shops, inns, cafes, golf, fishing, riding nearby. Sleep 2-6. Ideal touring base. Attractive rates. Open all year. Mount Brioni. Phone: (05035) 251.

LOOE. Centrally situated fishermans 18th cen- tury, 2 bedroomed cottage. On the level in quiet area. Most suitable for all age groups. Sleeps 5. Private patio, barbecue area. Colour television. From £88 weekly. Phone: (0503) 262881.

LOOE. Superior tasteful centrally heated apartments. Superb sea views. Overlooking Looe Bay Island. Sleep 2-8. Open all year. Cornish Tourist Board/West Cornwall Tourist Board inspected. Equipped to high standard. Free parking. Beautiful grounds. Peaceful location yet close beach, shops and amenities. Phone: (0503) 262073.

LOOE, Polperro Fowey. Cottages, house, apartments. Sleep 2/10. Indoor pools. Also outdoor pools (shared). Linen provided, heating. Early - late season. Coloured brochure S.A.E. Mrs Pendry, Penton Lanreath, Looe, Cornwall PL13 2NU. Phone: (0503) 220404, 16th April 1995 (010503) 220404.

LOOE 2 miles, hillside picturesque valley Sandy bay, sports, watersports club amenities. Parking. Children welcome. No pets. Sleeps 4 plus. Chalet bungalows. One hilltop, one bottom. Phone: owners (0462) 453942 ansaphone for written details.

LOOE. Cosy fishermans cottage, sleeps 4. In the heart of village. Level walk within 100 yards of beach, quay and shops. Bed linen and electricity included. Personally supervised. Family pet welcomed. Phone: (0726) 842577 after 6pm.

LOOE. Cottage style house overlooking popular fishing harbour, with super river and valley views. Quiet, hillside position but close to shops and beach etc. Microwave, colour television, text. Own parking. Prices from 2/4 persons. Phone: (0503) 264126.

LUDGVAN, near Penzance. Cosy cottage with panoramic views of St. Michael's Mount and Bay. Rural situation. Inglenook fireplace, beams, multi-fuel stove, electric heaters. Comfortable, well cared for. Ideal centre for coasts and country. Phone: (0227) 700554.

LUXULYAN. Idyllic holiday cottage, sleeps 2. Converted granite farm building in 3 acre gardens in the heart of the Cornish countryside. Ideally situated for North and South coasts. Supervised by owners. For brochure Phone: (01726) 851702.

MARAZION, St. Michael's Mount. Three bedroom terraced cottage, sleeps five. Near beach and shops. Three miles Penzance. Well appointed and fully equipped. Parking nearby. Convenient for touring and coastal path walks. Available all year. Phone: (0114) 249 8265.

MARAZION area. Bungalow, 2 bedrooms (double and twin). Beautiful views over Mounts Bay and St. Michael's Mount. Own gardens, parking. All electric. Children and pets welcome. April to October. £140 - £265 per week. Phone: Boase (0736) 710361.

MAWGAN. Spacious self-contained wing of former rectory in peaceful surroundings near Helford River. Sleeps up to 6. Glastan House, Mawgan, Helston. Phone: (0326) 221261.

MAWGAN PORTH. Luxury flat, international style, privately owned. Large, comfortable, carpeted, colour television, balconied, sea views. Garden. 100 yards beach, mini golf, residents swimming pool, tennis courts. Parking. 2 - 6 Trenalt, Mawganporth, Newquay, Cornwall TR8 4DB. Phone: (01637) 860296.

MAWGAN PORTH BAY. Surfside holiday flats. 1 acre garden. 100 yards sandy beach, glorious views, coastal walks, swimming, surfing. Accommodating 2 - 6. Parking. Colour television. Fully equipped. Children welcome. Sae brochure, Blakemore, Trenalt, Mawganporth, Newquay, Cornwall TR8 4DB. Phone: (01637) 860296.

MAWGAN PORTH, between Newquay - Padstow. 2 bedroom flat, sleeps 4/5. Fully equipped, microwave, television. Heated swimming pool, patio, tennis courts. 100 yards beach, shops. Lineman, 'Brynn', Indian Queens, Cornwall TR9 6QN. Phone: (0726) 860600 or (0726) 861199 (ansaphone).

MAWGANPORTH BEACH. Well equipped, heated two bedroom flat. Sleeps six. Coastal views. Balcony. Parking. Swimming pool. Newquay approximately six miles. From £60 per week. Phone: David Ball (01637) 871005.

MAWNAN SMITH, Falmouth. Luxurious olde thatched cottage. Near Helford River, beaches. Coastal walks. Sleeps 5. Jacuzzi, bath, shower, elegant 4 poster canopy bed. Secluded garden. Village pub. Book early August 1995. Phone: (0326) 250806.

MERRYMEET. Two delightful cottages, each sleeping two people. Situated in peaceful idyllic countryside. Excellent for couples wishing to visit different areas of Cornwall and nearby Devon. Very clean and fully equipped. Phone: Liskeard (0579) 348308.

MERRYMEET. Tin miners' cottages. Well appointed with most interesting gardens. Above a beautiful valley. Peaceful, relaxing, yet central to moors, coastal walks and golf. Also many historic houses and gardens. Reasonably priced. Phone: Liskeard (0579) 344111.

MEVAGISSEY, Cornwall. Charming character fisherman's cottage, sleeps 4. Minutes from harbour. Ideal Summer or Winter breaks. Pets welcome. Phone: 081 761 0480.

MEVAGISSEY, Cornwall. Ideal for couples, mini self-contained flatlet. Television. Private parking. Small dogs welcome. All year round bed and breakfast. Christopher and Kathleen Richards, Phone:/Fax: (0726) 843161.

MEVAGISSEY. Quaint 300 years old ex-fishermen's cottages. Approximately 70 yards from harbour. Parking available. One sleeps 2/4 and one sleeps 7 people. Sorry no pets. Mrs. R. D. Smith, Lindridge Farm, Six Ashes, Bridgenorth, Shropshire, WV15 6EP. Phone: (0384) 873202.

MEVAGISSEY. Comfortable spacious bungalow, sleep 5. Magnificent sea view. Near beach, harbour, shops. Central for touring all Cornwall. Linen, electric inclusive. Parking. Personally cleaned. Reduced rates early/late. Ford, 'Colraine', Beach Road, Mevagissey. Phone: (01726) 843460.

MEVAGISSEY. 17th century farm courtyard cottages. On working dairy farm in quiet rural location. Cleanliness guaranteed. Beach 2 1/2 miles. Sleep 2/4 plus cot. No pets. From £125 per week including electricity and bed linen. Phone: (0726) 843505.

MEVAGISSEY, near. Situated in peaceful hamlet, spacious 4 bedroomed house. Sleeps 6. One bathroom, one shower room, large living room, piano, colour television. Private secluded garden, own parking. For details and booking Phone: (0637) 880748.

MEVAGISSEY. Comfortably furnished house. Superb position, overlooking harbour and bay. Two double bedrooms, kitchen, dining room, lounge, bathroom, conservatory. Private car space. Linen provided. Personally supervised. Kendall, Panorama, Kiln Close, Mevagissey, St. Austell, Cornwall. Phone: (01726) 843164.

MEVAGISSEY. Luxury 2 bedroomed apartment. 100 yards from the beach at Portmellon Cove. Sleeps 4. Colour television, dishwasher, microwave. Parking. Superb garden. Free electricity and linen. Brochure Rising Sun Inn, Portmellon, Mevagissey PL26 6PL. Phone: (0726) 843235.

MEVAGISSEY, Cornwall. Waterside cottage available for holidays. Looking over the harbour, boats and bay. Superb location. Comfortable accommodation. Recently refurbished. Enquiries please Phone: (0726) 842073.

MEVAGISSEY. Comfortable, spacious bungalow, sleep 5. Magnificent sea view. Near beach, harbour, shops. Central for touring all Cornwall. Linen, electric inclusive. Parking. Personally cleaned. Reduced rates - early late. Ford, Colraine Beach Road, Mevagissey. Phone: (0726) 843460.

MEVAGISSEY. 4 ground floor luxury apartments. High on the hill. Each with patios. Overlooking harbour and bay. Ideal for touring Cornwall. Private car park. No pets. Polhaun, Polkirt, Mevagissey PL26 6UU. Phone: (0726) 843222.

MILENDREATH. Holiday village, near Looe, Cornwall. Villa, sleeps 4 - 6. Colour television. Lovely views. Private sandy beach. Excellent family facilities, indoor swimming pool, woodland walks, clubhouse. Mrs. Austin, 44 Orient Road, Lancing, Sussex BN15 8JZ. Phone: (0903) 766455.

MOUSEHOLE. Three bedroom cottage on working farm, near Mousehole. Views of Mounts Bay. Large lounge with colour television, kitchen, bathroom and garage. Phone: (0726) 731204.

MOUSEHOLE, in Cornwall. Delightful self-contained apartment. 2 bedrooms, sleeps 4. Own garden. Sea and country views. Set in small hamlet. Open all year. Tariff £70 to £200. Phone: Mrs Richards for brochure (01736) 731289.

MULLION. Self-contained flat, sleeps two adults. Single caravan (own shower/toilet). Sleeps two adults. Both excellent sea views. Beach nearby. Large garden. Regret no pets. Parking. Flat from £100, caravan £70 all inclusive. Phone: (0326) 240423.

MULLION. Detached two bedroomed bungalow to sleep 4/5. Colour television, video recorder, fridge-freezer, microwave, oven, washing machine, tumble dryer. Close to village centre. Linen supplied. Enclosed garden. D. Michell, Phone: (0326) 240243 evenings or (0326) 572434 daytime.

MULLION harbour. Beaches, fishing. Sleep 4 to 6. Linen supplied. Pets allowed. Parking, garden. Picturesque, rural. Tourist Board registered. Open all year round. Cots, highchairs. Good touring centre Lizard to Land's End. £100-£255. Phone: (0326) 240226.

NEWLYN. All year round self-catering apartment, sleeps 2/4 plus cot. Modern conveniences. Centrally heated. Superb sea and country views. Coastal walks and beaches nearby, local amenities. Large garden, parking. No smoking, no pets. Phone: (0736) 68007.

NEWQUAY. St. Michael's Court Holiday Flats. Situated town centre, two minutes beaches and shops. Also superb three bedroom bungalow near Tolcarne beach and two bedroom apartment overlooking Fistral Beach. Families/couples only. Brochure Phone: (01637) 876969.

CORNISH MILL HOUSE
Self Catering Accommodation

Sleeps up to 8, ideal large, or 2 families. Swimming pool, golf, tennis, games barn, play meadow, laundry, telephone, centrally heated, linen provided, electricity included. Pretty wooded valley, situated close to coastal resorts and Bodmin moor.

For more details and brochure telephone Liskeard (01579) 346521

NEAR LOOE
TREDINNICK FARM

Half of large Farmhouse. Sleeps 10. Bed linen, microwave, dishwasher, washing machine, colour TV, central heating makes this an ideal base for all tourist attractions.

MRS A. E. BARRETT
TREDINNICK FARM, DULOE, LISKEARD, CORNWALL PL14 4PJ
TEL: (01503) 262997

PADSTOW. Two delightful, well furnished cot-tages. One near harbour, sleeps four, has small sunny garden. Second near cliffs and beaches, sleeps 6, with nice garden for children. Peaceful yet close amenities. Phone: (0202) 697780.

PADSTOW (Petherick Creek). Holiday bunga-lows, alongside wooded Tidal Creek within three miles.Glorious sandy beaches. Quiet spot. Ideal spot, walking birdwatching and all holiday activities. Pets are accepted. For brochure and prices/available dates Phone: (0208) 812475.

PADSTOW, St Merryn. Modern bungalow. 3 bedrooms, sleeps 8. Colour television, microwave, freezer, washing machine. Quiet site. Close 5 beaches, riding, golf, outdoor pool, play areas. Ideal touring base. Available 12 months from £78. Phone: owner (0384) 214646.

PADSTOW area. Superb holiday bungalow, fully equipped for family of 4 with 2 single beds and bunks. Bed linen supplied. Close to sandy beaches and golf course. No pets. Reasonable prices. Phone: (0841) 521053.

PADSTOW. Lodenek Cottage. Self-catering cot-tage available from November to 18th March. £150 per week. £95 three day break. Sleeps 6. All amenities. Open fire. Rayburn and wall heaters throughout. Linen provided. Phone: Renals (0208) 75548.

PADSTOW, North Cornwall. 4 bedroom house - 2 bedroom courtyard cottage - double studio apart-ment. Shared garden, situated 80 metres. Beautiful working harbour. Close beaches, walks, golfing, sailing and fishing. SAE Lantern House, Duke Street or Phone: (0841) 532566.

PADSTOW, near. Comfortable Cornish cottage in small village. All facilities, television, washing machine, etc. Sleeps 4/6. Available throughout the year. Near many beautiful sandy beaches, golf course, pubs and restaurants. Phone: day or evenings 081 870 1221.

PADSTOW. Constantine Bay. Secluded bunga-low in own garden, also flats. 200 yards from large sandy beach. Adjoining scenic coastal footpath and golf course. Properties furnished and equipped to a high standard. Sleep 2/4. Pets welcome. Phone: Mrs. Harris (0841) 520262.

PADSTOW. Traditional Cornish cottage with garden. Comfortable and well equipped, including dish-washer, fridge freezer, washing machine, television, barbecue, cot, central heating. Close to harbour and shops. Ideal for beaches, walking, golf, water sports. Phone: (0725) 518441.

PADSTOW. Fully furnished, 3 bedroom bunga-low. Gardens, garage, detached. 1 1/2 miles Padstow town, 1/2 mile beaches approximately. Vacant March to November £85 - £230 per week. Electric extra. Details Phone: (01841) 520294.

PADSTOW. Detached farmhouse, sleeps 8 plus cot. Rural position but close to many sandy beach-es and golf courses. Large garden, barbecue and picnic area. All modern conveniences including dishwasher and automatic washing machine. Phone: (0841) 540518,

PADSTOW. Self-catering ground floor flat. In lovely fishing town. Estuary views. Close to beaches, cliff and river walks. Sleeps 5. Laundry facilities. Heating. Garden, street parking. Lesley Mills, 34 Dennis Road. Phone: (0841) 533361.

PADSTOW, Mellingey. Charming detached cot-tage. Spacious. Fully equipped. Garage and parking. Situated small picturesque hamlet, surrounded by beau-tiful countryside yet only 3 miles Padstow and beaches. Suit all ages. Sleeps 4. No pets. Phone: (0386) 860550.

PADSTOW. Quietly situated period cottage. Close harbour/beaches. 3 bedrooms, sleeps 6/7. Washing machine, fridge freezer, colour television, microwave. Barbecue. Cot, high chair. Pet welcome. Gas central heating. Walled patio, garden. Phone: (0722) 328823 evenings.

WIN A PERSONAL CD PLAYER

To find out how simply turn to the readers' questionnaire at the back of this guide

PADSTOW, St. Ervan. Cottages and apartments. ETB 3 key commended. Electricity, linen included. 1840 rectory in 4 acres. Secluded position. Easy access sea, coastal walks, golf, Padstow. £150-£390. Contact Mrs Lloyd (01841) 540255.

PAR. Attractive comfortable bungalows, mid Cornwall, sea and country views. Secluded Carlyon Bay beach with Coliseum and recreational facilities 1 1/2 miles. Other beaches short distance. Good touring centre. Cliff walks. Personal supervision. Phone: (0726) 812492/815352.

PENDEEN. Three bedroomed stone cottage on coast between St Ives/Land's End. Sleeps seven. All modern conveniences. Quiet situation/gardens/parking. Village amenities including pubs and eating. Excellent for touring, local, historical interests. Reasonable rates. Phone: (0277) 224592.

PENTEWAN near Mevagissey. Picturesque fisherman's cottage. Two bedrooms, sleeps four/five. Well equipped, cosy, comfortable. Peaceful setting. Lovely walks, sandy beach. Village amenities. Small garden, parking. Sailing, golf, sports nearby. Sorry no pets. Phone: (0726) 843130.

PENZANCE. Nanceddan Farm, Ludgvan. Comfortable farmhouse flat in rural position. Superb views of St. Michael's Mount. Three bedrooms, sleeps six. Children's play area. Complimentary grocery pack. Free colour brochure available. Phone: Mrs Richards (0736) 740165/740238.

PENZANCE. Well equipped two bedroomed detached private bungalow. Garden, patio area. Parking. Conveniently located for town centre and promenade. Colour television, linen, electricity. Night storage heating included. Reasonable rates. Available all year. Phone: (0736) 64159.

The Land's End Vineries

Fifteen modern holiday bungalows, in a quiet rural location near the Minack Theatre, beaches and the coastal path. All bungalows are fully equipped with electric cooker, microwave, toaster, colour TV, bedlinen. Large car park and gardens. Set away from the road. Special rates for Winter break holidays.

Licensed restaurant on-site serving meals and snacks through the day during the Summer.

Phone or write for our brochure:
The Land's End Vineries, Poljigga, St. Levan, Penzance, Cornwall TR19 6LT Tel: (01736) 871437

PENZANCE SEAFRONT COTTAGES
25-yards from the sea, overlooking Mounts Bay. Sleeps 1 to 6 persons. Fully equipped; garage, garden, colour TV, heating. Open all year.
S.a.e. Mrs M. Blewett, 5 Reens Road, Heamoor, Penzance, Cornwall TR18 3HP. Tel: 0736 61741

PENZANCE. Village overlooking sea. Pretty local cove, St. Just area. Enchanting period cottage, inglenooks and beams. Inclusive of electric, linen, hot water, television, night storage heating. Sleeps 5-6. No pets. Private parking. Comfort, cleanliness guaranteed. Phone: (0736) 787223.

PENZANCE, near. 5 minutes drive Mounts Bay, beaches. Comfortably furnished bungalow in two self-contained units. Sleep 4/5 and 2/3. Parking, garden. All electricity and linen provided. £115 - £220. Village location. Phone: Drew (0736) 763200.

PENZANCE 6 miles. Comfortable flat, sleeps 2/4. Ideally situated. Close to beautiful beaches and coastal footpath. Parking. Garden. Private heated pool by arrangement. Babysitting. Laundry service. Also learn to swim holidays available. Phone: (0736) 787339.

PENZANCE. Gulval Bal. Farm cottage with magnificent views over Mounts Bay, set in secluded garden. Well equipped. 3 bedrooms, colour television, washing machine. Personally supervised. Parking. Linen available. Heating, open fire. Sleeps up to 6 people. Phone: (0736) 66254.

PERRAN COOMBE
Four to six berth bungalows on secluded wooded site. Night storage heating. 1.5 miles from Perranporth, ideal for bird watching, walking or as a base for touring.
Saxon Holidays, Lexcroft, Perrancombe, Perranporth TR6 0QJ Phone: (01872) 571505

PERRANPORTH. Self-contained flats, fully equipped and comfortably furnished. Colour television. Parking. One minute level walk to beach and shops. Sleeps two to eight people. Curtis 'Bel-Fiori', The Gounce, Perranporth, Cornwall TR6 0JW. Phone: (0872) 573478.

PERRANPORTH
SEASIDE HOLIDAY FLATS AND BUNGALOW OPPOSITE SANDY SURFING BEACH
Comfortable family accommodation adjacent to shops and village amenities. Free parking, colour TV etc. Sleeping range 2-10 people. Please state numbers in your party. Reasonable rates.
PHONE: (0872) 572157
25 PENTREVE, WHEAL LEISURE PERRANPORTH, CORNWALL TR6 0EY

PERRANPORTH. Comfortable carefree moder- ately priced holidays in quiet country cottage, sleeps 4 - 5. 1 mile from village and beach. Colour television, bed linen provided. Brochure from Mrs Sally Penna, Waycroft Cottage, Perrancoombe Hill TR6 0JA. Phone: (0872) 573204.

PERRANPORTH. Self-contained luxury flat, sleeps six. 3 minutes walk to 3 miles beach. Colour television, video, satellite, microwave, washing machine, dishwasher, freezer, shower. Car parking. For leaflet Phone: evenings (01872) 572629, day, mobile (0585) 257570.

PERRANPORTH. Self-catering. Five bedrooms. Five minutes shops and beach on level. Parking. Bath, shower, electricity. Large garden. Well equipped. Automatic washing machine, two toilets. Bedrooms have hand basins. Jewell, Riverside, Perrancombe, Perranporth, TR6 0HT. Phone: (0872) 572018.

PERRANPORTH. Kestrel Holidays. Self-catering houses, flats, bungalows. Near the sea or in the country. Sleeps 2 to 10 people. Prices from £70 to £500 per week. Phone: (0872) 573368.

PLYMOUTH. 14 cottages and bungalows 8 miles West of Plymouth. Situated in 18 acres of beautiful grounds in the picturesque River Lynher Valley. Ideal for fishing, golf, riding, town and coast and exploring Cornwall and Devon. Short breaks and daily rates. Open all year. Phone: (01752) 842187 or 843407. See our colour advert.

POLPERRO. Picturesque fishing village. Fisherman's cottage, sleeps 2-4. Personally supervised. Village centre. Free parking 20 yards from cottage. Sorry no pets. Details from Mrs Hoskin, Ivy Cottage, Polperro. Phone: (0503) 72732.

POLPERRO. Beautiful detached one bedroom property with patio. In sunny position within yards of harbour and village centre. Very well equipped and maintained. Sleeps two. Bed linen provided. Heating. Parking. Non smokers only. Phone: (0503) 72271.

POLPERRO, Looe. Unique galleried Cornish cottage. Furnished and equipped to high standard. Glorious peaceful countryside. Close coast and moors. Ideal base to explore Devon and Cornwall. Open all year. Non-smoking. Phone: Mrs Stockley (0503) 220252.

POLPERRO. Crumplehorn Mill. 14th century Inn. Bed and breakfast, self-catering. Good food. Local fish, fine ales, farm scrumpy. Children, pets welcome. All rooms en-suite, colour television, film channel. Quaint fishing village. Lots of do nearby. Brochure. (0503) 72348.

POLPERRO. Ideal holiday cottage by the harbour in the picturesque village of Polperro. Sleeps 6 plus cot. Central heating. Secluded garden, free car parking space. No pets. Short stays available. Phone: (0233) 850219.

POLZEATH. Well maintained three bedroomed bungalow, sleeps five. Blue Flag sandy beach. Two hundred yards. Ideal surfing, bird watching, walking, traditional beach holiday. Television, video, electric heating. Available all year. £100 - £270 weekly. Phone: (0326) 574917.

POLZEATH. Self-contained 2 bedroom ground floor flat in modern block with launderette. Sleeps four plus cot. 5 minutes above safe sandy surfing beach. Adjacent National Trust coastal path. £80 - £250. Details Phone: Bradley (0208) 863633.

POLZEATH, Tintagel area. Comfortable and modernised old world cottage. Sleeps 2/4. Quiet coastal location with extensive sea views. Beach and cliff walks. Parking. Television. Garden. Mitchell, Abbey Cottage, Parrys Close, Bristol BS9 1AW. Phone: (0272) 682673.

POLZEATH. 16th century Shilla mill to let per week or weekend breaks. Early or late season. Sheltered garden. Just 5 minutes walk Polzeath beach, shops. Extensive National Trust coastline. Sleeps 7. Phone: (0208) 862326.

POLZEATH. Flat. Superb sea views, edge of safe sandy surfing beach. Chalets. 200 yards beach and shops. Rock house sleeps 8. Country views. Reasonable terms. V. Mably, Cala-Gracio, St. Minver, Cornwall PL27 6PY. Phone: (0208) 862203 or 862320.

PORT ISAAC. Picturesque fishing village. Sleeps 2. Sea, cliff views. Coastal country walks. Very comfortable. Electric, linen included also heating. Television. Parking. Out of season, mid-week, weekend specials. Good rates. Phone: (0208) 880168.

PORT ISAAC. Tourist Approved. Furnished bun-galows for 2 - 4 persons. House accommodating 5 - 7. 2 newly built bungalows for 2 - 5. Modern amenities. Parking, television. Over lovely bay, unspoilt village, beaches, scenery. Storage heaters. £85 - £125. Early - late season. Phone: (01208) 880283.

PORT ISAAC. High standard self-catering flat for 2. Use of garden and patios in superb peaceful position overlooking harbour, coastline and picturesque fishing village. Ideal base for touring, walking, beaches. Dogs accepted. Parking. Phone: (0208) 880416.

PORT ISAAC. ETB 4/5 key. Highly commended. Beautiful cottages. Working family farm. Very friendly animals to feed. Games, fitness rooms, tennis, volley ball courts. Also large period house near Camelford, sleeping 12. Golf, sea, moors nearby. Phone: (0208) 880248.

PORT ISAAC. Treharrock Farm Cottages. Two peaceful cottages. Superb views of countryside and coast. Washer dryer, fridge freezer, colour television, microwave, electric and linen included in price. Personally cared for by owner. ETB 4 key commended. Phone: (0208) 880517.

PORT ISAAC. Fisherman's cottage. Close harbour. Sleeps 6. Modern bungalow overlooking village. Studio apartment. South facing. Sleeping 4. Parking. Phone: (0752) 842170.

PORT ISAAC. Listed farm cottages in peaceful idyllic rural setting with outstanding views of the surrounding countryside. Golden sandy beaches and quaint harbours nearby. Farm animals. Sensible prices inclusive of electricity and linen. Phone: (01208) 880564.

PORT ISAAC. Cosy harbourside cottage. Available all year. Sleeps 4 to 6. All modern facilities. From £120 to £260 per week. In 'conservation' and 'area of outstanding natural beauty'. For details Phone: (0326) 372693.

PORT ISAAC. Bungalow, flats, chalet. Sleep 2-4-6-8-10. Close sea, shops. Parking. Well equipped comfortable accommodation. Near to coastal footpath. Surfing, sailing, golf. Open all year. Unspoilt fishing village. Sea views. D. Hicks, Locarno, Port Isaac, Cornwall. Phone: (0208) 880268.

PORT ISAAC near. Thatched Cottage. Four poster bed. Colour television. Tranquil setting. Private parking. Dogs welcome. Open all year round. Special off season rates. Horse riding, golf. Plenty to do or just relax. Phone: (0208) 851450.

PORT ISAAC. Slate and Stone Cottage in old part of lovely fishing village. Attractively furnished and well equipped. Sleeps 9 plus cot. Sea views. Parking. Nice garden. Cornish Tourist Board approved. Phone: (0403) 262810 or 240841.

PORTHALLOW, Gallentreath. Self-catering apartments. Small fishing village. Quiet and peaceful. Lovely coastal walks. Panoramic sea views. Equipped to a high standard. All modern, P. Peters, Gallentreath Porthallow, St Keverne Helston, Cornwall TR12 6PL. (0326) 280400.

PORTHALLOW. Cornish cove. One hundred yards beach. Completely renovated 2 bedroomed fisherman's cottage. Sleeps 4. Sitting room, kitchen, bathroom, television, wood burning stove, radiators. Sun terrace, garden. Private parking. Skewes, White Rocks, Porthallow, Helston. Phone: (0326) 280214.

PORTHLEVEN. Self-contained wing of spacious bungalow. Fully equipped. Sleeps three. Coastal location overlooking Mounts Bay. Close, comfortable National Trust walks, beaches. Pets welcome. Phone: (0326) 563330 or (0452) 856730.

PORTHLEVEN, South West Cornwall. Beautifully located. Converted fisherman's cottages. Cosy and comfortable, one overlooking beach. Sleeps 2, other at outer harbour edge, sleeps 2 plus 2. Colour televisions, central heating. Further details Phone: (0326) 564820.

PORTHLEVEN. Detached 2 bedroomed cottage. Gardens. Parking, tennis court. Picturesque harbour. Beaches. Coastal walks. Quiet village. Ideally situated for touring West Cornwall. Phone: (0326) 563789.

PORTHLEVEN, lovely house. Spectacular sea views directly overlooking the harbour. Tastefully furnished with every comfort. All modern facilities. Sleeps 5. 3 minutes walk to sandy beach, restaurants and amenities. Ideal location exploring Lizard, Falmouth, Penzance. Phone: (0326) 573051.

PORTHLEVEN area. Sunny stone cottage adjoining National Trust Cliffs. Spectacular views and safe sandy beach. All season comfort. Open fire. Washer/dryer machine (not August). Sleeps 4. Pictures/inventory sent. Hughes, Phone: (0736) 763565.

PORTHTOWAN. Self-catering cottages within short distance from sea and sandy beaches with scenic cliff walks. Colour television. Parking. Open January, December. Personally supervised. 9 miles Truro, Falmouth, Helston, Coniam. 4 miles Redruth, Cambourne. Phone: (0579) 62624.

PORTMELLON COVE, Mevagissey. Fisherman's cottages converted to self-contained apartments for 4 people. Only 10 yards and overlooking beach. Own car park and small boats. Colour television. Phone: (0562) 747196, 745082.

PORTREATH. 19th century coachman's house, sleeps 4/5 in picturesque village. Sea views near beach, enclosed gardens, children welcome. Spring, autumn short breaks. Pets by arrangement. Woodmason, 2 Hillside, Portreath, Redruth TR16 4LL. Phone: (0209) 842078.

PORTREATH. Quality character cottages in a peaceful wooded valley close to beaches and cliffs. A 'Home from Home'. Ideal for couples and small families. Open all year. ETB 4 key highly commended. Phone: (0209) 843377 for colour brochure.

PORTREATH. Cottage in village centre. 2 min- utes level walk to harbour, beach, shops. Sleeps 6. Television, video, microwave, washing machine. Winter heating. Pets by request. £150 to £295. Discounts for smaller groups. Phone: (0209) 842077.

PORTREATH. Cottage, sleeps six. Two minutes sandy beach. Level walk. Garage. Television, microwave, heating, double glazing, cot. Phone: (0923) 823012.

PORTREATH. Between St. Ives and Newquay. Large detached farm cottage. Modernised, sleeps 12-14. 2 miles from sandy beach and harbour. Close to local amenities. Fully equipped, quilts provided, linen available. From £350 per week. Phone: (0209) 710895.

PORTREATH, near. Cornwall. Superbly equip- ped 3 bedroom bungalow with enclosed garden. Central to both coasts & many tourist attractions, yet only 10 minutes to sandy beach. Automatic washing machine, video, satellite television. Phone: (0209) 831755.

PORTREATH. Primrose Cottage, sleeps four in two double bedrooms. Large garden with safe parking. Colour television. Linen and electric inclusive. One mile beach, golf course and country park. Colour brochure Phone: (0209) 842481 evenings are best.

PORTREATH. 10 yards from sandy beach on north Cornish coast. Ideal for cliff walking, surfing and family holidays. Excellent 2 bedroom apartment. Every possible comfort, sleep 4/5. Linen provided. Phone: (0209) 890488.

PORTSCATHO, Jacaranda. 3 bedrooms, sleeps 6, 2 bathrooms, fireplace, night storage heaters. Garage, parking. Overlooking Gerrans Bay in quiet cul-de-sac. Pets by arrangement. New 2 bedroom ground floor flat, sleeps 4. £100-£395 per week. Mrs I.-L. Radford, Treventon Close, Portscatho, Truro. Phone: (0872) 580517.

PRAA SANDS, Porthleven (between). Six self-catering bungalows on 1 1/2 acres in quiet country location. Linen, electric inclusive. Games room. Pets welcome. Parking outside your holiday home. Owners resident on site. The Hillsdale Holiday Bungalows. Phone: (0736) 763466.

PRAA SANDS, Penzance, West Cornwall. 2 superb bungalows, sleeping 6-9. In large gardens, with parking space. 1 overlooks sea, 1 not overlooked 2 miles from coast. Pets welcome. Sae, Laity, Chyrase Farm, Goldsithney, Penzance TR20 9JD. Phone: (01736) 763301.

PRAZE-AN-BEEBLE. Small, cosy farm cottage for 2. Non smokers. Quiet countryside. Panoramic views to coasts at St. Ives and Penzance. 0.5 mile to village shops, pub. Sorry no pets. ETB approved. £165 - £195 per week. Phone: (01209) 831030.

REDRUTH. 3 miles. North Coast 5 miles. Newly converted stone barn. Cosy and comfortable with colour television, video, microwave etc. Linen included. Quiet, secluded spot with lovely walks. Ideal for touring. Sleeps 6. Phone: (0209) 821147.

RESTRONGUET. Waterside cottages, near Mylor Bridge. Midway between Truro, Falmouth. Fully equipped, washing machine, bed linen. Sleeps (2-6). On-site parking. Fine scenery. Good walks, yachting, bird-watching. Personally supervised. Reduced rates off peak. Phone: Reid (0736) 710285.

ROCK. Comfortable family bungalow, 5 min-utes Rock/Daymer/Polzeath. Sunny large kitchen. Garden. Parking. Sleeps 6/7. Reasonable rates. Excellent beaches and sailing, golf, windsurfing, walks, surfing. Please Phone: 081 789 0840.

ROCK, North coast. Traditional well equipped comfortable cottages, sleeping 2/5. Secluded not isolated. Garden, parking. Near golf, sea, coastal walks. Area of outstanding natural beauty. Apartment, sleeps 5. Bed linen included. Phone: David Ray (01840) 212879.

ROCK. 'Studio' - Sleeps 2/4. Cosily furnished and equipped to very high standard. Two minutes walk to Porthilly Beach. Close to sailing, golf, coastal footpath. Set in lovely shared garden. Phone: Mrs Gregan, (0208) 815096 daytime/(0208) 862410 evenings.

ROSCROGGAN. 2 miles from sandy beach, between St. Ives and Newquay. Detached newly converted chapel with 2 1/2 acre field. Rural area. Sleeps 10-12. Local amenities nearby. Fully equipped, linen available. From £350 per week. Phone: (0209) 710895.

SAINT IVES. Town centre 4 bedroom flat. Lounge, kitchen, bathroom. Hot water provided. Includes beach hut on Porthminster beach (10 minute walk). Mrs White, Vivian House, Dove Street, St. Ives TR26 2LZ. Phone: (01736) 798919.

SENNEN. Land's End semi-detached bungalow, sleeps 6. Short walk sandy beach. Colour television. Refurbished to high standard. Non smoking. Puddiphatt, Care of Chy Byghan, Sunny Corner Lane, Sennen, Penzance, Cornwall TR19 7AX. Phone: (0736) 871459.

SENNEN. Modern detached 3 bedroomed bungalow, sleeps 6. Panoramic views from Cape Cornwall around to Sennen Cove. Large garden, garage and parking. All inclusive prices. Regret no pets. Brochure Phone: (0736) 871204.

SENNEN. Detached cottage in tranquil rural setting. Sleeps 4. 2 single bedrooms, 1 double bedroom, colour television, automatic washing machine, cosy solid fuel fire. Large garden. Sea views. Easy access to wonderful beaches. Phone: (01736) 871284.

ST. AGNES, Cornwall. Cottage or bungalow. Private gardens. Ample parking. Two minutes walk to village. Half-mile to beach. Lovely coastal walks. Colour televisions. Mrs J. Sharp, West Kitty, St. Agnes TR5 0SU. Phone: (0872) 552829 or (0872) 553718.

ST AGNES. Charming cottage in village approximately 1 mile from beach. Sleeps 5. 3 bedrooms, 1 en-suite. Comfortable lounge, television, video. Well equipped kitchen, microwave, washing machine, etc. Separate shower room and w.c. Sunny garden with patio. £85 - £285 per week. Phone: (0932) 246952.

ST AGNES. Charming, well equipped 3 bed-room period cottage. Sleeps 6 comfortably. Garden. Sea views. Close village amenities. Ideally situated on North Coast for beaches, surfing, walking, touring, golfing, fishing, riding. Discounts available outside school holidays. Phone: (0306) 881372.

ST. AUSTELL. Bosinver cottages. Thatched farmhouse, sleeps 12. Other properties sleep 2-7. In garden surroundings. 30 acres, including fishing lake. Swimming pool, tennis, games room. Shops, pub nearby. Children, dogs welcome. Some discounts given. Phone: (01726) 72128/70438.

ST. AUSTELL BAY. Charming harbourside cot-tage and lovely countryside cottage at Charlestown. Also luxury detached bungalow with secluded rear garden at Carlyon Bay. ETB 3 keys commended. All completely refurbished and nicely furnished. Parking. Phone: (0726) 815566/(01726) 815566.

ST. AUSTELL. Modern self-contained garden flat. Situated in quiet countryside yet within easy reach of North and South coasts. Sleeps 2/4. Colour television, central heating, bed linen provided. No smoking. Ample parking. Phone: (0726) 850457.

ST. ERTH. Cottage in pretty village near sandy beaches of Hayle and St. Ives. Three bedrooms, sleeps six. All electric and modern conveniences. Linen and electricity included in rental. Colour television. Sorry no pets. Phone: (0494) 451316.

ST. IVES. Spacious apartment with panoramic sea view overlooking harbour. On quiet private road, free parking in front. 3 double bedrooms, sleeps up to 6. Near beaches, shops, stations. No pets, no smoking. Phone: (0736) 795657.

ST IVES. Holiday flat. Suit couple/family. Sup- erb position overlooking Porthmeor beach. Quiet spot, level to beaches, harbour. Glorious sea views. Patio, parking. Colour television, linen. £105 - £225 weekly. Phone: (0736) 797969.

ST. IVES BAY, Cornwall. Holiday bungalows. Close to sandy beach, near golf course. Sleep 4/6. Children and pets welcome. Colour television. Private parking. Available April to October. Apply Maureen Richards, Springfield, Lelant Downs, near Hayle, Cornwall. Phone: (0736) 753625.

ST. IVES. Superb ground floor flat, almost on waters edge with magnificent view over harbour and bay. Just minutes walk to Porthminster beach, harbour and shops. Sleeps 2 - 4. Phone: (0736) 794996 for more details.

ST. IVES. Exceptionally well furnished and equipped self-contained flat in a peaceful valley with superb sea views. Sleeps two, no children. No smoking. Dogs by arrangement. Car parking. Near beach. Central heating. Rates £95 - £250. Phone: (0736) 793124.

ST. IVES. Town centre. One two bedroom self- contained holiday flats. Bathroom, living room. All electric, heating with cooker, fridge, colour television. Fitted carpets, double glazed. Central shops, beaches, harbour. Uren, 'Alaunia', 12 Trennith Place. Phone: (0736) 795710.

ST. IVES. Superior, modern holiday cottage. Sleeps 6/8. Parking. Close to town and Porthmeor surf beach (50 yards). Available all year. £80 - £395. Short breaks. No pets. Details - Hurst, 25 Kilburn Close, Bramcote Moor, Nottingham. Phone: (0115) 9287748.

ST. IVES BAY (Gwithian village). Quiet attrac- tive granite and beamed cottage. Well furnished and fully equipped. In acre of secluded garden by three mile sand and surfing beach. Sleeps 4. Phone: (0736) 754701.

ST. IVES. Delightful 4 bedroomed cottage, sleeps up to 10. Full of character and perfectly situated, being within 80 yards (level walking distance) of three beautiful beaches, harbour and shops. Morey, 4 Burrow Road, St. Ives, Cornwall. Phone: (0736) 797014.

ST. IVES. Glentworth apartments. Just a few minutes from beach and town. Well appointed. Parking. Sea views. Central heating. From £80 per week. Sorry no pets or smoking. For details and availability Phone: (01736) 797892.

St. Ives

Tiny fisherman's cottage situated in the narrow streets of "Downalong." 100 yards to beach, on level for harbour, shops, etc. Sleeps 4.

Carbis Bay

Self-contained flat with superb view over the bay. Ideal location for touring and just a 20 minute walk to St. Ives.

Telephone: Penzance (01736) 794177

ST. IVES. Harbourside self-catering flat, sleeps 4-6. Panoramic view of harbour. Central for shops, railway and bus station. Write 24A Halsetown, St. Ives, Cornwall or Phone: Dorothy Tristram (0736) 797435.

ST. IVES

CORNWALL

Cottage, sleeps 4, with car park. Only 3 minutes from town and harbour.

For brochure phone:

Colin (01209) 717772

From £225 per week

ST. IVES. Enjoy the breathtaking scenery and beaches, golf, horse-riding etc. Or just relax in one of our superb properties situated in and around St. Ives. Most have sea views and parking. Personally inspected. Brochure Phone: (0736) 794495.

ST. IVES. Houses, sleeps 9-11, 4-6. Flatlet sleeps 2. Panoramic views over town, harbour, bay. On site parking. Award gardens. Full double glazing, central heating. Quiet area near centre. Pets accepted. Owner lives on site. Highly recommended. Phone: (01736) 795871.

ST. IVES, Cornwall. Seafront holiday flats overlooking harbour, beach. Fully equipped. Sleep 2-7. Mr and Mrs Phillips, Carn Brea, Talland Road, St. Ives, Cornwall TR26 2DF. Phone: (0736) 795335.

ST. IVES BAY. Chyreene Court. Comfortable, 2 bedroom, self-contained apartments. Overlooking magnificent sandy beach (two minutes walk). Excellent sea views. Balcony/patio, parking. Cornish Tourist Board approved. Short breaks from £60. Weekly £80-£300 per flat. Brochure Phone: (0736) 756651.

ST. IVES. Holiday flat sleeps two. En-suite, kitchen/diner, lounge, colour television. Linen, bedding, towels, electric all inclusive. Free parking. Near shops, beaches and on bus route. Phone: (0736) 796358 or 795433. Non smokers preferred. No pets.

ST. IVES BAY. Luxury detached bungalow style chalet. From £30 per week to £200 per week. Self-catering. Overlooking magnificent beach and beautiful St. Ives. 3 bedrooms. Colour television. Pine kitchen, bathroom etc. Mrs Gunningham for free brochure. Phone: (0509) 414329.

ST. IVES. Over 150 cottages, houses, flats. All in St. Ives. Short breaks off season. For extensive free colour brochure: W. Parsons, St. Ives Self-Catering Holidays, 9 High Street, St. Ives, Cornwall TR26 1RS. Phone: (0736) 794686 (24 hours). Fax: (0736) 794818.

ST. IVES, Cornwall. Carbis Bay. Luxury bunga- low, sleeps 4/6. 2 bedrooms, television, microwave, complete kitchen. Near beach, golf, restaurants. Free electricity and gas. Car parking. Phone: (0736) 797804.

ST. IVES. 'The Cliffs', Carbis Bay. Holiday Flats. Furnished and equipped to high standard. Colour television. Superb sea views. Spacious garden. 9 hole putting green. Private gate to cliff walks and beaches. Parking. Colour brochure Phone: (01736) 796121.

ST. IVES, Cornwall. Holiday flat for 4 persons. Overlooking Porthmeor beach, with extensive coastal views. Parking. Linen. Television and heating. Open all year. Phone: Mrs Williams (0736) 752231.

ST IVES, Cornwall, Wharf Road. Hobblers House. A 17th century listed building on the harbour. 3 bedrooms only. Above our well known sea-food restaurant. 5 minutes from Tate Gallery. Phone: (0736) 796439.

ST. IVES. Carbis Bay. Superb holiday flats. Magnificent sea views. Personally supervised. Highly recommended. Many repeat bookings. Car parking. Ask about our free golf offer for parties of two or four. For brochure Phone: (0736) 795966.

ST. JUST area, Penzance. Three bedroomed house, sleeping five. Coastal location. Panoramic views to Atlantic. Ideal walking, riding, golfing, beaching, birdwatching or relaxing. Large private garden. Well behaved pets welcome. From £85. Phone: 081 531 7392.

ST. JUST/PENZANCE. 2 self-catering holi- day cottages. Each sleep 6. Near Sennen Beach and Lands End. For particulars Phone: (0736) 787251.

ST. KEVERNE. Tregoning Manor. Cottages, bright, cheerful, well equipped character cottages. Woodburners, beams, linen and welcome pack included. Set in ten acres. Millpond, stream, woodland walk. Close to good beaches and Helford River. Phone: (0326) 280222.

ST. MAWES. Newly built luxury house, sleeps 6. Three double bedrooms (two en-suite). Double garage, balcony, garden. Secluded residential area. Fabulous view across water. Adjacent bungalow, sleeps 2/4. Fabulous view, almost waters edge. Brochure Phone: (0637) 830213.

ST. MAWGAN, North Cornish coast. Six holiday bungalows and stone single storey cottage set in 9 acres in secluded valley. One mile large sandy beach, 6 miles Newquay, 10 miles Padstow. Tourist Board approved. Retorrick Hill Phone: (01637) 860460.

ST MELLION. Beautifully converted oak beamed stone Barn. In peaceful country setting. Ideal for touring Cornwall and Devon. Sleeps 2/5. Central heating, colour television. All bedding etc. included. No hidden extras. Children welcome. Brochure Phone: (01579) 350855.

SENNEN COVE

Self-contained flat overlooking Sandy Cove. 3 minutes to sea. Sleeps 6 plus cot. Colour TV. Sorry no pets. From £125 per week. S.A.E. to:

Mrs. J. L. Bullamore, 2 Samworths Close, Castor, Peterborough PE5 7BQ

Tel: (01733) 380794

SENNEN COVE, CORNWALL

$2^1/_2$ miles from Lands End. Holiday Flat sleeps 6. Overlooks beautiful fishing cove and miles of golden sands. Private stairs to flat. Loads of extras, including colour TV and microwave. Close to Porthcurno and Minack Theatre, Marazion, Penzance and St. Ives.

Prices starting £120 to £180. Open all year.

Phone: (01736) 871410 for details

Please mention

Daltons Directory

when replying to advertisements

THE LIZARD. Spacious, modern 3 bedroomed bungalow, set in large garden. Facilities include washing machine, microwave, fridge/freezer and dishwasher. Sleep 6 plus cot. Bed linen supplied. Beach 2 miles. Cleanliness guaranteed. Phone: (0726) 843505.

TINTAGEL. Fully licensed four crowns commended ETB offering high quality en-suite accommodation, four poster honeymoon suite, extensive menu's and wine stock. Write colour brochure. The Wooton's Country Hotel, Tintagel, Cornwall PL34 0DD. Phone: (0840) 770170.

TINTAGEL. Village. Three comfortable furnished properties within 3 acre grounds. Sleeping 2/4 people. Minutes walk picturesque cliffs and shops. Pets welcome. Ample parking. From £100 per week. For brochure Phone: (0840) 770264 evenings.

TINTAGEL. Charming old stone cottage. Beautifully modernised and comfortably furnished with 3 bedrooms to sleep 6. Set amid glorious scenery on the dramatic North coast. Legendary land of King Arthur. Pets welcome. Phone: (0840) 250417.

TINTAGEL. 2 luxury one bedroom apartments in heart of village. Ideal base for exploring North Cornish coast, Bodmin Moor. Easy access to golf, riding, surfing, swimming, fishing. Available all year. Short and long breaks. Phone: (0840) 770430.

TINTAGEL/Boscastle. Seven stone cottages with beautiful sea and rural views in quiet hamlet. Sleeping from two to ten. Gardens and children's play area. Linen provided. Dogs welcome. Halgabron Holiday Cottages. Phone: (01840) 770667 for brochure.

TINTAGEL one mile. North Cornwall. Luxury fully equipped bungalow. Open all year. Sleeps two plus cot. Magnificent coastal views. Situated in peaceful hamlet, surrounded by beautiful walks. Colour television, heating. Regret no pets. Phone: (0840) 770454.

TINTAGEL. 3 cosy cottages, sleeps 2/4/6 in coastal hamlet with sea views. Colour television. Bed linen provided. Beautiful coastal walks. Near many beaches. Riding centre. Golf course. Phone: M. Nute (01840) 770437.

TREBARWITH STRAND, near Tintagel. selfcatering properties, sleep 2 to 12. Close sandy beach. Area of outstanding natural beauty. Ideal for surfing, walking. Many places of interest within easy driving distance. Pets welcome. Phone: (01840) 770585.

TRELIGGA, North Cornwall coast. Two selfcatering cottages, near beach. Sleeps 7/9. Car park, garden. Games room, cots, highchairs, colour television. Barbecue, golf, clubs, sea views. Colour brochure Phone: (0344) 774361 or (0840) 212003.

TREVONE, near Padstow. Spacious Victorian cottage. 3 bedrooms, sleeps 4-6. Well equipped. Small secluded garden. Close to dog free sandy beach and only minutes' by car Trevose. Golf courses and sailing at Rock. Phone: (0734) 535544.

TRURO near. Mid Cornwall. Luxury character cottage. Quiet rural location. Ideal both coasts, touring, country walks. Open beamed ceilings. Large lawns, garden, patio, barbecue. Very well equipped. Cornwall Tourist Board approved. Sleeps 6/8. Phone: (0872) 510248 for brochure.

TRURO. Modern 2 bedroom bungalow. Close city centre in quiet cul-de-sac. Sleeps 4. Kitchen with fridge, cooker. Dining room, lounge, table, chairs, television, pay phone. Secluded gardens, parking. Phone: (01872) 77374. Fax: (01872) 41666. Central for touring Cornwall.

TRURO. Modern bungalow, sleeps 6 and traditional cottage, sleeps 4. On separate sites in beautiful quiet countryside, 1 mile from Truro. Central heating and fully equipped to a high standard. Ample parking. Phone: Truro (01872) 73000.

WADEBRIDGE. Beautiful Cornish Stone Cottages overlooking River Camel, Bodmin Moor, with sea views. Very comfortable, central heating. Near Padstow and beaches. Sleeps 2 to 16 people. From £75 week. Ideal touring base. Phone: (0208) 813341.

CARAVANS, CHALETS & HOLIDAY PARKS

BOSSINEY COVE, Tintagel. Three family owned six berth caravans. Fully equipped, privately maintained. Scenic coastline views. Heated indoor pools, shop, club, evening entertainment, children's games room. Parking by your caravan. 'No hidden extras'. Information Phone: (0703) 771962, (0831) 899458.

BUDE, near. Luxury caravans on quiet rural park. All with two bedrooms, shower and toilet and colour television. Swimming pool. Licensed bar. Close to Tamar Lakes for fly/coarse fishing. Lufflands Caravan Park. Phone: (0409) 241426.

BUDE area. Devon, Cornwall border. Modern 6 berth caravan. Fridge, colour television, shower, flush toilet. Beaches approximately 3 miles. Lovely countryside. Gas heater, cooker and geyser. Phone: (0288) 331397. Mrs Cleave, Marsborough, Morwenstow, Bude, Cornwall EX23 9PD.

BUDE, near. Large well appointed holiday chalet near Widemouth Bay. Surfing beach, south of Bude. Heated outdoor pool. Sleeps 6. Ideally situated for exploring the spectacular coast and scenic countryside of north Cornwall. Phone: Mrs Jones (0288) 361646.

BUDE. St Tinney Farm Holidays. Luxury bunga- lows. New caravans on tranquil site. Coarse fishing, two lakes, children's riding, friendly farm, animals, bar, cafe, shop, laundry, nature walks. Four miles to beach. Free brochure Phone: (01840) 261274.

BUDE, Kilkhampton. Modern bungalow. Lovely setting. Superb modern sports facilities. Heated in, out pools, badminton, squash, tennis, bowls, sauna. Restaurant, bars. Pet welcome. Phone: 081 643 7230, 081 715 7843.

BUDE. Superb rural and coastal views. Many beaches nearby. Ideal touring location. Small, peaceful, friendly site with shop, laundry, logland play area, level sites and statics. Cornish Coasts Caravan and Camping Park, Widemouth Bay. Phone: (01288) 361380.

BUDE, Wooda Farm Caravan Park. Quiet Family park in the country by the sea. Excellent facilities for touring and camping. Luxury holiday homes for hire. ETB 5 ticks. AA 4 crown. Please contact Mrs D.D. Colwill, Wooda Farm, Bude, Cornwall EX23 9HJ. Phone: (01288) 352069.

BUDE. Luxury 3 bedroomed pine lodge. Overlooking sea and countryside. Equipped with colour television, fridge, microwave, etc. Near beaches and all facilities including heated indoor pool. Book direct and save pounds. Phone: (0420) 82785.

BUDE. Caravan, sleeps eight. Private site over- looking sea. Colour television, refrigerator, separate shower. From £80 per week, including gas and electricity. Phone: (0288) 361348.

CRACKINGTON HAVEN, near Bude, Hentervene. New pinelodge. Super park. Near sea. Luxury caravans, all facilities. Walkers paradise, beautiful country. Swimming, surfing, fishing, riding, golf. Short breaks available. Children, pets welcome. Open all year! Phone: (0840) 230365.

FALMOUTH. Retanna Holiday Park. Small, quiet park between Falmouth and Helston. Holiday caravans and touring facilities. Good location for beaches and exploring Western Cornwall. Low season, short breaks and OAP discount available. Brochure Phone: (01326) 40643.

HARLYN BAY. Between Newquay/Padstow. 1, 2 and 3 bedroomed caravans. Shower, toilet, colour television. Shop, licensed club, restaurant, bar meals, takeaway. Safe sandy beach 400 yards. Coastal walks, surfing, riding, golf. Local market. Phone: (01566) 773199.

42 CORNWALL Caravans etc.

HAYLE, Riviera Towans. Well appointed holiday chalet. 1 double room, 1 single room, with bunk beds. All linen provided. Beach approximately 400 yards. Situated in St. Ives Bay with many facilities within easy reach. Phone: (0736) 756387.

HAYLE RIVIERE TOWANS, Cornwall. Fully equipped 4/5 berth chalets. Colour television. Few minutes walk beach and shops. Ideal for touring. Coarse fishing, go-carting, pitch and putt nearby. Competitive rates. Phone: Mrs Terrill (0209) 612214.

HAYLE (near St. Ives). 4/5/6 berth chalets to let. Fully furnished and equipped including shower, toilet, colour television. 2/3 bedrooms. Only 3 minutes walk to beach! Fabulous views. Full details/brochure on request. Phone: (0752) 843241.

HAYLE, Riviera Towans. Excellent 2 bed- roomed chalet. Fully equipped, shower and colour television. Near beach with beautiful sea views. Ideal central spot for visiting many Cornish attractions. Personally supervised. Details Phone: Exeter (0392) 466327.

HAYLE (near). 5 and 6 berth in spacious area. Freedom for children. Shower and toilet facilities beside caravans. Parking. Linen, television, fridge. Ideal for touring both North and South coasts. Phone: (0736) 762407.

HAYLE. Sunny Meadow Holiday Park. 2 bed- room caravans. Toilet, shower. Colour television. Tent and caravan pitches, toilet and shower facilities, laundry, small shop. Dogs welcome. Ideally situated for touring Cornwall. Smith, Lelant Downs. Phone: (01736) 752243.

HAYLE. St Ives Bay Holiday Park. Family holidays with private access to huge golden beach. Caravans, chalets, camping. Indoor pool. Entertainment for all in peak season. For colour brochure Phone: (01736) 752274.

HELSTON. Immaculate six berth caravan on dairy farm. Central for many beaches and major tourist attractions. Ideal for touring Lizard Peninsula. From £75 to £125. For details Phone: (0326) 561946.

SILVER SANDS HOLIDAY PARK KENNACK SANDS
Peaceful landscaped family park in unspoilt, natural surroundings. Holiday caravans, tourers and tents set in individual pitches bounded by trees and shrubs. Short woodland walk to safe, clean, sandy beach.
Telephone: 01326 290631

KENNACK SANDS, Lizard Peninsula. Cornwall at its best. Small, secluded park. Safe, clean beaches. Panoramic views. Shop, takeaway food, games room, launderette. Heated indoor pool, sauna - solarium. Sea view, Chalet & Caravan Park, Gwendreath, Helston TR12 7LZ. Phone: (0326) 290635.

LAUNCESTON. Between Dartmoor and the sea. Caravan, sleeps six in private half-acre paddock. Modern chemical toilet, shower and basin with hot and cold. Golf, fishing, horse riding, surfing etc close by. £150 per week. Phone: (0566) 785369.

LAUNCESTON. Quiet park. Between Bude and Dartmoor. 5 miles A30. Budget family accommodation. Deluxe caravans. Pets welcome caravans. Discounts for singles and couples. Golf, fishing, lots to do and see locally. Brochure Phone: (01409) 211382.

LAUNCESTON near. Cornwall. Idyllic peaceful, quality accommodation, surrounded by nature trails, coarse fishing, games and gym room, farming activities. Golfing, sea and moors within easy reach. Mrs Jones, Tredidon Barton, St. Thomas. Phone: (01566) 86288.

CUTKIVE WOOD CHALETS LISKEARD
Six self-catering chalets in 41 acres of woodland. 2/3 bedrooms, fully equipped including linen, colour television, fridge, cooker, microwave. On site shop, pets corner for children, dogs welcome.
Mrs. E. Coles, St. Ive, Liskeard, Cornwall PL14 3ND. Phone: (0579) 62216

LISKEARD. Trenant Caravan Park. 6 berth caravans. Quiet country park in sheltered valley. Upper reaches Fowey River. Close Bodmin Moor. Ideal walking, touring centre. Campers and dogs welcome. £60-£115 per week. Phone: Liskeard (0579) 20896.

LISKEARD. Small privately owned terraced caravan and camping park. Maintained to a very high standard. Within easy reach of beaches and moorland. 50 pitches. Many with electric hook-up. Hard standing available. ETB 4 ticks. Phone: (0271) 328981.

LISKEARD. Static 4 berth caravan on small privately owned terraced caravan and camping park. Within easy reach of beaches and moorland. With own garden and parking. 1 double bedroom, duvets and pillows provided. ETB 4 ticks. Phone: (0271) 328981.

LOOE, Fowey. 6 berth Caravan. Private site, owner maintained. 4 miles from coast. End bedroom, shower room, separate toilet, kitchen and lounge area. Colour television, microwave. Mrs Lee, The Mowhay, Trevollard, Lanreath, Looe, Cornwall PL13 2PD. Phone: (0503) 220206.

LOOE, Polperro. Trelay Farmpark. Quiet, tran- quil, pretty park. 3 open acres, lawns - tourers. Holiday caravans for sale/hire. Open Easter - end October. Graded - very good 4 ticks. Friendly, personal service. Trelay Farmpark, Pelynt, Looe PL13 2JX. Phone: (0503) 220900.

LOOE. Luxury caravans, quiet site. Sea views. Shop and off-licence. Family run between Looe and Polperro. Whatty, The Bungalow, West Wayland, Looe, Cornwall PL13 2JS. Phone: (0503) 262410/264070.

LOOE. Privately owned superior villa. Millendreath holiday village. Sleeps 6. Superb beach, panoramic views, marvellous walks. Cable television, microwave. Many on-site activities: indoor pool, parascending, clubhouse, shop etc. Bed linen included. Competitive rates. Phone: (0892) 553570.

LOOE, Polperro Countryside. Graded 'very good', 4 ticks ETB. Quiet, pretty with friendly caring management. Reasonable rates for caravan holiday homes, tourers, tents, motor caravans. Open Easter/end October. Trelay Farmpark, Pelynt-by-Looe PL13 2JX. Phone: (0503) 220900.

LOOE. Polborder House. Peaceful park with excellent facilities. Situated in beautiful surroundings the park is extremely well maintained and noted for its tranquillity and cleanliness. Luxury caravans for hire. Tourers and campers welcome. Phone: (01503) 240265.

NEWQUAY. Trebellan Park, Cubert in quiet val- ley with fishing lakes, 4 flats, 1 bungalow. Touring site. Free showers, heated pool, play area. Games room. Pets corner, shop, laundry, public telephone. 16th century thatched inn. Phone: (0637) 830522.

Millendreath HOLIDAY VILLAGE

Fully equipped villas and bungalows in secluded valley, all with colour TV and satellite. Indoor heated swimming pool, clubhouse and entertainment, bar, cafe, supermarket. Situated next to beach with watersports and parascending. Ample parking.

Weekend and Bank Holiday Special Breaks Available

FREE SWIMMING POOL USAGE
FREE CLUB MEMBERSHIP
FREE ENTERTAINMENT

Free brochure: Dept DD, Millendreath Holiday Village, Looe, Cornwall PL13 1NY
Tel: (01503) 263281 (24 hours)

Very Special Places!
Cornwall - Looe Bay & Mullion

Fantastic Fun Family Holidays located in areas of outstanding natural beauty with the very best in luxurious accommodation and all weather facilities. Heated indoor pools • Outdoor pool • Sauna and Solarium • Fun factory and ball pool • Adventure playgrounds and daily activity programmes for children and teenagers. A host of eating, dining and takeaway meals, good food and all day pubs • Shop • FREE Clubs and Nightly Live Entertainment and Cabarets • FREE Gas and Electricity (Caravan Holiday Homes) • FREE Bed Linen • FREE Colour TV • Lots to see and do including Bike Hire and even Scuba Diving! • Discounts at Local shops and attractions.

WESTSTAR HOLIDAY ★ PARKS

Ring for FREE Colour Brochure (quote D1)
(01392) 447 447
8 Abbey Court, Eagle Way, Sowton, Exeter, Devon EX2 7HY

TREKENNING MANOR TOURIST PARK

New Ownership

A delightful, select family run park, exclusively for touring caravans, motor caravans and tents. One of the most attractive parks in Cornwall, set in the secluded grounds of a 15th century manor house. Adjacent to A39 by the St. Columb Major roundabout, 10 minutes drive to Newquay and north coast beaches. All modern facilities, including family showers and bathrooms. Heated swimming pool, childrens play area, games room, shop, gas, launderette, public telephone, licensed bar and restaurant/take away.

Please contact John, David or Tracey for our colour brochure

Phone/Fax: (01637) 880462

NEWQUAY, CORNWALL

NEWQUAY. A small elite site of bungalows and chalets set in sheltered valley. Only a short distance from the sandy beaches of Porth and Whipsiderry. Brochure E. Wakeley, 17 Rainyfield, Padstow, Cornwall PL28 8EZ. Phone: (0841) 532779.

NEWQUAY. Two berth newly refurbished tour-er sited holiday park. Use of all facilities. Few minutes drive from beaches, Atlantic rollers. Duvets, pillows supplied, no linen. Awning. Free gas, linked electricity. Phone: (0209) 861042. Swimming pool.

THE MEADOW

Holywell Bay, Newquay, Cornwall

Bungalows, caravans, chalets on small private site by large sandy surf beach. All services, parking, some touring.

Colour Brochure

Phone (01872) 572752

NEWQUAY. Six berth modern caravans on Trenance site. Ideal family site adjoining leisure park. Swimming pools and zoo. 1/2 mile town centre. Sae Mrs B. Reynolds, 68 Henver Road, Newquay TR7 3BN. Phone: (01637) 873891.

NEWQUAY two miles. One only four to six berth large caravan fully equipped. Colour television, shower, flush toilet in pleasant peaceful country setting. Central for touring beaches, cliff walks and golf nearby. Phone: (0637) 871102.

NEWQUAY. Treloy Tourist Park, Newquay, Cornwall. Touring caravans, tents and motorhomes. Heated swimming pool. Licensed bar, family room. Shop, laundry, free showers. Electric hook-ups. Adventure playground, own golf course, concessionary green fees. Phone: (01637) 872063.

NEWQUAY. Holiday in pleasant surroundings in caravans on Trenance Park. 6-berth, 1 and 2 bedrooms, shower, colour television. Near town, beaches and entertainment. Competitive rates. Harris, 'Waye', Rue Des Buttes, Saint Mary, Jersey JE3 3DE. Phone: (01534) 482619.

NEWQUAY. Luxury holiday caravans for hire. Sleeping 2-8. Award winning family park. From £125 per week. Supermarket, cafe. Free heated swimming pool. All caravans fully equipped. Also touring/camping pitches. Free brochure. Trevella Park Phone: (0637) 830308.

NEWQUAY. Trencreek Holiday Park, Cornwall TR8 4NS. Superior spacious houses and bungalows. Touring and camping level site. Licensed bar, swimming pool, shop, cafe, amusements, launderette, showers, toilets. Coarse fishing. No pets. Nearby golf. Mrs Hautot. Phone: (01637) 874210.

PADSTOW. Seagull Tourist Park. Small, quiet park on working farm. Showers, toilets, washing machine, dryer, payphone, gas, ice packs. Near to shops, entertainment, riding, golf, surfing, fishing. Caravans to let. Contact Warden. Phone: (0841) 520117.

PADSTOW, Harlyn Sands, Cornwall. 6 berth caravan, fully equipped. 400 yards from safe sandy beach. Clubhouse with family entertainment. Shop and restaurant on site. Ideal for touring this lovely area of North Cornwall. Phone: (0837) 810444.

PADSTOW (near). 2 bedroomed chalets, sleep-ing 4/6 persons. Well equipped and fully self-contained. Bar, shop etc. on site. No pets. Coast 2 miles. £60 - £210 weekly. Williams, 'Veryun' Spearcey Close, Taunton TA3 7HN. Brochure Phone: (01823) 337316.

MUSIC WATER CARAVAN PARK

NEAR PADSTOW

Close to beaches. Small swimming pool, licensed bar, children's play area, level pitches, electric hook-ups, clean & friendly, everyone welcome. Also Caravans for hire. Rallies welcome.

TELEPHONE FOR BROCHURE 0841 540257

TREGUSTICK FARM HOLIDAY PARK

PORTH, NEWQUAY, CORNWALL

Situated in rural setting yet only 3 miles from Newquay (Town Centre). 1 mile beach.

Amenities include Swimming Pool, Solarium, Games Room, Children's Play Area. Caravans & Chalets 4-7 Berth with modern amenities.

COLOUR BROCHURE

Mrs. D. Hoskin, Tregustick Farm Holiday Park, Porth, Newquay, Cornwall TR8 4AR.

Tel: (01637) 872478

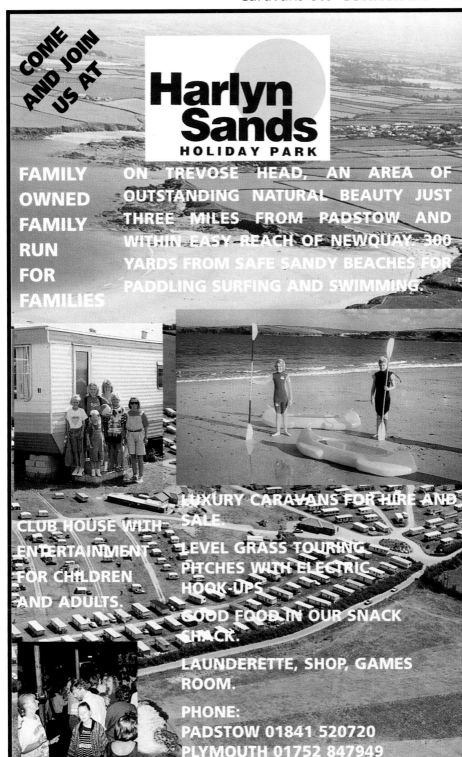

PAR SANDS. Luxury fully serviced caravans. Close to safe sandy beach and in spacious gardens of country inn. Colour televisions. Large beer garden, family room. No pets. For colour brochure Phone: (0726) 812540.

PENTEWAN SANDS, near Mevagissey. Personally managed caravans with showers, toilets, on lovely private beach site. Clubhouse entertainment, pirates, kids club, heated pool. Restaurant, snack bar, supermarket. No dogs. Mrs. E. Bartlett, 141 Tregonissey Road, St. Austell, PL25 4DS. Phone: (0726) 74543.

PERRANPORTH, Perran Sands. Chalets with cot, microwave, shower, colour television, Nintendo and Haven membership included. Book 2 weeks during first 12 weeks of season and have first week at half price. Osgood. Phone: (0637) 880329.

PERRANPORTH (Newquay coast). Blue Seas holidays. Luxury caravans all with showers, colour television. Sea or beach views. Peaceful family park. Approximately 10 minutes walk on pavement to shops and golden sands. Free gas, electric. Phone: (01872) 572176.

PERRANPORTH. Ocean view holiday caravans. Luxury caravans with sea views. Peaceful family park. Walk on pavement to town and superb sandy beach. Low season discounts. Free gas and electricity. No VAT. Phone: Hudspeth (0872) 571045.

PERRANPORTH. Perransands Holiday Village (Haven complex). Private, cosy chalets. Sleeps six. Fully carpeted, colour television, fully equipped kitchen including microwave. Entertainments, indoor and outdoor pool, spectacular beach. Warm welcome. Perran Bay Holidays. Phone: (Bob) (01392) 57659.

PERRANPORTH. Silverbow Park. AA, Calor, ETB awards for excellence. 14 superior leisure homes and touring pitches in beautiful landscaped parkland. Swimming pool, tennis, bowls. Special discounts. Colour brochure Phone: (01872) 572347.

PERRANUTHNOE, near Penzance. 6 berth caravan. Shower, fridge, toilet, television. Quiet site. Near beach. Pets accepted. Details Phone: (0736) 710452.

POLPERRO. Caravan and camping site on dairy farm. Sea views. 6 berth caravans for hire. Mains services, colour television. Ideal for those seeking a peaceful holiday. Brochure, contact Williams, Phone: (0503) 72387.

POLZEATH. Modern 6 berth caravan. 2 bedrooms, bathroom and shower, hot and cold water, full size cooker and fridge, colour television, fully equipped kitchen, gas fire. Pets allowed. Quiet farm site. Near beaches. Phone: (0803) 297272.

POLZEATH, North Cornwall. Six berth modern caravan. Toilet, shower, cooker, fridge, colour television. 2 minutes beach, good surf. Clean family site with shop, launderette. Ample parking. Phone: (0566) 782456 evenings, weekends for details.

PORT ISAAC, four miles. Large luxury caravan. All services in pretty orchard on working farm. Quiet and peaceful but easy reach beaches, shops, Moors. Children welcome. No pets. From £95 per week. Brochure Phone: (0208) 841202.

PORTHTOWAN FARM. Luxury caravan. Near coast. Panoramic views end bedroom. Hot and cold shower, toilet. Television. Fridge, mains services. From £85 per week. Also bed and breakfast accommodation in farmhouse. From £12 person. Phone: Simmons (0209) 890343.

PORTHTOWAN near. 200 yards main A30. Whealrose Camping Caravan Park, nr. Porthtowan, Scorrier TR16 5DB. Beautiful level 6 acre secluded valley setting. Country walks, beaches close by. Full disabled facilities. Free showers, awnings, dishwashing. Sorry no entertainment. Phone: (01209) 891496.

REDRUTH. Caravans and chalets on small, quiet park offering the peace and tranquillity your holiday deserves. Extremely central for exploring Cornwall. Special reductions and short breaks available. Hedged touring pitches. Tresaddern Holiday Park, St. Day. Phone: (01209) 820459.

REDRUTH. Caddy's Corner Farm. Small family farm with static caravan accommodation and excellent tourer/camping facilities. Children's areas. Animals. Television. In rural setting, centrally located for all Cornish coasts. Pets welcome. Davis, Carnmenellis. Phone: (0209) 860275.

ROCK two miles. North Cornish coast. 6 berth two bedroomed mobile holiday home. Shower, television. Select, quiet beautiful woodland site. Fine sandy beaches, all water sports, golf nearby. Variety of coastal and moorland walks. Phone: (0428) 683786.

ROCK, near Polzeath. Luxury caravans on lovely secluded park overlooking the River Camel. Golden sandy beaches and quaint harbours nearby. Heated swimming pool. Terms from £80, June £120, July from £150 per week. Phone: (01208) 880564.

ST. AGNES. Woodlands chalets. Timber chalets, sleeping 2-5 in secluded woodland setting, just 350 yards from sandy beach. Close to Cornish coast path and wonderful views. Small family site, pets welcome. Phone: Mrs B. Thompson (0872) 553593.

ST. AUSTELL. Carlyon Bay Camping Park. A family park with luxury facilities. Footpath to golf-course and Cornwall's Blue Flag award sandy beach. ETB graded excellent. AA Britain's best sites. Practical Caravans Top 35 video. Phone: (01726) 812735.

ST. AUSTELL. Trencreek Farm Holiday Park. Chalets, caravans, camping. Heated swimming pool, tennis court, fishing lakes etc. Special offers Easter to mid July. Self-catering. Second week half price. Touring £35 per week including electric. Phone: (01726) 882540.

ST. BURYAN between Penzance and Land's End. Near unspoilt beaches, fishing, coves, Minack open air theatre. Modern 6 berth caravans. Spacious camping and caravan pitches on peaceful family park. Tower Park, St. Buryan, Cornwall. TR19 6BZ. Phone: (01736) 810286.

ST. IVES. Polmanter Tourist Park, St. Ives, Cornwall TR26 3LX. Touring caravans, tents and motorised only. AA 4 pennants, ETB 5 ticks. Families and couples. Swimming pool, tennis. Family lounge, lounge bar, games room. Hook-ups. Phone: for brochure (01736) 795640.

ST IVES, Penzance. Choose from 4 self-cater- ing holiday villages. Clean sandy beaches. Superb value 2 bedroom cottages and 3/4 bedroom lodges sleeping 2 to 10. Free entertainment, sports, indoor, outdoor pools. Pets. Ben Bowers, Phone: (0115947) 6927, (0500) 026222 (Freefone).

POLPERRO, CORNWALL
(photograph courtesy of West Country Tourist Board)

ST. IVES BAY. 5 berth, 3 bedroom chalet. Sea views. Ideal family holiday. Only 400 yards from Hayle, Towans, golden sands. Bus services, shops and pub nearby. Microwave, colour television and video. No pets. Phone: (0736) 757034.

ST. IVES, Cornwall. Small friendly farm site. 1 mile town centre, beaches. Cottage - 6 berth caravans available. Tourers, campers welcome. Coastal, countryside, walks, golf course and pony trekking nearby. Laundry facilities. Sae Rogers, Hellesveor Farm. Phone: (01736) 795738.

ST. IVES BAY. Chalet, situated at Riviere Towans overlooking St. Ives Bay area. Fantastic views. This spacious chalet on the sand has three bedrooms, sleeps up to six adults. Fully equipped including television, microwave, blankets. Phone: (01209) 712821.

ST. IVES BAY. Hayle and Saint Erth. Holiday and long lets, spacious fully equipped chalet and cottages, available summer and winter. Close to sea. Families welcome. Dogs by agreement. For further precise details Phone: (01736) 756976.

ST. JUST
Near Penzance
Caravans for hire. Camping with electric. Licensed bar, food, childrens play ground. Close to Lands End and beaches. Caravans from £90. Camping from £4.
For brochure
Phone: (01736) 788571

ST. MERRYN, near Padstow. 2 bedroomed 6 berth holiday chalet on quiet site with clubhouse. Situated between Bodmin Moor and the sea. It is ideal for exploring Cornwall. Sorry no pets. Details Phone: (0993) 775730.

TREVEAN CARAVAN & CAMPING PARK
ST. MERRYN, PADSTOW, CORNWALL PL28 8PR
MRS. M. J. RAYMONT
TEL: 01841 520772
Quiet family park near sandy/surfing beaches. 3 luxury caravans to let. 36 touring caravan/tent pitches. Modern toilet/shower block/launderette. Electrical hook-up-points. Childrens play area.
AA, Camping Club, RAC & English Tourist Board Graded. Q ✓✓✓

TINTAGEL. Single self-contained, all electric chalet in elevated position with coastal view. Separate bedrooms (double and bunkroom), shower, toilet, washing machine, dryer, colour television, electricity. Bed linen included. Pets welcome. £90 - £170. Chylean, Tintagel, Cornwall PL34 0HH. Phone: (0840) 212262.

TRURO. Close Fal Estuary. One only, secluded all electric 4-6 berth caravan. Double bedroom, toilet, shower room, colour television. Fire, microwave, fridge, cooker. Bed linen provided. Mains services, fine country views and lovely walks. Phone: (evenings) (0872) 863303.

TRURO. Leverton Place. Family run caravan park. Awarded Rose Award for excellence. 15 caravans, each set in their own hedged garden. Heated swimming pool, comfortable bar and bistro, and children's games room. Phone: (0872) 560462.

WHITSAND BAY Holiday Park. In Cornwall, and only 6 miles from Plymouth. With spectacular views on historic site. South East Cornwall's award winning park. It's a little different. Phone: (01752) 822597.

LITTLE BODIEVE HOLIDAY PARK
Wadebridge, Cornwall PL27 6EG
Telephone: (01208) 812323.
ROSE AWARD FAMILY PARK. 20 acres of level well mown areas. Ideal touring centre, close to superb beaches. Fully tiled toilet & shower blocks, Baby Room, Launderette, Electric Hookups, Heated Outdoor Pool, Watershute Splash Pool, Shop, Crazy Golf, Pets Corner, Play Area, Games Room, Licensed Club House, Bar Meals, Takeaway, Entertainment in main season. Luxury caravans for hire.
Early and Late Season Breaks
Resident Proprietors:
Dennis Hills, Chris Berry & Families.
BROCHURES ON REQUEST

WIDEMOUTH BAY, near Bude, Cornwall. Panoramic sea - coast. Modern holiday chalet. Accommodates 6. Fully furnished, colour television, microwave. Club, bar, sports facilities inclusive at £300 weekly. Cousins, Moneviere, Holsworthy, North Devon EX22 6HQ (United Kingdom). Phone: (0409) 253423.

WIDEMOUTH BAY, Bude. Spectacular panoramic sea views from this family run camping, touring site. Modern facilities. Laundry shop, play area, pool table, hook ups and telephone. ETB graded 3 ticks. Penhalt Farm, Cornwall. Phone: (0288) 361210.

WHERE TO GO

Dobwalls Family Adventure Park
Liskeard.
Tel: (0579) 20325

Mini-American railroad complex, 'live' experience of Archibald Thorburn's (1860-1935) wildlife paintings, children's adventure playground, braille facilities. Picnic areas, barbeque, cafes, shops. Disabled visitors welcome.

Flambards Triple Theme Park
Culdrose Manor, Helston.
Tel: (0326) 574549

Recently extended award-winning authentic life size Victorian village with fully-stocked shops, carriages and fashions. Britain in the Blitz exhibition, Aero Park with original helicopters, aeroplane and Exploratorium. Restaurants, mother and baby facilities. Disabled visitors welcome.

St. Agnes Leisure Park
St. Agnes.
Tel: (087255) 2793

Cornwall in miniature, Dinosaur World, Fairyland, Haunted House, Grand Circus. Restaurants, camera loan. Disabled visitors welcome.

Tintagel Castle
Tintagel, Cornwall.
Tel: (0840) 770328

Medieval ruined castle on wild, windswept coast. Famous for associations with Arthurian legend.

Lands End
Lands End, Sennen, Penzance, Cornwall.
Tel: (0736) 871501

Attractions include, Last Labyrinth, Man against Sea, Spirit of Cornwall, Little Cornwall, Greeb Farm, Galleon play area and land train. Life boat exhibition.

Bodmin and Wentford Railway
Bodmin General Station, Lostwithiel Road, Bodmin.
Tel: (0208) 73666

Nostalgic branch line old country town to BR mainline station by River Fowey. The normally steam hauled trains pass through lovely countryside and give access on foot to Lanhdrock (NT) and Cardinham Woods (FC). Refreshments and gift shop.

DEVON

HOTELS & GUEST HOUSES

ASHBURTON, Ilsington. Dartmoor National Park. Superior bed and breakfast in lovely detached Edwardian house. One mile from Hay Tor. En-suite bedrooms, colour television, tea making facilities. Super pubs and eating places nearby. Sorry no smokers. Phone: (0364) 661277.

AYLESBEARE, East Devon. 16th century farmhouse. Tranquil surroundings. ETB. All rooms en-suite, colour television, tea, coffee, central heating. Guest lounge, log fires. Coarse fishing, riding, golf, nature reserve nearby. Woodland walks. Brochure available. Phone: (0404) 822771.

BARNSTAPLE. Comfortable accommodation in 17th Century farmhouse. Bed and breakfast from £11, evening meal optional. Near coast and Exmoor. Tea, coffee making facilities. Children welcome, babysitting available. Pony rides. Phone: Mrs Friend (0271) 850286.

BARNSTAPLE. Beautiful country manor hotel in glorious woodland setting. All rooms en-suite and all facilities. Heated pool, tennis court, cosy bar. Close Exmoor and coast. Let us spoil you. Phone: (0271) 850262.

BARNSTAPLE, North Devon. Farm bed and breakfast. Tea and coffee making facilities, hot and cold in room, shower, television lounge. Convenient to beaches and moors. Open May to October. Phone: Mrs Cherry Prideaux (0271) 830442.

BARNSTAPLE, Devon. Listed Farmhouse. 2 miles from Barnstaple. Working farm with calves, sheep, ponies and goat. Children welcome. Hot and cold in bedrooms. Bed and breakfast. Evening meal optional. Traditional farmhouse cooking. Reductions for children. Phone: Jenny Rogers (0271) 830253.

BIDEFORD. Farmhouse accommodation in small Parish of Welcombe on Devon, Cornwall border. 2 miles off coast where one of Britain's cleanest beaches in Readers Digest Guide 1994. Bed and breakfast, evening meal optional. Phone: (0288) 331391.

LARGE WORKING FARM

BECKLAND FARM
Hartland, North Devon

A delightful old farmhouse situated on the coast between Clovelly and Hartland. Direct access to National Trust coastal walks and within easy reach of many coves and beaches. Comfortable centrally heated accommodation comprising of 1 large family room with en-suite, 1 twin bedroom with H&C, private use of bathroom, also bunk bedroom. All with sea views and tea and coffee facilities.

Further details: **Mrs Debbie Symons, Beckland Farm, Hartland, Bideford, N. Devon EX39 6AP. Tel: 0237 441289**

BIDEFORD, North Devon. Small country hotel. Quiet, peaceful location, overlooking spectacular countryside. 1.5 miles from town. Beautifully decorated, spotlessly clean. All en-suites with television, beverages. Superb traditional food, everything homemade. Non smoking establishment. Phone: (01237) 472962.

BIDEFORD. Splendid roundhouse barn conversion amidst beautiful peaceful countryside. All rooms en-suite with colour television, tea making facilities. Family room with special rates. Sea ten minutes. Mrs Smith, The Roundhouse, Guscott, Huntshaw, Torrington, Devon. Phone: (0271) 858626.

GREENLAKE FARM
Hartland, Bideford

B&B, evening meal optional. Family and double room including hot and cold. Tea/coffee facilities. Children welcome. **Mrs. Heard – Tel: (0237) 441251.**

BIDEFORD, North Devon. Small country hotel. Peaceful picturesque location overlooking spectacular countryside. Excellent accommodation with emphasis on quality, comfort, cleanliness. En-suites - colour television, beverages, superb food, everything homemade. Book with confidence in non-smoking establishment. Phone: (01237) 472962.

BRIXHAM. 19th century licensed country hotel, Sandy beaches nearby. Overlooking Dart Valley Steam Railway. Excellent cuisine, all rooms colour television, radio, beverage facilities. En-suites available. Dogs, children welcome. Special out of season rates. Phone: (0803) 842381.

BRIXHAM. Delightful 15th century Guest House. Excellent home cooking. Wealth of beams and cottage style bedrooms. Pets welcome. Ample coastal walks. Bed and breakfast from £13. Black Cottage, 17 Milton Street. Phone: (01803) 853752.

BUCKFASTLEIGH. Woodholme Guest House. Spacious Victorian home providing comfortable bed and breakfast. Twin, double and luxury en-suite rooms. Close Buckfast Abbey, South Devon Steam Railway and Dartmoor. 20 miles Exeter, Plymouth, Torbay. Phone: (01364) 643350 for brochure.

BUCKFASTLEIGH, South Devon. Dairy farm. Comfortable/relaxing atmosphere. Bed and breakfast, evening meal available. Overlooking Dartmoor, close to beaches. Delicious food, excellent accommodation, tea/coffee facilities. Enclosed garden with children's play area. ETB commended. Phone: (0364) 643775.

BUDLEIGH SALTERTON, Devon. Bed, breakfast. Family run. Minutes from beach, coastal path, bus route. Children and pets welcome. Colour television in rooms. Phone or sae (0395) 444100. Vegetarian or English breakfast. No smoking. Self catering available.

BUTTERLEIGH. Mid Devon. £125 weekly. Bed and breakfast with delicious evening meals. Generous farmhouse hospitality. Peaceful relaxing atmosphere overlooking the beautiful Burn Valley. Ideal for coast, moors, M5 (J28). Coarse trout fishing. Free cycle hire. Phone: (0884) 855463.

CHAGFORD. 17th century farmhouse. Bed and breakfast and home cooking in peaceful Devon countryside. Large garden. Swimming pool. Fields and woods. Edge of Dartmoor. Historic Exeter nearby. Central for all coasts. Tents and caravans welcome. Phone: (0647) 24110.

CHAGFORD, Throwleigh Manor. Beautiful country house in idyllic setting in Dartmoor National Park, offers excellent bed and breakfast from £15.50. Also self-catering cottages. Swimming pool, games room, lake. Children welcome. ETB commended. Phone: (0647) 231630.

CHAGFORD. Glendarah House. Beautifully re-furbished Victorian country house in Dartmoor National Park. Lovely en-suite rooms. Peaceful. Ideal walking/touring centre licensed. Parking. ETB 2 crowns. Highly commended. AA 4 Q's selected. RAC acclaimed. Phone: (01647) 433270.

CHALLACOMBE. High quality en-suite (non-smoking) bedrooms, panoramic views, superb cooked breakfast and a warm welcome for you to enjoy the beauty of Exmoor. Excellent walking, fishing, riding nearby. Dogs by arrangement. Stabling. Enquiries Phone: (05983) 568.

CHULMLEIGH. Fox Hounds Hotel. Mid Devon country house hotel. Set in 30 acres. Taw Valley. 7 miles salmon, sea-trout, trout fishing. Par 3 golf in grounds. Comfortable bar. Log fires. Elegant restaurant. Snooker. Clay shooting. Excellent food. Fine wines. Phone: (0769) 580345.

CLEARBROOK. Dartmoor Guest House. 8 miles north of Plymouth. Bed and breakfast, evening meal optional. Village pub 100 yards. All rooms have wash basins, colour television and drinks facilities. Private parking. Dartmoor Tourist Association members. Phone: (0822) 852130.

CLOVELLY. 'The Old Smithy'. Comfortable bed and breakfast. Some en-suite. All with tea making facil-ities and colour television. Near coastal footpaths. Short drive to Dartmoor and Exmoor. Phone: (0237) 431202. Vanstone, Sierra, Clovelly, Bideford, Devon EX39 5ST.

**Attractive 17th Century Cottage
with sea views**
Overlooking picturesque village of Clovelly.
Tea/coffee facilities and TV in all rooms. 1 family,
1 double, 1 twin rooms. Children and pets welcome.
Mrs. B. May. 0237 431209

CLOVELLY (near). Peace, quiet and good food available in spacious character L-shaped cottage with modern facilities. Panoramic views. Ideal base for get-ting away from it all. For bed and breakfast details and brochure Phone: (01237) 431513.

COLYTON, Sunnyacre. Restful accommodation on farm in beautiful scenic countryside. Good local beaches. Plenty of interesting amenities. Ample home cooking includes traditional roasts, all home-made desserts. Games room. Children welcome. Phone: Norma Rich Farway (0404) 87422.

COLYTON, Wiscombe. Linhaye Farm. Ground floor. En-suite and private bathroom. Bedrooms, televi-sion and tea facilities. Quiet countryside, five miles from sea. Home cooking with local produce. Lovely coast walks, small working farm. Phone: Rabjohns (0404) 87342.

COLYTON. 15th century thatched fully licensed hotel. Resident proprietors. Excellent cuisine. One 4-poster bedroom. Also available luxury holiday cottages, sleeping 2/3. Sorry no children/pets. White Cottage Hotel, Colyton. Phone: (0297) 552401.

COMBE MARTIN. Panoramic sea views. Fully en-suite rooms. Excellent food. Real ales, wines. Good service, atmosphere. Family suite. Parking. Central for Exmoor, Cornwall touring, walking, relaxing. Open all year. Brochure Focsle Inn Phone: (01271) 883354.

CROYDE, St. Helens Priory Hotel. Thatched 17th century former priory. Small family-run hotel in relaxing, friendly atmosphere. Set in acre of beautiful gardens. All facilities, most rooms en-suite. Beaches, golf, riding nearby. Phone: (0271) 890757.

DARTMOOR. Mardlewood House. A listed 18th Century woollen mill in secluded valley of River Mardle, on edge of moor, yet just 3 1/2 miles from Buckfastleigh and A38. For brochure Phone: Mrs Bellows (0364) 643152.

DARTMOOR. Farmhouse, bed and breakfast. Peaceful, unspoilt countryside. All rooms en-suite, tea making facilities, colour television, games room. Farm animals. Ideal walking places of interest. Beaches. Newcombe Farm, Scoriton, Buckfastleigh, South Devon TQ11 0JE. Phone: (0364) 643734/642724.

DARTMOOR. Teign Valley. Country house. Bed and breakfast, evening meal. Beautiful, peaceful sur-roundings. En-suite facilities, tea making facilities, home cooking. Lounge, dining room, television. Homely atmosphere. Long established. Phone: Rachel Waddilove. Phone: (0392) 811559.

DARTMOOR. Away from everything! 2 self-catering properties for 4 and 8. In isolated part of Southern Dartmoor. Beautiful walking, riding country-side. Local beauty spots and places to visit. Streams, rivers. Moorland. Booty, Poundsgate. Phone: (0364) 631223.

DARTMOUTH. Bed, breakfast. En-suite avail-able. Family, double, twin, single, colour televisions, tea, coffee facilities all rooms. Fully central heated, double glazed. Two minutes Quay and town centre. Lovely views river from dining room. Phone: (0803) 833069.

DAWLISH. Walton Guest House. Grade II listed property. All bedrooms en-suite, with colour tele-vision, beverage facilities. Four poster bedroom. Private parking in grounds. Short walk to beach, town centre, station. Colour brochure. Phone: (01626) 862760.

DITTISHAM. Near Dartmouth. Unspoilt village inn. Overlooking the peace and beauty of the River Dart. Offering comfort, fine cooking and friendly old bar. Reduced golf fees nearby. Winter, The Red Lion Inn TQ6 0ES. Phone: (01803) 722235.

ERMINGTON. In peaceful countryside, perfect for touring, high standard bed and breakfast accommo-dation, en-suite, own front door, colour television, tea/coffee facilities. Outdoor heated swimming pool. Price from £15. Sorry no pets. Phone: (0752) 830427.

EXETER. 17th Century farmhouse in tranquil countryside with extensive views. Three spacious en-suite bedrooms with hospitality tray. Farmhouse break-fast cooked on Aga. Television lounge with woodburn-er, central heating. Children welcome. Parking. Bolt, Wood Barton, Farringdon. Phone: (0395) 233407.

EXETER near. Discover a beautiful part of Devon. Character farmhouse in peaceful setting. Dartmoor 15 miles, sandy beach 4 miles. Bed and full English breakfast £14 per night, weekly £85. Chiverstone Farm, Kenton, Exeter. Phone: (0626) 890268.

EXETER. 2 crown ETB rated licensed hotel. 10 minutes walk cathedral, stations and university. En-suite rooms with satellite television, telephone and free tea and coffee. Brochure. Morris, Clock Tower Hotel, New North Road, EX4 4HF. Phone: (0392) 424545.

EXETER. Oakcliffe Hotel. Small friendly hotel, convenient to city centre, railway/coach stations and university. Tea/coffee facilities and televisions in all rooms. Showers in some. Full English breakfast. 73 St Davids Hill, Exeter. Phone: (0392) 58288.

EXETER 6 miles. Farmhouse in delightful Devon countryside. Rooms with hot and cold, central heating, tea making facilities. Lounge with colour television. Bed and breakfast from £14. Glanvill, Higher Bagmores Farm, Woodbury, Exeter. Phone: (0395) 232261.

EXMOOR, Scatterbrook Farm. Working farm in National Park. Good facilities for disabled. Warm friendly welcome. Good home cooking. Dogs welcome. Bed, breakfast £10 to £15. Two en-suite. Evening meal £6.50. Please Phone: Dulverton (0398) 23857.

HOLNE, Ashburton. Bed and breakfast. Personal service, vegetarians, children, pets welcome. ETB listed. Panoramic views, walking on Dartmoor, canoeing, horse riding. 45 minutes sea. Pub and shop handy. Phone: (0364) 631235.

HOLSWORTHY. Working farm on Devon, Cornwall border. En-suite rooms with tea making facilities. Close to Clovelly, coast and moors. Excellent cuisine. Bed and breakfast from £13.00. Optional evening meals. The Barton, Pancrasweek, Holsworthy. Phone: (0288) 381315.

HOLSWORTHY, Devon. Farmhouse accommodation. Hot/cold all rooms, tea facilities. Free horse riding. Games room. 8 miles from beach. Golf. Child minding. Margaret Hayes, Little Knowle Farm, Pyworthy, Holsworthy, Devon, Bude Beach. Phone: (0409) 253544.

HONITON. Ann and Doug Rickson welcomes you to farmhouse bed and breakfast. Television and tea and coffee making facilities in rooms. Lovely views, 25 minutes to coast. Pets welcome. £11 per night. Phone: (0404) 43489.

HOPE COVE, Fern Lodge. ETB 2 crowns. All rooms en-suite, tea and coffee facilities. Good home cooking, table license, extensive sea views. Brochure and tariff Phone: (0548) 561326.

HOPE COVE. Fern Lodge. Family run guest house. 200 yards from the beach. Good home cooking. 2 lounges. Licensed. All rooms en-suite. Parking available. Children over 5 and pets welcome. ETB 2 crowns. £19.50 and £29. Phone: (0548) 561326.

ILFRACOMBE. Friendly RAC acclaimed hotel. En-suite rooms with television and tea making facilities. Car parking. Children and pets welcome. Short breaks from £46.00. 7 days dinner, bed and breakfast £140 to £174. St. Brannocks House. Phone: (0271) 863873.

ILFRACOMBE, Strathmore. Licensed hotel. AA, RAC, ETB 3 crowns. All rooms en-suite. Excellent choice of menu. Parking. Bargain breaks and special offers. For brochure/tariff Phone: (0271) 862248.

ILFRACOMBE. Sherbourne Lodge. Licensed hotel. Torrs Park. Within walking distance of tunnel beaches, harbour and main shopping area. En-suite with colour television, tea making facilities. Walks, golfing and shooting nearby. Car park. ETB 2 crowns. Phone: (0271) 862297.

ILFRACOMBE. Highlands Hotel. Comfortable, licensed family hotel. Most en-suite. Colour televisions all rooms. Games room. 2 minutes seafront. Home cooking. For brochure please Phone: (01271) 865004.

ILFRACOMBE, Devon. Perfectly situated licensed hotel. Car park. Opposite National Trust walks, close beach, amenities. Our 10th successful year. Don't be disappointed. Phone Floyde Hotel on (0271) 862594, ask for Jeff or Sue. Best Devon bed and breakfast.

LYNMOUTH. 'Tregonwell' an elegant Victorian riverside guest house snuggled into the sunniest side of Lynmouth's wooded valleys amidst dramatic scenery and enchanting harbour. Ideal base for exploring Exmoor/Doone Valley. Parker, 1 Tors Road. Phone: (01598) 753369.

LYNMOUTH. Tregonwell Hotel. Elegant Victorian riverside house. Snuggled into the sunnyside of Lynmouth's wooded valleys, amidst dramatic scenery and enchanting harbour. Beautiful bedrooms, drawing room, en-suites. From £16.50 nightly. Garage parking. 1 Tors Road, Lynmouth, Devon. Phone: (01598) 753369.

LYNTON, North Devon. Visit the Switzerland of England on the edge of Exmoor and stay at the Fairholme Hotel, enjoying breathtaking sea views. Heated indoor swimming pool. Bed and breakfast from £20.50, dinner £9. Phone: (0598) 52263.

LYNTON. 'Fernleigh', Park Street. Modern Guest House with warm and friendly atmosphere from the resident proprietors, Patricia and Louis Emmerson. Luxury bedrooms with private bathrooms, colour televisions, tea makers, radio alarms, central heating. Two crowns commended. Phone: (0598) 53575.

LYNTON. Gable Lodge. An elegant Victorian hotel with comfortable, pretty bedrooms. Both standard and en-suite. Lovely views. Cosy lounge with open fire. Warm welcome and special offers for out of season. Short breaks. Phone: (01598) 752367.

LYNTON, Exmoor. Comfortable, quiet non-smoking hotel. Ample parking. Wonderful views. Bar, imaginative home cooking. Pretty en-suite, well-equipped rooms. 3 nights, dinner, bed, breakfast £99. ETB 3 crown commended. Phone: Judith or David (01598) 752279.

MODBURY. Dairy beef farm. Comfortable farm-house accommodation with picturesque views across valley at breakfast. Tea, coffee facilities. One double, one family bedroom. Parking. Ideal touring, beaches, riding, fishing. Reasonable rates. Good eating places. Reasonable. Phone: (0548) 830219.

MORTEHOE. Smugglers Inn, near Woolacombe. Rooms from £20 per room, some en-suite. Licensed bar, family room. Good pub food. Horse riding, golf nearby. Beautiful country walks, beaches. Good village pub atmosphere. Dogs and children welcome.

OKEHAMPTON eleven miles. Bed and break-fast accommodation. Glorious views. Small village central for touring Dartmoor, North Devon and Cornwall. Large bedrooms, 1 twin, 1 double. Shared shower room. Evening meal by arrangement. Ample parking. Phone: (040923) 1298.

OTTERY ST MARY 2 miles. Farm bed and breakfast and evening meal. One week £120. Delightful country position. Home cooking. Children, pets very welcome. Phone: (0404) 822980.

CAT LOVERS PARADISE
FLUXTON FARM HOTEL
Ottery St. Mary Devon EX11 1RJ
Telephone: (01404) 812818
ETB ☼ ☼ ☼ Lovely 16th century farmhouse in beautiful Otter Valley, with two acre gardens including stream, trout pond and garden railway. Only four miles from beach at Sidmouth. Beamed candlelit dining room; two lounges with colour TV, one non-smoking. Log fires, central heating; 'Teasmade' in all rooms, all double rooms en-suite, with colour TV. Good home cooking our speciality, using all local fresh produce, superbly cooked. Children and pets welcome; pets free of charge.

Cat lovers welcome.
Parking. Licensed.
Open Christmas. AA Listed
Terms from £210 per person
per week, DB & B
Proprietress: Mrs E. A. Forth

PAIGNTON. Rosslyn Hotel. A cosy and friendly licensed hotel on the level close to all amenities, 100 yards to beach. Old worlde bar, en-suites, televisions, tea making facilities. Brochure. Val, Bob, 16 Colin Road. Phone: (01803) 525578.

PAIGNTON
CRANMERE LICENSED HOTEL
200 yards safe sandy beach, overlooking beautiful park. Colour televisions (satellite), teamaking. Free parking. Half-board £104-£134 weekly. Large discounts early bookings, senior citizens and children. Credit cards.
16 Youngs Park, Goodrington
Brochure and details: 01803 557491

PAIGNTON, Devon. Beautiful guest house. Close to beach on level. Bed and breakfast from £12. Evening meal optional. May/October specials, over 55's £79 weekly. Half board. ETB commended. Excellent food. Phone: brochure (0803) 525729.

PAIGNTON. Cliveden Guest House, 27 Garfield Road. Open all year. Excellent home cooking. All rooms central heating, teamaking, television. Own car park. 100 yards level seafront. Close to coach, rail stations. Brochure Phone: (01803) 557461.

PAIGNTON. Bayview Hotel. Friendly family run licensed hotel. Ideally situated for town centre and beaches. Tea - coffee facilities, colour television, lounge. Ample parking. En-suite available. From £84 per week, bed and breakfast. Phone: (0803) 557400.

PAIGNTON. The Haywood Guest House. Close to all amenities. Good home cooking. Excellent accommodation. Central heating, colour television all rooms. Reductions on out of season bookings. Long, short breaks. Mrs Howe, 8 Kings Road. Phone: (0803) 525907.

FRIENDLY FAMILY RUN
LOVELY GUEST HOUSE
Tea making, some en-suites, TV's, choice of menu with sumptuous food. Beach, stations, theatres, shops, etc. 300 yards. Special offers and short breaks.
Send or phone for details: 0803 555810
Easton Court, St. Andrew's Road,
Paignton TQ4 6HA

PAIGNTON. Waverley Guest House. Situated in a quiet cul-de-sac. 200 yards level walk to promenade. Short walk through park to other amenities. Some en-suite. Choice menu, tea making facilities. Parking. Reductions for OAP. Phone: (0803) 551027.

PAIGNTON. Richmond. Quality guest house. Quiet position, 75 yards seafront and near all amenities. Colour television. Tea making all bedrooms. Car park. Ample food. Reasonable terms. Cleanliness assured. Special terms early and late. Phone: (0803) 558792.

PAIGNTON. Family run hotel. Home cooking, tea and coffee facilities, hot and cold water all rooms. Close to all amenities. Located between park and beach, 100 yards. Phone: (0803) 551044.

PAIGNTON, St. Weonards. Licensed Hotel. Level position close to all amenities. Excellent varied menu. Clean and friendly environment. Out of season specials. We pride ourselves on giving value for money. RAC, AA. ETB. Phone: (01803) 558842.

PAIGNTON. Glenavon Hotel. A friendly family run hotel. Level position. 80 yards from beach. Good home cooking, tea making facilities. Full central heating, fire certificate. Car parking on premises. Under new management. Brochure Phone: (0803) 524877.

PLYMOUTH. Allington House, The Hoe. Clean comfortable and welcoming. Some rooms en-suite, all with television and beverage facilities. Excellent touring centre for Devon and Cornwall. 6 St James Place East. For information Sae please. Phone: (0752) 221435.

PLYMOUTH. Close to seafront and Channel fer-ries, coach and railway stations. Colour television, tea - coffee making facilities, evening meals available. Central heating and very comfortable. St Malo Guest House. Phone: (0752) 262961.

PLYMOUTH. The Breakaway Guest House, 28 North Road East, PL4 6AS. Phone: (0752) 227767. Centrally situated, comfortable rooms with television, tea making facilities, full English breakfast. Single rooms £13, doubles £25. Reductions for children sharing.

PLYMOUTH. Small friendly bed breakfast. Full traditional English breakfast, early for ferry passengers. Colour television, complimentary tea, coffee facilities. Ideal University, Brittany Ferries, city attractions and places of interest. £11 per person. Phone: McEvoy (0752) 550909.

SALCOMBE. Romantics/walkers paradise. Superb en-suite rooms. Outstanding sea views. Excellent cuisine. Real ale. Log burner. Pets welcomed. 'National Trust at its best'. Bargain breaks. Port Light Hotel, restaurant, inn. Bolberey Down, Salcombe, South Devon. Phone: (0548) 561384.

SALCOMBE. Lovely Victorian villa over-looking the magnificent Salcombe Estuary. Twelve en-suite bedrooms. Excellent candlelit dinners with local fish a speciality. Home cooked desserts. Miles of coastal walking. Dogs accepted. AA/RAC 2 star. Grafton Towers Hotel, Salcombe. Phone: (0548) 842882.

SALCOMBE, The Wood. Offers Luxury, en-suite accommodation. Some with balconies, overlooking the mouth of the estuary and South Sands beach. Home grown produce used in tasty home cooked meals by Pat Vaissiere, De Courcy Road. Phone: (0154) 8842778. Fax: (0154) 8844277.

SEATON, Devon. Truffles, friendly seafront Guest House. Reputation for good food. En-suite rooms, tea making facilities, colour televisions. Children and dogs welcome. Open all year. 3 day breaks from £54. 6 Marine Crescent, Seaton. Phone: (0297) 20225.

SHALDON. Farm accommodation. We have the best view for miles - come and see!! Home cooking, games room, central heating. En-suites, family rooms, singles, tea making. Bed, breakfast, evening meal from £19. Brochure Mrs Pengelly, Phone: (01626) 872796.

TEIGNMOUTH. Delightful seaside resort within easy reach of Dartmoor. Bed and breakfast from £85 per week. Excellent food and accommodation. Parking. Television, hot and cold all rooms, tea making facilities. Non-smoking. Phone: West (0626) 774273.

TIVERTON. Angel Guest House. ETB two crown. Comfortable, friendly accommodation in town centre. En-suite available. Colour television, drinks facilities in rooms. Bed and breakfast from £14. Evans, 13 St. Peter Street. Phone: (0884) 253392.

TIVERTON. Landrake. Situated at the 900 foot level. 4 miles north of Tiverton. Working farm, peaceful yet within easy reach of north and south coast and moors. Traditional farmhouse cooking. Kerslake, Landrake, Chevithorne, Tiverton EX16 7QN. Phone: (01398) 331221.

TORQUAY. 'Sunnybrae' Guest House. Good food, great company. Near shops, seafront. Tea making facilities free. Non smoking. Open May, September. Prices bed and breakfast, evening meal £85 to £105 inclusive. Bed and breakfast £65. Phone: May, (0803) 296073. 38 Bampfylde Road.

TORQUAY. Torcliffe Guest House. Central. Completely refurbished. En-suites available with shower, toilet, colour television, tea making. Separate tables. Silver service. Own keys, access all times. Full English breakfast. Bed and breakfast from £14. 55 Lymington Road. Phone: (0803) 213787.

TORQUAY. Shirley Hotel. Elegant detached licensed hotel. Quietly situated only 500 yards from harbour, shops. En-suite rooms, colour televisions, satellite. Heated outdoor swimming pool, sauna, jacuzzi. RAC acclaimed. Phone: (01803) 293016, Braddons Hill Road East, TQ1 1HF.

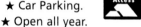

TORQUAY
LINDUM HOTEL

A family run licensed hotel, centrally situated for seafront, main shopping area, theatre, harbour and conference centre. Bedrooms mostly en-suite with televisions, radio/intercom and teamaking facilities. Central heating. Choice of menu. Car parking. Brochure and tariff with pleasure.

Phone: (01803) 292795
ABBEY ROAD, TORQUAY, DEVON TQ2 5NP.

RAC LISTED | AA LISTED

TORQUAY. Kingsway Lodge Guest House assures a warm welcome. Recommended for superb food. Level walking distance to beach and shops. Satellite television all rooms. Short breaks. Children welcome. We care about your holiday. Phone: (0803) 295288.

TORQUAY. Comfortable Guest House near all amenities. Good home cooking. Television, tea makers all rooms. For brochure Beverley Hurren, Treander, 10 Morgan Avenue, Torquay TQ2 5RS. Phone: (01803) 296906.

TORQUAY, Torbay. Star Hotel. Friendly family run hotel. Some en-suite and family rooms with television. Tea, coffee making facilities in all rooms. Children under 5 free. Close to beach. Phone: Lynn or Pete (0803) 293998.

TORQUAY. Rosemarie, 2 Bridge Road. Central. Bed and breakfast daily from £10. Evening dinner £5. Special weekly prices, children half price. Satellite/video link, colour televisions, teamaking all bedrooms. En-suite available. Sae, brochure. Phone: (0803) 297975.

TORQUAY. Mount Nessing Hotel, Saint Lukes Road North. All rooms en-suite, televisions, teamakers. Car park. Central all amenities. Conservatory lounge bar, choice menu. ETB three crowns. Access, Visa accepted. Three night specials, £69, £129 to £179 weekly. Phone: (0803) 294259.

TORQUAY. Welcome to Walnut House! Small select guest house, non-smoking. Offering quality bed and breakfast accommodation. All rooms have showers, television, teamakers. Comfortable lounge. Conveniently situated (seafront, station) in pleasant location. £12 - £14. Phone: (0803) 606854.

TORQUAY, Abbeyfields. Small homely hotel. Close to town/station, conference centre and seafront. Open all year. En-suites, televisions, kettles. Bed and breakfast from £12 daily. Smokers welcome. Also special diets. Flexible atmosphere. Bridge Road. Phone: (0803) 294268.

TORQUAY. Walnut Lodge. Small, friendly hotel located in tree lined avenue. ETB 2 crowns. Televisions, tea making, en-suites. Car park. Close to sea, gardens, theatres. Child and senior citizen reductions. Terms from £77/week. Phone: (01803) 297402.

TORQUAY. Kelvin House Hotel. Comfortable licensed hotel. Near seafront and Riviera centre. En-suite rooms with colour televisions and tea making facilities. Excellent cuisine. Private car park. Phone: (0803) 297313 (Discounts for senior citizens and children).

TORQUAY. Hotel Protea. Non-smoking, licensed hotel. ETB 4 crowns, highly commended. Elegant Victorian villa with sea views to most rooms. Luxury en-suite with bath - shower, television in all rooms. Car parking. Pool. Seaway Lane, Torquay. Phone: (0803) 605778.

TORQUAY. Small friendly guest house, main bus route, close to harbour, town centre and all amenities. Bed and breakfast from £70 per week per adult. Evening meal optional. Phone: (0803) 293469.

TORQUAY. Guest House at Babbacombe. Colour televisions and tea making all rooms. Some en-suite. Bed and Breakfast from £11 daily. Seacliff House, 154 Babbacombe Road, Torquay. Phone: (0803) 326042.

TORQUAY. Woodgrange Hotel. Licensed, with warm friendly atmosphere. En-suite available. Remote colour television, radio alarm. Tea - coffee in all rooms. Open all year. Large residents lounge. 18 Newton Road. Near town and beach. Phone: (0803) 212619.

TORQUAY. Oaks Guest House. Bed and breakfast. All rooms have coloured television and tea making facilities. Large car park. Excellent 4 course breakfast. Comfortable rooms and friendly hosts. Hurdiss, 156 Newton Road, Torquay. Phone: (0803) 612446.

TORQUAY. Beautiful elegant detached warm hotel. All en-suite. Close to beach, town. Bed and breakfast from £13. Delicious 4 course evening meal £5.50. Free car park. We promise you an enjoyable stay. Please Phone: (0803) 297212.

TORQUAY. Welcome to Walnut House. Small, select, non-smoking guest house. Conveniently located, offering high standards of comfort and hospitality. All rooms have private shower, television, tea makers. Bed and generous breakfast £12-£14. Please phone: (0803) 606854.

TOTNES. Thatched cottage. Bed and breakfast, evening meal if required in a lovely part of Devon. Close to sea and moors, 2 miles from Totnes. A peaceful environment for relaxation and unwind. Phone: Michael (0803) 868157.

TOTNES. ETB listed farmhouse bed/breakfast, 2 miles from Totnes. 2 bedrooms with wash basins, drink facilities. Guest bathroom. Guest lounge with colour television. Evening meals by arrangement, home cooking. Central heating. Sorry no pets or smoking. Phone: (0803) 863718.

WESTWARD HO! Close to beach, shops, golf course and horse riding. Central for touring. Modern, comfortable accommodation with en-suite. Plenty of good food. Ample parking. From £12.50 per night. Phone: (0237) 479773.

WESTWARD HO! Bideford, Devon. Victorian guest house. Own grounds. Parking. Sea views. Colour television, tea - coffee facilities. Licensed. Evening meal optional. AA, RAC, ETB. Buckleigh Lodge, Bay View Road, Westward Ho! Devon EX39 1BJ. Phone: (01237) 475988.

WIDECOMBE-IN-THE-MOOR, Dartmoor, Devon. Bed and breakfast. Share our extensive knowledge of Dartmoor and make your holiday unforgettable. High standard of cleanliness and comfort. Warm friendly atmosphere. No smoking. Phone: Pauline Boyes (03642) 264.

ETB
♛♛♛

Caertref

Beach Road
Woolacombe
North Devon EX34 7BT
Phone: 0271 870361

RAC
ACCLAIMED
AWARD

Caertref is ideally situated approx. 3 minutes walk from Woolacombe's beautiful beach and close to shops and amenities. Cosy bar, full central heating, colour TV lounge, free car parking, some en-suite rooms. Our aim is to give you a good holiday in a friendly relaxed atmosphere, feed you well and look forward to your return next year.

WOOLACOMBE. Combe Ridge Hotel. Family run, licensed. Situated directly opposite Combesgate beach. ETB 3 crown facilities. Open all year. Private parking. Special reductions OAP, children and for early - late season breaks. Sea views most rooms. Phone: (0271) 870321.

SELF-CATERING

APPLEDORE, North Devon. Cottage. 2 bed- rooms, sleeps 4. All modern conveniences. Near beach, golf course, shops. Very comfortable. 2 single beds, 1 double bed. Colour television. Reasonable rates. Phone: (0271) 43759.

APPLEDORE. Personally restored and tended fisherman's cottages. In unspoilt village at the estuary of the Rivers Torridge and Taw. Linen, towels, fuel included. Shopping and meal service. Call Barbara Potter. 'Potter about in Appledore'. Phone: (0237) 474628.

APPLEDORE. Traditional fisherman's cottage in conservation fishing village. Sleeping six and having panoramic views across the estuary to Exmoor. Colour television with video and films. Microwave, autowasher. Garden. Pets. 50 yards from slipway. Phone: B.H. Smith (0237) 476154.

MARINERS COTTAGE
Irsha Street, Appledore

Elizabethan fisherman's cottage right at the sea edge – the high tide laps against the garden wall. Extensive open sea and estuary view of ships, lighthouses, fishing and sailing boats. The quayside, beach, shops, restaurants and fishing trips are all close by. Riding, sailing, tennis, golf, sandy beaches, historic houses and beautiful coastal walks, and the Country Park, are all close. Mariners Cottage (a historic listed building), sleeps six plus baby, in three bedrooms and has a modern bathroom, fitted kitchen, childrens playhouse, tumble dryer, dining room and large lounge with colour TV. Gas central heating makes Mariners good for winter holidays from £95 per week. Pet welcome. Picture shows view from garden. SAE, please for a brochure of this and other cottages to:
Mrs. D. Barnes, Boat Hyde, Northam, Bideford, Devon EX39 1NX or phone: (Bideford) (0237) 473801 for prices and vacancies

APPLEDORE/Westward Ho! Home from home. Immaculate, comfortable, well equipped listed cottages. Ideally situated for exploring or simply relaxing. The beach, Exmoor, Tarka trail minutes away. Many visitors return regularly. Friendly welcome assured. Phone: (0237) 472042.

APPLEDORE. 2 bedroom cottages. Furnished. All amenities, all electric. Situated on estuary of Tarka's 2 Devon rivers, Taw and Torridge. Williams, Ivy Cottage, Ivy Court, Appledore, Devon EX39 1RP. Phone: (0237) 472066.

ASHBURTON. Fully furnished self-contained flat. 2 bedrooms (1 double, 1 twin beds), lounge, fully equipped kitchen - diner. Coloured television, hoover. Beautiful area, convenient for Moors and coast. No objection to dogs. Phone: Ashburton (0364) 652589.

ASHWATER, Braddon Cottages. Six English country cottages, equipped to high standard. Devon countryside, facing south to fishing lake and Dartmoor. Tennis court. Wood fires, central heating. From £40 off season. Colour brochure, Ridge, Beaworthy EX21 5EP. Phone: (0409) 211350.

AXMINSTER near. Devon Dorset border. Four character self-catering stone cottages, fully modernised, high standard. Beautiful countryside location, spectacular valley views, convenient coast. Large gardens. Children welcome. Gas central heating. Ample parking. Bed and breakfast available. Phone: (0297) 34731.

AXMINSTER. Cosy self-catering bedsit, sleeping 2 within 14th century farmhouse. Completely independent with separate outside door. Situated in Yarty Valley, near river and coast. Mrs Johnson, Brays Farm, Dalwood, Axminster, Devon EX13 7HG. Phone: (0404) 881203.

AXMINSTER. 3 bedroom farm cottage. Beautiful countryside setting with good local walks around 250 acre farm. Bed linen, electricity, microwave, oven included. Lyme Regis 5, Seaton 4 miles. Dogs allowed. Ample parking. Excellent rates. Phone: (0297) 553450.

AXMINSTER. Country cottage, sleeps 4. Pleasant garden parking facilities. Dogs very welcome. Village post office, stores nearby. Sea 5 miles. Central for touring. Local tramways, gardens, fishing trips. Mrs Brown, Woodhayne Cottage, Whitford, Axminster EX13 7NW. Phone: (0297) 552590.

AXMOUTH is a charming village on River Axe. Close to Seaton town and beach. Cottage, sleeping 4 - 5. Has its own garden. Centrally located but overlooking fields. Covered parking. Pets welcome. Phone: 081 946 9453 (answerphone).

BABBACOMBE, Torquay. Self-contained holi- day apartments. 200 yards sea front and Downs. Level walk and close to all amenities. Garden for visitors use. Ample parking. Pets welcome by arrangement. For brochure please Phone: (0803) 327203.

BABBACOMBE, Torquay. Self-contained holi- day flats, pleasant, level, parkland area. Convenient for seafront, shops, bowls, tennis, putting, golf. Garden, parking. Reduced terms, early and late season. Ludwell House, Cary Park, Babbacombe, Torquay TQ1 3NH. Phone: (01803) 326032.

BANTHAM BEACH, 1.5 miles. Small site of five pinelodges and two apartments in a peaceful secluded valley near Kingsbridge, and many tourist attractions. Prices from £75 - 375. Open all year. Brochure Sue and Chris Miller. Phone: (0548) 560253.

BANTHAM, near Kingsbridge. Comfortable detached house. Within easy walk of large sandy beach and river estuary. All machines. Colour television, video. Garden with games barn and barbeque. Sleeps 8 plus cot. Phone: Mrs Kirvan (0395) 233265.

BARNSTAPLE. Ground floor flat. Goodleigh, few miles from Exmoor and beaches. Quiet position on edge of small village. Sleeps 2. Overlooks our private garden, off-road parking. Please phone for brochure. Phone: Mrs C. Oatway (0271) 71827.

BARNSTAPLE. Farmhouse cottage near Swim- bridge. Set in 7 acres river valley. Colour television. All modern conveniences. Sleeps 5 plus cot. Extensive landscaped gardens with river running through grounds. Coarse fishing available. Ample parking. Phone: (0271) 830555.

WILLESLEIGH FARM

GOODLEIGH, BARNSTAPLE, DEVON EX32 7NA

Superb self-catering in our traditional Cottage and unique Gatehouse. Cleanliness, quality and privacy assured. Family run farm in glorious countryside.

English Tourist Board
HIGHLY COMMENDED

FARM HOLIDAY BUREAU

For detailed brochure please phone

01271 43763

BARNSTAPLE. ETB self-catering cottages and farmhouse bed and breakfast accommodation. In peaceful rural setting, one mile from town. Within easy reach local beaches, Exmoor and other amenities. Weekly and daily terms per person. Phone:(0271) 45039.

BARNSTAPLE. Comfortable 3 bedroomed cottage. Centrally heated and well equipped. In rural setting, yet only 1 mile from town. Within easy reach of beaches and moorland. Garden and ample courtyard parking. Available May to October. Phone: (0271) 73021.

BEER, Devon. 1 bedroom self-contained flat. (Washing machine). Sleeps 2, 4 (bed settee). Car parking. 5 minutes' walk to shops, beach. No pets. Very reasonable rates. Phone: (0297) 625446, (0297) 21416.

BEER

Modernised semi-detached fully equipped 3 bedroomed former fisherman's cottage with garden in picturesque village, near shops, restaurants and hotels. 4 minutes walk from safe beach. Swimming, fishing, delightful coastal walks.
For further details, please ring Mrs. Light
0297 80335

BEER. Restored 16th century cottage. Close to sea and shops. Comfortably furnished. 3 bedrooms, luxury bathroom, inglenook fireplaces. Farmhouse pine kitchen. Full central heating. Small garden. Regret no pets or smokers. Phone: (0256) 760120 evenings.

BELSTONE, Dartmoor. Large converted barn, sleeps 12. 4 bedrooms. Central heating. Ideal family, adult or youth groups. Good centre Devon, Cornwall. Outdoor swimming pool. Sorry no pets. Martin, The Lees, Belstone, Okehampton. West Cornwall Tourist Board approved. Phone: (01837) 840008.

BERRYNARBOR, near Combe Martin. Self-contained flat, 2 double bedrooms, sleeps 5 plus cot. Fully equipped, all electric, colour television. Linen provided. Large garden. Hillside setting with valley views. Parking. No pets. Coast 2 miles. Phone: (0271) 882491.

BIDEFORD. Enjoy the sea, moors and towns and come back to 'Rendles Down', secluded pleasant old four bedroom farmhouse on its own in beautiful countryside. Mrs Beer, Ley Monkleigh, Bideford EX39 5JZ. Phone: (0237) 473336.

BIDEFORD, North Devon. Bungalow, sleeps six centrally heated and double glazed. Nice garden. Numerous local attractions, close to sea and golf course. Very reasonable rates. Phone: (08054) 211, evenings after six o'clock.

BIDEFORD. Locality, charming four bedroomed country cottage. Sleeping 8. Large garden overlooking River Torridge. Peaceful countryside. Easy parking. Beaches 15 minutes. £125 - £330. Also 4 berth caravan. Own secluded garden overlooking river. Pets welcome. Phone: (0237) 475057.

BIGBURY-ON-SEA, near Kingsbridge. Comfortable self-contained flatlets. Sun terraces overlooking beach with extensive uninterrupted coastal views. Golf nearby. Ideal walkers. Suitable couples or young families. Maximum 4 people. Open all year. Phone: (0548) 810446.

BIGBURY BAY. Family fun holidays in cedarwood bungalows. 200 lazy yards from waterside. Fishing, windsurfing, aqua diving from clean sandy beaches. Indoor pool and golf nearby plus superb cliff walks. Beachdown, Challaborough TQ7 4JB. Phone: (01548) 810089.

BIGBURY ON SEA. Self-catering accommodation, sleeping 4-6. Close sandy beaches, golf club and Devon beauty spots etc. For brochure please write Mrs Saunders, 'Merriville', Ringmore Drive, Bigbury on Sea, South Devon or Phone: (0548) 810556.

BRIXHAM. Superior luxury self-contained balcony flat overlooking Golden Hind. Outstanding harbour and sea views. Equipped to highest standards including microwave, freezer, balcony loungers, payphone and all usual facilities. Sleeps four. No children, pets. Phone: (0803) 323532.

Please mention
Daltons Directory
when replying to advertisements

BRIXHAM. Good selection of harbourside cottages, houses, flats. Many with excellent views and parking, close to beaches and town. Colour television. Children and pets welcome. Holidays Torbay, 26 Cotmore Close, Brixham TQ5 0EF. Phone: (0803) 854708.

BRIXHAM. Modern house, sleeps 6. Sea views. £130 - £260 per week. Regret no pets. Windycot, Deans Lane, Tadworth, Surrey KT20 7TT. Phone: (0737) 813324.

BRIXHAM. Comfortably furnished fisherman's cottage. Two bedrooms, lounge, television. Fully equipped kitchen, fridge, gas cooker. Will sleep five. approximately 100 yards from harbour and shops. Phone: 081 686 1902.

BRIXHAM. Penthouse flats near harbour and town centre. Self-contained and spacious with satellite, colour television. Some sea views. Children and pets welcome. Open all year for holidays and short breaks. Free brochure. Phone: (01803) 854005.

BRIXHAM. Three bedroomed town houses with roof terraces/balconies overlooking sea and close to beach and Berry Head Country Park. Also flats adjacent to town and harbour. Suit 2/4 persons. Phone: (0803) 844820.

BRIXHAM. Fisherman's cottage overlooking inner harbour. Sleeps 6. Pet welcome. No parking. No garden. Close to public car park and shops. Phone: (081) 304 4395

BRIXHAM. Memorable holidays for all seasons. Listed barn transformed into 2 self-catering character homes sleeping 2/4/6 comfortably. Garage. Dogs welcome. Convenient local shops. Close to coastal footpaths and beaches. Ideal touring centre. Phone: (01803) 854560.

BRIXHAM. Holiday bungalow. Detached brick built, privately owned. 2 bedroom, sleeps 2-6. Private parking. Colour television, fully equipped. Superb sea views. Use of outdoor heated pool and clubroom. For details please Phone: Canterbury (01227) 751633.

BRIXHAM. Detached holiday bungalows above sheltered coves. Easy scenic walk to harbour and town. Available all year. Spring, autumn, winter breaks or long lazy summer holidays. Heated pools. Licensed bar. Colour brochure with pleasure. Phone: (01803) 851800.

BRIXHAM. Self-contained first floor flat with balcony. 2 bedrooms. Superb sea and harbour views from all rooms. Bed linen provided. Well equipped. Close to harbour and town. Available all year. Phone: (0602) 728242.

BROADHEMPSTON, South Devon. Delightful country cottage, self-catering. Sleeps four. Dartmoor, Cornwall and the coast easily accessible. Comfortably furnished. Conservatory. Garden and television. All electric. For further details Phone: (0295) 710124.

BUCKFASTLEIGH (near). Get away from it all! 2 very comfortable, well equipped 2 bedroom cottages in lovely rural setting. Near Dartmoor. Garden. Colour television, central heating, microwave. Short breaks also available. Brochure: Phone: Mrs C. Richardson (0364) 643848.

BUCKFASTLEIGH. Granary conversion on Family farm. Unspoilt countryside in Dartmoor National Park. Self-catering. Fully equipped, sleeps 4 plus cot. Pets by arrangement. Details sae Andrews, Zempson, South Brent, Devon TQ10 9DX or Phone: (0364) 73112.

BUCKS MILLS, near Clovelly. Comfortable traditional cottage in picturesque coastal village. Area of outstanding natural beauty. Honest 4 minutes walk beach - coastal path. Garden. Sleeps 4 plus cot. Open all year. Off season short breaks. No pets. Phone: (0458) 50349, (01458) 850349 after May 1995.

BUDLEIGH SALTERTON, East Devon. Immaculate, seaside character cottage. 3 bedrooms, sleeps 5, cot. 2 living rooms. Enclosed secluded garden, patios, driveway, balcony views, barbecue. Four poster bed. Beach, golf, riding. Common close by. £240 to £289 inclusive. Phone: (01395) 445529.

CHAGFORD, Dartmoor National Park. Farm cottages and flats, sleep 2 - 10. Children welcome. Pets accepted. Ideal walking, fishing, golf, riding, touring. Close to open Moor. Central for North and South coasts. Beechlands, Chagford, Devon TQ13 8HF. Phone: (0647) 433313.

CHALLABOROUGH, Bigbury Bay. Detached bungalow. Large garden. Four double bedrooms, sleeps eight. Magnificent position directly overlooking first class sandy beach. Very well furnished, automatic washing machine, tumble dryer. No pets. Brochure available Phone: (0548) 550511/810704.

CHALLACOMBE, North Devon. Three bedroom cottage, sleeps six. Log fire. Pets welcome. Large enclosed secluded garden. Ample parking. Ideal for walking, touring or visiting local beaches. Board games, table tennis and colour television. Phone: (0474) 834215.

CHUDLEIGH. Three cottages converted from stone buildings. Non-working farm. Beautiful unspoilt countryside between Dartmoor and sea. Colour television, electric cookers, microwaves, washing machines. Bed linen provided. Children welcome. Regret no dogs. Phone: (0626) 853334

CHUDLEIGH KNIGHTON, South Devon. Comfortable 2 bedroom detached cottage. Close to Dartmoor and coast. Quiet village location. Sleeps 5. Sunny gardens. Ample parking. No pets. Phone: (0626) 853434 evenings.

COMPTON POOL FARM – COMPTON, SOUTH DEVON

Nestling in a sheltered, sunny valley, surrounded by red Devon hills, these tastefully converted, comfortably furnished stone cottages surround a pretty garden courtyard.

Games Barn. Indoor heated pool, tennis, trout lakes, friendly farm animals, lots more, close to sea.

JOHN & CATHY SONGER
Compton Pool Farm, Compton, Devon TQ3 1TA
Tel: 01803 872241. Fax: 01803 874012

CLOVELLY. Luxury chalet, outstanding view over bay. Patio, small garden. Bathroom, separate toilet. Sleeps 5. Comfortable, well equipped, television, fridge/freezer. Very reasonable rates. Reduction for 2 visitors. Short breaks arranged. Regret no pets. Phone: (0548) 856296.

COLYTON. Luxury holiday cottage. Sleeping two. Washing machine, dryer, microwave, television. Parking. Optional pub/hotel facilities. Weekly or long lets. Sorry no children or pets. Hotel brochure also available. Colyton Cottages, Colyton. Phone: (01297) 552401.

COLYTON. Bonehayne Farm. Annexe on working farm. Picturesque setting, large lawn, overlooking fields, river and woodlands. Centrally heated, oak beams, inglenook fireplace. Good trout fishing. Coast 4 miles. Phone: (0404) 87396 or 87416. Brochure available. Caravan also.

COMBE MARTIN. Detached bungalow, faces south. Views across to hills other side of valley. Large garden. Two minutes sea and shops. Gas central heating available. Phone: Combe Martin 883538, Miss Willis.

COMBE MARTIN. Spacious and comfortably furnished holiday houses overlooking beach with delightful sea views. Central heating. Available all year. Sleeps 7/8. Discount for smaller parties. Mrs Lovering, Loverings Flat, Borough Road. Phone: (0271) 882008.

COMBE MARTIN 4 miles. Two semi-detached bungalows and mobile home set in beautiful countryside. Everything provided including microwaves, colour televisions and duvets. You only need bed linen. Sleeps 4/5. Parking. No pets. Phone: (05983) 242.

COMBE MARTIN. High standard, well maintained self-contained flat. Two bedrooms, lounge, kitchen, bathroom. Accommodate 2 - 6 persons. Minute walk beach. Fridge, colour television. Parking. Storage heating for Winter breaks. Further details Phone: (0271) 882522.

COMBE MARTIN 4 miles. Luxury country cottages. Beautifully maintained. All amenities. Sleeps 5. £140 - £300 weekly. Short breaks. Linen inclusive. Cot, highchair. No pets. Details Phone: Combe Martin (01271) 882376. D.M. & R. Heath, Northcote, Near Patchole, Kentisbury, Barnstaple, Devon.

COMBEINTEIGNHEAD. Cottage on beach, overlooking River Teign. Garden. Ideal watersports enthusiasts. Sleeps 6. Washing machine, refrigerator, colour television. Available April to October. Pets allowed. Details from Mrs R.J. Price, Vale House, Slapton, Kingsbridge. Phone: (0548) 580669.

CROYDE. Holiday bungalows. "Seashells". Private entrance into dunes, wonderful views to Baggy Point. Secluded lawned gardens. Personally cleaned. Linen included. 5 minutes' walk to beach and village. Also farmhouse accommodation. Ley, Stock Farm, Brayford. Phone: (0598) 710498.

CROYDE BAY, Devon. Modern chalet bungalows. 2/3 bedrooms, sleep 4/6. Colour television, refrigerator. Adjacent golden sandy beach. Bathing, surfing, golf course near. Also olde worlde village and National Trust walks. Clatworthy, Randwick, Ilfracombe. Phone: (0271) 865820.

CROYDE. Chapel Farm offers self-catering holiholidays. The Old Smithy Cottage, Chapel Farm Apartment, or Goldenhours Holiday Bungalow. All within 5 minutes of Croyde's sandy surfing beach. J. Windsor, Chapel Farm, Croyde, North Devon EX33 1NE. Phone: (0271) 890429.

DARTMOOR. 3 miles Tavistock. Character cottage nestling peacefully in Dartmoor National Park. Self-contained two bedroom, one bathroom. One shower/toilet. Central heating. Beams. Woodburner. Pets welcome. Ideal to bring own horses. Phone: Tavistock (0822) 615093.

DARTMOOR DEVON

For the ultimate in self-catering accommodation we have a choice of properties to suit all tastes and ages. All have superb views across Dartmoor, are set in private gardens yet are only a level walk from the centre of a Dartmoor stannary village.
From **Padley Hey**, set in its own garden of 1 acre, sleeping six and featuring a four poster bed, to **The Old Stables,**

a character stable conversion sleeping four with private outdoor heated pool, and **Lookover,** a quiet, charming bungalow with private garage and gardens.
They are all fitted and equipped to the highest standard to ensure your holiday will be unforgettable.
You want what we provide, the best!

Contact 01803 290673
for details

DARTMOOR. Horrabridge village with shops and pubs. Near Tavistock. Well furnished self-catering cottage. Sleeps 6. Use of garden. Quiet, no through road. Parking. Beautiful views. Available July - September. £170 per week. No pets. Phone: (0822) 854793.

DARTMOOR NATIONAL PARK. 2 bedroomed cottage, sleeps 5. Large self-contained 3 bedroomed flat, sleeps 6. Central for touring. £115 - £185 per week. Phone: Buckfastleigh (0364) 643689.

DARTMOOR Buckland in the Moor holiday cot-tage. Sleeps 6. Own grounds. Parking within. Well behaved dogs welcome. For further details contact Wendy Gill, 'Ruwendor', Hares Lane, Ashburton, Devon TQ12 7AU or Phone: (0364) 653075.

DARTMOUTH. Small select secluded site. Smart holiday bungalows. Only one mile lovely Blackpool Sands. Situated in old walled garden surrounded by lawns. Private car park. Park West, Stoke Fleming, Dartmouth TQ6 0RZ. Phone: (0548) 580072.

DARTMOUTH 2 miles, beach 1/2 mile. lovely fully modernised cottage in secluded courtyard in coastal village. Sleeps 4 plus cot, high chair, linen, electricity, heating, garden all inclusive. Very reasonable rates. Phone: (0803) 835328.

DARTMOUTH. Studio flat on ground and first floors of large Georgian house. Two minutes' walk from town centre and riverside. Sleeps two. All electric, television, shower etc. Linen and electricity included. Details Phone: Jestico (0803) 832133.

DARTMOUTH. The Mates House. Dating from 1628 in centre of town and close River Dart. Sleeps four/six. Fully equipped. All electric, television, cot. Linen included. Details and photo, Phone: Jestico (0803) 832133.

DARTMOUTH, South Devon. 3 bedroomed house, accommodates 8. Located in quiet, slightly elevated area. Within walking distance of town with views to River Dart and countryside. Regret no pets. Private parking. Phone: Gloucester (01452) 529066.

DARTMOUTH. 2 superb flats over river. 5 minutes walk town centre. Ideal base for touring, walking, fishing, boating. Short breaks too. Sleeps 2/5. Dogs ok. Phone: 081 878 9336, (0803) 834462.

DARTMOUTH. Hillfield Farm Cottage, Hillfield. Fully furnished, sleeps 4 plus cot. Garden and parking. 3 1/2 miles Dartmouth and beach. Golf club and leisure centre 2 miles. Babysitting if required. Phone: Joan (0803) 712279.

DARTMOUTH. Nicely furnished holiday house on farm. Close Slapton Sands. Sleeps 10. Linen. Colour television. En-suite facilities. Microwave, dishwasher, washing machine, tumble drier. Garden. Brenda Wall, Lower Fuge Farm, Strete, Near Dartmouth. Phone/Fax: (0803) 770541.

DAWLISH. Bungalow in quiet, residential area. Close to lawns, shops, beach. Equipped and furnished to high standard. Sleeps 4. Lounge, large kitchen - dining room. Bedroom, bathroom. Private parking. £100 - £240 per week. Brochure Phone: (01785) 54341.

DAWLISH Holiday flat. 2 bedrooms, sleeps 4. Own bathroom. Panoramic sea and town views. Own patio. Colour television. Secluded private residential area. Car parking. Fully equipped. Mrs Brown, 7 Mayflower Close. Phone: (0626) 863016.

DAWLISH, South Devon. Holiday cottage, fully equipped with colour television, microwave and dishwasher. Central for shops, sea. Send for details, Mrs Foster, 7 Southlands Grove, Leaventhorpe, Thornton, Bradford, West Yorkshire. BD13 3BG. Phone: (0274) 818235

DAWLISH WARREN. Villas. Sleep six. Welcome family holiday park. Electricity, linen, television inclusive. Leisure facilities include, indoor heated swimming - play pools, sauna, club, restaurant, cinema, children's entertainment. Phone: 9 - 5.30 weekdays, 10 - 12.30 Sundays (0420) 82376.

DAWLISH WARREN. Well equipped holiday apartment, sleeps 5. Pleasant location. Close all amenities, sandy beach, lovely walks. Golf course nearby. Easy access from M5, A30. Book early for summer. Off-season offers available. Phone: (0323) 720176.

DAWLISH. Superior apartment, sleeps 2/3. Self-contained. Own entrance with patio. Modern kitchen. Panoramic views, residential area. Central heating, colour television, hot and cold, bed linen inclusive. 'Highfield', 56 Westcliff Park Drive, Dawlish, Devon EX7 9ER. Brochure Phone: (01626) 865818.

DITTISHAM
NEAR DARTMOUTH
Pretty cottages and luxury houses in delightful unspoilt riverside village. Superb location for sailing, walking, painting, birdwatching, golfing or just relaxing. Open all year, short breaks out of season. Hire boats available.
PHONE: (0803) 722561

DOLTON, North Devon. Spacious, secluded, picturesque thatched cottage. Lovely garden and view. Children and dogs welcome. Near friendly village, nature reserve and Rosemoor Garden. Convenient for moors and coast. Phone: (08054) 278 evenings. From £90.

DREWSTEIGNTON. Bowbeer Farm. Wing old farmhouse. Full character charm. Sleeps 4. Large garden, swing and slide. Children welcome. Cot, highchair available. Colour television, microwave, washing machine. Linen included. Pony. Spacious accommodation. Sorry no pets. From £75 per week. Phone: (0647) 281239.

EAST BUDLEIGH. Old world thatched cottage. Situated in charming historic village. Amidst lovely countryside. 2 miles from sea. Sleeps 4. (4 poster bed and 2 singles). Garden, parking. Dogs welcome. Phone: Budleigh Salterton (0395) 445446.

EAST PORTLEMOUTH, near Salcome. Well appointed self-contained flat in modern house. Country views. Beaches 1.5 miles. 1.5 acre gardens, patio, barbecue. Ample parking. Sleeps 5. All home comforts. No pets. No smoking. Phone: Davis (01548) 511277.

EXETER 4 miles. Peacefully situated character cottage. 2 bedrooms, sleeps 4/5, large comfortably furnished lounge, well equipped kitchen. Enclosed rear garden. Lovely walks locally through National Trust land. Convenient moors/sea. £145 - £225. Phone: (0392) 841369.

EXETER. Comfortable farm cottage next to working dairy farm. Lovely views as far as Dartmoor. Village half mile. Two bedrooms. Golf, riding, fishing all found locally. Mary Brown Cottles Farm, Woodbury, Exeter EX5 1ED. Phone: (0395) 232547.

EXETER. Self-contained part of farmhouse on working dairy farm. Easy access towns - beaches - moors. Quiet location. Well equipped. Electricity, linen included in price. Children welcome. Sleeps 6. ETB 4 key approved. Brochure available. Phone: (0404) 822276.

EXMOOR COASTAL. Choose from. House, own indoor pool, jacuzzi. House on own beach. Riverside cottages. Own enchanted 80 acre valley. Four posters, log fires. Dogs welcome. Breaks from £98. Phone: (05983) 339.

EXMOOR, North Devon. Charming wing of farmhouse, sleeps four plus own free pony to ride on. Friendly family farm, completely refurbished, giving comfortable, high standard spacious accommodation. Fishing, riding, golf, shooting nearby. Phone: (03984) 546.

EXMOOR NATIONAL PARK. 17th century long-house cottages and 2 barn conversions in 3 acres grounds. One cottage suitable for some disabled. Riverside with views over Moors. Beautiful walking/riding country. Brochure Phone: (05983) 320.

EXMOOR. Coastal hideaways. Choose from house, own indoor pool, jacuzzi. Riverside cottages, own enchanted 80 acre valley. House on beach. Luxury 6 bed house, Croyde. 4 posters, log fires. Breaks from £98. Dogs welcome. Phone: (0598) 763339.

EXMOUTH. Comfortable self-catering holiday homes. Quiet residential roads, near sea and shops. Two to ten people. Children welcome. Wheelchair access. Dogs accepted. Reasonable terms. July to September only. Please Phone: Mrs Christine Duncan (0395) 266967.

EXMOUTH near. Comfortable 3 bedroom house available April onwards. Quiet village. Sleeps 6. Central heating, colour television. Within easy reach of coast and moors. Riding, fishing and golf. Reasonable rates. Phone: Woodbury (0395) 232471.

HARTLAND. Olde worlde thatched holiday cottage in an unspoilt corner of Devon. Scenic beauty, unspoilt coastline. Sleeps 6. 3 bedrooms, lounge. Colour television. Modern conveniences. Garage parking 2 cars in village. Phone: Cole (0237) 470725.

HOLBETON. Beautiful conservation village, near Plymouth, Cornwall, sea, river, Dartmoor. Three charming modernised cob cottages. Two, three, five bedrooms, sleep four, six, nine. Television, microwave, washing machine, electric heating. Gardens, parking. Open all year. Phone: (0993) 881228.

HOLNE, Ashburton. Period cottage, own seclu-ded garden, parking, fully equipped for four/five people. Lounge with open hearth and beamed ceiling. Well equipped kitchen. Pub, post office. Dartmoor, River Dart within easy reach. Phone: (0364) 631235.

HOLSWORTHY, Kingslake. 4 coarse fishing lakes. 1 trout lake surrounded by woodland. 7 lovely cottages in idyllic setting on 46 acre estate. Come and enjoy our peace and tranquillity. For colour brochure Phone: (0409231) 401.

HONITON. Comfortable, detached bungalow with country views. Easy reach of Sidmouth, Seaton and Lyme Regis. Sleeps 4, plus cot. Fully equipped, bed linen included. Swimming pool, horse riding and golf nearby. No pets. Phone: (0404) 841341.

HONITON. Secluded working farm in an area of outstanding natural beauty. Fully equipped 16th century farmhouse annexe. Sleeps 7 (seven). Central beaches, moors, sports facilities. Farmhouse dining service. Wyatt, Odle Farm, Upottery, Honiton. Phone: (0404) 861272.

ILFRACOMBE five miles. One bedroom cottage adjoining owners. Sleeps 2/4. Situated on village outskirts, easy walk to village stores and pub. Beautiful outlook over small valley. Ideal walking, touring. Short drive to beaches. Phone: (0271) 864755.

ILFRACOMBE. Self-contained ground floor holi-day flat, sea views. Sleeps 2/5. Parking. Lounge, colour television, bedroom sheets supplied. Separate kitchen, fridge-freezer, shower, toilet. Mrs Ley, Old Slade Quarry, Slade, Ilfracombe, Devon EX34 8LQ. Phone: (0271) 863798.

ILFRACOMBE. Detached central heated modern bungalow with garage. Garden with views of Tors. Sleeps six. Few minutes seafront. Prices include heating and hot water. From £100 per week. For further information Phone: Mrs Willis (0543) 374195.

ILFRACOMBE, North Devon. Three bedroom town cottage. Close to harbour. Fully equipped, all basic facilities, bathroom, kitchen, all electric. Non-smokers only. Mr France, 16 Grove Road, Burgess Hill, Sussex RH15 8LF. Phone: (01444) 232017.

ILFRACOMBE. Four minutes walk to town and harbour. Spacious four bedroom house. Good sea views. Shower, television, microwave, heating. Off season bargain breaks available. Summer holiday enquiries welcome. Further details Phone: (01932) 857073. Answerphone sometimes.

ILFRACOMBE. Lynden Holiday House. Spacious. Near shops and sea. 6 bedrooms. All hot and cold water. Colour television and video. Kitchen with washing machine, microwave, fridge freezer. Back garden and barbeque. Sleeping 6 - 12 persons. Bartlett, Tower Cottage, Berrynarbor. EX34 9SE. Phone: (0271) 883408.

KENTON, Exe Estuary, near Exeter. Period cottage, overlooking village green. Three bedrooms, two reception, two bathrooms. Parking, own garden. Very comfortably furnished. Convenient moors and coast. ETB 4 key commended. £155 - £360 per week. Phone: (0929) 480461.

KINGSBRIDGE, South Milton in South Hams. Cottage, sleeps 4. Garden, parking. Close to 'clean' beach. Salcombe 4 miles, for sailing, fishing, Kingsbridge 3 miles ops. Turner, Beach Cottage, South Milton, Kingsbridge, Devon TQ7 3JR. Phone: (0548) 560354.

KINGSBRIDGE. Lovely farmhouse, sleeps 12. Also barn. Set in beautiful South Hams countryside. Very comfortable. Excellently equipped. Duvets, linen, recreation barn. Farm walks. Central for beach and moors. Short breaks available. Brochure Phone: (01548) 521327.

KINGSNYMPTON, North Devon. Comfortable, well equipped farm cottages in beautiful countryside. Ideal walking, riding. Children love to feed animals and join in farm activities. Adventure playground, laundry, clay pigeon shooting. Open March - December. Brochure Phone: (0769) 572448.

LUSTLEIGH. Picturesque 16th century thatched cottage on pretty village green in Dartmoor National Park. Excellent pub, tearooms, dairy and gift shop. Perfect walking country. Golf, fishing, riding, beaches nearby. Sleeps 4. Phone: (0803) 605295.

LYNMOUTH, Clooneavin holiday apartments and chalet. Self-catering accommodation. Spectacular views. Where Exmoor meets the sea. Ideal for walking/touring/fishing or relaxing. Short distance sea/ shops/ pubs/ restaurants. Short breaks available. Phone: (01598) 753334, G. Davidson.

LYNTON near. Comfortable and clean, well equipped cottage. An excellent base for exploring Exmoors beautiful countryside and coastline. Open all year. For brochure Phone: (0598) 752286. Mrs Bowen, East Ilkerton, Lynton, Devon EX35 6PH.

MERTON, near Torrington. Cosy, well equip-ped cottage in quiet position on village edge. Sleeps 4 plus cot. Oil central heating included. Washing machine, microwave, duvets. Ideal for Moors, sea, fishing and walking. Phone: (08053) 279

NORTH MOLTON, North Devon. Cosy, well fur-nished, 2 bedroom cottage. Accommodates 4. Friendly village, edge Exmoor National Park. Pretty garden. Lovely countryside, convenient coast. £120 to £235 per week, including electricity. No pets. Phone: (0598) 740622.

OKEHAMPTON near. Self-contained wing of 16th century thatched farmhouse. Quiet location with easy access to A30. Ideal for exploring Dartmoor and West Country. Sleeps 4 plus cot. Pets welcome. Phone: (01837) 86470 (home), (01837) 54344 (office).

OKEHAMPTON. East Hook Cottages. Scenic location. 1 mile Okehampton, fringe Dartmoor National Park. 2 cottages, 3 bedrooms. Each comfortably furnished. Quiet, peaceful, spacious grounds. Open all year. Reasonable prices. Stevens, West Hook, Okehampton. Phone: (01837) 52305.

OKEHAMPTON. Self-catering farmhouse. 3 bedrooms. Sleeps 8. Close to Dartmoor Coast. Easy access. Quiet position. Good views. Phone: (0837) 87325.

PAIGNTON. Wide selection of self-contained flats, sleep 2-8. Close to beach. Some with panoramic views. Ample parking. Accommodation to suit all budgets. Bargain prices for early season. Free colour brochure. Baker Leisure Holidays Phone: (0923) 261111.

PAIGNTON. Waterside house. Self-catering quality flat. Fully equipped, colour television. 2 bedrooms, spacious lounge, large kitchen/diner. Own bathroom and toilet. Parking in grounds. Near beach and shops. Phone: (0803) 528369.

PAIGNTON. Superb 2 bedroom holiday home. 5 minutes stroll to beach. Easy walk to town centre and harbour. Sleeps 4/5 with large safe garden for children. For brochure Phone: (0803) 556285.

PAIGNTON. Big Tree Holiday Flats. Self-contained, modern, purpose built. 1 or 2 bedroomed flats, ample parking. Colour television. Ideally situated for beaches, harbour, leisure centre, water park, shops. 68 Fisher Street. Phone: (01803) 559559.

PAIGNTON. Holiday apartments. Superb level position. 150 yards beach/amenities. Fully self-contained with bedrooms, bathroom, lounge, kitchen. Parking. Television. Sea views, balconies or garden. 2-5 persons. Central heating. Open all year. Alcudia, 22 Adelphi Road, TQ4 6AW. Phone: (0803) 554022.

PAIGNTON. Family holiday flat near shops, sea front. August, September. 26 Elmslegh Road, Paignton, South Devon. Phone: (0803) 554228.

PAIGNTON. 250 yards Goodrington beach. Shipwreck leisure park. Pool centre. Close to shops, pubs, buses. Fully equipped chalets, caravan, flats. Large garden, parking. Mrs Jean Jackman, 'Tregarth' Cliff Park Road, Goodrington, Paignton, Devon TQ4 6NB. Phone: (01803) 550382.

PAIGNTON. Superior self-contained, centrally heated apartments. Superb position, between harbour and beaches. Adjacent beautiful headland garden. Satellite channel and video link to colour televisions. Laundry room. Parking. Payphone. Serena Lodge, 15 Cliff Road. Phone: (01803) 550330.

PAIGNTON. Stanley House, 17 Cliff Road, TQ4 6DG. Near beach and harbour. Self-contained apartments, some sea views. Own parking. Special rates early and late season. Night storage heater. Colour television. Resident proprietors. Phone: (01803) 557173.

PAIGNTON Seafront. Holiday apartments. Superb sea views. Includes bed linen, central heating, hot water, colour television. Parking. Warm welcome, cleanliness assured. From £60 per week. Wulfruna Apartments, 9 Esplanade Road, Paignton TQ4 6EB. Phone: (01803) 212660.

PLYMOUTH HOE. Self-catering flats. Comfortable, well equipped, pleasantly decorated. Central position. Adjacent The Hoe, Barbican, city centre, theatre, bus terminal and marina. Suitable for 2-4 persons. 231 Citadel Road East PL1 2NG. Phone: (01752) 667896 or 851101.

PLYMOUTH HOE. Superb self-contained flats, Sleeps 2-6 persons. Colour television. 200 yards sea front. Available all year. Colour brochure Carsons, 5 Regent Street, Plymouth PL4 8BA. Phone (0752) 254425 or 404171. Member of Plymouth Tourist Board.

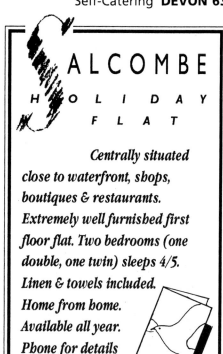

SALCOMBE. Character cottage. Carefully reno-vated to retain original Victorian fittings. Panoramic views over harbour from all front rooms and large terrace. Very convenient for town centre. Three bedrooms. Garden, parking. Gas central heating. Phone: (0548) 842120.

SALCOMBE. Delightful family holiday home. Sun patio, modern kitchen, washing machine. Lounge, television, 3 bedrooms. 30 metres water, town centre. Ideal for sailing, walking, touring. Car parking available. Details Phone: (0432) 870255.

SALCOMBE. Waterfront central location. Comfortably furnished. Lounge, separate kitchen with eating area, 2 bedrooms, sleeps 5. One with south facing balcony. All electric. Telephone and use of boat with outboard motor. Brochure Phone: (01989) 564444.

SALCOMBE, South Devon. Pretty self-con-tained holiday flat. Available all year. Centrally heated. Sleeps 2. Lounge/dining kitchen, luxury bathroom, double bedroom. Estuary glimpses. 5 minutes town centre. Garden, parking, barbecue. Reasonable rates. Phone: Roberts (0548) 843218.

SALCOMBE. Delightful family holiday home. Patio, modern kitchen, washing machine, microwave. Lounge, television. 3 bedrooms. 30 metres water, town centre. Ideal for sailing, walking, touring. Car parking available. Sorry no pets. Details Phone: (0432) 870255.

SEATON, Devon. Lovely cottage style flat. Quiet location. Equipped to a high standard. Sleeps 2. Colour television. Parking. 5 minutes walk to beach and shops. £165 maximum. Phone: (0297) 442198.

SEATON, near. Higher Cownhayne Farm. Colyton, Devon. Self-catering apartments in large farmhouse. Colour televisions, bathrooms, kitchens, dining combine sitting rooms. Apartments fully equipped. Trout fishing, model aircraft flying. Caravanning, camping. Available all year. Elsie Pady. Phone: (0297) 552267.

SEATON. Quiet cottage, centrally situated. Also flat overlooking Axmouth harbour, offer an ideal opportunity for exploring the beautiful Axe Valley. Both sleep 2/5. Comfortably furnished. Parking. Colour television. Brochures: Daniel, 5 Trevelyan Road. Phone: (01297) 20966.

SEATON, Devon. Luxury bungalows. Overlooking the beautiful Axe Valley. One mile from sea. Sleeping 4 and 5. They are beautifully equipped and furnished to high standard. Tariff from £175 per week. For brochure Phone: (0460) 64069.

SEATON. Just off seafront. Comfortable well equipped modern two bedroomed first floor end flat (in small block), sleeps 4. Colour television, washer/dryer. Level walk to town centre. River, countryside nearby. Excellent walking area. Phone: (01297) 680 364.

SHALDON, Teignmouth, Torbay. Lovely selection of coastal cottages, bungalows and apartments, many with sea views. Children and pets welcome. Short breaks available. For brochure Phone/Fax (0626) 872314. 9 a.m. - 7p.m. Monday-Saturday. 24 hours answerphone.

SIDMOUTH near. Charming olde worlde detached cottage. Sleeps 6. Well equipped, delightfully furnished. Inglenook, beams. Hot and cold and television all rooms. Garden, parking. Lovely countryside and walks. Convenient coast and shops. Excellent value. Phone: 081-440 8031.

STOKENHAM VILLAGE. Mile from sea, Slapton Sands. Three charming courtyard cottages, sleeping two to eight. Walled garden. Parking. Near pubs, church, sailing, golf, bird watching. Rent includes constant hot water and electricity. Brochure available. Phone: (0548) 580655.

TAVISTOCK. Dartmoor country cottages. Timeless views, peaceful modern amenities. Central heating, woodburning stoves, colour television. Gardens. Ideal getting away from it all. Resting comfortably. Walking, birdwatching, touring. Pets and price! Open all year. Mrs C. Stacey. Phone: (0822) 810392.

TEIGNMOUTH. Comfortable fully fitted self- contained annexe to Victorian seaside villa. 8 miles from Torquay. 10 minutes walk seafront and town centre. Sleeps 2/3. No pets. Use of garden. £80 - £175 per week. Brochure. Phone: (01626) 778507.

TEIGNMOUTH, South Devon. Holiday flats. 10 yards safe clean beach. Superb views. Comfortable, fully equipped, colour television. Close to all amenities. Level walking. Sleep 2/4/6. Most self-contained. Sae Bella Vista Seafront. Phone: (0626) 774134.

TEIGNMOUTH. Self-contained annexe to large Victorian house. 10 minutes walk from beach, shops and station. Well equipped for 2 - 4. Separate off road parking and private entrance. Regret no pets. £80 - £165 per week. Phone: (01626) 778645.

TEIGNMOUTH. Self-contained holiday flats within 10 minutes walk to town and beach. Colour television and linen included. Sea or garden views. Residential area. Private drive for parking. Tolvarne, First Drive, Exeter Road. Brochure Phone: Mrs J. Beatty (0626) 773559.

THURLESTONE, South Devon. Converted barn. Quiet country location. Close to sandy beach. Sleeps 4-6. Good garden for children. Linen provided. Dogs welcome. Well equipped. Golf, walks, riding, sailing close by. Handy for Salcombe. Phone: (0548) 560524.

TIVERTON. Cottage, beautiful Exe Valley. Sleeps nine in four bedrooms. Oak beams, log fire, storage heaters, colour television, very well equipped. Salmon and trout fishing. Mrs B. MacDonald, Hatswell, Washfield, Tiverton, Devon. Phone: (0884) 253016.

TIVERTON. Cider cottage. Delightful comfort- able well furnished cottage on 150 acre dairy farm. Overlooking beautiful unspoilt countryside. Sleeps five. ETB 4 key highly commended. Phone: (01884) 256946. Brochure available. Mrs Hann, Great Bradley Farm, Withleigh, Tiverton EX16 8JL.

TORQUAY. Self-contained flats in quiet area near to shops and beach. Low rates early and late season. Private parking. Small dogs by agreement. Lewis, Harlowen Lodge, 11 St. Margarets Road, Torquay TQ1 4NW. Phone: (0803) 313536.

TORQUAY. Spacious holiday flats with quality furnishings, colour television, shower rooms. Set in large gardens, quiet area with car park. Laundry room, barbecue. Sleeps 2 to 9, bed linen included. Easy walk to harbour, beaches, shops, theatres. Phone: (0803) 293555.

Holiday Homes & Cottages S.W.

TORQUAY, PAIGNTON, BRIXHAM AND SURROUNDING AREAS

Houses, Bungalows, Cottages, Apartments, Chalets & Caravans

* Realistic Affordable Prices
* Off Season Bargains
* Free Cancellation Insurance
* No Booking Fee
* Pets Welcome

The
Torbay Holiday Agency
Dept 28, 365A Torquay Road, Paignton, Devon. TQ3 2BT

For Free colour brochure phone **(01803) 663650**

Fax (01803) 664037

TORQUAY. Seafront first floor flat. 2 bed-rooms with sea views, lounge/diner, kitchen, bathroom with bath and shower. Colour television, off road parking. Apply Mrs Ballard, Pendennis, Seaway Lane. Phone: (0803) 297676.

TORQUAY. Waldon Hall. Comfortable self-contained apartments. All with colour television, cookers, fridges. Linen included. Many have sea views. Easy reach to town, beach, harbour. Separate kitchens, bathrooms. Slee, St Lukes Road South. Phone: (0803) 297784.

TORQUAY. Rosa Torina superior apartments. Completely self-contained, sleep 2 - 6. Couples, families only. Excellent location, easy walk to beaches, shops, harbour, entertainments. Linen, colour television included. Early/late season bargain breaks. ETB approved. Phone: (01803) 296995.

TORQUAY. Kimberley Court Holiday Flats, TQ1 4NS. 1-8 persons. Comfortable, spacious, well equipped. Linen, colour television, cots. Parking provided. Cleanliness assured. Level walk to seafront. Shops nearby. Pets by arrangement. No VAT. Resident proprietors. Phone: (0803) 325704.

TORQUAY. Self-contained holiday flats, cen-trally situated for beach and shops and amenities. Own showers and toilets. Coloured television. Car park. Bed linen provided. Phone: (0803) 293164 or write to Kingswood, 22 Morgan Avenue, Torquay, Devon.

TORQUAY. Thatched cottage, sleeps four. In quiet village, six miles from coast. Fully equipped with dishwasher, microwave, washing machine, telephone, gas barbecue. Patio, large garden and car parking. Sorry no pets. Colour brochure Phone: (0626) 872436.

TORQUAY. Clydesdale Holiday Flats, Croft Road. Super central position. Close to seafront, main shops, riviera centre, entertainments. Self-contained, fully equipped, beds made for arrival. Heating provided. Open all year. Phone resident Manager (01803) 292759.

TORQUAY. Self catering apartments, uniquely situated approximately 200 metres harbour, town, beaches and entertainments. Self-contained units with colour televisions, fully equipped for 1-6 persons. Cleanliness assured. Launderette. Parking. The Beulah, Meadfoot Road. Phone: (01803) 297471.

TORQUAY. Comfortable holiday cottages. Ideal for families. Equipped for 6. Colour television, linen. Three bedrooms, lounge, kitchen, bathroom. Parking. Garden. Quiet position not far from shops, harbour, beaches. No VAT. Colour brochure Phone: (0803) 294023.

TORQUAY. Alexandra Lodge. Superior self-contained holiday apartments. Set in own grounds. Overlooking Torbay. All flats fully self-contained for 2 to 6 people. Large car park. Contact resident proprietors Pat and Tim Walton. Phone: (01803) 213465.

TORQUAY. 'Kathleen Court'. Holiday apart-ments in lovely Italian villa. Well appointed, spacious and fully self-contained. Nicely situated in quiet area overlooking bay. Large gardens. Parking. Launderette. Close harbour. Friendly hosts. Phone: (01803) 293470.

TORQUAY. Babbacombe. Luxury clifftop cot-tage, sleeps 4. Both bedrooms en-suite. Lounge, colour television, dining room, fully equipped kitchen. Garden. Convenient all amenities, cliff walks and beaches. Very comfortable and well furnished. Phone: (0803) 200333 evenings.

TORQUAY. Great value. £104 for 2, £165 for 4. En-suite, self-contained holiday flats. Fully equipped, linen, Sky/colour television. Parking. Quiet location, close beach, town. Ideal holiday home away. Free brochure. Phone: (0803) 296430.

TORQUAY. Detached family 4 bed bungalow. Secluded patio, garden. Enviable position. Overlooking Cockington village. Seaviews. Televisions, microwave. Bathroom, shower room, laundry room. Bed linen. Local shops, inns. Horse riding nearby. Beaches 1 mile. Parking. Gayton, 16 Walnut Road. Phone: (0803) 605658.

TORRINGTON. Away from the crowds, luxury attractive and well equipped cottages in peaceful countryside. Four with heated indoor pool, two with open log fire. Sleep 4-6. Pets welcome. ETB 4 keys highly commended. Brochure Phone: (01805) 601540.

TORRINGTON. Three bedroomed country cottage. 2 double, 2 single beds, bathroom/toilet upstairs. All electric kitchen. Television lounge. Linen supplied. Large garden in peaceful setting. Convenient Moors and coast. Brochure Millman, Winscott, St. Giles, Torrington. Phone: (0805) 623120.

TORRINGTON. Self catering cottage on farm. Working farm with ducks, hens and other farm animals. Dartington Glass Factory, Rosemoor Gardens and Tarka Trail nearby. Cottage sleeps six. Colour television. Wood, Lake Farm, Langtree. Phone: (0805) 601320.

TOTNES. Converted cider house on working farm, 2 miles from Totnes. Sleeps 7 in 3 bedrooms plus cot. Kitchen/diner with fridge/freezer, microwave. Washer/dryer. Bathroom, separate showeroom, toilet. Lounge with television. Parking. Garden. No pets. Phone: (0803) 863718.

TOTNES. Clean, comfortable, bungalow accom-modation on dairy farm, situated between Totnes and Kingsbridge. Peaceful and secluded with garden and beautiful view. Centrally placed for coast and Dartmoor. Ample parking. For details Phone: Mrs Parker (0548) 521307.

TOTNES. Large spacious 17th century house sleeps 9 plus cot. 4 bedrooms, 2 bathrooms. Large gardens. Central to moors and coast. Gas central heating. Washing machine, linen and baby sitting available. Personally supervised. Mrs. Anning. Phone: (0803) 863918.

WEST WORLINGTON. Discover Devon in 16th century thatched cottage. Situated in area of outstanding beauty, overlooking Little Dart Valley. Between Dartmoor and Exmoor. Large south facing garden adjoining open countryside. Sleeps 6. Linen provided. Phone: (0494) 674866.

WESTWARD HO!, Inglebrook. Fully equipped apartments in l 1/2 acres. Breathtaking views. Ideal base in Tarka country for touring, walking. Sandy beaches, tourist attractions, golf, fishing, riding, cycling, surfing, tennis, indoor bowls, swimming. Overlooking country pack. Phone: (0237) 473819.

WOOLACOMBE. Cliffside. Well equipped self-contained flats. Seafront. All with sea views. Free parking, level walk to village. Clean sandy beaches, safe bathing, garden. Resident proprietors. Bowen, Cliffside Esplanade, Woolacombe, Devon EX34 7DJ. Phone: (0271) 870210.

WOOLACOMBE. Comfortable holiday flats, self-contained and fully equipped, including bed linen and colour television. Spectacular sea and country views. Parking. Pets accepted. Nearby leisure facilities available. Scott, Sea View House, Seymour Villas, Woolacombe. Phone: (0271) 870630.

WOOLACOMBE, North Devon. Superb spacious private two bedroomed flat. Sleeps four. Close magnificent Blue Flag beach. Self-contained, fitted to high standard. Heating, full kitchen plus microwave, colour television. £90 - £275 per week. Phone: (0271) 870216.

WOOLACOMBE. Superb seafront position self-contained flats, sleep 2 - 5 plus cot. All flats have wonderful sea views. Comfortable and fully equipped. Bed linen included. Parking. Pets by arrangement. Barricane, Esplanade, Woolacombe EX34 7DJ. Phone: (0271) 870444 evenings.

WOOLACOMBE. Spacious self-contained two bedroomed apartment. Spotlessly clean. Well equipped throughout. Three minutes from beach and all amenities. Sea views. Drying area. Garage. No pets. Prices inclusive of hot water and electricity. Phone: (0271) 870529.

CARAVANS, CHALETS & HOLIDAY PARKS

AXMINSTER (near). 2 bedroom mobile home in quiet lawned area of small cottage complex in 7 acres with super panoramic views. Heated outdoor pool, games room, fishing. Special early - late terms. Phone: (0297) 32385.

BARNSTAPLE. To let 6 berth caravan on fam-ily run dairy farm. Close to beaches. Children and dogs welcome. For details Phone: Angela (0271) 43679.

BARNSTAPLE 6 miles. North Devon Farm. One 7 berth caravan, self-contained. Colour television, fridge, Calor gas cooker, shower room. Adjoining wash basin, toilet. Ideal for children. Reasonable rates. Phone: Mrs Ford for details (0271) 858262.

BEER, Devon. Caravans, lovely views, all with full services. Personal service. Quiet site. No club. Good shop. Mrs S. Beresford, Forston Lodge, near Dorchester, Dorset DT2 7AB. Phone: (0305) 266332.

BIGBURY BAY, near Challaborough. 1993 cara-van 6 berth. Two bedrooms, bath, shower, gas, electric included. Close to beach, coastal walks, shops. Available April to October reasonable. Private. Phone: (0752) 253968.

BISHOPSTEIGNTON. Luxury caravans (6 berths). On peaceful site, overlooking River Teign. Fully fitted with toilets, showers, colour television, fridge. Details from Mrs R.J. Price, Vale House, Slapton, Kingsbridge or Phone: (0548) 580669.

BRIXHAM. Six berth caravan. Two bedrooms, bathroom with shower, toilet, wash basin and shaver point. Electric cooker, refrigerator and water heater. Colour television. All electricity free. On well known south bay holiday park. Reasonable. Phone: (0392) 55739.

BRIXHAM, Paignton. Excellent holiday chalets. Quiet country site overlooking beautiful River Dart. Sleeps 4. Fully equipped, fitted kitchen, colour television, microwave. Parking. 1 1/2 miles to beach. Pets welcome. Brochure Phone: (0803) 752497.

BRIXHAM, Torbay. Holiday chalets. Fishcombe Cove. Quiet family run site. Panoramic views across Torbay. Self-catering, fully furnished flats. Sorry no pets. For brochure write or Phone: (0803) 853313.

BUDLEIGH SALTERTON. 'Ladram Bay'. 6 berth caravan overlooking sea. Television. Shower. Fridge. Cooker etc. Free electric, gas. Entertainment. Pool. All amenities on site. Shop, pub, launderette. cafe. Play area etc. Pets welcome. Phone: (0823) 663326.

BUTTERLEIGH. £80 - £140 weekly. Holiday in beautiful mid Devon. Spectacular views, lovely walks. Spacious 6 berth mobile home. Modern conveniences. Colour television, fridge, shower. Coarse trout fishing, cycle hire. Easy reach coast, moors, M5 (J28). Phone: (0884) 855463.

CHALLABOROUGH BAY. Near Bigbury, South Devon coast. Fully equipped luxury 3 bedroom caravan with colour television. Free amenities, entertainment, children's club. Private secluded bay, indoor pool. Country walks. Phone: (0626) 852715 evenings or weekends.

CHALLABOROUGH BAY. Large comfortable 8 berth caravan. Colour television, microwave, gas, electric inclusive. Close to all site facilities and beach. Parking next to van. Phone: (01752) 701725.

COLYTON. Bonehayne Farm. Working farm. 6 berth luxury caravan in secluded spot on farmhouse lawn. Overlooking fields, river and woodlands. Good trout fishing. Sea 4 miles. Brochure available. Cottage also available. Phone: (0404) 87416/87396.

COMBE MARTIN. Enjoy caravan holiday in a large garden on a farm. Wonderful views of the countryside. Dogs welcome. Ideal all beaches, Exmoor beauty spots. Quiet. Sleeps 6. Television. Shower. Phone: (0271) 883609.

DARTMOOR VIEW CARAVAN PARK

QUIET 5 ✓ GRADED HOLIDAY PARK IN WEST DEVON

Excellent facilities, beautiful views, caravans and tents. Easy access from M5 via A30. Ideal centre for touring and walking in Devon and Cornwall.

DARTMOOR VIEW CARAVAN PARK

Whiddon Down, Okehampton, Devon EX20 2QL.

Phone: (0647) 231545

DARTMOUTH. Small quiet level site. Hire fleet 6 berth/holiday homes. Welcomes tourers, tents/motor homes. Toilet/shower block, laundry, barbecue, electric hook-ups. Colour televison, heaters, fridges, cookers, showers, toilets every unit. Phone: (0803) 770535.

DARTMOUTH. One only large caravan, near Blackpool and Slapton beaches. Colour television, fridge, hot and cold water, shower, flush sanitation. Large enclosed patio. Clean, comfortable. Private, moderate terms. Mrs Wall, Hillaway, Strete, Dartmouth, Devon. Phone: (0803) 770213.

DARTMOUTH. Quality I and 2 bedroom chalets suitable for 2 - 6 people and under our personal supervision. Site facilities include heated pool, bar, restaurant etc. Wychwood, Swannaton Road, Dartmouth, Devon TQ6 9RL. Phone: Una or Jim (0803) 835008.

DARTMOUTH. Luxury holiday chalet, sleeps 6. Colour television. On site with amenities. Close to beaches and places of interest. Ideal touring centre. For details Phone: (0494) 714593.

DARTMOUTH. Holiday Chalets. Owner maintained. Double glazed. Lovely country views towards Dart Valley. Superb holiday area. Beaches, coastal walks, boating, golf, easy reach. Art holidays and guided walks available by arrangement. Phone: (0803) 845196/(0803) 844587.

DAWLISH WARREN

Brick built chalets. Sited at the Welcome Holiday Park. Col. TV. 2 indoor heated pools. Club with family entertainment. Pets welcome.

Phone: 01275 834626

DAWLISH WARREN, Devon. Well equipped six berth caravan sited on holiday park with all facilities. Close to beach. Ideal base for discovering the beauty spots of South Devon. Phone: (0202) 578133 for further details.

DEVON Cliffs Holiday Centre. Three bed- roomed caravans. Phone us for competitive rates. Also, Costa Brava apartment, sleeps seven, and hotel accommodation, Calis Beach, Turkey. Just £49 per week bed and breakfast. Duxbury, Hele, Exeter. Phone: (0392) 881363.

EXETER, five miles. Super six berth caravan to let. All amenities. Lovely rural area. Sea sixteen miles. For details Phone: (0404) 822409.

PEACE & TRANQUILLITY NR. EXETER

Delightful setting for 42ft., 2 bedroom, 6 berth caravan. Situated in a private & friendly park. Relax & enjoy the scenery or choose to stroll along the many forest lanes. Very reasonable charges. Pets welcome. 15 minutes from sea. (Dawlish).

MR. D. L. SALTER Haldon Lodge, Kennford, Nr. Exeter EX6 7YG

Ph.: (01392) 832312

EXMOOR NATIONAL PARK. Quiet peaceful caravan park. Beautiful wooded valley banks, trout stream. Luxury apartments, caravan. Self-service shop, licensed restaurant, launderette. Trout fishing, games room. Sunny Lyn Caravans, Lynton, North Devon. Phone: (01598) 753384.

EXMOOR National Park. Touring caravans and tents. Small unique park with lovely views on working farm. Moorland walking within 400 yards. One mile from Winsford. Good access. Loos and showers. Electric hook ups. Phone: (01643) 85259.

EXMOUTH. Sandy Bay. Eight berth luxury caravan. Sea views. Close to beach. Shower, television, microwave. All amenities on site. 2 swimming pools, night club, restaurant. Haven site. 25% off list price. Phone: (0202) 574925.

EXMOUTH, Devon Cliffs. Haven site 1994. Three bedroom, six berth caravan on concrete base. Free gas, electric and entry swimming pools, clubs. Microwave, television, radio, quilts. Plus covers, pillow slips. Plus extras. No pets. Phone: (01752) 778885.

EXMOUTH, Devon. Cliffs. 6 berth caravans on Haven's holiday park. Colour television, showers, gas and electricity included in price. Excellent site facilities. Free entry to entertainment and swimming pools. Close to sandy beach. Phone: (0823) 461285.

EXMOUTH. Sandy Bay, Devon Cliffs. 6 berth caravan, two bedrooms, colour television, microwave, shower. Price includes clubs, pools etc. Loads of entertainment for all ages. Big discounts off Haven prices. Book early to save disappointment. Phone: (0793) 436717.

EXMOUTH. Sandy Bay. Modern holiday caravan to let. All amenities, all facilities at Devon Cliffs Holiday Park, Sandy Bay, Exmouth, Devon. Competitive rates. Childrens clubs, cabaret clubs, indoor/outdoor swimming pools, shops. Phone: (0395) 273070.

EXMOUTH. Devon Cliffs, Sandy Bay. 1992 3 bedroomed luxury caravan with all amenities. On site facilities include free indoor/outdoor heated pools, sandy beach, children's fun palace. Late night cabaret, disco. Phone: (0752) 601207.

EXMOUTH. Devon cliffs holiday caravan. All amenities and entertainments on site. Microwave and colour television. Free club and pools. For details Phone: (0272) 658275 or (0831) 243811 mobile.

EXMOUTH, Devon Cliffs. Haven's premier site 1995. Two bedroomed 35 foot caravan. All amenities. Quiet position overlooking sea. Safe bathing, private sandy beach. Free pools and family entertainment. Personally cleaned. Discounts families of four. Phone: (0305) 848676.

EXMOUTH, Devon Cliffs, Sandy Bay. Luxury three bedroomed caravan. Shower, colour television, microwave. Patio furniture. Sea views. Very reasonable rates. All amenities on site including beach, swimming pools and children's club. Phone: (01392) 430201 or (01392) 433149.

EXMOUTH, Devon. Sandy Bay Haven site. Lux- ury caravan. All conveniences. Colour television, heated swimming pools. Excellent entertainments, shops, restaurants. Inclusive prices. Safe sandy beach. Reduction for two consecutive weeks. Phone: (0703) 293257.

EXMOUTH. Devon Cliffs. 'Havens best site' Luxury 3 bedroom caravan with television and microwave. Near pools, entertainments and beach. Discount on Haven prices. Pools and entertainments free. Privately owned. Phone: (0242) 517460.

EXMOUTH, Devon Cliffs. Haven site. Luxury caravans for hire. Colour television. Shower, fridge. Clubs, swimming pools, shops, restaurants. Sorry no pets. Phone: (0395) 222029.

EXMOUTH, Devon Cliffs. Sandy Bay. Fabulous 3 bedroom caravan. Amazing sea views. Colour television. Shower, entertainment. Swimming pools on the haven site. For more details Phone: (0395) 274425.

EXMOUTH, Devon. Sandy Bay. 6 berth luxury caravan on Haven Holiday Site. Facilities include nice beach, clubs, bars, swimming pools and much more. Ideal family holiday. Phone: (01980) 611830, (01722) 332445.

EXMOUTH, Devon Cliffs. Sandy Bay (Haven). 8 berth caravan. Close to free amenities. Discount prices. Sorry no pets. Phone: (0793) 616458.

EXMOUTH, Devon. Cliffs Haven site. Caravan, all amenities available. 6/8 berth. Television, music centre, video, microwave, fridge, gas and electricity free. Sea view. Easy location to clubs and beach. Reasonable prices. Phone: (0684) 298943.

EXMOUTH. Haven Holiday Park. Private luxury 3 bedroom caravan at seafront. Swimming pool, clubs and children's entertainment included. Excellent family site. Phone: (0438) 815035.

HELE BAY. Near pretty fishing market town of Ilfracombe with its famous tunnels leading to beach. Privately owned caravan. Golf, fishing, riding, swimming pool all near. Lovely walks, quiet site. Pets allowed. Phone: (0424) 425517 for more information.

HONITON/SIDMOUTH. Very comfortable mobile home in picturesque countryside. Approved riding school and 260 acre sheep farm. Fully equipped. Double room, bunk room, water closet, shower etc. Ideal family holiday. Cottage also available. 4 miles coast. Phone: (01404) 87200/355.

ILFRACOMBE. Near sea. Large caravan, sleeps 6-8. Microwave, barbecue, pub, carvery, shop. All facilities. Duvets. Low season £75, high £200 plus gas. Children's area, Blue-Flag beaches. Details Phone: Mrs White (0271) 867432 evenings. Popular site. Newly refurbished.

ILFRACOMBE. Family size caravan. Seaside, country, valley, park. 500 yards beach, 1 mile town centre. Horse riding, golf, indoor swimming pool nearby. Bargain weeks early - late season. Details John's Caravans Phone: (01271) 863229.

LYNTON, Devon. Sunny Lyn Caravans. Stay in one of our caravans or luxury apartments and enjoy the tranquil surroundings of our park. Ideal centre for touring Exmoor National Park. Shop, launderette, restaurant. Near sea. Phone: (01598) 753384.

LYNTON, North Devon. Twixt Exmoor and coast. 6 berth caravan with shower, wc. Television etc. On small farm, offering peace, tranquillity in glorious countryside. Riding stables nearby, fishing, surfing in area. Excellent walking country. Phone: (0598) 763258.

OKEHAMPTON, Olditch. Caravan and camping park. Holiday units for hire. Tourers and tents welcome. Hard standings, electric hook ups. Licensed restaurant. Ideal for walking, Dartmoor and touring West Country. Bailey, Stickle Path, Okehampton, Devon EX20 2NT. Phone: (01837) 840734.

OKEHAMPTON. For a quiet, restful holiday. Luxury 6 berth caravans. Fully equipped. Colour television, shower, toilet, refrigerator, hot water. ETB very good grading. Bridestowe Caravan Park, Bridestowe, Devon EX20 4ER. Phone: (01837) 86261. From June Phone: (01837) 861261.

PAIGNTON - Grange Court. Modern holiday caravans including luxury caravan. All with bathrooms, gas and electric included in rental. Clubhouse with entertainment on site. Shop, pool, launderette. Close to beach. No pets. Phone: (01225) 316578.

PAIGNTON. Situated on the A385 between Paignton and Totnes. Central to all attractions. 13 caravans and 3 flats. Open all year on a small quiet site. 4 ticks graded. Phone: (0803) 551971. Bona Vista Holiday Park.

PAIGNTON. Holiday caravans, all with showers toilet, coloured television. Swimming pool, family entertainment, licensed supermarket. Near beaches, shops, award winning park. Free brochure Sonia Hopkins, 18 Bidwell Brook Drive, Goodrington, Paignton, Devon. Phone: (0803) 843741.

PAIGNTON. Grange Court Holiday Centre. Wide range of luxury and budget caravans on award winning park near sandy beaches in centre of Torbay. Pool, club, entertainment, licensed restaurant. Adventure playground. Colour brochure Phone: (0803) 812949.

SALCOMBE. Family run caravan park, set amidst National Trust land. Easy walking distance of Sandy Cove. Fully equipped, modern caravans with all facilities. Children's play area and games room. Sun Park Caravan and Camping. Phone: (0548) 561378.

SANDY BAY, Exmouth, Devon Cliffs. 8 berth, 3 bedroom luxury caravan. Private beach, colour television, microwave. Pools, clubs all free. Beautiful panoramic view from caravan. Haven site. Bookings April to November. Phone: 021 603 9512.

SEATON, Lyme Bay Holiday Village. 6 berth chalet, all facilities. OAP's discount early season. Free club membership and electricity, colour television. Phone: (0676) 532888.

SEATON, Devon. Lovely chalet on excellent Haven park. New decor, carpets etc. etc. Sleeps six. Close beach, shops, harbour, river. All amenities and entertainments. Two heated swimming pools with flumes. Sports facilities. Phone: Townsend (0242) 232060/574431.

SEATON, East Devon. Chalet sleeps 6. Bath-room, 2 bedrooms. Colour television. Pet allowed. Quiet site. Mile from sea, shop. Fine walking country for Beer, Lyme, Branscombe, Sidmouth. Open March to October. For brochure Phone: 021422 0746.

SIDMOUTH. Rose Award. Luxury caravans on quiet rural park. In an area of outstanding natural beauty. Sidmouth's closest caravan park. Graded excellent. Salcombe Regis Caravan Park, Sidmouth, Devon. For free brochure Fax:/Phone: (0395) 514303.

SIDMOUTH. All electric holiday caravans on peaceful site. No club. Adjacent coastal footpath and East Devon heritage coastline. Next to donkey sanctuary. De-luxe caravans sited for sale with 10 year lease. Dunscombe Manor EX10 0PN. Phone: (01395) 513654.

TAVISTOCK area. Comfortable, fully serviced caravan in Dartmoor National Park. Small family-run site in beautiful countryside, minutes' walk from open moorland. Ideal walking, touring. Sleeps six. Rates inclusive of gas, electricity, colour television. Phone: (0934) 742976.

TORBAY, near South Devon. 6/8 berth luxury caravans and pinelog chaletta. All with bathroom, colour television, fridge. Launderette, shop, pay phone. Ball, Higher Well Farm Holiday Park, Stoke Gabriel, Totnes, Devon. Phone: Stoke Gabriel (01803) 782289.

TORQUAY. Holiday caravans. Select site situa-ted in area of outstanding landscape. Value good touring centre for coast and moors. Fully equipped, television, showers. Special rates for two. Cutts, Kingsland Farm, Marldon Road, Torquay. Phone: (0803) 613496.

UMBERLEIGH. Single caravan on family farm in the unspoilt beautiful Taw Valley. 2 bedrooms, kitchen/diner, lounge. Sleeps 6. Gas and electricity free. Children and pets welcome. £135 per week peak season. Phone: Chittlehamholt (0769) 540661.

WESTWARD HO! Small select caravan site overlooking sea and Bideford Bay. All caravans comfortable with mains facilities, showers, toilets and coloured television. Free coloured brochure apply Phone: (0237) 475281 or 471663 (evening).

WOOLACOMBE, Twitchen Park. 34 foot luxury 3 bedroom caravan. Colour television, shower. Excellent award winning site. Near sea. Beautiful safe beaches. Heated pool, entertainment. Big reductions for small families and senior citizens. Illustrated brochure from Mrs L. Hughes. Phone: 081 546 8137.

WOOLACOMBE, Devon. Rose Award site near sea, Blue Flag beach. Heated pool, bars, entertainment. Adjacent golf course. Deluxe 2 and 3 bedroom caravans with all facilities. Early/late discounts. Mrs Oldham, Mortehoe, Woolacombe. Phone: (0271) 870423/890550.

WOOLACOMBE. 2/3 bedroom 6-berth caravans with own showers, toilets, colour televisions. Most with sea views. Superb 'Rose Award' park with excellent facilities. Entertainment, pool, children's club. Close Blue Flag beach. Phone: Mrs Sprason (0562) 883038.

WOOLACOMBE. Caravan sleeps six. Privately owned and maintained. Well equipped. No linen. Near Exmoor and beautiful coastline. Excellent Rose Award site. Swimming pool. Club house. Restaurant. Special early and late rates. Brochure. Phone: (0271) 870700.

WHERE TO GO

Once Upon a Time
Woolacombe.
Tel: (0271) 870999

Wild Boar adventure trail. Fantasy train ride. Twista bikes, plastic ball ocean, animated fairy tales. Restaurant. Disabled visitors welcome.

Watermouth Castle
Ilfracombe.
Tel: (0271) 863879

Peter Petz Steam Swing Boats. Model railway, mechanical music, doll collection, crystal ball, smugglers' dungeon, dungeon maze, pets corner, aviaries, crazy mirrors, gnomeland, merrygoland, peddle snails and mystic phone box.

Combe Martin Wildlife Park and Monkey Sanctuary
Higher Leigh Manor, Combe Martin.
Tel: (0271) 882486

Monkey sanctuary, otters, seals and the largest enclosure of meerkats in the world. Garden and indoor model railway.

Dartmoor Wildlife Park
Sparkwell, Plymouth.
Tel: (075537) 209

Over 1,000 species of animals, reptiles and birds. 'Close encounters of the Animal Kind', talk, touch and learn all-weather facility. Falconry displays, pony rides, adventure playground, restaurant and shop. Disabled visitors welcome.

Rosemoor Garden,
Torrington, Devon.
Tel: (0805) 24067

Garden of rare horticultural interest. Trees, shrubs, roses, alpine and arboretum. Nursery of rare plants.

Killerton House
Broadclyst, Nr Exeter, Devon.
Tel: (0392) 881345

18th Century house built for the Acland family, now houses collection of costumes shown in various room settings. 15 acres of hillside garden with rare trees and shrubs.

Buckfast Abbey
Buckfastleigh, Devon.
Tel: (0364) 42519

Large Benedictine monastery rebuilt on medieval foundations. Many art treasures in the abbey.

Lundy Island
Lundy, Bristol Channel, Bideford, Devon.
Tel: (0237) 431831

Unspoilt island, tavern and restaurant, shop, marine reserve, archaeology, wildlife, spectacular walks and sea crossing.

DORSET

HOTELS & GUEST HOUSES

LOXWOOD HOTEL
**6 ALUMDALE ROAD, ALUM CHINE,
WESTBOURNE, BOURNEMOUTH**
A warm and friendly welcome awaits you at our delightful family run hotel. All bedrooms are tastefully furnished. Only 5 minutes walk to the sea. ● Parking ● Colour TV Lounge ● Tea/Coffee making facilities in all rooms ● Full English Breakfast ● Evening Meal optional ● Some en-suite available ●
B&B from £12.50-£15.75 per night. H/B from £129-£150 per week.
Tel: 01202 765394

BLANDFORD, Brook Farm, Winterbourne, Zelston. Ideally situated for coast and countryside, this working farm offers two spacious family rooms. Basins, television, chairs, beverage facilities. One with en-suite shower. Excellent eating places nearby. Phone: Irene Kerley (0929) 459267.

BOSCOMBE, Bournemouth. Family hotel. Licensed. Parking. Television, tea making facilities all rooms. Fourteen pounds, bed and breakfast. Eighty five pounds weekly. Half price children. First under five free. Special arrangements for babies. Near sea. Phone: (0202) 396876.

BOURNEMOUTH. Alum Chine Bella Vista Hotel. Friendly, family run by Gwen and Wallace. Licensed bar, en-suite, televisions, tea coffee facilities. Pool table, darts. Three minutes from sandy beach. For brochure or more information phone (0202) 763591, many thanks.

BOURNEMOUTH
ASHLEIGH HOTEL
6 SOUTHCOTE ROAD
Small family run licensed hotel offering an ideal location for a relaxing holiday or mini break. All rooms enjoy tea/coffee making facilities, colour TVs with Satellite. En-suites available, forecourt parking, lounge bar and television lounge, garden and sun patio. Centrally situated, close to sea, shops, rail/coach stations and entertainment.
**Room Only from £12.00
B&B from £14.50 B.B.&E.M. from £18.50.**
TEL: (0202) 558048

BOURNEMOUTH. Amberwood Grange is situated in town centre in a quiet environment within walking distance of sea-front, shops, gardens. Attractive apartments with on-site parking. Resident proprietors. Open all year. 30 Dean Park Road, BH1 1HY. Phone: (01202) 290920.

BOURNEMOUTH CENTRE
Come and be spoilt! Forget the dishes and relax. En-suite rooms (deluxe and 4-poster available for that special occasion). Licensed bar and car park. Beautiful sandy beach, town centre, with its selection of shops and department stores, the B.I.C., and Pavilion Theatre, are just a few minutes walk away.
Bed and breakfast from £17 per person per night Half board from £138 per week
2 THE MANOR BOURNE HOTEL
2 WEST CLIFF ROAD BH2 5EY
Tel: 01202 299645

St. GERMAINE HOTEL
**24 Derby Road, Bournemouth BH1 3QA
Telephone (01202) 557923**
A spacious detached hotel surrounded with greenery and standing well back from the road.
❖ Close to sea and town centre ❖ Large private car park ❖ Overlooking public tennis courts, bowling green and lovely park ❖ Spacious dining room ❖ Home cooked food highly recommended ❖ Spacious rooms ❖ Ground floor bedrooms ❖ All rooms colour TV ❖ Tea and coffee facilities in all rooms ❖ Most rooms ensuite ❖ Games room ❖ Full central heating ❖ Pets welcome
**Terms: B&B from £12.50 p.n.
H/B from £95 to £159 p.w.**

BOURNEMOUTH. Chine Cote Hotel. Friendly family run near beach. Beautiful area. Televisions, tea making facilities. En-suites available. Reduction children sharing. Open all year. Book early for 1994 prices. 25 Studland Road. Phone: (0202) 761208.

HIGHCLERE HOTEL
■ All bedrooms have en-suite facilities ■ Private telephone all bedrooms ■ Colour TV/radio all bedrooms ■ Licensed ■ Children very welcome over the age of 3 ■ 4 minutes walk to beach ■ Ample free parking ■ Garden with play area ■ Sea views ■ Bargain breaks early or late ■ Delicious choice of menu, for all meals.
Terms: Half Board from £145 per week inclusive.
Brochure from: **David and Averil Baldwin, 15 Burnaby Road, Bournemouth BH4 8JF. Tel: (0202) 761350**

BOURNEMOUTH. Sandy Bay Guest House. Close to sea and shops. Excellent food. Free colour televisions and tea making facilities all rooms. Licensed. Parking. From £40 bed, breakfast, half board from £85 weekly. Phone: Boscombe(0202) 309245.

BABBACOMBE COURT HOTEL
**28 WEST HILL ROAD,
BOURNEMOUTH BH2 5PG
TEL: 01202 552823
FAX: 01202 789030**

Friendly family run hotel, close to beach, B.I.C. and shopping centre. Telephone, TV, tea making in all rooms, most rooms en-suite, ample parking. Renowned for our good home cooking. Whether on conference, business or just a break away, a warm welcome awaits from resident proprietors David and Jackie Dyer.
**Terms: B&B £18-£25 per day
B&B and Evening Meal
£145-£190 per week**

The Vine Hotel

A family run licensed hotel only 3 minutes walk from cliff top and path or lift to beach. All rooms en-suite bath or shower and w.c., teamakers and colour TV. Comfortable lounge, attractive bar, full central heating, parking. Short breaks and midweek bookings. Dogs welcome. For the safety and comfort of all guests bedrooms and dining room are non smoking.

22 SOUTHERN ROAD, SOUTHBOURNE, BOURNEMOUTH, DORSET BH6 3SR
TEL: 01202 428309

BOURNEMOUTH. Hawthorns Hotel, West-bourne. 3 crown commended family hotel, offering high standards of comfort, cleanliness and cuisine. Refurbished, all rooms en-suite. Parking, licensed bar. Close to Westbourne, Alum Chine and town centre. Discounts available. Phone: (01202) 760220.

NEWFIELD HOTEL
29 BURNABY ROAD, ALUM CHINE, BOURNEMOUTH BH4 8YF
AA QQQ recommended. Licensed hotel of character and charm. 3 minutes to sandy beaches, through tranquil wooded chine. En-suite rooms, colour TV, Tea/coffee facilities. Evening dinner is regarded as an occasion for good food and wine.
TERMS FROM £18.50 BB. FROM £25.50 HB.
01202 762724

BOURNEMOUTH. Recession offer still stands. Pensioner offers holiday beds for families. 500 yards clifftop, Southbourne, near Fishermans Walk. Tea making facilities. June to September only. Adults £8, children £4 per night. Clean beach award. Phone: (0202) 430529.

BOURNEMOUTH Central. Ten minutes pier. Non- smoking house. Garaged parking if required. Single, double and family rooms. Private bathroom. Television lounge, cot available. Concessionary prices for children. £12.50 out season, £15 mid season. Phone: (0202) 396835.

Bournemouth ALUM CHINE
Small family run hotel, near beach and shops. Home cooking. Prices from £99 per week half-board. Also mid-week and weekend breaks, en-suite available.
FENN LODGE HOTEL
Rosemount Road, Bournemouth BH4 8HB
Phone: (01202) 761273

WEST BAY HOTEL
West Cliff Gardens
BOURNEMOUTH BH2 5HL
Proprietors Sylvia & George Lang
welcome holiday & conference guests. George offers varied menus, including vegetarian-special diets no problem. En-suite, TV, teamaking. Licensed. Parking. Nr. golf.
Pets welcome by prior arrangements.
Prices: BB from £20; BBEM from £25 daily.
Weekly BB from £150; BBEM from £170
Special breaks Spring & Autumn
CHRISTMAS & NEW YEAR PROGRAMMES
0202 552261 OR 556949

BOURNEMOUTH (Southbourne). Stella Maris. Friendly welcome at our family run guest house. Tea making, colour television with Sky all bedrooms. Some en-suite. Excellent home cooking. Guest lounge. Car park. Close to amenities. Reasonable charges. OAP reductions. Phone: (0202) 426874.

BOURNEMOUTH. Southbourne Grove Hotel. Friendly, family run. 14 bedrooms, en-suites available. Family rooms. Discounts for families/OAP's. Excellent cuisine. Close beach. Licensed bar. Car park. Children very welcome. Bed and breakfast from £15. Phone: (0202) 420503.

FIRCROFT HOTEL
Bournemouth
Licensed family hotel all en-suite. Free entry to sports and health club. Free £100 entertainment vouchers. Childrens discounts. Near to beach and shops. Table d'Hote menu. Bowls/dancing.
For details
(01202) 309771

BOURNEMOUTH. Glenthorne licensed Guest House. Opposite park. Near beach and shops. All rooms have colour television, tea making and central heating. Bed and breakfast from £70 per week, evening meal optional. Child reductions. Phone: (0202) 397532.

BOURNEMOUTH. Sea Breeze Hotel. Comfortable licensed hotel with sea views. All rooms en-suite with colour television and tea making facilities. Excellent home cooking. Dogs welcome. Good walks nearby. Fowler, 32 St. Catherines Road, Southbourne. Phone: (01202) 433888.

BOURNEMOUTH. Pine Lodge Guest House, 200 yards beach and gardens. Close shops, buses. Sea views, tea making, home cooking. Half board from £92-£119 weekly. 47 St John's Road, Boscombe, Bournemouth BH5 1AQ. Phone: (01202) 393134.

BOURNEMOUTH, Boscombe. Aulevant Hotel, 15 Westby Road. Two crown, residential licence. Sky, games room, tea, coffee facilities. Excellent cuisine. Near sea, shops, transport. Golf, fishing nearby. Further details, brochure Phone: (0202) 394884. Open all year.

BOURNEMOUTH. Clifton Court Hotel. 3 crowns. All rooms en-suite with sea view. Residential licence, car park, garages. Tea/coffee facilities, colour television, radio. Excellent home cuisine with varied menu. Open all year. Central heating. Phone: (0202) 427753.

BOURNEMOUTH. Waterside holiday apart-ments. Panoramic sea views. Tourist Board. 4 and 5 key approved. Registered category 3, wheelchair use. Sleep 3-10. Parking, gardens. Children play area. Prices £200 to £480. Phone: Ken on (01202) 300118.

BRIDPORT. Britmead House Hotel. ETB 3 crown commended. Full en-suite rooms (including one ground floor), with many thoughtful extras. Lounge and dining room. Overlooking garden, beyond which is open countryside. Dinner optional. Short breaks. Phone: (01308) 422941.

BRIDPORT. Bed and breakfast. In 400 year old thatched cottage. Pretty village, near town. Comfortable rooms. Tea making facilities. Sitting room with colour television. Good food, pubs. Gorgeous countryside, coast, riding, golf. For brochure Phone: (0308) 422779.

CHRISTCHURCH. Ashbourne Guest House. Excellent well appointed, family run. Within easy reach of New Forest and Bournemouth. Close to beaches and fishing facilities. Evening meal optional. All rooms colour television etc. Weekly discount 10%. Phone: Hamilton (0202) 475574.

DORCHESTER. Sixteenth Century thatched cot-tage. Stream front and back. Quiet village in wonderful countryside. Beaches 20 minutes by car. Excellent touring area. Good walking. Prettily furnished bedrooms, Inglenook fireplace in dining room. Willis, Cerne Abbas. Phone: (0300) 341659.

LULWORTH COVE, Dorset. Bed and breakfast from £13. Television, tea and coffee making facilities in all rooms. Open all year. Central heating. 10 minutes walk to Lulworth Cove. Phone: Jan Ravensdale on West Lulworth (01929) 400467.

LULWORTH COVE. The Orchard. Comfortable bed and breakfast. Off-road position and parking. Large garden. Full English vegetarian vegan breakfast, tea, coffee facilities. Close coastal path, beaches. Central South Dorset attractions. From £12.50. Phone: (0929) 400592.

LYME REGIS, near. Quiet farmhouse, bed and breakfast. 2 miles from coast. Tea making facilities and television lounge. One family room and one double room. Sea and pond fishing, fossil hunting and country walks. Phone: (0297) 560464.

MARTINSTOWN. Old Brewery House, near Dor-chester DT2 9JR. Family run bed and breakfast, in old house. Full of character and charm. 2 double, 1 twin bedrooms. £15 per person. Large shared bathroom. Phone: Cooke (0305) 889612.

PIDDLETRENTHIDE. Attractive former coach-house in rural Piddle Valley. Peaceful and private location. Beautiful views. Excellent, tastefully furnished accommodation. Sunny walled patio. Cosy woodburner. Centre of Hardy country. Easy access to coast. Tourist Board commended. Phone: (0300) 348253.

POOLE, Vernon. Small Guest House. Rural setting. Ideal base for touring Dorset. All rooms ground floor hot, cold, television, tea, coffee facilities. Own key. Parking 7 days for price of 6. ETB listed. Phone: Rendell (0202) 625185.

POOLE, Tangletrees. Modern bungalow. ETB listed. Rooms with television, tea makers, shower room. Own drive parking. Traditional or vegetarian breakfast. Easy reach quay, beaches and town. Ideal holidays. Mrs Ruffle, 32a Creekmoor Lane, Creekmoor. Phone: (01202) 681909.

POOLE. Passing through, staying a while. Looking for good bed and breakfast. Close ferry and beaches. Sea views. En-suite. Tea making facility. Television. Safe parking. Open all year. From £16. Interested? Phone: Rita (0202) 679470, mobile (0585) 319931.

SOUTHBOURNE, Bournemouth. Pennington Hotel. Small friendly hotel. Ideal position, close cliff top and shops. All rooms television, tea making facilities. Some en-suite. Good cooking assured. Parking. 26 Southern Road. Phone: (0202) 428653. ETB two crown commended.

SOUTHBOURNE, Bournemouth. The Osprey bed and breakfast. Stay longer - stay cheaper! Three nights from £39. Tea, coffee. Sky television, video link-up all rooms. Close to Fishermans Walk and sea. Friendly family atmosphere. Ring us! Phone: (0202) 423673.

STUDLAND. Bed and breakfast in 17th century National Trust farmhouse. Colour television and tea, coffee making facilities all rooms. Lovely coastal walks. Five minutes safe, clean beaches. Phone: (092944) 254.

STURMINSTER NEWTON, North Dorset. Bed and breakfast £16.00. Relax in our Georgian home. Spacious accommodation and friendly atmosphere. Explore Bath, Salisbury or discover picturesque villages. Wonderful walks and the coast. Many National Trust properties. Details Phone: (0258) 820778.

STURMINSTER-NEWTON. Sheila Martin, Moorcourt Farm, Marnhull DT10 1HH. Friendly, welcoming farmhouse. Colour co-ordinated bedrooms with tea/coffee. Keys, television, washbasins, flowers. Lounge, dining room, shower room, bathroom, toilets. Gi-normous breakfast menu. Children over 10. £13 - £14. Phone: (0258) 820271.

SWANAGE. Bed and breakfast. 17th century house in picturesque village. Full English breakfast. All bedrooms hot and cold and tea making facilities. Horse riding holidays arranged all year. Golf nearby. Phone: Mrs Coe (01929) 426066.

SWANAGE. Nethway Hotel. Very close, safe sandy beach and town centre. Quietly situated on level ground overlooking steam railway station and town. Excellent English cuisine, licence, television lounge, bar. Car park. Children welcome. Brochure Phone: (0929) 423909.

SWANAGE. Sunny Bay Guest House. Superb views of bay and Downs. Close town centre, beach and country park. Bargain breaks available. Reductions for children sharing. Open all year. 17 Cluny Crescent, Swanage. Phone: (0929) 422650.

SWANAGE. Beachway. Small family run hotel. 2 minutes beach. Television, satellite, tea making facilities all rooms. Some en-suite. Machine - knitting courses, ramblers, school parties, families welcome. Bed and breakfast from £15.50. Ulwell Road. Phone: (0929) 423077.

SWANAGE. 'Easter Cottage'. 2 crown bed and breakfast. Cosy, quietly situated. 250 yards beach/amenities. Log fires in guest lounge. Bedrooms have hot and cold/en-suite. Colour television. Complimentary beverages. Open all year. Bargain breaks available. Phone: (0929) 427782.

WAREHAM. Bed and breakfast bungalow. Natural centre for exploring Dorset. Secluded surroundings. Safe off road parking. All bedrooms have hot and cold, tea making facilities, colour television. Mrs Gegg, 1 The Merrows, Sandford. Phone: (01929) 552313.

WAREHAM. Farmhouse. Bed and breakfast. Most en-suite. Television all rooms. Peaceful surroundings. Beautiful views. Many beaches. Tourist attractions nearby. Camping available Summer. AA RAC listed. Reduction for weekly bookings. From £15. Phone: Barnes (0929) 463098.

WEYMOUTH. Comfortable and homely bed and breakfast with evening meal if required, in quiet village setting. Cat lovers and mothers union especially welcome. Field, 'Selwyns', Puddledock Lane, Sutton Poyntz, Dorset DT3 6LZ. Phone: (0305) 832239.

WEYMOUTH. Fairlie House, Holland Road. Personally run Guest House near seafront, town centre. Colour television, tea making facilities all bedrooms. Car space. OAP's reduced rates, low seasons. Phone: Christine Sweet (0305) 783951 for brochure.

WEYMOUTH. Greenacre, Bed and Breakfast. 83 Preston Road. Spacious house, close to Bowleaze Cove. 5 minutes drive town centre. Tea making, colour television all rooms. Own keys. Parking £14.50 per person. En-suite £16.50 Phone: (0305) 832047.

WEYMOUTH. Fir Court Guest House, 18 Dorchester Road. Close beach. All rooms en-suite. Television and tea-making. Car park. Bed and breakfast only, from £19 nightly or £120 weekly. Phone: Mrs P. Diffey, (0305) 788510.

WEYMOUTH. Seaways Guest House, town cen- tre. Near beach, trains, buses, car parks, ferries. Colour television, tea making facilities in all bedrooms. Clean, good food. 5 Turton Street, Weymouth, Dorset DT4 7DU. Phone: (0305) 771646.

WEYMOUTH. Small family run bed and break- fast hotel. All rooms en-suite, colour televisions. Close to beach, harbour, condor and all amenities. Berolina, 20 Esplanade, Weymouth. Proprietors Roy and Janet Lyones. Phone: (0305) 784172.

WEYMOUTH. Close to harbour, sea and main shops. Overnight or longer. Television and hot drinks facilities in all rooms. Bar. Discounts for parties and pensioners. No petty restrictions. Beverley Guest House, 19 East Street. Phone: (0305) 782129.

WEYMOUTH, Wessex. Guest House. Large double/family rooms. Free car park. Free tea making facilities, lounge. Access all times. Full English breakfast. Bed and breakfast from £11. Also holiday flats. Mrs Lambert, 128 Dorchester Road DT4 7LG. Phone: (0305) 783406.

WEYMOUTH. Guest House overlooking bay. Glorious views. All rooms have hot and cold water, shaver points, tea making facilities, colour televisions. 10 yards to beach. Packed lunch if required. No evening meals. Phone: (0305) 784916.

WEYMOUTH. Quiet homely cottage. Bed and breakfast. Unspoilt village of Langton Herring on heritage coastline, Chesil beach. Walking, fishing, birdwatching, riding, leisure pursuits. For one night or weekly. Terms open all year. Log fires. Phone: (0305) 871627.

WEYMOUTH. Premier Hotel. Seafront position. Close to all amenities. En-suite facilities. Residents bar, choice of menu. Special rates for senior citizens midweek breaks. Child reductions. For details and brochure Phone: Sue or Mike (0305) 786144.

WEYMOUTH. Kings Acre Hotel. Situated on the Esplanade. Superb sea views. Close all amenities. Lovely, comfortable rooms, many en-suite. Delicious quality home cooking of renown. Any diets catered for. Offering friendly hospitality. AA, QQQ, BTB 3 crowns. Phone: (0305) 782534.

THE HAVEN
147A PRESTON ROAD, WEYMOUTH
Cosy and comfortable accommodation. Car parking, own key, central heating, separate toilets. Hot and cold. Shaver points. Tea and coffee facilities. Hospitality trays. Colour TV. Comfortable lounge. Hearty English breakfast. Evening meal available.

(01305) 833469

WEYMOUTH. Kenora Licensed Hotel. English Tourist Board three crowns. Choice of menu. Clean, comfortable en-suite bedrooms with television and tea-makers. Award winning garden, free parking. All just 500 metres from sands, town and harbour. Phone: (0305) 771215.

WEYMOUTH. Adjacent harbour. AA/RAC. 2 star. All 77 rooms en-suite. Colour television, tea/coffee makers. Lift. Choice menu, entertainment/dancing nightly, licensed. Crown Hotel, 51 St Thomas Street, Weymouth, Dorset DT4 8EQ. Tel: (0305) 760800.

WEYMOUTH. Fir Trees Guest House. Rooms en- suite, satellite television, tea - coffee making. Parking. Close to harbour. Relax and enjoy your stay. Continental or English breakfast. Details Mrs Stuart-Brown, 27 Rodwell Avenue, Weymouth DT4 8SH. Phone: (01305) 760190 (days), (01305) 772967.

WEYMOUTH. Old Wyke Bakehouse Hotel. Converted Victorian bakery. Family run. All bedrooms with private facilities. Ideal for Weymouth, Portland, and for exploring the beautiful Dorset coast and countryside. Excellent restaurant. Licensed. For brochure Phone: (0305) 772580.

WICKHAM. Select bed and breakfast, peaceful country house. Guests lounge. Excellent breakfast. Parking. No smoking. Free tea/coffee as required. Close to pubs, shops, restaurants, Portsmouth continental ferries. Open all year, £14 per person. Phone: (01329) 832457.

SELF-CATERING

ABBOTSBURY. Coastguard cottages. 1823. Outstanding position on heritage coast. Magnificent walking in Hardy country. Full comforts in coastal/rural situation. Extensive gardens to Chesil Beach. Weekly. Also Winter weekends. Phone: (0305) 871335 (home), (0305) 871746 (office hours).

BEAMINSTER. Two bedroomed fully modern- ised character cottage. Sleeps four. Colour television, storage heating. Garden, parking. Pets welcome. Small selection of shops and country walks nearby. Beaches and coastal walks eight miles away. Phone: (0308) 862034.

BEAMINSTER. Self-catering cottages, sleeps four. In beautiful Hardy country. Ideal for walking and within easy reach of coast. Pet welcome. Phone: (0308) 862661.

BEAMINSTER 8 miles. Farming family offer, comfortable cottages for holidays for 2/7, created from traditional stone farmyard buildings. Relax with peace of mind whilst children play safely in a natural environment with freedom and space. Phone: (0460) 30207.

BEAMINSTER. Delightful 2 bedroom bungalow in peaceful location. 200 meters from town centre. 8 miles from coast. Kitchen/diner. Separate bathroom and wc, lounge. Garden. Sleeps 5 plus cot. Watts, 53 Hogshill Street. Phone: (0308) 863088.

BOSCOMBE, Bournemouth. Comfortable self- contained flats and flatlets. Sleeps 2-12. Few minutes walk beach and shops. Close to New Forest, Purbecks, golf courses and entertainments. Terms from £70 - £295 per flat per week. Phone: (01202) 396788.

BOURNEMOUTH, Boscombe. Flat, first floor, self-contained, two bedrooms, lounge, kitchen, fridge-freezer, electric cooker, bathroom. Near town centre and 15 minutes sea. Bed linen inclusive. Car space. Lawrence, 5 Grosvenor Gardens, Boscombe, Bournemouth. Phone: (0202) 302194.

BOURNEMOUTH and New Forest. Thatched cottages, bungalows, houses and apartments on the west side of the Forest in seaside and rural village settings. Cleaned and maintained by their owners. Sleep 2-10. Phone: (0202) 707885. Mobile: (0850) 800858.

BOURNEMOUTH. 4 comfortable, completely self-contained holiday flats. Bargain prices. Close sea and shops. 1-3 bedrooms. Parking, garden, central heating, colour televisions, wheelchair access. Children and pets welcome. £85-£240. 'Longmoor', 23 Harvey Road, BH5 2AD. Phone: (0202) 432064.

BOURNEMOUTH. Garden flat, self-contained, 2 bedrooms, sleeps 5. Very close River Stour and Redhill Common. Fishing, walks. Easy reach New Forest and Bournemouth Centre. Ample off-road parking. Registered Bournemouth Tourism. £95 - £200. Phone: (0202) 514793.

BOURNEMOUTH, SOUTHBOURNE. Superior small cottage, ideal family accommodation. One bedroom (twin beds), large lounge (twin beds, double sofabed), kitchen, bathroom. 5 minutes walk, sea, shops, opposite park. Television, cot, linen provided. House-trained pet welcome. Phone: (0202) 420025.

BOURNEMOUTH. Alum Chine. Burnham Lodge. Spacious, comfortable, self-contained holiday flats. Fully equipped, sleep 4/6. Colour television. Forecourt parking. Close sea and shops. Prices £100 - £300 per week. Phone Mrs Walmsley for brochure (0357) 21210.

BOURNEMOUTH. Spacious, high standard fam- ily holiday flat, sleeping 6 to 7. Close to town centre, shops and beach. Fully fitted kitchen with washing machine and tumble dryer. Telephone and garden. Phone: (0202) 730090.

BOURNEMOUTH, Alum Chine. We specialise in accommodation for couples. Clean, modern en-suite flatlets with own shower, toilet, kitchenette, colour television. Parking. Close sea, shops. £48 - £74 per person weekly. Low rates May - June. Phone: (0202) 763827.

BOURNEMOUTH centre, Westcliff Mews. Lux- ury modern cottages and garages. Patio, lounge/diner, fitted oak kitchen, two bedrooms, two bathrooms/shower. No meters. Central heating throughout. Quietly run. Minutes sea, amenities. Daisley, 17 Clarendon Road. Phone: (0202) 764450.

BOURNEMOUTH. Town centre. Self-catering flat, flatlets, 2-6 persons. Quiet cul-de-sac. Near beach, shops, gardens. Well equipped. Gas cooker, fire, refrigerator, colour television, linen. Free parking rear premises. Open all year. Phone: (0202) (change 01202 from 16th April) 554828.

BOURNEMOUTH (Southbourne). Delightfully situated between shops and fine sandy beach (3 minutes). Clean, modernised flats. Attractive rates. Early, 1 late season. Terms from £50 - £280 per unit, weekly. Seaway Holiday Flats, 41 Grand Avenue, Southbourne, Bournemouth BH6 3SY. Phone: (0202) 300351.

BOURNEMOUTH, Southbourne. 2 spacious self- contained ground floor flats. 2 double bedrooms, fully equipped for up to 6 people. Quiet position. Close to Fisherman's Walk, sea and shops. Resident proprietors. Parking. From £80. Phone: (01202) 422719.

BOURNEMOUTH. Lovely clean, quiet, comfort-able self-contained flat. Sleeps 2/6. 2 bedrooms, lounge, separate well-equipped kitchen. Garden. Colour television. Parking. Dogs, children welcome. From £90-£250 per week. Woodhouse, 30 Somerley Road, Bournemouth BH9 1EN. Phone: (01202) 517489.

BOURNEMOUTH, Southbourne. Holiday flats. Self-contained, 2 to 7. High standard. 3 minutes sea, shops. Parking. Television, hot water, central heating. From £80 per week. Open all year. Low season breaks. Norcliffe, 33 Grand Avenue, BH6 3SY. Phone: (0202) 499067.

BOURNEMOUTH, New Forest area. Bungalow, chalets. Comfortably furnished, central heating. Sleep 2/6. Fenced gardens, small attractive park. Pets welcome. Ideal centre, local fishing, riding, golf, walking, coast. 9 miles village shop and club. Phone: (0425) 473750.

BRIDPORT. Self-catering cottages in conver-ted barns, 4 miles from sea. Set in 10 acres, wonderful views, tame animals for children. Linen provided. ETB four keys approved. Lancombes House, West Milton, Bridport. Phone: (0308) 485375.

BRIDPORT near. Farmhouse ground floor flat, sleeps 2/4. Panoramic views of National Trust countryside and sea. Terms £85/140. Fry, Wanehouse Farm, Morcombelake, Bridport DT6 6DJ. Phone: Chideock (0297) 89405.

BRIDPORT. Country farmhouse. Self-catering accommodation, sleeps 4/6. Peaceful location, lovely walks and scenery. 3 miles from Charmouth. Phone: (0297) 560439.

BRIDPORT. Bungalow, modern and spacious. ETB 3 key commended. Situated between Bridport and West Bay Harbour, with its beaches and coastal path. Available all year. £128 - £300 per week, all included. Sleeps 4/6. Brochure Phone: (01308) 422941.

BRIDPORT. Attractive 2 bedroomed terraced mews cottages set in heart of historic market town. Within easy reach of beaches and beautiful Dorset countryside. No pets. ETB inspected. From £130 to £180 per week. Phone: (0308) 488611.

BRIDPORT. 3 bedroomed bungalow, sleeps 6. Central heating. Delightful peaceful location in heart of Marshwood Vale, on working dairy farm. Unusual pets. 6 miles to sea. Superb walking countryside to enjoy Symes. Phone: (0308) 867660.

BRIDPORT near. Cosy character cottage, in quiet West Dorset village. Sleeps 5 adults plus baby. Inglenook, coal or log fire. Off-road parking. Nearby beaches with superb country and cliff walks. Brochure Phone: (01935) 706353.

CHARMOUTH. Charming Georgian coach house. Tranquil walled courtyard. Parking. Three bedrooms, comprehensively equipped. Colour television, microwave, washing machine. All linen, towels and electricity included. Close to beach and amenities. Children welcome. Sorry no pets. Phone: (0297) 560139.

CHARMOUTH. Holiday flat. Quiet village location with countryside views. Situated in centre of village. Level walk to shops and beach. 2 bedrooms, kitchen, diner, lounge, shower room. Garden, parking 2 cars. Phone: Mrs C Pielesz (0297) 560221.

CHIDEOCK, Dorset. Tollhouse cottage. Sleeps 2, near National Trust coastline. Comfortable, fully equipped, reasonably priced. Available all year. Phone: Chideock (0297) 489585.

CHRISTCHURCH. Luxury flats. Lounge, 2 bed-rooms, bathroom with shower, kitchen, fully equipped with fridge, washing machine, microwave. Situated in Christchurch between 2 rivers. Leisure and town centres, beaches, New Forest. Takeaways within easy reach. Parking. Phone: (0202) 477226.

CHRISTCHURCH. Harbourside bungalow. Superb view. Huge windows. Patio, good garden, private slipway. Mooring. Ideal for windsurfing and dinghies. Sleep 5/7. Near sandy beaches, New Forest and Bournemouth. Suitable for wheelchairs, children and pets. Phone: (0635) 43602.

CHRISTCHURCH, Friars Cliff. Self-contained self-catering studio flat, close to sandy beach, near New Forest. Well equipped. Television, safe parking. £75 per week low season to £150 high season. Open throughout year. Details Phone: (0425) 270204.

CHRISTCHURCH. The Causeway. Flats and flatlets. Some en-suite. Ideally situated between town and harbour of Christchurch and Mideford Quay and beaches. Near New Forest. Colour television, linen provided. ETB approved. 32/34 Stanpit. Phone: (0202) 470149.

FISHPOND, near Lyme Regis. Comfortable self-contained annexe. Sleeps 4. All facilities, parking. Quiet location, lovely view, walks, country pubs. From £160 per week. Phone: (0297) 678475.

FORDINGBRIDGE. Beautiful lodges in secluded position overlooking private lake. Cosy and warm. Ideal for Summer and Winter holidays. Centrally situated for Bournemouth, New Forest, Salisbury and Pool. ETB highly commended. Phone: (0425) 653340.

GILLINGHAM. Scandinavian style lodge. Sleeps 6. All comforts. Colour television, carpeting, heating, microwave. Superb location overlooking trout, carp lakes. Very quiet. Fishing, golf, cycles, walking. National Trust. Visiting. Campbell, Whistley Waters, Milton, Gillingham, Dorset. Phone: (0747) 840666.

GILLINGHAM. Cole Street Farmyard Cottages. Self-catering. Ideal touring centre for families. Small animals and free-range poultry kept. Bed and breakfast in 300-year-old farmhouse. Open all year. No pets. Brochure Phone: (0747) 822691.

GWITHIAN - 7 miles from St. Ives. Spacious self-contained and fully modernised holiday flat. Close to sandy beach. Lounge, kitchen, bathroom, 2 bedrooms, hallway, separate toilet. Private parking. Garden, pets welcomed. Mrs Patchett. Phone: (0736) 752564.

LULWORTH COVE. Lovely apartment situated above owner's small shop. Just two minutes beach. Fully equipped for six. Television, fridge, linen included. £200 per week. May to September. Photographs available. Phone: (0929) 400379.

LULWORTH COVE and The Purbecks. 7 cot-tages some with log burning stoves. Sleeps 1/11 people. All tastefully furnished and maintained to a high standard personally by owner. All in idyllic country settings. Pets welcome. Phone: (0305) 854094.

LULWORTH COVE, near Dorset. Modern detached 3 bedroom bungalow in secluded streamside garden. Garage and off road parking. Central heating and colour television. Sleeps five plus cot. Modern kitchen appliances. Phone: (0929) 462739.

LULWORTH. Modern two bedroom flat in the picturesque village of West Lulworth. One mile from Lulworth Cove. Ideal for touring, lovely scenic coastal walks, sandy beaches at Swanage and Weymouth. Reasonable rates. Phone: (0737) 832282.

LULWORTH COVE. Comfortable, furnished 3 bedroomed house. Available April to October in this beautiful coastal village. 10 minutes walk from sea and Dorset coastal path. Accommodates 6. With central heating. Colour television. Garage and gardens. Phone: (0929) 400 201.

LYME REGIS. Holiday apartments, sleeps 2 to 4. All have balconies, sea views and central heating. Mrs Cross, 33 Silver Street. Phone: (029744) 3809.

LYME REGIS. Large chalet, sleeps 6. Overlook-ing safe sandy beach. Ideal family holiday. Lovely walks, fishing, golf. Dogs and children welcome. Large kitchen, fridge freezer, microwave, bath, flush toilet, hot water. Please phone for details (01823) 412269.

LYME REGIS. Flat, sleeps six. 100 yards Cobb. Superb sea views. Parking. Colour television. Garden. Pets accepted. Phone: (0225) 465430.

LYME REGIS. Sleeps 6. Separate part farm-house dairy farm. Two miles sandy beach, one mile village shops. Three bedrooms, one double, four singles. Duvets. Two bathrooms. One pet. Electric heating, 50p slot meter. Plenty parking. Phone: (0297) 443223.

LYME REGIS 3 miles. 2/3 bedroomed house, bungalow, luxury caravans in rural valley 10 minutes level walk beach. Facilities include swimming pool, bar/family room, shop, launderette, playground. Sae Manor Farm Holiday Centre, Charmouth, Dorset DT6 6QL. Phone: (01297) 560226.

LYME REGIS 3 miles. Semi rural. Spacious bungalow, sleeps 8 plus. Reduced terms for smaller families, except July - August. Children welcome. Large, secluded mature garden. Short walk to shop. Ideal beach, touring, walking, garden holiday. Phone: (0297) 34124.

MILTON ABBAS. Luccombe Farm. Several con-verted cottages in beautiful quiet rural setting. ETB commended, three keys. Games room, riding, sailing and other activities available. Also baby sitting, maid service and good local pub. Phone: (0258) 880558.

MORCOMELAKE, near Chideock. Picturesque sunny hillfarm cottage. Views over heritage coastline. Area of outstanding natural beauty. Sleeps 5. Large, quiet, safe garden. Sea 1/2 mile. National Trust and horse riding nearby. Phone: (0297) 89303.

MOUSEHOLE. Village centre, off main road. Janie's cottage. Three bedrooms, sleeps six. Colour television, washing machine/drier. Central heating. Richards, 13 Longhurst Lane, Marple Bridge, Stockport. Phone: 061 427 1426 (evenings), 061 406 8717 (days).

MUDEFORD, Christchurch. Modern comfort-able house. Close harbour, beach, forest, golf, bird sanctuary. Colour television, microwave, washing machine. Garden. Central heating, balcony. Sleeps 6. All types of boating - fishing available nearby. 105 Stanpit Cooke. Phone: (0703) 455823.

PIDDLE VALLEY, Dorset. Exceptionally com-fortable, well equipped cottages on peaceful sheep farm. Near Dorchester and glorious coast. Tennis court, games barn, large, safe central lawn for small children. Dogs welcome. ETB commended, 5 keys. Brochure Phone: (0305) 848208.

POOLE QUAY. Luxury fully self-contained 2 bedroomed apartments, sleeps 2-6 persons. 2 minutes level walk to historic quay. Quiet location. Car park in grounds. Tourist Board highly commended, 4 keys. Phone: Mrs. Ellison (0202) 708195.

POOLE. Spacious apartments in 18th century mill on the quay. Also mews house in the old town. All are fully furnished with laundry and private parking. Sleep 2-8. Fun whatever the weather. Phone: (01258) 857328.

PORTLAND BILL, near Weymouth. Comfortable coastguard cottage, sleeps four. Walking, fishing, bird-watching. Quiet 'out-of-the-way holiday'. Available April - October. Sorry no pets or children under ten. For full details please Phone: (0903) 785052.

SANDBANKS, POOLE

Ideal for children and family holidays. 4 bedroomed houses. Fully equipped. Fridge/freezer, washing machine, central heating, private gardens and parking. 400 yards easy walk to beautiful sandy beaches. Excellent water sports. Beautiful scenery. Bournemouth/Poole 5 miles.

Colour brochure

Phone: (0604) 717071

SHAFTESBURY. Comfortable cottage tucked away on working dairy farm. All amenities. Sleeps 6, plus cot. Beautiful countryside. Superb central touring area. Visitors welcome to explore mixed farm. Well behaved pets welcome. Details Mrs Martin. Phone: (01747) 811183.

SHAFTESBURY. Family dairy farm in glorious countryside. Charming character cottages and farmhouse flat. Sleep 2-5 plus cot. ETB 4 keys commended. Linen, central heating, laundry room. Farm animals. Pretty thatched villages. Excellent walking. Suitable disabled. Brochure: Phone: (0747) 811830.

SOUTHBOURNE. Bournemouth. Three bedroom detached house, sleeps seven plus cot. Downstairs toilet/shower, colour television, central heating, double glazing. Balcony sea views. 100 yards sandy Blue Flag beach. Garage, parking, secluded garden. Contract cleaned. Phone: (0273) 477885.

STURMINSTER NEWTON. Sheila Martin. 'Moorcourt Farm', Marnhull DT10 1HH. Friendly flat, sleeps four. Two double bedrooms, kitchen/diner, lounge leading to garden. Bathroom, toilet. Watch Sunny the White Donkey and his friend Buster the Horse. Phone: Marnhull (0258) 820271.

STURMINSTER NEWTON near. Far from the madding crowd. Cider house conversion. Snug low ceilings. Log fire, central heating. Quiet. 4 poster. Short break. £80. Phone: (0258) 817735.

STURMINSTER NEWTON. Exceptionally com- fortable cottages, sleeping 2/2/2/2/4 in converted barn on working farm. Peaceful, off beaten track. Colour televisions (remote), games room (pool/table tennis), swimming pool. Clay shooting, large garden, laundry room. No dogs. Phone: (01258) 817348.

SWANAGE. Kinnaird holiday flats. Self-con- tained flats with garden and communal lounge. Overlooking safe sandy beach. Ideal for beach or walking holidays. Friendly atmosphere. Personal supervision. Parking. 18 Burlington Road. Phone: (0202) 423058.

SWANAGE

5 bedroom spacious detached house. Sleeps 10 in comfort. Huge sun terrace overlooks bay. 2 minutes beach and centre but secluded. All comforts. No pets.

081-441 7070
07072 63020

SWANAGE. Superb sea views from modern 2nd floor apartment (lift). Accommodates 2-3 persons. Regret no children under 5 or pets. Centrally situated 200 yards, level sea and shops. Available all year. (Heating). Phone: (01929) 422263.

SWANAGE. Avalon Holiday flats/flatlets. 200 metres beach, town. Self-contained. Accommodating 2/10. Central heating, colour television. Car park. Fully inclusive terms. Details, stamp please, Mrs M. Snook, Avalon, 5 Rempstone Road, Swanage, Dorset BH19 1DN. Phone: (0929) 424779.

SWANAGE. Stone built self-contained annexe, between Corfe Castle, Swanage. Large garden. Two bedrooms, lounge, bathroom, toilet, kitchen, microwave, fridge/freezer, washer/dryer, colour television, video, telephone, storage heaters. Children, pets welcome. Phone: (0929) 480668.

SWANAGE. Alrose Villa. Four self-catering flats in Victorian villa. Close to seafront. Fully equipped including microwaves. Self-contained. Comfortable with colour television. Parking. 2 Highcliffe Road. Phone: Don and Pam Jacobs (0929) 426318.

SWANAGE. Very comfortable, spacious well equipped 2 bedroom flat. Sleeps 6. Linen provided. Central heating, colour television. 5 minutes level walk town centre, beach. Children welcome. Parking. Regret no pets. Non smokers preferred. Phone: (0929) 422535.

SWANAGE. 100 yards from beach. Sleeps 8. Fully equipped, modernised luxury flat. With 4 bedrooms, 2 bathrooms, sitting/dining room with balcony. Private parking in spacious garden. Phone: (0202) 768908.

SWANAGE. Centrally situated for sea and Shops. Sleeping 2/6. Fully self-contained. Colour television and parking. Open throughout the year. Special low season terms. Phone: (0929) 422637 or write to Westland Flats, Northbrook Road, Swanage, Dorset.

SWANAGE. Superior, 8 room house, sleeps 10. Also ground floor flat, 5 rooms, sleeps 6. Colour television/garage each. Panoramic view. Close town/beach. Personal supervision. No pets. Phone: Mrs Haysom (0202) 694157.

SWANAGE. The Gables Holiday Apartments, Victoria Avenue BH19 1AN. Fully equipped self-contained apartments, having 1, 2 or 3 bedrooms. Excellent location, just 200 yards from beach with easy access to the shopping centre. Phone: (0929) 422968.

SWANAGE, Dorset. Comfortable, well fur- nished detached house. Large garden. Quiet location. 3 bedrooms, sleeps 6. Large living rooms. Colour television. 5 minutes from sands. Car parking. For further information Phone: Mrs Fuller 081 946 6037 or (0929) 421009.

★★★★★★★★★★★★★★★★★★★★

DALTONS
DIRECTORY
AND
DALTONS WEEKLY

The Winning Combination
for all your holiday needs

★★★★★★★★★★★★★★★★★★★★

SWANAGE. 3 self-contained 2 bedroom flats. Spacious, comfortable, clean. 2 overlooking sea. Quiet situation. Near sea and path to beach. Reduced rates spring, autumn. Children 7 years minimum. Brochure "Marston", 16 Burlington Road. Phone: (01929) 422221.

SWANAGE. Glenthorn Holiday Flats. Fully furnished, comfortable flats, sleeping 2/7 people. 150 yards safe sandy beach. Colour televisions. Cots, high-chairs all provided. Large car park. Ring or write for brochure. Clifford, 15 Ulwell Road. Phone: (0929) 422432.

UPWEY (4 miles Weymouth). Superb little south-facing cottage in heart of village. Restored to high standard. Ideal for Winter or Summer holidays. Sleeps 2/3. Please Phone: (0305) 812241.

WAREHAM, Ridge. Rural cottage. Close Poole harbour/bird reserve. Convenient Studland, Swanage etc. Sleeps 2 - 6. Modern, well equipped and furnished including colour television. Large garden. Parking. Personally run by owner. From £185 per week. Phone: (0202) 622780.

WEST BAY. Bungalow, sleeps six. Linen, colour television, central heating, electrics all included. Ample car space. Close to beach and fishing harbour. Big garden facing fields and river beyond beautiful setting. Small pets welcome. Phone: (0308) 422294.

WEST BEXINGTON. Equi-distant Lyme Regis, Weymouth, Dorchester. Detached bungalow, sleeps 6. 150 yards Chesil beach. Popular walking, fishing area. Mainly National Trust land. Parking for three cars. Sorry no pets. Phone: (0249) 651378 or (0308) 897806.

WEYMOUTH. Bungalow cottage and caravan. Beautiful countryside by the sea. Facilities available adjacent camping parks. Swimming pool heated, club house. Good value food, entertainment. Main season brochure. West Fleet Holiday Farm, Fleet, Weymouth. Phone: (01305) 782218.

WEYMOUTH at Preston. Spacious 3 bedroom bungalow. Glorious panoramic views of Weymouth Bay, from Overcombe to Portland. Overlooking Lodmoor Reserve. Enclosed rear garden. Fully equipped. Dog by arrangement. Sleeps 5/7 plus cot. Phone: (0305) 837398.

WEYMOUTH. Osmington Village. New spacious bungalow. Glorious rural views. Fully fitted kitchen, 2 bedrooms, large lounge, diner with patio doors to garden. Own garage. ETB. 3 key commended. Phone: (01035) 853591.

WEYMOUTH HARBOUR. Adjacent town centre. Luxury 3 bedroom, 2 bathroom, 1 en-suite flat. Comfortably sleeps 8. Open plan lounge/diner, French doors give Vista view harbour, fitted kitchen, washer/dryer, fridge/freezer, central heating and garage space. Phone: (0305) 832134.

DREAM COTTAGES

Self catering holidays in beautiful coastal or country locations. Visit National Trust properties. Enjoy the picturesque villages, history and unspoilt areas of outstanding beauty.
Dream Cottages
41 Maiden Street, Weymouth DT4 8AZ
Tel: 01305 761347

WEYMOUTH. Comfortable stone cottage with extensive views towards sea. Set in beautiful countryside, sleeps maximum 6. Available for holiday lets from September to April. For details and booking Phone: (0258) 880278.

WEYMOUTH, Dorset. Olde worlde furnished cottage. Mid-week breaks, mini weekends or week. Near the sea and shops. From £20. G. Parkhouse, Barleycorn Cottage, Mill Lane, Preston, Weymouth, Dorset DT3 6DE. Phone: (0305) 832211.

WEYMOUTH/CHICKERELL VILLAGE

Cosy period cottage, 2 bedroom, equipped 4 persons, use of nearby hotel facilities, indoor pool, bowls, tennis, squash, snooker, children's play areas.
DAISY COTTAGE – (01305) 786948

WEYMOUTH. Christopher Robin Holiday Flats. Fully self-contained. Colour television, bed linen provided. Glorious sea views. Free car parking. Brochure from Mr Gregory, 70 The Esplanade, Weymouth, Dorset DT4 9RD. Phone: (0305) 777345.

WEYMOUTH. Ace holiday flats, 48-50 Spa Road. Self contained comfy and clean. From 2-6 persons. Well behaved dogs and children welcome. Large garden. Colour television and car parking for each flat. Phone: (01305) 779393.

WEYMOUTH. Spacious cottages and holiday flats. Ideal 4/6 persons. All comfortably furnished, high standard of cleanliness, maintained. Car parking. Television. Brochures on request. Dunvegan Holiday Flats, 75 Rodwell Road DT4 8QB. Phone: (01305) 783188.

WEYMOUTH, Old Harbour. 2 spacious self- contained flats at Water's Edge, near Brewers Quay. Fully equipped to sleep 5. Parking available. Small pets welcome. Sae Mrs Roberts, 7 Cove Row, Weymouth DT4 8TT. Phone: (0305) 789737 or (0392) 56664.

WEYMOUTH. 2 and 4 bedroomed cottages. With television, video, microwave, washing machine. Gas and electric included. Close to picturesque harbour, town and seafront. For details Phone: (0836) 619148.

WEYMOUTH. Old harbour holiday flats. Ideally situated. Adjoining harbourside, seafront and town centre. Close to sea and beach. Central for all amenities. Can sleep 2/6 persons. Sae 451 Chickerell Road, Weymouth DT3 4DG. Phone: (0305) 776674.

WEYMOUTH. Ideally situated on beach. Lovely self-contained 1 bedroom apartments, sleeping 4 to 5. Magnificent uninterrupted sea views and direct access to beach. Available Easter to October season. Booking and information, Phone: Kermani (0305) 782520.

WORTH MATRAVERS, Dorset. Purbeck. Stone bungalow, in picturesque village. 2 double bedrooms, fitted kitchen, bathroom, shower, separate toilet, large lounge. Views over Downland to sea. Garden, garage. Good walking. Cobb, Stonecroft, Durlston Road, Swanage BH19 2DL. Phone: (01929) 424761.

CARAVANS, CHALETS & HOLIDAY PARKS

BOURNEMOUTH, Christchurch. Excellent river- side site. Luxury 4/6 berth caravans. Mains facilities, showers, heater, fridge, colour television. Fishing. Musker, 44 Hurn Way, Christchurch, Dorset BH23 2PB. Phone: (0202) 482425.

BOURNEMOUTH. 8 berth caravan in quiet cottage garden. Close to sea and New Forest. Fully equipped. Clean and comfortable. Very private. Ringwood 5 miles, Christchurch 5 miles. Pets welcome. Phone: (0225) 672417.

BRIDPORT, near. Dorset. Picturesque Marsh- wood vale farm, sited mobile home. Sleeps 4. All modern conveniences. Own private garden. Four miles beach. Colour television. From £70 week. Phone: Rosie (0308) 867535.

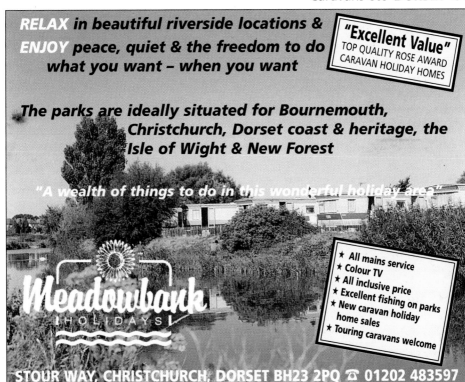

MANOR FARM HOLIDAY CENTRE
CHARMOUTH, DORSET DT6 6QL
Luxury 6 berth caravans. Sleeps 6. Colour TV, toilet, shower, etc. Swimming pool, bar on site. Situated in rural valley, 10 minutes level walk to beach.
S.A.E. to D. W. Loosmore
Tel: 01297 560226

CHARMOUTH. Luxury 2 bedroom caravans. Microwave, colour television, duvets, pillows, cot provided. Indoor, outdoor pools, bar, shop. Excellent facilities, close sea. Ideal for all age groups. Panoramic views. Special offers. Short breaks available. Phone: (0789) 400796.

CHRISTCHURCH. Hoburne Caravan Park. Privately owned 6 berth caravan. Fully equipped including microwave, colour television, video. Licensed clubhouse, sauna, solarium, steam room, indoor outdoor heated pools, children's play area. Walking distance to beach. Phone: (01256) 467586.

CHRISTCHURCH. Hoburne Park. Fully equipped luxury 4 berth caravan. All electric. Site facilities include bar, family room, pools, children's play area. For further details Phone: Mrs Rolfe (0494) 441130.

CHRISTCHURCH. Hoburne Park. Fully fitted 6 berth caravan. Colour television, microwave, full cooker etc. Club, swimming pools, tennis, shop, launderette. 15 minutes walk from beach. Phone: (0455) 842364.

DURDLE DOOR. 2 bedroom, 6 berth caravan. Mains services, bathroom, kitchen, gas fire, colour television. Shops, clubhouse on picturesque coastline. Good beaches. £125 off peak to £250 peak. Phone: (0980) 611639 evenings.

DURDLE DOOR, Lulworth, Dorset. Unspoilt clifftop campsite. Super mobile home, sleeps 6. All amenities, colour television. Close to 3 beautiful beaches. Many country walks. Pets welcome. £100-£250 weekly, deposit, £25 weekly. Phone: (0895) 833245/674296.

HIGHCLIFFE, near Bournemouth and New Forest. 4 berth chalet on cliff top site. Indoor and outdoor swimming pools. Club and entertainment. All modern conveniences. £90 - £225 per week. Phone: Farnborough (0252) 542649.

HIGHCLIFFE. 6 berth caravan, family site. Full facilities. Near shops, beach. At Cobbs Holiday Camp situated between Bournemouth, New Forest. Licensed club, children's play area. Personally supervised. Open Easter, October. Brochure Spurrier, 145 Chestnut Avenue, Eastleigh, Hampshire SO50 5BB.

HIGHCLIFFE-Bournemouth-New Forest. Well equipped detached holiday chalets. Sleep 4/6. On Naish holiday village. Clifftop site. Club, entertainments, indoor, outdoor pools, children's adventure play area etc. Access to the beach. No pets. Phone: (0590) 683572.

HIGHCLIFFE, Dorset. Well equipped six berth caravan sited on holiday park with all facilities. Close beach. Easy reach of Bournemouth, Southampton and New Forest. Phone: (0202) 578133 for further details.

LULWORTH, Durdle Door. Breathtaking sea views. Modern 6 berth caravan. Mains facilities. Colour television. Close beach, farm shop, clubhouse. Ideal family holiday. No smoking or pets. Weekly £90-£250. Phone: (0929) 471879.

LYME REGIS. Panoramic sea view, peaceful countryside. Only two modern fully equipped caravans on one acre. Well-kept private field. Cleanliness guaranteed. Free range eggs and home baked bread. Details Phone: Mrs Grymonprez (0297) 443216.

LYME REGIS 12 miles. One only 6 berth cara-van. Secluded views, enclosed garden. Children and pets welcome. Barbeque, en-suite, shower, toilet. Good area for walking and local attractions. P.J. Rudkin, Lower Oathill, Crewkerne TA18 8PZ. Phone: (0460) 30235.

POOLE, Rockley Park. Fully equipped large 2 bedroomed caravan. Colour television, microwave. All bedding supplied, duvets etc. Beds made up for your arrival. Free gas and electricity. Privately owned and maintained. No pets. Phone: Mrs Howlett (0202) 682416.

POOLE, Dorset, Rockley Park. 1994 super lux-ury caravan. 6 berth. Close to beach. Colour television, fridge, microwave, electric kettle, toaster, gas heated. Good entertainment, bars, shops, restaurant. Swimming pools. Phone: Stephen (0734) 812775.

POOLE, Rockley Park. Privately owned lux-ury 4/6/8 berth caravans on super beach site. Weekend/midweek breaks all season. Indoor/outdoor swimming, tennis, bowls, sailing, windsurfing, fishing, club entertainment. Phone now! Hilary Morris Caravans (0202) 745255.

POOLE, Rockley Park. 6 berth caravan. Fully equipped. Indoor and outdoor pools, clubs, shops, children's club, tennis, bowls, amusement arcade. Burger King restaurant. Ideal for touring around Dorset beauty spots. Close to Bournemouth. Phone: (0225) 704621.

POOLE, Dorset. Privately owned caravan. Rockley Park. Shops, restaurants, indoor - outdoor pools. Launderette. Amusements, entertainment. Caravan fully equipped. Heating, lighting all included. Full weeks and midweek bookings taken from March to December. Phone: Godalming (0483) 421080.

POOLE, Rockley Park. Luxury 6 berth, 2 bedroomed privately owned caravan. Colour television, radio/cassette. Shower, toilet. Main services. Picnic table. Small sandy beach. Outdoor - indoor pools. Full entertainment. Various sports available. Phone: (0425) 655192.

ROCKLEY PARK is one of 19 holiday parks coast to coast. Our luxury holiday homes, sleep 2-8 people. Prices start from £9 per person per night, based on 6 sharing. For a free colour brochure Phone: Lo-Call (0345) 508 508.

SWANAGE. Luxury caravan, 3 bedrooms, 6/8 berth. All services, colour television, fridge, microwave, shower, bathroom, toilet. Privately owned. Overlooking Swanage Bay. For booking details Phone: 081-892 0313.

SWANAGE. 6 berth luxury caravan on Rose Award park. Quiet, secluded position, magnificent sea view. Free gas, electric, colour television, shower. Licensed club, fitness centre, indoor bowling green. 10 minutes walk to beach. Phone: (0935) 71592.

SWANAGE. Luxury six berth caravans. Services, television, refrigerator, shower and toilet. Overlooking Swanage Bay and Purbeck Hills. Sae C. M. Davis, 87 Bloxworth Road, Parkstone, Poole, Dorset BH12 4BL. Phone: (0202) 749539.

SWANAGE. Superb caravans - personally supervised. Toilet, shower, fridge, colour television, heater. Beautiful site, excellent shop, bar, restaurant, play area, indoor heated swimming pool. Near sandy beaches, town. Brochure D. D. Lund, 8 William Road, Bournemouth BH7 7BA. Phone: (0202) 394260.

SWANAGE, Dorset. Priestway Holiday Park. Extensive sea views of the sea and the Purbeck Hills. 6/8 berth. Full mains caravans. Fridge, colour television. Camping and touring pitches. Shop, launderette. 1 mile beach. Pets welcome. Phone: (0929) 424154.

SWANAGE. 35 foot 6 berth caravan. Sea views. 2 bedrooms, sofabed, separate shower, toilet room, launderette. Clubhouse, shop. Bedding provided. Studland naturist beach 3 miles. Shaw, 12 Lemon Grove, Whitehill, Bordon, Hampshire GU35 9BE. Phone: (0420) 473683.

WEYMOUTH. Haven Littlesea Holiday Park. Cobb's luxury caravans for hire. 10 feet and 12 feet wide. All sizes available. Fully equipped. Excellent amenities. Indoor, outdoor pool, club etc. Cleanliness guaranteed. No pets. Phone: (0708) 459954 or (0850) 602437.

WEYMOUTH. Luxury caravan 1994 model. Sleeps 8. Weymouth Bay Holiday Park. Available Easter to October. Competitive rates which include use of facilities on this Haven Park. For brochure Phone: (0932) 561748.

WEYMOUTH. Luxury holiday caravans. Relax-ing exclusive park. Pets welcome. Colour television, shower, toilet, kitchen. 2 bedroom, 6 berth. For brochure Phone: (0747) 824617.

WEYMOUTH BAY (a Haven park). Holiday Cara-vans 6 and 8 berth. Fully equipped, colour television, shower, microwave, club entertainment, indoor and outdoor heated pools. Short breaks early and late season. Phone: (0305) 834987 evening, (0305) 834715.

WEYMOUTH. Waterside Bowleaze Cove. 6 berth caravan for hire. All facilities including colour television, microwave, shower. Site has indoor and outdoor pools, 2 clubs. Shop, beach across road. No pets. Phone: (0275) 834785.

WEYMOUTH, Littlesea Haven Holiday Park. 6 berth caravan for hire with indoor and outdoor swimming pools, bowling, nightclub with evening entertainment, cafe and launderette. Discount prices. Phone: (0256) 54947.

WEYMOUTH, Littlesea. Haven Park. Luxury private caravans. Wc, shower, cooker, fridge, colour television. Free gas, electricity. Indoor - outdoor pools. Adult bar, family bar, children's clubs, playground, ten-pin bowling, food court, shop. From £100 per week. Phone: (0992) 561424.

WEYMOUTH, Bowleaze Cove. New 6 berth lux-ury caravan. Colour television, microwave, shower. Clubhouses, indoor and outdoor swimming pools, jacuzzi, solarium. Horse riding site. 100 yards from sandy beach. No pets. Phone: (0797) 363948.

WEYMOUTH, Littlesea (Haven). 2 and 3 bed-roomed luxury caravans. Family owned, well equipped. Sea views. Free gas, electricity. Clubs and pools. Superb positions, most with own private gardens. Excellent site. Lovely walks. Phone: (0703) 253113 or (0850) 263606.

Spend your holiday by the sea, surrounded by the beautiful Dorset countryside.

Osmington Mills is a delightful hamlet, 5 miles from the busy holiday town of Weymouth.

We can offer the following accommodation and facilities:

● **Fully Serviced CARAVANS** ● **BUNGALOWS** ● **2 FLATS**
● **ALSO 1ST CLASS CAMPING PARK** ● **OLDE WORLDE FARMHOUSE**
● **LOG CHALETS FOR SALE OR HIRE**

Fishing Lake and Horse Riding on site. All visitors have FREE use of our Heated Swimming Pools and Club Complex·

Please write or phone NOW for your free colour brochure which will tell you more than this space will allow

OSMINGTON MILLS HOLIDAYS LTD

OSMINGTON MILLS, WEYMOUTH,
DORSET DT3 6HB
Tel: (01305) 832311

WEYMOUTH. Littlesea Haven. 6 berth caravan, all amenities. 2 clubs, 2 swimming pools. Tiger club for children, shops. Sorry no pets. Phone: (0272) 647312.

WEYMOUTH. Waterside Holiday Park, Bowleaze Cove. Luxury caravans. Fully equipped. Television, microwave. Two licensed clubhouses. Full entertainment, heated outdoor pool, excellent indoor pool complex, amusements. Takeaway, hairdressers, two shops. Beach is on our doorstep. Phone: (0305) 833451, (0272) 496126.

WEYMOUTH, Littlesea (Haven) Park. Luxury caravans. Indoor, outdoor heated pools, splash shoot, family and adult clubs both with entertainment. Gas, electric all free. Food, court, amusements, bowl lingo etc. Phone: (0860) 679997 or (0272) 663993.

WEYMOUTH BAY. Luxury 95 foot caravan. 3 bedrooms, television, hi-fi. Privately owned on Haven site. All facilities. 2 pools, clubhouse with full entertainment. Separate pub with food. Short walk to sea. Details Phone: (0703) 325691.

WEYMOUTH. Pebble Bank Caravan Park. Quiet family park in picturesque setting with superb sea views. Close to Weymouth centre. Caravans for hire and sale. Touring caravans, motor homes and tents. Modern facilities. Licensed bar. Phone: (01305) 774844.

WEYMOUTH. Waterside Holiday Park, Bowleaze Cove. Swimming pools, clubs, entertainment, shops, takeaway, bar food. 1994/5 2/3 bedroom luxury caravans with views. Microwave, full cooker, refrigerator, remote control television, all services free. For brochure Phone: (0788) 562543.

WEYMOUTH. Waterside Holiday Park. 2 and 3 bedroom caravans for hire. Fully equipped. Colour television. Swimming pool complex, clubhouses, shops, launderette. Close to beach and cliff walks. For brochure Phone: 081 942 7526.

WEYMOUTH. Waterside Park. Luxury two and three bedroom caravans. Microwave, colour television, duvets. Parking next caravan. Indoor fun pool, clubs, entertainment. Early breaks from £15 nightly. Holiday park opposite beach. Phone: Mrs Sanders (0305) 833749, (0374) 160604.

WEYMOUTH. Littlesea Holiday Park. 3 bedroom luxury caravan. Colour television, shower, hot,cold water, fridge. Haven site. Use of all amenities including indoor, outdoor pools, water shoot, bowling alley, restaurant, club, nightly entertainment. Phone: 081 527 7176.

WEYMOUTH. Littlesea Haven holiday park. Luxury 2 and 3 bedroom caravans with shower, toilet, fridge, cooker, microwave, gas fire, colour television. 2 clubs, live entertainment. Indoor, outdoor pools. Children's club, tenpin bowling. Mrs. Bolstridge. Phone: (0527) 61216 (0860) 580629.

WEYMOUTH, Bowleaze Cove. Luxury caravan for hire at Waterside Holiday Park, opposite beach. Two bedrooms, shower, television, microwave, fridge. Indoor and outdoor swimming pools. Free family entertainment. Takeaway shops, hairdressers. Cleanliness guaranteed. Competitive prices. Phone: (0963) 440431.

WEYMOUTH, Littlesea. 8 berth caravan holiday home for hire, April to October. 3 bedrooms, inside toilet, shower washbasin, fridge, microwave, toaster, cooker, dishwasher. All amenities on site. For details Phone: (0850) 130119, after 6 pm (0531) 822222.

WEYMOUTH, Littlesea. (Haven's most popular Dorset park). Modern super luxury family caravan. Privately owned. Colour television, microwave. Clubs, entertainment, pools, shop, launderette. Free gas and electricity. Phone early for best choice of dates. Phone: (Stafford) (01785) 47105.

WEYMOUTH: Waterside holiday park. Luxury caravan holiday homes on Dorsets premier independently owned holiday park. Licensed clubrooms, nightly entertainment, superb indoor and outdoor pool complex. Touring facilities available. Phone: (0305) 833103. Bowleaze Cove, Weymouth, Dorset DT3 6PP.

WHERE TO GO

Tower Park
Poole, Dorset.
Tel: (0202) 749094
Leisure, entertainment and retail complex comprising ten-screen cinema, water park, leisure ice pad, 30 lane megabowl, nightclub, bar and restaurant. The Water Park has flumes, tyre ride, 66-foot tower, lazy river ride, whirlpools, rapids and feature pools. Disabled visitors welcome.

Parnham House
Beaminster, Dorset.
Tel: (0308) 862204
Tudor manor house with additions and embellishments by John Nash in 1810. Home of John Makepeace and his famous furniture-making workshops. 14 acres of gardens.

Tales of Lyme' - The Experience
Marine Parade, Lyme Regis.
Tel: (0297) 443039
Historical tableaux and audio-visual display depicting the history of Lyme from the salt-boiling monks of 774 AD to the present day.

The Dinosaur Museum
Icen Way, Dorchester, Dorset.
Tel: (0305) 269880
Only museum in Britain devoted exclusively to dinosaurs. Fossils, full-size models, computerised, mechanical and electronic displays. Video gallery.

Weymouth Sea Life Park
Lodmoor Country Park, Weymouth, Dorset.
Tel: (0305) 761070
Spectacular marine life displays - shark observatory, fascinating tropical jungle and trail, Captain Kidd's Adventureland, pets' paddock and splashpool.

The Tank Museum
Bovington Camp, Wareham, Dorset.
Tel: (0929) 403463
Largest and most comprehensive museum collection of armoured fighting vehicles in the world. Over 250 vehicles on show, with supporting displays and video theatres.

Natural World Leisure Centre
The Quay, Poole. Dorset.
Tel: (0202) 68712
A walk through evolution starting from the primitive fish, sharks, to coral reefs, South American river fish, including the dreaded piranhas, beyond in time to amphibians, reptiles, massive snakes, crocodiles and alligators.

SCILLY ISLES

SELF-CATERING

HUGH TOWN. Fully equipped flat, sleeps up to six. Two bedrooms, lounge/diner, fully fitted kitchen with hob and oven, washer/dryer, bathroom with bath and electric shower. Garden. Linen hire available. Phone: (0634) 379705.

ISLES OF SCILLY. Holiday cottage, sleeps 5. Colour television. Garden. Pets welcome. Quiet corner of St. Mary's. F. Watts, Watermill, St. Mary's TR21 0NS. Phone: (0720) 422426.

ST MARY'S. Situated on main island in the Isles of Scilly. Centrally positioned in high town. Spacious first floor flat. Fully equipped. Overlooking small park. 3 key approved ETB. For further information Phone: (0424) 751446.

ST. MARY'S. Comfortable furnished two bed-roomed flat, situated near to three beaches and shops. ETB approved. Sleeps up to five people. For further details please Phone: Mrs Hogg (0203) 450455.

WHERE TO GO

Isles of Scilly Museum
Church Street, Hugh Town, St. Mary's.
Tel: (0720) 422337

Built in 1967 to house collections and display of all facets of past and present life on the islands. Also has a marine section containing treasures recovered from historic shipwrecks around the islands.

The Garrison & Star Castle
St. Mary's.
Tel: (0720) 422317

Garrison Gate was built in 1742 as part of the garrison wall and there are gun batteries and a promenade. Star Castle erected by Elizabeth I in 1593 as a defence against possible Spanish attack, has walls which form a 8 pointed star.

TRAVELLING BY COACH OR RAIL?

TURN TO THE BACK OF THIS GUIDE FOR USEFUL TELEPHONE NUMBERS

SOMERSET

HOTELS & GUEST HOUSES

ASHBRITTLE. Family working farm on Devon - Somerset borders. Noted for comfort, homeliness, good food. Ideal touring Exmoor, Quantocks, coasts. Peaceful scenic countryside. Character farmhouse with lovely valley views. ETB 2 crowns. Brochure Phone: Ann Heard (03986) 296.

AXBRIDGE. Manor Farm Cross. Working sheep and beef farm, adjoining Mendip Hills. 400 year old farmhouse, former stage-coaching inn. Ideal for touring and walking. Children and pets welcome. Tea, coffee making facilities. Phone: Dimmock (0934) 732577.

AXBRIDGE. Quiet guest house. Heart of county. Central for all types holiday. En-suite room with all facilities. Sun lounge with open country views. Brochure on request. Millard, Ferndale, Chapel Allerton, Axbridge BS26 2PJ. Phone: (0934) 712695.

BATH 15 miles. Spacious family home set in 2 acres of garden and paddock. ETB highly commended 2 crowns. 15 miles Bath, Bristol, 5 miles Wells. En-suite accommodation. Phone: (0761) 241519.

BREAN SANDS. Farmhouse bed and breakfast. 100 yards from beach. Comfortable rooms, tea, coffee facilities, guest television lounge. Relaxing atmosphere. Warm Somerset welcome from Rod and Jill Brake, Brean Farm, Brean, Burnham on Sea. Phone: (01278) 751055.

BRIDGWATER, Canalside. Family owned and run freehouse. Two minutes from Junction 24, M5. Friendly atmosphere. Excellent home baked cuisine. Ideal fishing and sightseeing base, travelling M5 weekend break. Idyllic surroundings. Children's play area. Phone: (0278) 662473.

BRIDGWATER. Farmhouse. Bed and breakfast. Quite peaceful location, overlooking lake. All rooms have colour television and central heating. ETB 2 crowns commended. Chappell, Cokerhurst Farm, Wembdon Hill. Phone: (01278) 422330, mobile (0850) 692065.

Withy Grove Farm

East Huntspill, Nr. Burnham-on-Sea.

A warm welcome awaits you.

Come and enjoy a relaxing and friendly holiday down on the farm. We can offer, at reasonable rates self-catering barns and cottages which are comfortably furnished with colour TV. We are central for touring and close to the River Huntspill famed for its coarse fishing.

Amenities for Guests include

★ Heated Swimming Pool ★ Games Room ★ Licensed Bar ★ Skittle Alley

Details on request from: Mrs Wendy Baker
Tel: (0278) 784471

CHARD. Wambrook Farm. ETB. An attractive listed farmhouse, two miles from Chard in beautiful peaceful village. Ideal for visiting Devon, Dorset and Somerset. Good pub food in village. Television, guest lounge. Mrs Eames. Phone: (0460) 62371.

CHARD. Bath House Hotel. Luxury rooms, en- suite. Excellent restaurant. Very reasonable priced. Ideal for touring the West Country. 5 minutes Crinckly Bottom Cricket St. Thomas, 15 minutes, Lyme Regis. Holyrood Street. Phone: (0460) 64106.

CHEDDAR and Weston-super-Mare just a short drive away. Banwell Castle, Banwell, Somerset BS24 6NX. Furnished in Victorian style. Outstanding views to Mendip and Welsh hills. Tranquil romantic setting. En-suite bedrooms, breakfast. £25 per night. Phone: (01394) 822263.

HILLTOPS   B&B FROM £13.00

Badger watching from the lounge most evenings. Magnificent views, good food, and a really friendly atmosphere. Approximately ¹/₂ mile from the Gorge and Caves. Tea and coffee making facilities in all rooms . Television in most rooms. Open all year round (except Christmas). Reduced rates for weekly booking and low season short breaks. Ample parking off the road.
Naidine and Hedley James, Hilltops, Bradley Cross, Cheddar
Telephone: 01934 742711

DULVERTON, Exmoor. 450 acre farm. Next to open moorland. See red deer and 60 mile views from attractively furnished rooms. Tea making facilities, visitors lounge. Quality farmhouse cooking. Pets. Babysitting. Evening meals. Phone: (0398) 23616.

DUNSTER. The Old Nunnery. Medieval House, beneath castle in beautiful ancient Exmoor village. Close West Somerset coast. Bed and breakfast £15 to £19 per person. Marian Frost, 6 Church Street, Dunster, Somerset TA24 6SH. Phone: (0643) 821711.

GLASTONBURY, Little Orchard. We are situa- ted on the slopes of historical Glastonbury Tor, with panoramic views over the Vale of Avalon. Centrally situated for touring West Country. All amenities available. Gifford, Ashwell Lane. Phone: (0458) 831620.

GLASTONBURY. Three minutes walk from town centre. Warm, friendly atmosphere. Bed and full English breakfast £14 per person. All facilities included. Ideal base for touring West country. Mrs D. Riddle, Hillclose,Street Road, Glastonbury BA6 9EG. Phone: (0458) 831040.

HIGHBRIDGE, near Laurel Farm, Mark- causeway, Mark, Highbridge, Somerset TA9 4PZ. Ideal touring centre or overnight stop. Full English breakfast, hot, cold. Television lounge, central heating. Open all the year. Cheddar, Wells, Glastonbury, Bath, Minehead. Phone: (0278) 641216.

LYMPSHAM. Traditional Somerset Farmhouse. Edge of picturesque village, Mendip views. Large gardens, parking and play area. 3 miles Junction 22, M5 and coast. Bed and breakfast £14, weekly £90. Children and pets welcome. Brochure Phone: (01934) 750206.

MARTOCK, South Somerset. Small, quality, bed and breakfast. ETB 2 crown highly commended. AA recommended. Visit the eight 'classic' gardens. Near Glastonbury Abbey, Wells Cathedral. Walk King Arthur country. 'Wychwood', 7 Bearley Road. Brochure. Phone: (01935) 825601.

MINEHEAD. Fernside, The Holloway. Delight- ful old cottage. Near shops and sea. Only three bedrooms ensures personal attention. Home cooked dinner. Television and heating all rooms. Special rates OAPs and children. ETB listed. Phone: Smith (0643) 707594.

MINEHEAD. Bournstream is surrounded by farmland. Easy reach of Exmoor and beaches. Comfortable accommodation. Hospitality tray. En-suite rooms. Log fires, sitting room. Adults £17.50 children welcome. Self catering and stabling available. S. Ansell Phone: (0984) 41048.

SOMERTON. Lower Farm, Kingweston. Working farm. Formerly a coaching inn. Combines old world charm with modern comfort. Attractive en-suite rooms with television, tea/coffee facilities, central heating. ETB 1 crown commended. Phone: (01458) 223237, Fax: (01458) 223276.

STATHE. Black Smock Inn. Traditional moorland inn. Overlooking River Parrett. Panoramic views. Large car park. Ideal fishing, birdwatching. Excellent accommodation. Colour television and tea making facilities all rooms. En-suite available. Home made food a speciality. Phone: (0823) 698352.

TAUNTON. Bed and breakfast in lovely 17th century farmhouse. Large garden. Children and pets welcome. 2 miles Taunton and 10 minutes motorway. Ideal for Exmoor and the West. Ground floor en-suite rooms. Suitable for disabled. Phone: (01823) 412269.

TAUNTON. 2 crown highly commended converted farmhouse in peaceful countryside. 10 minutes Taunton. Tea making facilities, colour television. Excellent breakfast menu. Golf, riding, fishing nearby. 30 minutes South coast. Good touring area. Phone: (01823) 601591.

TAUNTON. Blorenge Guest House, fully licensed. Most rooms en-suite, all colour television and tea making facilities. Swimming pool. 5 minutes to train and coach station plus town centre. Off-road parking. Mid Victorian house. Phone: (0823) 283005.

TAUNTON. 17th century farmhouse. Bed and breakfast only. 2 miles from M5 motorway. All rooms overlooking garden. 2 ground floor en-suite rooms, suitable disabled. Television, tea/coffee. Riding, fishing, golf nearby. Besley, Prockters Farm, West Monkton, Taunton. Phone: (01823) 412269.

WATCHET. Orchard House. Bed and breakfast in comfortable house in Boadwater village in Exmoor National Park. Close pub, shop. Television lounge, tea making facilities, radio all rooms. Ideal walking, riding, bird watching, fishing. Phone: (0984) 41011.

WATCHET. Caravans and chalets. Quiet, peaceful park, overlooking sea. Pets welcome. Half price for senior citizens. Early and late season. Personal attention. D.W. Howe, Helwell Bay, Watchet, Somerset TA23 0UG. Phone: (0984) 631781.

WELLS. Near this attractive cathedral city, a quiet country house. Convenient for visiting Cheddar, Glastonbury, Wookey Hole, Bath. Double rooms en-suite, tea making, lounge with television. Private parking. Bed and breakfast £15. Phone: Stevens, (01749) 342083.

WESTON-SUPER-MARE. Saxonia Guest House. All rooms en-suite. Ground floor bedroom. Suitable for disabled. Children welcome. ETB 3 crowns. For brochure write: 95 Locking Road, Weston-Super-Mare, Somerset BS23 3EW. Phone: (01934) 633856, Fax: (01934) 623141.

YEOVIL, near. Comfortable farmhouse offers warm welcome and peaceful relaxed atmosphere in the heart of countryside. Perfect location for touring, cycling, walking, fishing and visiting historic houses and gardens. Fresh home cooking. Phone: (0458) 250626.

SELF-CATERING

BREAN. Spacious three bedroom bungalow, sleeps 8. In own grounds with own access to 7 miles of sandy beach. Central heating, television, plus all facilities. Horse riding, fishing nearby. Phone: (0278) 751263 for brochure.

BRUTON. Ideal base for stately homes, gardens, cathedrals. Bath, Wells, Glastonbury, Dorset coast. Converted barn in rural courtyard. Flexibly priced. 2 - 8 ideal. Extended families (2 kitchens, 2 bathrooms) conservatory, garden. For brochure, prices Phone: (0749) 813246.

BURNHAM-ON-SEA. Peacefully situated. Grade II listed beamed cottages. Fully equipped. 1 mile from town and beach. Sleeps 4. Parking, garden. No pets. Available all year. ETB 3 keys commended. Sae for brochure. £90-£210. Phone: (01278) 782505.

CASTLE CARY. 1 bedroom cottage. En-suite. Sleeps four. Situated in the grounds of a public house with skittle alley. Golf and many more activities nearby. Only 90 minutes from Paddington. Bed and breakfast or self-catering. Phone: (0963) 350255.

CHARD. Quality country cottages. For 2-7. Spacious, comfortable, colour television. Children's play area. Family farm animals, stream, meadows, picnic tables, barbecue, croquet, table tennis. Dogs welcome. Lovely countryside/coast. Touring, walking, cycling. From £150 per week. Phone: (0460) 30207.

CHARD near, South Somerset. Cuttifords
Door. 1 mile Chard, 12 miles Dorset - Devon coast.
Luxuriously equipped barn conversion. Duvets, linen,
towels provided. 2 double bedrooms, bathroom.
Garage, garden. New 1994 short winter breaks available. Phone: (0460) 63047.

**YOUR LAST CHANCE TO BOOK A
FAMILY HOLIDAY WITH A
DIFFERENCE ...**
Over 200 PERSONALLY selected cottages and farmhouses
which offer the finest accommodation in the West Country.
Free colour brochure:
Farm & Cottage Holidays, Dept. DWG, 12 Fore Street,
Northam, Bideford, Devon EX39 1AW
Tel: (01237) 479698 (24 hours)

CHEDDAR. Ideal West Country centre. Small
Victorian house, sleeps 5. Fully equipped, comfortable.
Small pets allowed. Available short breaks £80 - £130
per week. Personally supervised. Brochure Phone: (0934)
743138.

COMPTON MARTIN. Spacious luxury Mendip
cottage. Sleeps two. Attractive gardens, parking. Easy
reach Bristol, Bath, Wells, Cheddar Gorge. Quiet rural
location, magnificent views over Chew Valley Lake.
Walking, fishing, birdwatching. ETB three keys commended. Phone: (0761) 221279.

EXMOOR. High quality cottages situated in a
rural setting with panoramic views. Ideal for children
and pets. Colour brochure available from Jane and Barry
Styles, Wintershead Farm, Simonsbath, Exmoor,
Somerset TA24 7LF. Phone: Exford 222.

EXMOOR. Winsford country holidays offer
country inns, guest houses and self-catering cottages in
this pretty village plus information on restaurants and
activities etc. For brochure and advice on your holiday
Phone: (01398) 23573.

ROADWATER

Enjoy your summer holidays, winter breaks in a large country cottage, situated in a secluded valley in the famed
Exmoor National Park. All
modern conveniences, 4 bedrooms, large gardens, outdoor
heated pool. Pets welcome.
E.T.B. 5 KEYS HIGHLY COMMENDED
Phone: 01984 40020

EXMOOR NATIONAL PARK. Georgian farm-
house on mixed working farm. ETB 3 keys. Sleeps 8.
Coast 5 miles. Good walks in beautiful countryside.
Horse riding nearby. £130. - £240. per week. Phone:
(01984) 640238.

GLASTONBURY near. Spacious accommoda-
tion, sleeps six. Three bedrooms, bathroom, kitchen,
diner, lounge. Garden, plenty of parking. Situated
between Mendip and Polden Hills on Somerset levels.
Easy reach of Bath, Wells, Weston. No dogs please.
Phone: Mrs Tucker (0278) 722321.

MENDIP COTTAGES

Two period cottages in picturesque villages.
Warm, comfortably restored and equipped to a high
standard. Sleep 2-6. Ideal for exploring Mendip Hills,
close Bath and Wells.
Telephone: (0373) 812879

NORTON-SUB-HAMDON. ETB 2 key com-
mended. Annexe of 18th century house in peaceful
Hamstone Village. Ideal for visit. Many classic gardens
and houses, walks and wildlife. Sleeps 2/4. Parking.
Lovely walled garden, (bus service). Phone: (0935)
881789.

Executive Holidays

(FROME) SOMERSET

Why not enjoy the independence of a self-catering holiday combined with the top
quality facilities that we offer.
All our properties are appointed to the highest standards and set in the peaceful
Somerset Countryside near Bath. The ideal centre for touring, walking or sporting
breaks with plenty for everyone to see and do.
OUR RANGE INCLUDES:

16th Century Mill Sleeping 10/12

Mill Cottage Sleeping 8

Both are set in their own individual grounds with trout streams, weir and mill race.
**For your free colour brochure ring 01373 452907 or 0860 147525 quoting DBH,
or write to: Executive Holidays, Iron Mill, Iron Mill Lane,
Oldford, Frome, Somerset BA11 2NR**

PORLOCK. Cottage. 3 Bedrooms, sleeps 6. 2 reception rooms, well fitted kitchen, colour television. Edge of village, 1 mile from sea. Excellent walking, riding, fishing. Beautiful countryside on edge of Exmoor. Reasonable rates. Phone: (0342) 893083.

QUANTOCK HILLS. Luxury wooden garden house. Beautiful forest garden setting, stream babbling by. Walking, West Somerset Steam Railway, red deer. Converted broom makers workshop. Heated all year. Truly special. 4 persons. Phone: Nether Stowey (0278) 733423.

QUANTOCKS, Somerset. Comfortable cottage, single/double bedrooms, Economy 7, television. £200 week. Also self-contained wing, country house. Single/double bedrooms, television. £150 week. Both near sea, golf, horse riding, fishing, steam railway. Country walks. Phone: (0278) 671548.

RODNEY STOKE, near Cheddar. 'Hollybrook Cottage'. Warmth and home comforts greet you in this tastefully restored period 2 bedroomed cottage with inglenook fireplace and picturebook garden. Tourist board approved. For further details please Phone: (0749) 870230.

SAMPFORD BRETT, Somerset. Self-catering flats in converted coach house. Two acres grounds with swimming pool. Ideal for touring coast, Exmoor, Quantocks. Naturists welcome. Details Phone: (0984) 632301.

STOGURSEY. Two bedroomed country cottage with garden. Sleeps four. In peaceful situation between the Quantocks and the sea. Fully equipped with television and microwave oven. Linen supplied. Owner supervised. For further information please Phone: (0278) 732779.

TAUNTON. Superior wing of farmhouse. Log fire. Also adjoining cottage, high standard accommodation. ETB 4 keys. Working farm. Small carp pond. Near Exmoor and Devon border. 30 minutes drive North or South coast. Reasonable terms. Phone: (0984) 62327,1.

TAUNTON, near. Semi-detached quiet cottage rural situation, close to Quantocks and Exmoor. Taunton 8 miles, Minehead 16 miles. Well equipped, sleeps 4. Car parking. Pets by arrangement and garden. Ideal country retreat or family holiday. Pullen. Phone: (0929) 423505.

WELLS near. Delightful barn conversion dairy farm. ETB 3 keys commended. Colour television, microwave, washing machine available, linen provided, electricity included. Family bedroom sleeps 2/4. Panoramic view. Peaceful location. Phone: (0934) 712367.

WEST CHINNOCK. 2/3 bedroom privately own-ed period cottages. Ideal base for Dorset coast. Walking, riding, golf, country houses. Everything provided including linen. Children - pets welcome. Phone: Peter Libby (0935) 881837.

WINSFORD. Heart of Exmoor. Attractive house. 500 yards from centre of Village. Sleeps 6. 2 Doubles, 1 twin, all modern conveniences. Enclosed garden. Plenty parking. Ideal for all country pursuits. Open all year. Pets welcome. Phone: (064385) 413.

CARAVANS, CHALETS & HOLIDAY PARKS

BREAN BEACH. Luxury holiday caravans with all facilities. Private access to sandy beach. Licensed club with entertainment. Also luxury caravans for sale on park. Coloured brochure. Three Acres Caravan Park. Phone: (0278) 751313.

BREAN. Dolphin Caravan Park, Coast Road, Brean, Burnham-on-Sea TA8 2QY. Seashore family caravan park. Private access to sandy beach. Children's play area. Modern caravans with showers and colour television. Pets welcome. Parking by caravan. Phone: (01278) 751258.

CHEDDAR. Broadway House Holiday Touring Caravan/Camping Park, Cheddar, Somerset. Phone: (01934) 742610. Five star facilities. Luxury caravans. Shower, toilet, colour television. Shop, bar. Swimming pool, playgrounds, laundry. Archery, caving, abseiling, canoeing. One mile England's "Grand Canyon" Cheddar Gorge.

DONIFORD BAY (Haven site). Three bedroom, seven berth caravan. Colour television, microwave, free gas, electric. On site entertainment, indoor/outdoor swimming pool and many other activities. Very competitive prices. Phone: Burrows (0522) 689322.

NORTH CURRY. Peaceful, spacious 2 berth mobile home in own secluded garden. Mains services, colour television. Village shops and pubs within easy level walk. Ample parking. Friendly pets welcome. Working smallholding. Reasonable rates. Phone: (0823) 490686.

WATCHET. Luxury caravans, quiet park with coastal and hillside views. Close to harbour and steam railway station. Caravans are fully equipped to Rose Award standard. Pets welcome. Short breaks brochure from Mr Wilson. Phone: (0984) 631206.

WATCHET. 6 berth caravan. Small quiet site Shop, swimming pool, children's play area. Pets welcome. Close Exmoor/Quantocks, walking, riding, fishing or just explore this unspoilt coast. Turner, Yew Tree Cottage, Bishopstone, Buckinghamshire HP17 8SF. Phone: (0296) 748438.

WATCHET, near Minehead. 6 berth caravan. Shower, flush toilet, television, separate bedrooms, heater etc. Shop, laundry room, indoor swimming pool. Private beach. Pets welcome. Beautiful countryside on the edge of Exmoor National Park. Phone: (0643) 704223.

WATCHET near. 8 berth caravan. 3 bedrooms, bathroom, toilet. Colour television. Free gas and electric. Situated in Haven Holiday Village. Extensive sea views. Family entertainment, club. Indoor fun pool. Junior adventure playground. Amusements, shop. Phone: (0984) 631549.

WELLS-NEXT-THE-SEA, Norfolk. 6 berth caravan available from April - October. Near pines and beach. Also ideal for bird watchers, near Blakney Point. Phone: (0923) 675383.

WHERE TO GO

Cricket St. Thomas Wildlife Park
Cricket St. Thomas, Chard.
Tel: (0460) 30755

Wildlife valley, heavy horse centre, country life museum farm, tropical aviary, adventure playground, miniature railway. Restaurant and shops. Disabled visitors welcome.

The Tropical Bird Centre
Rode, Somerset.
Tel: (0373) 830326

Hundreds of exotic birds in lovely natural surroundings. 17 acres of woodland, gardens and lakes with childrens's play area, pet's corner, miniature steam railway and clematis collection.

Cheddar Showcaves
Cheddar Gorge, Somerset.
Tel: (0934) 742343

Beautiful caves located in Cheddar Gorge. Gouh's Cave with its cathedral-like caverns and Cox's cave with its stalagmites and its stalactites. Also 'the Crystal Quest' fantasy adventure.

Haynes Motor Museum
Sparkford, Somerset.
Tel: (0963) 40804

Motor vehicles and memorabilia covering the years from the turn of the century to the present day. Video cinema, exhibition.

Wookey Hole Caves and Mill
Wookey Hole, Wells, Somerset.
Tel: (0749) 672243

The most spectacular caves in Britain and home to the Witch of Wookey. Working Victorian paper mill, 'Fairground by Night' exhibition, Edwardian Penny Pier Arcade, archaeological museum and mirror maze.

Fleet Air Museum
Royal Navy Air Station, Yeovilton, Somerset.
Tel: (0935) 840565

Over 50 historic aircraft, displays and equipment, including Concorde prototype. Falklands campaign, Kamikaze, RNAS 1914 - 1918, The Wrens and Harrier Jump Jet story exhibitions.

WILTSHIRE

HOTELS & GUEST HOUSES

BURCOMBE, Salisbury. Manor Farm. Comfortable farmhouse in pretty village. Five miles West Salisbury. Ideal location for touring, including Bath, Dorchester, New Forest, Stonehenge. Rooms have tea facilities. Twin, double, single. Local pub for supper. Phone: (01722) 742177.

MALMESBURY. Stonehill Farm. 15th century farmhouse. Working dairy farm in lush and rolling countryside on the Wiltshire - Gloucestershire border. Ideal quiet location. Twin and double rooms. Full English breakfast. Tea - coffee facilities. Pets welcome. Phone: (01666) 823310.

NEWTON FARMHOUSE

(0794) 884416
Southampton Road, (A36), Whiteparish
Salisbury, Wiltshire SP5 2QL
Proprietors: John & Suzi Lanham

Grade II, Part 16c farmhouse, formerly part of the Trafalgar Estate, 8 miles south of Salisbury on the A36 Southampton Road. Convenient for Stonehenge, Winchester, Romsey and New Forest. 8 en-suite rooms (1 with 4 poster) with colour TV, tea/coffee facilities. Beamed dining room with flagstone floor. Large grounds, outdoor swimming pool. Evening meals by arrangement.

ETB Registered AA QQQ

SELF-CATERING

CHIPPENHAM. Detached bungalow with superb views in large enclosed garden. Easy parking. Colour television. Ideally situated for visiting Lacock, Bath, Salisbury, The Cotswolds, Wells. Sleeps 4/5 plus cot. Phone: (0249) 730297.

STONEHILL FARM
CHARLTON, MALMESBURY, SN16 9DY

COMMENDED
01666 823310
Self-catering in two well equipped converted barns. Sleeps 2/3. From £140.00 per week including electric and linen.

Cotswold edge and within easy reach by car of Bath, Oxford and Stonehenge. We offer a warm welcome in a relaxed atmosphere on our family run Dairy farm. Pets and children welcome.

Also B&B in charming 15th Century Farmhouse, & 3 pretty rooms, 1 en-suite from £14.00 per person per night.

WHERE TO GO

Longleat Safari Park
The Estate Office, Warminster, Wiltshire.
Tel: (0985) 844400

Lions, white tigers, elephants, zebras, giraffes, rhinos, monkeys and only white lion in Europe and many more endangered species. Disabled visitors welcome.

Bowood House and Gardens
Calne, Wiltshire.
Tel: (0249) 812102

18th Century house by Robert Adam collections of painting, watercolours, Victoriana, Indiana and porcelain. Landscaped park with lakes, terraces, waterfall and grottos.

Fox Talbot Museum of Photography
Lacock, Wiltshire.
Tel: (0249) 730459

Displays of apparatus and photographs related to Fox Talbot. Gallery with seasonal exhibitions.

Salisbury and South Wiltshire Museum
The King's House, 65 The Close, Salisbury, Wiltshire.
Tel: (0722) 332151

Grade 1 listed building. Stonehenge collection, the Salisbury Giant and early man. History of Old Sarum, Salisbury, Romans to Saxons ceramics, Wedgwood picture and costume exhibitions.

Iford Manor Gardens
Iford Manor, Bradford-on-Avon.
Tel: (0225) 863146

Great Western Railway Museum
Farrington Road, Swindon.
Tel: (0793) 526161

FOR YOUR CHANCE TO WIN A PERSONAL CD PLAYER
turn to the reader's questionnaire
at the back of this guide

SOUTH EAST ENGLAND

BEDFORDSHIRE • BERKSHIRE • BUCKINGHAMSHIRE
ESSEX • GREATER LONDON • HAMPSHIRE
HERTFORDSHIRE • ISLE OF WIGHT • KENT
OXFORDSHIRE • SURREY • SUSSEX

When I first moved to London to live, I did what I suppose most people do – I enjoyed many months discovering the sights and sounds of the great capital itself.

And what an adventure! The nightlife, the theatres and galleries, Buckingham Palace, the Tower of London, Regent's Park Zoo, tennis at Wimbledon.

Only later did I spread my tourist net wider and decide to explore the arts and parts (as we say in Ireland) of the rest of South East England. I have to say, my reaction was disappointment; disappointment that I hadn't treated myself sooner to the pleasures that the rest of this region has to offer!

So, if you don't want to make the same mistake as I did, why not begin at the obvious starting point – a trip down the River Thames itself. From Gloucestershire to the outskirts of London, the world-famous Thames courses for 124 miles through five counties – the perfect vantage point from which to view the vintage scenery of the South East.

But the Thames isn't the only water the South East has. Resorts like Southend and Margate are spoken of in the same breath as such timeless treasures as jellied eels, donkeys on the beach and sticks of rock. And who can talk of seaside attractions without mentioning Brighton? Who needs soft sand when you've got such charming narrow streets choc-a-bloc with antique shops, and that, oh, so, impressive Pavilion?

The other rock the region has to offer is the "White Cliffs" of Dover, one of the true icons of all things English. Other natural beauty spots to savour include the orchards of Kent, Woburn Park and the New Forest – once described as England's "Heart of Oak". And if the mythic "White Horse" isn't enough of a thrill, then feel free to feast your eyes on the real horses racing so majestically across the Epsom downs!

The South East is equally rich in culture and heritage. Winchester, Canterbury, Chichester, Rochester: rarely have I been able to visit, in such close proximity, such handsome Cathedral towns. Not to mention such impressive historical homes as Windsor Castle and Blenheim Palace. Then there is Oxford – perhaps the most famous seat of learning in the world. It's certainly been established long enough! The first colleges were founded in the 13th Century. Each has its own unique appeal, and among them are to be found many more venerable attractions. If it's your first visit, the exhibitions like 'The Oxford Story' put you in the picture with life-size models recreating eight centuries of the university's past through sights, sounds and even smells!

For the TV addicts amongst you, Oxford takes on added significance through the exploits of 'Inspector Morse' and locations familiar from the TV series make up guided tours. In sheer quantity, in terms of architecture the South East, perhaps more than any other region we cover in this book, probably offers the most splendid, and varied. One thing is for sure – you won't be stuck for anything to do or see.

"Any man who is tired of London is tired of life" wrote Dr Johnson. But why stop at London when the South East has much more to offer.

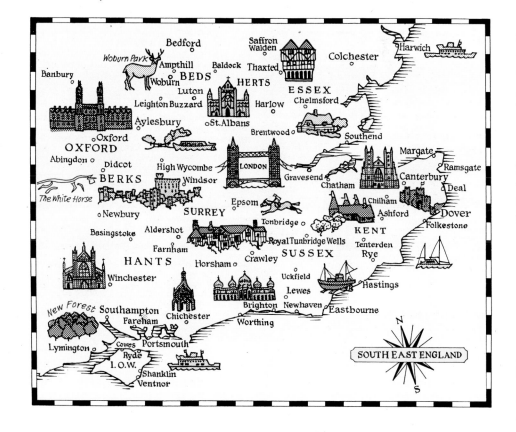

SOUTH EAST ENGLAND

BEDFORDSHIRE

SELF-CATERING

BEDFORD. Thatched cottages, barn conver-sions. Country views, lovely walks. Working farm with cows, horses, sheep, free range chickens, ducks and geese. Plenty to do and see. Bedford 5 miles. From £120 a week. Phone: (0234) 771996/772275.

WHERE TO GO

Whipsnade Wild Animal Park
Dunstable.
Tel: 0582 872171 - Open all year (except Christmas day) A large open zoo containing over 2,000 animals (200 different species). Steam railway. Special events in the summer, cafeteria and shop. Disabled visitors welcome.

BERKSHIRE

HOTELS & GUEST HOUSES

HENLEY ON THAMES near. Detached Victorian house overlooking fields. Colour television, tea - coffee facilities. 4 bedrooms. Pub food walking distance. Ideal for Windsor, Maidenhead, Reading, Heathrow. ETB listed. Ground floor en-suite room. Carver, Windybrow, Victoria Road, Wargrave, Berks. Phone: (01734) 403336.

WINDSOR. Trinity Guest House. In the town centre in a quiet cul-de-sac close to river, castle and stations. All rooms have colour television, clock radio, coffee/tea making facilities and hair dryers. Phone: (0753) 864186. Fax: (0753) 862640.

CARAVANS, CHALETS & HOLIDAY PARKS

HURLEY. Hurley caravan and camping park. Holiday homes for hire. Large area for tourers and tents. Situated on bank of River Thames. Touring centre for London, Oxford and Windsor. Brochure Phone: (0628) 823501. BH-HPA member, 3 ticks.

WOKINGHAM. California Chalet and Tour-ing Park, Nine Mile Ride RG11 3NY. Phone: (0734) 733928. Enjoy the peaceful lakeside location of our small family run park with comfortable chalets and secluded tourer pitches with full amenities. Ideal London - Windsor.

WHERE TO GO

Blake's Lock Museum
Gasworks Road, Reading
Tel: 0734 590630
Situated on the River Kennet, housed in a former pumping station, this museum focuses on the life and times of Reading and its waterways in the 19th and early 20th centuries.

Museum of Reading
The Town Hall, Blagrave Street, Reading.
Tel: (0734) 575911
Featuring the story of Reading, tracing the development of the area from its Saxon beginnings through to the present day and the Bayeux Tapestry. Reading's replica, exact in size and details, sewn by the Leek Embroidery Society in 1885.

ESSEX

HOTELS & GUEST HOUSES

CLACTON. Hamelin Hotel. Licensed, friendly family run. Some rooms en-suite. All bedrooms with television and tea making facilities. Special rates OAPs. Weekly bookings. 200 yards sea and town. From £14 bed and breakfast. Phone: (01255) 474456.

COLCHESTER. 16th century grade II listed farm-house within 420 acres. Fishing lake, swimming pool, tennis court, games room. Superb peaceful location. Lovely views. Caravans and camping. Excellent touring base. Kentishes Farm, Stisted, Ruth Corby. Phone: (0376) 325129.

HORNCHURCH. Essex. Very nice bed and break-fast accommodation in private house. Television, tea making facilities. Off-street parking. Convenient M25, M11. Central London, District Line tube 200 yards. Non smokers only. No pets. Phone: (0708) 438414.

MAYLANDSEA, near Chelmsford. Modern, detached comfortable residence. Country views. 1 double, 1 twin bedroom. Tea - coffee making facilities. Guests own bathroom. Colour television. Terms £15 - £17 per night. Clark, 25 West Avenue. Phone: (01621) 740972.

WALTON ON NAZE. West Lodge Guest House. Small and friendly. Close to beach, shops, stations. Good parking. En-suite available. Rooms have television, hot and cold, tea making. Family room. Bar meals. Reasonable rates. Phone: (0255) 677172.

SELF-CATERING

CLACTON. Spotlessly clean. Fully equipped self-catering holiday flats. First house from seafront, first road from pier. 3 minutes shops. Stamped addressed envelope Mr West, 19 Beaumont Close, Walton on Naze CO14 8TX. Phone: (0255) 672380.

CLACTON, Jaywick Sands. Seafront bungalow. Sun lounge with extensive sea views facing south. Clean, well equipped, good decorative order, night storage heaters. Garage. Open all year. Serviced by owners at each change over. Phone: (0206) 574166.

WHERE TO GO

Basildon Zoo
London Road, Vange, Basildon.
Tel: (0268) 553985

A small zoo set in five acres of pretty countryside. Big cats, aviaries, llamas, guanaco, rare poultry, pets corner, rare plants and trees, Cafeteria, shop, playground, Disabled visitors welcome.

Colchester Zoo
Stanway Hall, Maldon Road, Stanway, Colchester.
Tel: (0206) 330253

150 species of animals including leopards, lions chimpanzees, rhinoceros, zebras, elephants. Siberian tigers, childrens corner, miniature railway. Shop, cafeteria, 11th century church, picnic area, first-aid. Disabled visitors welcome.

House on the Hill Toy Museum
Stansted.
Tel: (0279) 813237

Fully animated toy museum housing one of the largest and most comprehensive toy collections in the country, presented as an entertaining and educational experience.

Never Never Land
Western Esplanade, Southend-on-Sea.
Tel: (0702) 460618

Fantasy Park where different styles of magic animation and illusion recreate familiar children's stories - Merlin the Magician, Model Railway, Masters of the Universe, Humpty Dumpty, Badger's House, Snow White and The Old Woman Who Lived in a Shoe.

Sea Life Centre
Eastern Esplanade, Southend-on-Sea.
Tel: (0702) 462400

Journey beneath the ocean waves and discover thousands of amazing sea creatures, everything from shrimps and starfish to conger eels and octopus. A dramatic walk-through tunnel creates the illusion of a walk on the sea bed with sharks, rays and many others gliding silently by, inches above your head.

Waltham Abbey
Waltham Abbey.
Tel: (0992) 767897

Fine Norman church founded in 1060 by King Harold, who is reputedly buried here. Visitor centre and shop. The Crypt Centre houses an exhibition about the history of the town and abbey.

GREATER LONDON

HOTELS & GUEST HOUSES

HAYES (near Heathrow). Homely Guest House with emphasis on comfort. All rooms with television, tea/coffee facilities. Satellite television, lounge. Parking for holidays. Bar, evening meals. Shepiston Lodge, 31 Shepiston Lane, Hayes, Middlesex UB3 1LJ. Phone: 081 573 0266. Fax: 081569 2536.

HEATHROW. Small, clean, comfortable guest house. 1 mile, but with no noise from flight path. In charming village, praised by all guests. ETB. Weekly parking, car service available. 9 Hollycroft Close, Sipson, W. Drayton UB7 0JJ. Phone: 081 897 9032.

LONDON. Kirness House. Students welcome. All European languages spoken. Service with a smile. From £20 each person. 29 Belgrave Road, Victoria, London SW1V 1RB. Phone: 071-834 0030.

LONDON. Family run guest house. Bed and breakfast from £25 singles, £33 doubles per night. All rooms with colour television and tea making facilities. Free street parking. Children welcome. ETB approved. Phone: 0171 226 5721 or 0171 226 3379.

LONDON W1. Glynne Court Hotel. Small, friendly bed and breakfast accommodation. Reasonably priced. All rooms with wash basins, colour television, telephone, hospitality trays. Centrally situated for all amenities. 3 minutes Marble Arch. Continental breakfast inclusive. Phone: 071 262 4344.

LONDON. Falcon Hotel, 11 Norfolk Square, London W2 1RU. Small family run hotel. Paddington station 1 minute. Shopping, sightseeing close by. All rooms en-suite. Television, tea - coffee facilities. Traditional English breakfast. Excellent rates. Phone: 071 723 8603.

LONDON. Gower Hotel, 129 Sussex Gardens, London W2 2RX. Small, family run hotel. Close to Paddington station. All rooms en-suite. Television, radio, telephone, tea - coffee, traditional English breakfast. Competitive rates. Excellent. Shopping, sightseeing close by. Phone: 071 723 8603.

COMPTON GUEST HOUSE
E.T.B./B.T.A. LISTED
Nearest to stations, situated in quiet, sought-after area. 20 minutes West End, Central London, 12 minutes walk to Wimbledon Tennis. Tea/coffee and colour TV's all rooms. Quality rooms and excellent service. Competitive rates.
Phone: 081-947 4488/081-879 3245
65 COMPTON ROAD, WIMBLEDON,
LONDON SW19 7QA

SELF-CATERING

LALEHAM ON THAMES. Burway House. ETB 3 keys commended. Self-catering holiday flats in Thameside village. Between Windsor and Hampton Court. Overlooking park. Near river. Open all year. Patmore, Ferry Lane. Phone: (0784) 457773.

LONDON. Baker Street W1. Self-catering holiday flats from £160 per week for 2 persons, including colour television, linen, phone and own bathroom and kitchen. 31 Crawford Street, London W1H 1PL. Phone: 071 402 6165.

LONDON. Baker Street W1. Self-catering holi-day flats. From £160 per week for 2 persons. Including colour television, linen, phone, own bathroom and kitchen. 31 Crawford Street, London W1H 1PL. Phone: 071-402 6165.

SELF-CATERING
All self-catering, fully furnished and equipped, including colour TV, linen, etc. Well situated for tourist attractions. High standard of cleanliness. Personal supervision. Flats inspected before every let. All flats situated with railway station close by.
Tel: (0181) 699 9055
1 bedroomed flat from £146 per week
2 bedroomed flat from £166 per week
3 bedroomed flat from £260 per week

LONDON. Self-catering holiday and long term flats, and studios with en-suite and cooking facilities. Linen, towels and television. Close to tube. Pleasant location. Reasonably priced. Cheap London Transport travel passes available. Phone: Don 081-505 0642.

LONDON W5. Stay bed and breakfast at my comfortable garden flat. Ideal location. 7 minutes underground, Piccadilly line. Double room £35 nightly. Self service. Convenient for Heathrow and central London, approximately twenty minutes. Off street parking. Phone: 081 994 8801.

WHERE TO GO

London Dungeon
28-34 Tooley Street, London, SE1.
Tel: 071 403 0606

World's first medieval horror museum. Now featuring two major shows "The Jack the Ripper Experience" and "The Theatre of the Guillotine".

London Toy and Model Museum
21-23 Craven Hill, London, W2.
Tel: 071 262 9450

One of the most extensive collections of commercially made toys and models in Europe dating from 1850 onward. Including trains, cars, planes and nursery toys.

Museum of the Moving Image
South Bank, London, SE1.
Tel: 071 928 3535

Celebration of cinema and television. 44 exhibition areas, offering plenty of hands-on participation and a cast of actors to tell visitors more.

Science Museum
Exhibition Road, South Kensington, London, SW7.
Tel: 071 938 8000

National Museum of Science and Industry. Full-size replica of Apollo II Lunar Lander, launch pad. Wellcome Museum of the History of Medicine, flights lab, food for thought, optics.

HAMPSHIRE

HOTELS & GUEST HOUSES

ASHURST, New Forest. Granby Manor bed and breakfast. Friendly family run Victorian house. En-suite family/double, twin/double with hot & cold, tea, coffee facilities. Comfortable lounge. Secluded garden. Close station. Forest walks, restaurants, parking. Phone: (0703) 292357.

The Old Coastguard Hotel

BARTON-ON-SEA

ENGLISH TOURIST BOARD THREE CROWNS

A very warm welcome awaits you at our small clifftop hotel – overlooking Christchurch Bay and the Purbeck Hills. The New Forest is only minutes away and many lovely walks and places of interest are all within easy reach. Most of our 7 bedrooms are en-suite – some ground floor – and all have colour TV and tea/coffee facilities. We offer genuine home cooking and personal service in a friendly relaxed atmosphere.

Brochure with pleasure from Resident Owners:

ANN & GERALD LONG

The Old Coastguard Hotel, 53 Marine Drive East
Barton-on-Sea, Hants. BH25 7DX

Tel: 0425 612987

(We regret that we cannot cater for children under 12)

BROCKENHURST
New Forest

Enjoy Summer and Autumn breaks in the friendly, relaxed atmosphere of a large Edwardian house right on the edge of the forest. Walking, cycling, riding – You name it, We can arrange it. Full board over Christmas.

Children and Dogs welcome, Goldfish by arrangement

Hayter 01590 623682

LYNDHURST, New Forest. For superb all year family holidays. Edwardian home bed and breakfast. Dogs welcome. Honeymoon, anniversary specials. Non smoking. Secure parking. 10 minutes from M27. Easy walk to quality eating establishments. Phone: (0703) 283584.

LYNDHURST (New Forest). Bed and breakfast in family home. Television, tea making facilities in rooms. Twin and double bedded accommodation. Children welcome at reduced price. Close village and forest. From £12.50 per night. Phone: (0703) 283397.

NEW FOREST. Ringwood. Large country house with direct forest access. Offering comfortable en-suite rooms with beverage facilities and choice of breakfast. Television lounge. Ideal for gardeners, walkers, riders. Horses accommodated. Overseas guests welcome. Phone: (01425) 476173.

NEW FOREST, Ringwood. Secluded bungalow. Small working farm. Guests may assist milking etc. Beverage facilities, colour televisions in large comfortable rooms. Helpful, friendly home. Short walk open forest. Phone: (0425) 472611.

NEW FOREST. Near Burley/Barton-on-Sea. Bed and English breakfast. 'Old fashioned courtesy'. Delightful country house, three acres. En-suites, tea/coffee facilities. Comfort. Quality. Relaxing setting, adjacent forest. Regret no children/smoking. Minimum two nights. Phone: (0425) 611101.

NEW FOREST, near Beaulieu. Mrs Stone, Heathlands, Lepe Road, Langley, Hampshire SO45 1YT. Bed and breakfast in bungalow. Two miles beach. Hot and cold, colour television, beverage facilities, shower. Parking. Non smokers only. £15 each. Phone: (0703) 892517.

NEW FOREST, BROCKENHURST
BED AND BREAKFAST

Delightful self-contained en-suite accommodation overlooking garden, a few minutes walk from this pretty New Forest village centre and Forest, 3 minutes walk mainline station. Full English breakfast served. Parking available for car and boat.

Tel: (01590) 622313

NEW FOREST, near coast and Lymington. Private house. Bed and breakfast. Homely accommodation. Colour television, tea, coffee making facilities in rooms. Mrs Harnett, Danewood, Sway Road, Tiptoe, Lymington, Hampshire SO41 6FQ. Phone: (0425) 612469.

NEW FOREST. Peacefully situated between Lymington and Beaulieu. Bed and large breakfast in comfortable friendly cottage accommodation with attractive en-suite rooms having tea making facilities and wonderful views. Fishing, riding, golf, swimming nearby. Phone: (0590) 676361.

BUSKETTS LAWN HOTEL
NEW FOREST

A delightful family run country hotel in quiet Forest surroundings. 14 en-suite bedrooms with colour TV; radio; central heating; trouser press; hairdryer; hospitality trays and direct dial telephones. Victorian four-poster suite. Excellent food, service, comfort. Licensed. Lounges (Dancing – some weekends). Secluded two-acre garden. Putting green. Croquet. Mini-football pitch. Seasonal outdoor heated swimming pool. Country house candlelit dinner. Children/pets welcome. Function and conference facilities. Ample parking. Open all year. Special weekend breaks. Christmas and New Year festivities.
Resident Proprietors: Con, Linda and Damian Hayes.

Terms – per person per night (inc. VAT)
Standard Rate (B&B) from £30. (D, B&B) from £40.00.
Special Breaks Available
AA ★★ RAC ETB ♨ ♨ ♨ ♨ Commended

WOODLANDS, NR SOUTHAMPTON, HAMPSHIRE SO40 7GL
Tel: (01703) 292272/292077
Fax: (01703) 292487

NEW FOREST, Brockenhurst. Small Country hotel. Superb position overlooking forest. All rooms en-suite, colour television. Mid-week breaks. 4 nights for price of 3. Licensed restaurant. Home cooking. Friendly service. Cloud Hotel AA ★★. STB 3 crowns. Phone: (0590) 622165.

NEW FOREST, Bransgore. Bed and breakfast. Delightful bungalow set in 7 acres farmland. Relaxed friendly atmosphere. Central for forest and Bournemouth. Riding, fishing, golf. Range of restaurants nearby. Tea making facilities, barbecue available. Phone: (0425) 672303.

NEW FOREST, Burley. Lovely en-suite bed and breakfast. Adjoining olde worlde tea rooms and pretty country garden. Beverage facilities, colour television. £40 nightly 2 people sharing including English breakfast. Golf, riding, fishing. Seaside nearby. Phone: (01425) 402305.

NEW FOREST, Lymington. Luxury 5 bedroomed house. 5 minutes forest, coast, Isle of Wight. Mountain bikes for hire. Comfortable accommodation and friendly atmosphere. Most rooms en-suite, colour television, coffee and tea making facilities. Price £16-£18. Phone: (0590) 678406.

NEW FOREST. Victorian Coaching Inn, in the heart of the New Forest. Excellent reputation for hospitality! Fresh home made dishes. CAMRA recommended. Caring staff who welcome and cater for families. Children's play area/garden. Phone: Malcolm Frow (0590) 682287).

NEW FOREST. Romantic breaks. Candlelit dining room, log fires. Wonderful walks. Gourmet cuisine. Rooms en-suite. Lovely views over open forest. Special any two-day break from £43 per person half board. AA 2 star highly commended. Whitley Ridge Hotel. Phone: (01590) 622354.

NEW FOREST, LYMINGTON
Lovely Edwardian Guest House in 14 acres. All rooms TV's and tea makers. Some en-suite or private bathrooms. £20 per person including full English breakfast, evening meals available. Continental and English cooking £12 inclusive of wines. Dogs and children welcome.
Phone: (0590) 673354
Gorse Meadow, Sway Road, Lymington SO41 8LR

NEW FOREST. Quality bed/breakfast en-suite rooms. Excellent beds and facilities in friendly home. Sea 1 mile. Pets welcome. Luxurious ground floor suite designed for disabled guests. Leisure facilities, golf, riding nearby. Phone: New Milton (01425) 613515.

NEW FOREST. Country cottage near Lymington. Rural surroundings. Every comfort. Morning tea, full English breakfast. Late night coffee. Television in all bedrooms. Bed and breakfast £12. Phone: (0590) 23051.

NEW FOREST, Bashley. Close sea, forest, riding. Comfortable accommodation. En-suite family room. Secluded garden, swimming pool. Guest lounge, television/games, tea making facilities. Special two day breaks from £50 per double room including breakfast. Phone: (0425) 619001.

NEW FOREST, Bransgore. 10 minutes Christchurch. Bed and breakfast. Victorian family residence. Informal, friendly accommodation. Secluded gardens. Parking. En-suite, colour television etc. Full English breakfast. Ideally situated for forest activities. From £14. Phone: G. Hooper (01425) 672450.

NEW FOREST, Brockenhurst. Bed and break- fast. Lovely Edwardian house in 2.5 acres of mature garden, 35 yards from open forest. Colour televisions, tea making. Horse riding arranged. Mountain bike hire. Good local pub. Phone: (01590) 623682.

NEW MILTON. Valesmoor Farm (Wootton). Bed and breakfast in horsey family home. Friendly welcome. Spacious accommodation. Television and tea-making facilities if required. New Forest across road. Towns and beaches within easy distance. Phone: (0425) 614487.

WATERFORD HOUSE
NEW MILTON
Relax in comfortable accommodation with good food and friendly service. Central for New Forest, beaches and local attractions.

Brochure on request
(01425) 614821

PORTSMOUTH/Southsea. Small family run guest house, 2 minutes from sea. Central for shops. Full English breakfast. All rooms hot and cold, central heating, colour television, tea trays. A warm welcome awaits you. Phone: Portsmouth (0705) 827173.

JEVINGTON
Family run B&B, situated in a quiet lane midway between High Street and Marina's. Ideal base for exploring lovely market town, New Forest and Isle of Wight. Excellent pubs and restaurants within walking distance.
Non smoking.
PHONE JUNE & IAN CARRUTHERS
01590 672148

RINGWOOD, Old Stacks. Warm friendly welcome assured in delightful non-smoking character bungalow, set in lovely garden. Twin en-suite/double with private bathroom. Both have colour television and beverage facilities. No evening meal. Inn nearby. Phone: (0425) 473840.

RINGWOOD. Lovely Victorian house. Quiet situation, 5 minutes walk town centre. Ample parking. Beautifully decorated 'Laura Ashley' style bedrooms. Breakfast in delightful sunny conservatory overlooking pretty gardens. Excellent New Forest base. AA QQQQ's selected. Phone: (01425) 476724.

RINGWOOD, New Forest. Fraser House, Blashford. Offers comfortable accommodation. All rooms colour television and tea making facilities. Some rooms en-suite. Excellent touring centre. Horse riding, fishing and water sports nearby. Non smokers preferred. Phone: (01425) 473958.

SOUTHSEA. Ashby's Hotel. Licensed public house. 1 minute from sea. Most rooms en-suite, Sky television, family room. Food from Karos kitchen. Real ales and lager from £1 per pint. Affordable prices, room only from £15 per night. Phone: (01705) 823497 24 hours.

SOUTHSEA. Licensed Victorian family run, 12 bedroom hotel. 5 minutes' walk seafront and shops. Ensuite available. Rooms have colour television, hostess tray, hairdrier. ETB, RAC listed. Security lit car park. 34 St. Ronans Road. Phone: (0175) 822872.

SWAY. String of Horses. Intimate secluded hotel. Mature grounds. Luxurious bedrooms, en-suite. Fantasy bathrooms. Candlelit award winning restaurant. Swimming pool. Regret no children. Excellent riding country. Mead End Road, Sway, Lymington, Hampshire SO41 6EH. Phone: (01590) 682631.

SWAY. The Forest Heath Hotel. Lively, traditional New Forest inn. Riding, fishing, walking. Close to all amenities. Good food, ale and company. Families welcome. Caring staff! 3 nights midweek, weekend £90. Double. Phone: (0590) 682287.

SELF-CATERING

BEAULIEU. The Ropeway Annex. Delightful part of riverside house. One acre garden. Jetty. Near Motor Museum, forest. Sleeps two, plus sofa bed. Bathroom, kitchen. OAP discount. Winter short breaks available. Enquiries Phone: (0590) 612545. Dogs welcome.

BROCKENHURST. New Forest. Mid-terrace cottage with immediate access to forest. Close to village centre. Coastal resorts, beaches and ferries easily reached. Sleeps 2. Fully equipped. Regret no children, pets or smokers. Phone: (0590) 22749.

EASTLEIGH, near Winchester, Romsey, Southampton. 'The Wren's Nest'. Modern, cosy, well equipped ground floor flat for couple (non-smokers). Kitchen - diner, bathroom, lounge, bedroom off - 4 poster. Large garden, parking. No dogs. Brochure Phone: (0703) 265758.

FORDINGBRIDGE, near New Forest. Exceptional ground floor flat. Sleeps 2. Own garden. Ideally suited for sightseeing, golf, riding, sea, walking. Trout fishing adjacent. Open all year. Part weeks out of season. Phone: (0725) 518360 (Hampshire).

HAYLING ISLAND, Winsor Holidays. Self-catering bungalows and apartments. Opposite 5 miles of beach (part Blue Flag awarded). Ample car parking, play/picnic area. Boating, fishing, golf, amusements nearby. Winsor Close, Hayling Island. Phone: (0705) 464443/463156.

HAYLING ISLAND, Hants. ETB registered selfcatering chalet in a quiet location. Sleeps four. Ample parking. Within easy reach of many places of interest and the beach. From £60 low season. Brochure available. Mason, Phone: (0635) 254744.

LYMINGTON, New Forest. Charming period thatched cottage with garden in quiet village beside open forest, 3 miles from sea. Open fires. Sleeps 6/7. Excellent walking, sailing, swimming, riding, historical places to visit nearby. Phone: 071 727 5463.

LYMINGTON. Country cottage, edge of the New Forest. Sleeps 4. Gas, heating, colour television. Patio, gas barbecue. Available all year. Pets welcome. Short breaks out of season. Please phone for details (0590) 682025 evenings.

LYNDHURST near, New Forest. Comfortable, Modern 4 bedroomed detached house in quiet close. Well equipped, including colour television, central heating. Separate dining room. Secluded garden, patio, garage and parking. Sleeps 7 and baby. Phone: (0703) 842226.

MILFORD-ON-SEA. Comfortable, well equipped flat, sleeps 2 people. Beach nearby. Easy reach of New Forest and ferry to Isle of Wight. Splendid area for walking, relaxing, riding, wind surfing. Regret no smokers. Phone: (0590) 642238.

NEW FOREST. Luxury log cabins. Some 3/4/7 night breaks available in 2 or 3 bedrooms, open all year on forest holiday centre with full facilities, including indoor swimming pool, shop, restaurant, inn. Phone: (0245) 321048.

NEW FOREST. Near Burley/Barton-on-Sea. Delightful, spacious, self-contained 'garden studio flat'. Tasteful furnishings, colour television. Private sunny patio. In country house, grounds three acres. Peaceful setting. Access forest. Country lovers recommended. Couple only. Phone: (0425) 611101.

NEW FOREST. Twin Oaks, Red Lynch. Sleeps 8/9. Comfortably furnished, equipped 4 bedroom house, bedding supplied. Central for Beaulieu, Salisbury, Wilton, Stonehenge, Romsey, Breamore, Mottisfont, Winchester, Marwell, Christchurch, Bournemouth, Weymouth. Country walks. Garden. Colour television. J. Leach, Newton, Whiteparish, Salisbury. Phone: (0794) 884428.

NEW FOREST, Romsey, Salisbury. Secluded country cottage. ETB recommended. Dogs welcome. Furnished, equipped high standard. Perfect location. Electric included. Phone: (0794) 341667.

NEW FOREST (Lyndhurst). Choice of well located and furnished cottages, sleeping 4 to 6. All modernised. Centrally heated and inclusive of linen, gas, electricity etc. Pay phones. Phone: (0703) 768620.

NEW FOREST, Sway. Top quality self-catering accommodation for 2/12. ETB 4 keys highly commended. From cosy studio to beautiful country house. Idyllic secluded setting. Ideal children and pets. Short or long lets. Brochure Phone: (0590) 682532.

NEW MILTON/BASHLEY. Bungalow, sleeps 5. Central heating, television, washing machine, microwave, linen. Pets and children welcome. Garden. £125 - £185 per week inclusive. Mrs C. Loader, Cherrydene, Marks Lane, Bashley, New Milton, Hampshire. Phone: (0425) 611713.

NEW MILTON outskirts. First floor flat on forest edge. Linen supplied, sleeps 4 plus cot. Children and pets welcome. Available all year round. For further details Phone: (0425) 619639.

PORTSMOUTH AND SOUTHSEA. Large holi-day flats in excellent position. Write D. Parker, Owl Cottage, Hoe Gate, Hambledon, Hampshire or Phone: (0705) 632568.

PORTSMOUTH. Stoneycroft holiday flats. Spacious self-contained 2 and 3 bedroom flats. Colour television and linen provided. Will accommodate 2 to 6 persons. 5 minutes to seafront, shops and entertainments. Fry, 32 Lennox Road South, Southsea PO5 2HU. Phone: (01705) 874871.

RINGWOOD, New Forest. Superbly located modern bungalow in own large flat secluded garden. adjacent to open forest with wonderful walks. Excellent location for golf, fishing and beaches, sleeps 4. Garage. Phone: (0425) 473809.

SOUTHAMPTON. Self-contained apartments. Completely equipped. Separate kitchen, bathroom, lounge. Colour television. Private veranda or patio. Sleeps 2/3. ETB 4 key commended. From £145 weekly. Pinewood Lodge, Kanes Hill, Southampton SO19 6AJ. Brochure Phone: (01703) 402925.

ROBINS COURT
Luxury fully self-contained Holiday Flats, Southsea. Ideally situated for seafront and Southsea's main shopping area's. Spacious flats with 2, 3 or 4 bedrooms. Accommodate 2 to 10 persons in complete comfort. Each flat has its own bath/shower room with toilet. Your beds are made ready for your arrival, be sure of a warm welcome! 5 minutes from seafront, free private car park.
Tel: or Fax: (01705) 737941 or (0973) 204609

SOUTHSEA, Portsmouth. Victorian terraced house. Sleeps six. Central heating, double glazed. Cooker, microwave, washing machine, fridge, colour television. Bath, shower. Linen provided. ETB three key commended. Open all year. Near amenities. No pets. Phone: (0705) 730433.

ST. IVES
RINGWOOD
Bungalow decorated, furnished and equipped to a high standard. Sleeps 2/6 people. Edge of New Forest. Ideal for walking, fishing, riding, touring and the seaside resorts of Bournemouth/Poole. Very good rates.
For information
Phone: (01425) 472906

ST. LEONARDS. New Forest border. Holiday house, 3 bedrooms, fully equipped, colour television, washing machine, microwave, payphone. Country setting. Close to Bournemouth and many places of interest. Families welcome. Sorry no pets. Parking. Phone: (0202) 893306.

WINCHESTER 3 miles. Self-contained fully equipped farm holiday flat. Overlooks fields and forestry. Lovely walks. 30 minutes drive from New Forest. Sleeps four and cot. Garden with patio and barbecue. Phone: (0962) 776355.

WINCHESTER/ROMSEY - Delightful farm cot-tage. Sleeps 5 plus baby. Fully equipped. Colour television, washer drier, garage, garden. Lovely walks. Good touring base for New Forest, Salisbury and coast. From £150 per week. Phone: (01794) 368265/368513.

Daltons Directory and Daltons Weekly
The winning combination for all your holiday needs

CARAVANS, CHALETS & HOLIDAY PARKS

HAYLING ISLAND. Brick chalet near sea and shops. Quiet location. Car parking in front. Secluded back garden. Sleeps four in two bedrooms. Shower. Pet allowed. £60 - £135 per week. For details please Phone: (0638) 743190.

LYMINGTON. Six berth caravan. Shower, toilet. Colour television on site. Indoor/outdoor pool, jacuzzi, sauna, steam room, gymnasium, bars, entertainment, restaurant, takeaway, supermarket. Pets welcome. Phone: (0256) 55009 anytime up to 10 pm.

MILFORD ON SEA. Luxury 3 bedroomed, well equipped caravan. Excellent position with parking space. Colour teletext television, video, microwave. Indoor, outdoor pools, jacuzzi, sauna, gymnasium, entertainment. Restaurant, takeaway, shop. Sorry no pets. Phone: (01285) 651423.

MILFORD ON SEA (near). Comfortable caravan, sleeps 7. With colour television and microwave. Indoor and outdoor pools, bars and entertainment. Dogs welcome. Sae Brown, 6 St Clements Close, Romsey, Hampshire SO51 8FF. Phone: (0794) 516391.

NEW FOREST
MILFORD-ON-SEA
Downton
Holiday Park
Shorefield Road
Mildford-on-Sea
Hampshire SO41 0LH
Tel: (01425) 476131/
(01590) 642515
✓✓✓✓

Lovely peaceful park. Near sea and New Forest. Bournemouth close by. Luxury caravans with all facilities. Pets welcome. Very competitive prices. Swimming, sailing, riding and forest walks are nearby. Prices include gas and electricity.
Open: March-October
No. of Acres: 3½   No. of Static Vans for Hire: 21
Static Vans . . . . .Low Season £53.00 (Min)
      to High Season £312.00 (Max) per van per week

NEW FOREST, near coast and Lymington. Small touring caravan site in paddock setting. Hook ups, showers, toilets. Plus touring, static caravan to rent. Terry Harnett, Danewood, Sway Road, Tiptoe, Lymington, Hampshire. Phone: (0425) 612469.

NEW FOREST. Mobile home. Ideal walking, riding, fishing, birdwatching. Secluded. Sleeps 2. Fully equipped. £90 weekly. Phone: (0425) 656824 evenings only.

Glen Orchard
HOLIDAY PARK
Edge of New Forest, close to beaches, centrally positioned for Bournemouth, Southampton and Isle of Wight.
■ Secluded rural site
■ Luxury 1/2/3 bedroomed caravans, 2/6 berth
■ Mains services ■ Showers ■ Toilets
■ Colour TV ■ Fridge ■ Heater
■ Laundry room ■ Games room ■ Children's play area
■ Early and late mini breaks ■ Sorry, no pets
Registered English Tourist Board
Colour Brochure on request
Walkford Lane, New Milton, Hants BH25 5NH
Tel: (01425) 616463

NEW MILTON. Bashley Park, 6 berth caravan. Colour television, shower and all mains services. Swimming, snooker and golf on site. Horse riding, sailing and wind surfing nearby. Family entertainment every evening. Phone: Cyril Derbyshire (0279) 723540.

NEW MILTON, Hampshire, Dorset border. 2 bedroom clifftop chalet. Sleeps 3 adults, 2 children plus 2 bed. Holiday village. 2 swimming pools. Lovely coastal views. Close New Forest, Bournemouth, Lymington. Reasonable. No pets. Phone: (0732) 351458.

NEW MILTON, New Forest. Near sea. Beautiful luxury caravan on lovely secluded holiday park. 2 bedrooms, duvets. Double bedroom has en-suite shower, toilet, kitchen, fridge, colour television, lounge. Sorry no pets. Phone: 081 805 2132.

WARSASH. Private caravan, fully equipped. Television. Patio. Ideal quiet holiday. Solent views. Beach, club, launderette, shop, tennis. Children's play area. Darts, pool table. Entertainment most weekends. Swimming pools planned 1995. Coastal walks. Phone: Hunter (0489) 600015.

WHERE TO GO

New Forest Butterfly Farm
Longdown Ashurst, Hampshire.
Tel: (0703) 292166

Large indoor tropical garden housing numerous exotic free-flying butterflies and moths from all over the world. Dragonfly ponds, adventure playground and insectarium.

Mary Rose Ship Hall and Exhibition
HM Naval Base, Portsmouth, Hampshire.
Tel: (0705) 812931

Reconstruction and conservation of Henry VIII's warship, and exhibition of the ship's treasures.

Beaulieu Palace House
Beaulieu, Hampshire.
Tel: (0590) 612345

Home of Lord and Lady Montagu, the house has been in the family since it was acquired in 1538 following the dissolution of the monasteries by Henry VIII. National Motor Museum, monastic life exhibition shops.

Royal Navy Submarine Museum
The Royal Navy Submarine Museum, Gosport, Hants
Tel: 0705 52917

The story of underwater warfare is told from the earliest days with a full-scale model of Bushnell's Turtle (1776) to the present nuclear age. The principal exhibit is the large submarine Alliance, built for World War II and modernised in the 1960's.

New Forest Museum & Visitors Centre
New Forest
Tel: 0703 28391

Delightful museum which tells the story of the New Forest, its history, traditional characters and wildlife. Enjoy the "Changing Forest" audio-visual show - see life size models of forest characters.

LYMINGTON TOWN QUAY,
HAMPSHIRE
(photograph courtesy of Southern Tourist Board)

ISLE OF WIGHT

HOTELS & GUEST HOUSES

GATCOMBE. Beautiful 17th century farmhouse on working farm. Central. Secluded. Ideal walking area. En-suite available. Tea making facilities, television, lounge with inglenook fireplace. Easter to October. Mrs Harvey, Newbarn Farm, Gatcombe. Phone: (01983) 721202.

RYDE, Binstuad. Comfortable Bed and (English) breakfast accommodation. Year round. 10 minutes from all attractions, ferries etc. From £15 per person. 2 single, 1 double room available. Weekenders welcome (minimum 2 nights). Phone: Mrs Hutchinson (0983) 611172.

DORSET HOTEL
RYDE
Family run licensed hotel. All with colour TV, tea and coffee making facilities. Solarium and outdoor swimming pool. 3 minutes shops and seafront. B&B and E.M., short breaks, 2 nights for 2 people from £60. 3 nights from £70.
Phone: (0983) 564327 for enquiries

SANDOWN. Family run Guest House. Near sea and shops. All rooms colour television and tea making facilities. Families welcome. Free baby sitting, en-suite available. Senior citizens reduced rates. Early and late season. Brochure available. Phone: (0983) 403485.

CLIFFWAYS HOTEL
39 RANELAGH ROAD, SANDOWN
E.T.B. ☆☆☆ COMMENDED
Charming and very select Bed and Breakfast Hotel. Extensive comforts to include in-house colour T.V., satellite T.V. Excellent breakfast menu. Central beach and all amenities. From £17.50 daily.
**PH.: SYLVIA BAX (0983) 403659
For further details**

SANDOWN. Small bed and breakfast, 200 yards beach. £80 per week. All rooms with shower, colour television with satellite, tea makers, central heating. All fully inclusive. W.C. en-suite available. Phone: (0983) 402523. S.a.e., 98 Station Avenue, Sandown, Isle of Wight.

SANDOWN. Three crowns detached guest house. Overlooking Sandown Bay on cliff path. En-suite rooms. Colour television, tea making. Good English food. Separate tables. Car park. Near Lake rail halt. Special offers low season. Phone: (0983) 402969.

SANDOWN
ALENDEL HOTEL
1 LEED STREET
SANDOWN
Family-run licensed hotel, full centrally heated. En-suite available. Colour TV, tea and coffee all rooms. Good home cooking and personal attention. Close station and all amenities. Children welcome at reduced rates. Family rooms available.
Short breaks available

Access   Members of Southern Tourist Board   **0983 402967**   Members of Sandown Hotel Association   BARCLAYCARD VISA

Royal Cliff Hotel
**Beachfield Road
Sandown, Isle of Wight
PO36 8NA
01983 403157**
The Royal Cliff Hotel is run personally by the resident proprietors Mr. and Mrs. P. H. Brown. The hotel is situated over looking Sandown Bay. It is within easy reach of piers, pavilion, shops and bus routes, etc. Facilities inc.: Licensed Bar with Dance Floor • Beautiful Garden, with Patio and Swimming Pool • Large Dining Room with sea views • Good Varied Menu • Ample Free Parking • Fire Certificate • Brochure available on request.

SANDOWN. Carisbrooke House Hotel. Licensed Family hotel. En-suite rooms, colour television, tea, coffee making facilities. Sea views. Close to beach, shops, leisure centre and cliff walks. For details Phone: (0983) 402257.

ALTAVIA HOTEL
SANDOWN
Lovely 32 bedroom hotel overlooking bay. Separate lounge. Drying facilities. Dance floor, private pathway from hotel to beach, 100 yards leisure centre. Colour TV, Satellite, videos shown on request,  board games. Hair dryers available. Rooms with a beautiful view. Car park. Crazy golf.
**18 Beach Field Road, Sandown, IOW PO36 8NH
Tel: (0983) 403767**

SANDOWN, Culver Lodge. Comfortable, licensed Hotel. Close to all leisure facilities. Most rooms have pleasant views. All rooms en-suite and have colour televisions, radio, tea - coffee facilities. Garden, parking free. AA QQQ recommended. For brochure Phone: (0500) 121252.

SANDOWN I.O.W.
Albion House Hotel
Fully licensed. Happy and friendly atmosphere. I minute from safe sandy beach and very close to all other amenities. Plenty of good home cooking. B&B from £13 per night. B&B evening meal from £16 per night. Prices are plus VAT.
**Phone: (0983) 402346
Make our home your home for your 1995 holiday.**

SANDOWN. Brackla Family Hotel. Close to beach, town. Licensed bar, tea facilities, television lounge with satellite. Car park. Half board from £119 per week. 1 child free. 7 Leed Street, Sandown. Call Freephone: (0500) 121283. Ref/GF3.

WOODSIDE PRIVATE HOTEL
Attractive family run 16 bedroomed hotel. Set in a quiet street, 2 minutes walk sandy beaches. Good home cooking, choice of menu, special diets catered for. Short breaks available. Full central heating, en-suite rooms, tea/coffee facilities. Also honeymoon suite available. Discounts early/late season.
Ring Maureen (0983) 405416

SHANKLIN. Whitegates Guest House. Small and friendly. Plentiful home cooking. All rooms have tea making facilities and colour televisions, some en-suites. Parking. Close to all amenities. ETB 2 crowns. I8 Wilton Park Road. Phone: (0983) 866126.

SHANKLIN. Licensed family hotel. Excellent home cooking, no dieting here. Home from home with no household duties. Tea/coffee facilities, televisions, central heating, separate dining tables. Children welcome. Prices held for 1995. Brochure Phone: (0983) 862494.

SHANKLIN. Warm welcome at licensed family hotel. Near shops, beach, station. All rooms with tea/coffee facilities, colour television. Excellent home cooking. OAP reductions. Val and Mike, Brooke House Hotel. Phone: (0983) 863162.

SHANKLIN. Kenbury Hotel. 3 crown ETB. All rooms en-suite. Colour television, tea makers, radio, clock. Excellent 5 course choice menu. Licensed bar, pool table. Reduced rates for OAPs (off season) and children sharing. Phone: (01983) 862085.

VENTNOR. Small, friendly hotel. Close to sea. Bright rooms, most en-suite with teasmades, heating and double glazing. Bar and comfortable television lounge. Any day bookings. Short breaks including car ferry arranged. For brochure Phone: (01983) 852656.

SELF-CATERING

BEMBRIDGE, Isle of Wight. Holiday semi bungalow, sleeps 5. Near sea, shops. All amenities. Children and pets welcome. Sae, Mrs Brown, Newcot, 7 Egerton Road, Bembridge, Isle of Wight.

BONCHURCH, Ventnor. Holiday flats in picturesque seaside village. Good walking and touring area. Private parking. Dogs by arrangement. For colour brochure please write 'Woodlynch', Shore Road, Bonchurch, Isle of Wight PO38 1RF or Phone: (0983) 852513.

BRAMBLES CHINE, Isle of Wight. Bungalow holiday complex. Sleeps 4 to 6. Two bedrooms, open plan lounge, kitchenette, bathroom, toilet, colour television. Good sea view. Safe beach, clubhouse. Quiet location. Sorry no pets. Brochure Phone: 081-642 5045.

BRIGHSTONE, Isle of Wight. Luxury farm cottages. Sleep 2/8. Linen included. Garden, patio. Barbecue. Trout fishing, tennis court. Five minutes walk to beach. £99 - £400. Bargain breaks. Beautifully quiet country setting. Details, Susan Fisk. Phone: (0983) 740338.

PLAISH FARM

CARISBROOKE, ISLE OF WIGHT PO30 3HU
BED AND BREAKFAST OR SELF CATERING
on working farm in peaceful Bowcombe Valley. In Lee of
Carisbrooke Castle. Newport, 2 miles. Ideal centre for beaches,
country walks, cycling. Friendly family atmosphere,
children of all ages welcome.
For further information, brochure contact: Mrs. Penny Chick.

Tel: 0983 520397

COLWELL BAY, Freshwater. Holiday bungalow.
Two bedrooms for 4/6 persons, privately owned, comfortably furnished, fully equipped, personally supervised. In quiet location, near beach and club facilities.
Rural and sea views. No pets. Brochure Phone: (0983)
529901.

COWES. Gurnard Pines Holiday Village.
Privately owned bungalow. Extensive Solent views. Fully
refurbished including luxury kitchen. Central heating,
colour television, stereo unit, microwave. Full bathroom. Sleeps 6/7. Heated pool, health, country and children's clubs. Phone: (0983) 840678.

COWES. Gurnard Pines holiday village. Attrac-
tive bungalows in picturesque surroundings. Colour
television, microwave. Heated swimming pool, excellent
club entertainment, children's play area, bistro, gym.
Short breaks and full weeks available. £70-£265 weekly.
Phone: (0203) 468841.

FRESHWATER BAY. Bayclose Holiday Flats.
Each has two bedrooms and full amenities. Open all
year. Private car park. Part weeks out of season.
Alongside National Trust downland. Well behaved dogs
welcome. For brochure Phone: (0983) 753531.

FRESHWATER, Brambles Chine. Holiday bunga-
lows, sleep six. Two bedrooms, bathroom, open plan
lounge-diner, kitchenette. Colour television. Indoor
heated pool. Shop, clubhouse. No pets. Fish, 104 Eastern
Avenue, Shoreham by Sea. Phone: (0273) 454741.

FRESHWATER. Modern, detached, three bed-
room house with all facilities, lounge, dining room,
large patio and garden, all south facing. 15 minute walk
to beach and beautiful countryside by Tennyson Downs.
Available July - September. Phone: (0983) 755599.

FRESHWATER BAY. Overlooking sea. Two
bedroom apartment. One shower room, en-suite. Fully
equipped for 4. Fantastic position with wonderful views
of sea and surrounding countryside. Golf course, horse
riding, swimming pool all nearby. Phone: (0983) 761548.

FRESHWATER, Brambles, Chine, Isle of Wight.
Comfortable brick-built holiday bungalow. Two bedrooms plus Relyon bed-settee. All amenities. Sandy
beach. Ample parking. Telephone, shop, laundry, clubhouse on site. Car ferry space booked from Lymington.
Phone: (01737) 765718.

FRESHWATER. Cosy cottage. Secluded manor
grounds. Plentiful wildlife. Close beach, shops, village
pub. Wood burning stove. Sleeps 2 plus child. Phone:
(0983) 756111.

LAKE, Isle Of Wight. Luxuriously furnished
annexe. Sleeps 2/3. Parking. Central heating. Non smokers. Use of patio, linen, television, video. 10 minutes
Sandown station. Swimming pool, golf, bowling nearby.
Views over Brading and Ventnor Downs. Phone: (0983)
402674.

LAKE, SANDOWN. Self-contained flats. Sleep
2-4. Fully equipped to high standard. Free linen. Colour
television. Car park in drive. Near beach, shops, station.
Briar Knoll, Sandown Road, Lake. Resident proprietors.
Phone: (0983) 402997.

LAKE Flatlets. Edge of open country
Well equipped en-suite facilities, colour television.
Ample parking, pleasant garden. 2-4 people. Open all
year. Resident owners. Excellent supermaket nearby,
cinema, bus route. Phone: (01983) 402004.

NEWBRIDGE. Comfortable, well equipped four
bedroom house in quiet rural village. Sleeps 8. Large
garden. Parking. Well stocked shop, post office. 3 miles
beach, country walks, local pubs, lovely views. Phone:
(0983) 760640.

NITON. Distinctive Victorian farmhouse ann-
exe. Three bedrooms, bathroom, living room and large
kitchen - diner. Comfortably furnished and well
equipped. Private entrance, parking, garden with patio.
Spectacular countryside views. 3/4 mile from Niton village. Phone: Mrs Dabell (0983) 730872.

PORCHFIELD. Attractive detached 4 bed-
roomed brick/stone cottage, sleeps 7/8. Well equipped,
modern kitchen. Rural location. Lovely views. From £250
- £350 inclusive. Horse riding nearby. Also bed and
breakfast available in cottage residence. Phone: (0983)
522817.

RYDE. 2 cottages. 2 bedroom cottage, sleeps
4/5; 1 bedroom cottage sleeps 2/4; cot, colour television. 400 yards to safe sandy beaches. Close to shops and ferries. Phone: (0703) 849565.

RYDE. Cosy flatlet for 4 persons. Walking dis-
tance beach, shops, theatre. Colour television. Garden,
parking. Linen supplied. £90 per week. Details from Mrs
Ferguson, Fern Cottage, 8 West Street, Ryde, Isle of
Wight. Phone: (0983) 565856.

RYDE. Victorian villa divided into flatlets for
2/4 persons. Also cottage sleeps five. All situated near
safe sandy beach and five minutes from town centre.
Dennis and Janet Mulhern, 54 The Strand PO33 1JD.
Phone: (0983) 565447.

RYDE. Upwood has 5 attractive apartments in
large Victorian house. Situated in pleasant area
between park and woods. Within easy reach of all
amenities. Distant sea views from some flats. Sleeps 2 -
8 persons. Phone: (01983) 568965.

SANDOWN. Holiday Chalets. Stone built
chalets accommodate up to six persons. Reductions
early and late season for three people or less. Situated
near sea and town. Short breaks available. Mrs Clemens,
Avenue Road. Phone: (0983) 404025.

SANDOWN. Our beautifully decorated self-
contained flats are highly recommended for cleanliness.
Colour television. Own car park. Delightfully situated
near beach, shops and leisure centre. Flats from £70 per
week. For colour brochure Phone: (0983) 403555.

SANDOWN, Isle of Wight. Sea-front holiday
cottage. Three bedrooms, sleeps six. Linen provided.
Colour television. No meters. Close to all amenities.
Sorry no pets. Reduced terms early and late season.
Phone: (0983) 404298.

SANDOWN. Fort Spinney Holiday Centre. Self-catering holiday flatlets and chalets, accommodate 2 to 8 persons. Quiet family park. Opposite safe sandy beach. No dogs. Large gardens. Brochure Yaverland Road, Sandown. Phone: (0983) 402360.

SANDOWN. Detached 2 bedroom bungalow, sleeps 4/5. Central heating. Television, microwave, fridge, washing machine. Bed linen provided. Secluded garden, quiet area. Near beach, shops, leisure centre. Golf, fishing, water sports, sailing, flying nearby. Phone: (0983) 407983.

SHANKLIN, Isle of Wight. Laurel Court self-catering apartments. Swimming pool, barbeque, garden. Near town, beach, sleeps 2 to 8 persons. May, June, July £95 to £150. Phone: (0983) 406468.

TOTLAND BAY. Quality residential chalet bun-galow. Some sea views. Private road. Garden, garage, colour television, sleeps 2-6. Children welcome, no pets. Fair rates, cheap out of season. Night storage heating. Dimmick, Pontivvy Lodge, Broadway. Phone: (0983) 753384.

VENTNOR. Delightful chalet bungalow, four bedrooms sleeping nine, bathroom and loo upstairs, also shower room and loo downstairs. Lounge 26 x 15 nicely furnished. Pleasant secluded.garden looking out to sea. Very quiet. Lots of parking. (0243) 267014.

VENTNOR. Holiday flatlets, overlooking sea. Sleeping 2/4. Fully equipped, televisions, fridges, etc. Near park and botanic gardens. From £60 per flatlet per week. Pat and Stan Dodd. 'Ventor Villa', 22 Zig Zag Road. Phone: (0983) 852490.

VENTNOR. All self-contained apartments. Free car parking in grounds. All apartment bedrooms are comfortably furnished with en-suite facilities. Beds made for your arrival. Fully centrally heated. Proprietors on site. Phone: for brochure (01983) 852283.

VENTNOR. Fisherman's cottage, situated in the charming resort of Ventnor. Sleeps up to 6. Phone: (0983) 854030.

VENTNOR, Isle of Wight town. Cottage, sleeps 5. Parking. En-suite, shower, deluxe kitchen, washing machine. Pleasant gardens, patio, barbecue. Television, video. Our home from home. 500 yards beach. Near all attractions. Saturdays - midweek/weekends. Phone: 081 394 0652.

WEST WIGHT. 2 holidays in 1. Beautiful countryside and sandy beaches nearby. Fully equipped, self-catering houses, cottages, bungalows, all privately owned. Holiday Homes, Whittingham Place, Avenue Road, Freshwater, Isle of Wight PO40 9UT. Phone: (0983) 753423 24 hours.

𝔚hitwell 𝔕ailway 𝔖tation

Whitwell, Isle of Wight, a Victorian branch line station, tastefully converted, self-catering to a high standard and well equipped. Glorious countryside, excellent walks/country pursuits. Beaches nearby. Large gardens. Sleeps 5. Winter short breaks.

Member of Isle of Wight Tourist Board

CARAVANS, CHALETS & HOLIDAY PARKS

ARRETON. Mobile home. Two double bed-rooms, bathroom. Kitchen with gas cooker, electric fridge. Lounge with colour television. Private rural site. Details Mr. J.T. Cooper, Dairyman's Daughter Cottage, Arreton, Isle of Wight PO30 3AR. Phone: (01983) 865318. Mobile (0850) 715050.

BEMBRIDGE. Whitecliffe Bay. Luxury caravan with sea view, two double bedrooms, shower, toilet, colour television, fridge and cooker. Quiet family site with shop and laundry. Sandy beach, two minutes walk. For terms Phone: (0705) 468996.

BEMBRIDGE, Whitecliff Bay. Caravans, clean, comfortable. Colour television, toilet, shower, fridge, heater, launderette, playground, shop, takeaway. Sea views, adjoins lovely beach. Sorry no pets. Mrs Ridett, 85 High Street, Carisbrooke, Isle of Wight PO30 1NT. Phone: (0983) 524476.

BEMBRIDGE. Whitecliff Bay. New caravan, 3 bedrooms, bathroom, television. Front pitch with panoramic sea views overlooking secluded bay. Minutes walk to sandy beach. Quiet site. Easy reach of local attractions by car. Coach tours available. Phone: (0983) 296168.

BEMBRIDGE. Whitecliff Bay. 6 berth luxury caravans, personally cleaned by owners. Showers. Colour television. Flush toilets. Full size cookers. 1 or 2 bedrooms. Shop, off-licence, takeaway on site. Overlooking sandy bay. Phone: (01983) 873630.

GURNARD PINES Holiday Village. Chalet bun-galow in delightful country setting. Sleeps 6. Heated swimming pool, colour television, shower, entertainment, childrens' club, bar and restaurant. Available February - November. Reasonable rates from £75 per week. Phone: (0923) 835971.

SANDOWN. Cheverton Copse Holiday Park. Award winning family park set in delightful wooded parkland. Licensed clubhouse entertainment high season. 1.5 miles to beautiful beaches and amenities. Tourers and campers welcome. Free colour brochure. Phone: (01983) 403161.

VENTNOR - Family site, 40 static caravans and 100 pitches. Shop, bar and heated outdoor pool. Disabled toilet/bathroom. Dogs permitted. Appuldurcombe Gardens Caravan and Camping Park, Wroxall, Ventnor, Isle of Wight PO38 3EP. Phone: (01983) 852597.

WHITECLIFF BAY, Isle of Wight. Six berth caravans, nearby beach, golf, fishing, activity centre, entertainment, water sports. Equipped with microwaves, television, baby equipment. Weekend and middle week breaks, low season. Rates £50 - £235. Phone: Heath (0785) 48450.

WHITECLIFF BAY. Isle of Wight. Caravan, sleeps 6. Clean, comfortable, well equipped. Colour television, fridge, hot water, flush toilet. Lovely views. Overlooking safe sandy beach. Shop, launderette, showers, children's playground on site. Phone: (0983) 402233.

WHITECLIFF BAY. 28 ft. BK82 six berth cara-van. One double bedroom, one bunk bedroom. Two lounge area. Full size fridge, toilet, shower and cooker. Sea view, beach access. Phone: 071 733 4092.

WHITECLIFF BAY. Luxury caravans. 2 bed-rooms, showers, fully equipped, including all bedding. Owner cleans to high standard. Parking alongside vans, Cliff top site. Tariff from £40 low season. Phone: (0983) 866321 or (0983) 528615.

WHITECLIFF BAY, Isle of Wight. 6 berth fully equipped caravans on quiet picturesque site. Safe sandy beach within 100 yards. Shop and showers on site. All linen provided. Phone: (0983) 526791 evenings and weekends.

WOOTTON. 2 modern caravans, sleeps 4. Colour television, bathroom with shower, balcony with seaviews. 50 yards from safe beach. Secluded woodland setting. Ideal for quiet holiday. Club, bar, cafe. Phone: (0983) 566579/612372.

WHERE TO GO

Osborne House
East Cowes, Isle of Wight.
Tel: (0983) 200022
Queen Victoria and Prince Albert's seaside holiday home. Victorian carriage service to Swiss Cottage where royal children learnt cooking and gardening.

Butterfly World and Fountain World
Staplers Road, Wootton, Ryde, Isle of Wight.
Tel: (0983) 883430
Tropical indoor garden with butterflies from around the world. Fountain World has water features and huge fish. Italian and Japanese gardens.

Isle of Wight Steam Railway
Railway Station, Haven Street, Ryde, Isle of Wight.
Tel: (0983) 882204
Five mile steam railway using Victorian and Edwardian locomotives and carriages. Souvenir shop, refreshments and children's playground.

Blackgang Chine Theme Park
Near Ventnor, Isle of Wight.
Tel: (0983) 730330
Frontier land, Nurseryland, Adventureland, Smugglerland, Fantasyland, water gardens and maze.

Haseley Manor
Arreton, Isle of Wight.
Tel: (0983) 865420
Historic manor house dating from medieval times through to the Victorian period. Large working pottery, sweet factory with demonstrations, craft village and gardens.

Calborne Watermill and Rural Museum
Newport, Isle of Wight.
Tel: (0983) 78227
Fine example of an early 17th Century watermill still in working order, Granary, waterwheel, water and pea fowl.

KENT

HOTELS & GUEST HOUSES

ASHFORD. 'Waterkant' Guest House. Headcorn provides tranquil setting within olde worlde charm of Wealden village. Relaxed informal atmosphere is complemented by fine cuisine. Comprehensive facilities and interesting surroundings. From £15. ETB registered. Phone: (0622) 890154.

BROADSTAIRS. Westfield Lodge, Granville Avenue. Comfortable guest house. Tea making facilities. Central heating. Colour television, lounge. Road parking. Painting holidays also available. Five minutes to sea and shops. Send for brochures. Mrs McKinnon. Phone: (0843) 862615.

BROADSTAIRS. Gull cottage. Non-smoking hotel. Overlooking sea and sandy beaches. Close to harbour, town centre. A character Victorian property. Ensuites, colour television, tea, coffee facilities. AA, RAC. For colour brochure Phone: (0843) 861936.

BROADSTAIRS. Cintra Hotel. Small family run hotel on main seafront. Near town and bus stops. Sally Ferry five minutes away. Bedrooms, en-suite, tea making facilities, television lounge, bar. Richardson, 24 Victoria Parade CT10 1QL. Phone: (0843) 862253.

BROADSTAIRS. Devonhurst Hotel. A warm wel-come awaits you at our fully en-suite, licensed, seafront hotel, overlooking a sandy bay. Home cooking. Any diet. Open all year including Christmas. Short breaks anytime. Phone: (01843) 863010. ETB 3 crowns.

BROADSTAIRS. East Hornden Hotel. Comfortable, licensed. Extensive sea views. Most rooms en-suite with colour television. Excellent cuisine. Recommended. Miller, 4 Eastern Esplande, Broadstairs, Kent. AA, RAC. Phone: (0843) 868306.

BROADSTAIRS. Non smoking hotel. Character property overlooking sea. Sandy beaches. Close to town centre, harbour, station. En-suite rooms. Colour television, tea, coffee facilities. AA, RAC, ETB 3 crowns. Gull Cottage Hotel, 5 Eastern Esplanade CT10 1DP. Phone: (0843) 861936.

CANTERBURY 6 miles. Delightful 16th century country house. Comfortable rooms. Friendly atmosphere. In 3 acres of gardens. Television and tea makers in rooms. Central for coast and country. Canterbury, Dover, Ramsgate, Folkestone all within easy reach. Phone: (0227) 750973.

CANTERBURY, Tyler Hill. 1.5 miles city from city centre. Spacious house in rural setting. Double, twin, single, tea making facilities. Car parking. The Bield, 2 Canterbury Hill, Canterbury, Kent. Phone: (0227) 464621.

CANTERBURY. Saint Stephen's Guest House. Comfortable accommodation with lounge and dining room. All 12 rooms are equipped with colour television, tea, coffee facilities. Private car park. ETB. 100 Saint Stephen's Road CT2 7JL. Phone: (01227) 767644.

CANTERBURY VILLAGE. Period beamed property. Comfortable beds and delicious breakfasts. All you need for a relaxing break (midweek specials). Close to channel ferries and many different interests. Resident official tourist guide. Phone: (0304) 812217.

CLIFTONVILLE. Crescent House. Licensed. Central seafront position. Good food and friendly personal service. Tea making facilities. Some en-suite and television available. Weekly terms or special short breaks. 24 Fort Crescent, Kent CT9 IHX. Phone: (0843) 223092.

CLIFTONVILLE, Margate. Innsbrook Hotel, Dalby Square. Friendly family run hotel. Adjacent to seafront. In picturesque Square. Adequate car parking. Good home cooked food. Television and tea making in all rooms. Licensed bar, pool table. Phone: (01843) 298946.

CLIFTONVILLE, Margate. Small seafront hotel En-suite shower and toilet, television, tea making. Close winter gardens, indoor bowls. Easy reach channel ports (daytrips!). Any number of nights. Open all year. Access/Visa, telephone bookings. Details 'Malvern'. Phone: (01843) 290192. ETB.

DOVER. Talavera House. Friendly service and high standards. Short breaks or holidays. Close ferries, Channel Tunnel and attractions. ETB one crown, commended. Adult prices from £13 bed and breakfast. 275 Folkestone Road, CT17 9LL. Phone: (0(1)304) 206794.

DOVER. Elmo Guest House. 120 Folkestone Road. Family run. Conveniently situated near town centre and priory station. Single, double twin family rooms. Colour television, tea making facilities. RAC, ETB one crown. Bed and breakfast £12 - £17 per person. Phone: (0304) 206236.

DOVER. Maison Dieu Guest House. Town centre. Family run home with a big welcome. Colour television and tea making facilities in all rooms. Only 5 minutes to all ferries. 89 Maison Dieu Road. Phone: (0304) 204033.

DOVER. Wallett's Court Hotel. Lovely old manor house in scenic countryside, close to Dover. All rooms en-suite and highly commended by ETB. Notable restaurant, licensed. Gardens. Tennis court. West Cliffe, St. Margarets, Dover CT15 6EW. Phone: (0304) 852424.

DOVER. Clean, comfortable Victorian house. En-suite available. Tea/coffee making facilities. Private car park. Conveniently situated for Dover, Priory railway station, town centre and 5 minutes drive to docks and Hoverport, 10 minutes to Channel Tunnel. Phone: (01304) 202422.

DOVER. Whitmore Guest House. Small family run. Colour televisions, tea making facilities. Family rooms. En-suite double room. Near docks, station, town. 261 Folkestone Road. Special 2/3 day breaks. RAC, ETB. Phone: Annie and Steve Waymark (0304) 203080.

DOVER. 'Valjoy' Guest House. Pleasant, friendly family home near rail ferry terminals. Children welcome. Television lounge. Private car park. Cooked breakfast from 6.30am. Late arrival, early departure. Internationally recognised. Bowes, 237 Folkestone Road. Phone: (01304) 212160.

FAVERSHAM. Delightfully converted granary, in peaceful countryside. Close to Canterbury. All rooms en-suite. Guests lounge with balcony. Easy access to motorways and Channel terminals. Highly commended. The Granary, Plumford Lane, Off Brogdale Road. Phone/Fax: (01795) 538416.

FOLKESTONE. Wycliffe Hotel. Family hotel, near amenities, within easy reach of Dover, Canterbury and other interesting places. Near Channel Tunnel/Seacat. Private parking, own keys, home cooking, special diets. For brochure and details Phone/Fax: (01303) 252186.

FOLKESTONE. Family run hotel. Clean and friendly. Televisions and hospitality tray all rooms. Some en-suites. Central heating throughout. Sun lounge with bar. Near to all amenities. Short walk to promenade. For brochure Phone: (0303) 243433.

FOLKESTONE. Augusta Hotel. 3 crown. Friendly atmosphere. Well appointed accommodation. En-suite rooms, televisions, mini bars, telephones, tea and coffee facilities. Licensed. Phone: Folkestone (0303) 850952, Fax: (0303) 240282.

MARGATE. Somerville Hotel. Family run. Licensed, clean, comfortable. Overlooking sea. Excellent cuisine. Some rooms en-suite. Open all year including Christmas. For brochure write 9 Canterbury Road, Margate, Kent CT9 5AQ or Phone: (0843) 224401.

MARGATE. Bay View Guest House. Small, clean. Sea views. Near rail station. Colour television, tea making all rooms. Toilets, showers on all floors. Close to beach and town centre. Own room front door keys. Phone: (01843) 297188.

MARGATE. Bed and breakfast overlooking beach. Television satellite, tea making facilities all rooms, some rooms en-suite. 2 minutes from station and coach stop. Good food, clean and friendly. The Happy Dolphin, Phone: (0843) 296473.

RAMSGATE, Kent. Family run guest house with en-suite facilities, colour televisions and tea and coffee supplied. Offers mini breaks or summer/all year round holidays. Close to beach and all facilities. Please Phone: (0843) 589940.

RAMSGATE. Detached Regency Hotel with private car park. Licensed bar. Television, tea and coffee facilities in all rooms. Evening meals available by arrangement. Close to all attractions. Westcliff Hotel, 9 Grange Road. Phone: (0843) 581222.

RAMSGATE. Spencer Court Hotel. Listed build- ing. Quiet square overlooking gardens, tennis courts and sea. Beautiful en-suite rooms with colour television and tea making facilities. Highest standards of hygiene and cleanliness possible. Two crown commended. Phone: (01843) 594582.

RAMSGATE, Kent. Small, comfortable guest house, with en-suite and shower facilities. All rooms with televisions and tea/coffee supplies. Close to harbour and town centre. Special rates all year. Phone: The Gentle Breeze (01843) 589940.

ABBEYGAIL GUEST HOUSE
17 Penshurst Road, Ramsgate CT11 8EG
Family run in quiet residential area, near seafront, ferries and shops. Ground floor rooms, all ages welcome. Tea/coffee, colour TV all rooms. From £12.00 per person.
Contact Hazel & John Nash.
Tel: (01843) 594154

WESTGATE. Argyle Hotel. Comfortable family licensed hotel. Excellent home cooking. Tea facilities all rooms. Television lounge. Two minutes walk beach, shops, station. Barbara Mann, 63 Westgate Bay Avenue, Westgate, Kent CT8 8SW. Phone: (0843) 831808.

WESTGATE-ON-SEA. Beautiful late Victorian detached guest house. Single double and family rooms. En-suite. 100 yards from beach. Close shops. Delightfully peaceful. Single room £24, double room £40, family £50 discounts. Phone: Eve or Tony Cutler (01843) 831828.

EDGEWATER PRIVATE HOTEL
99 Sea Road, Westgate-on-Sea, Kent CT8 8QF
Tel: (0843) 831933
Contact: Eileen and Graham Colgate

Seafront position. Warm friendly welcome.
Heated indoor pool – sauna – bar.
Large lounge overlooking sea – 18 hole golf course nearby. Swimming lessons – plus scuba diving lessons.
Open all year. All rooms ensuite.

SELF-CATERING

APPLEDORE
COTTAGES AND DETACHED PINE LODGES
Idyllically situated in woodland overlooking tranquil waters, panoramic view of fields, and nearby unspoilt village. Colour TV, central heating, parking. Children and pets welcome. Facilities for coarse fishing and rough shooting.
Ashby Farms, Appledore, Ashford, Kent.
Phone: (01233) 758378

BIRCHINGTON, Minnis Bay. Well appointed sunny bungalow. Two twin bedrooms. Spacious living room with colour television. Kitchen with fridge, microwave, gas cooker. Close sea, shops, buses. Secluded garden. Regret no children or pets. Phone: 071 821 7842.

BROADSTAIRS. Three bedroom house or cot-tage, both with central heating. Sleep six plus cot. Own parking. Five minutes from sea. Clean and comfortable. Write 34 Smithamdown Road, Purley, Surrey or Phone: 081 660 1925 for further information.

BROADSTAIRS. Cliffedge, seafront, holiday flatlets. Sleeps two and three persons. Family flatlet for four. Self contained flat for four, colour televisions, centrally heated, linen supplied. No pets. Sae please. Mr Arnold, 3 The Parade. Phone: (0843) 863245.

BROADSTAIRS. Light and spacious self-cater-ing apartment with panoramic sea views. Three double bedrooms. Large garden, parking. Close to beach and golf course. Phone: (0843) 862824.

BROADSTAIRS. Self-contained, self-catering flats in middle of main bay with balconies overlooking the sea, sleep up to 6 people. Some parking available. Sae to 'Blades', 9/10 Victoria Parade, Broadstairs, Kent CT10 1QS or Phone: (0843) 861060 9 to 10.30 a.m.

BROADSTAIRS, Kent. Detached 3 bedroom house. Near beach, shops, bandstand. Central heating. Double glazed, garden. Pets allowed. Long, short let. Please Phone: (01843) 861689 or 862704.

CANTERBURY. Cottage. Quiet and comfortable. ETB inspected. 3 keys commended. Sleeps 2-4. Central heating. Furnished and decorated for a relaxing holiday. Near railway and bus stations. Details Mr Allcorn, 115 Whitstable Road, Canterbury CT2 8EF. Phone: (0227) 450265.

KNOWLTON COURT
The Estate Office, Knowlton Court, near Canterbury, Kent CT3 1PT
Tel: (0304) 842402 Fax: (0304) 842403

Self-catering properties available all year. Sleep 1-19. In quiet countryside 9 miles south-east of Canterbury and within easy reach of Channel ports. Fully furnished. Also cottages in Dorset.

CANTERBURY. Self-catering, well appointed bungalow. 1 double bedroom plus sofabed, situated in lounge. Sleeps 3. Views of cathedral from patio and garden. Short walk to city centre and cathedral. Off street parking. Phone: (01227) 471914.

VALE VIEW
RHODES MINNIS, CANTERBURY CT4 6XP
TEL: 0303 863266
Quietly situated, self-contained bungalow/annexe, sleeps 2. In area of outstanding natural beauty with lovely views. Easy reach of Canterbury, Dover and Folkestone for Channel crossings. Car essential. **£180-£198 weekly.**

CANTERBURY. Self catering Victorian mid ter-race house in quiet street in city centre. Accommodates 4/5. Available 7/7/95 to 23/9/95. £220 per week. Comfortable beds, good appliances. Convenient for the many interests in east Kent. For further details Phone: (0304) 812217.

CLIFTONVILLE. Self-contained garden flat. Adjacent seafront, shops. Fully furnished and equipped. Microwave, freezer, colour television, bedroom, kitchen, lounge, shower, toilet. Sleeps 2/5. Free linen, gas and electricity. For very reasonable terms Phone: (0843) 223506.

DEAL. Cottage, newly refurbished, sleeps 4. 300 yards from the sea. Good central position, open all year. Good for golf and fishing, but would suit all age groups. Sorry no pets. Phone: (0304) 361728.

DOVER, White Cliffs country. Holiday bunga-low at St. Margarets Bay. Sleeps 4 adults. Bedding provided. Bring own towels. Club facilities available. £75 - £260 per week. Phone: (01304) 852761.

DYMCHURCH. Honeysett Cottage, sleeps six. Comfortable and quaint, fully equipped, linen provided. Colour television. Garden, beside seaside and country-side, sandy beach. Ideal for cycling and walking. Convenient for day trips to France. Phone: (0303) 875293 evenings.

FOLKESTONE, Sandgate. Seafront self-con-tained holiday flats, sleep 2-7. Uninterrupted sea views. One or three bedrooms, lounge, colour television, kitchen, bathroom. Terms from £95. Mini breaks October - May from £50. Sae 7 Wellington Terrace CT20 3DY. Phone: (01304) 852369.

FAIRHAVEN
HOLIDAY COTTAGES
**Derby House, 123 Watling Street,
Gillingham, Kent ME7 2YY.
Phone: (01634) 570157 (24 hours)**

An extensive selection of personally inspected holiday homes. Various shapes, sizes and locations in Southern England and Wales. Available throughout the year. Featuring Kent and the Kingsdown Leisure Park nr. Deal.

COTTAGES IN THE SOUTH OF ENGLAND AND WALES

GREATSTONE, Kent. 3 bedroom detached bun-galow. Large garden. Close to sea, shops and country-side. Colour television, washing machine, microwave, central heating, double glazing, fully fitted carpets. Very good for Winter breaks. Competitive prices. Phone: 081-864 9454.

KENT·SUSSEX
SELF-CATERING SPECIALISTS
- ● Oasts & Barns
- ● Granaries
- ● Cottages

Freedom Holiday Homes
**Frittenden, Cranbrook, Kent TN17 2EP
BROCHURE Tel: (01580) 852 251
Fax: (01580) 852 455**

MARGATE. Minnis Bay. Charming, spacious, seaside cottage (former fourteenth century farmhouse, fully modernised). Five bedrooms, sleeps nine. Colour television. Large garden adjacent shops. Ample parking. Children and well behaved pets welcome. Further details Phone: (0628) 524158.

MARGATE. Self-contained holiday flat. Close to Margate beach, Dreamland and station. Sleeps 4. All facilities including linen. Clean and comfortable. Mrs D.W. Wright, 27 Canterbury Road, Margate CT9 5AW. Phone: (0843) 221966.

RAMSGATE. 2 houses and 2 apartments. Near seafront. Sleeping 3-6. ETB commended, 3-4 keys. Comfortable, well equipped. Gardens, parking. Payphones. Open all year, short breaks available out of season. Phone: (0843) 592945.

RAMSGATE. Hamilton House. Excellent posi-tion overlooking picturesque harbour and sea. Close to town centre and beaches. All apartments spacious, comfortable and well-furnished with their own facilities. Contact Mrs E.A. Burridge, 5 Nelson Crescent, Ramsgate. Phone: (01843) 582592.

ST MARY'S BAY (Dymchurch). Very large, com-fortable furnished bungalow. Sleeps 8/10 plus cots. 5 bedrooms, 2 bathrooms. Exceptionally well equipped. Washing machine, dryer, dishwasher, microwave etc. Central heating. Maintained garden, parking. Few minutes beach, shops. Realistic rents. Phone: 081 455 2577.

SUTTON VALENCE. Luxury cottage, sleeps two. Non-smokers. Panoramic views Kentish Weald. Picturesque village. 'Darling Buds of May' country as featured in television series. Within easy reach of Leeds Castle, Hever, Sissinghurst and Canterbury. Phone: (0622) 843303.

WESTBROOK (Margate approximately 1 mile). Comfortable, spacious three bedroomed house situated in quiet road. 2 minutes from Westbrook Bay and sandy beach. Lawned garden. Parking facilities. Regret no pets. Further details please Phone: 081 440 7546.

CARAVANS, CHALETS & HOLIDAY PARKS

ALLHALLOWS is one of 19 holiday parks coast to coast. Our luxury holiday homes, sleep 2-8 people. Prices start from £9 per person per night, based on 6 sharing. For a free colour brochure Phone: Lo-Call (0345) 508 508.

CANTERBURY. Small picturesque country park, overlooking Chartham Downs. Ideally situated to enjoy country walks, historic sights, coastal resorts and cross channel excursions. 4 tick graded chalets and caravans. Large outdoor swimming pool. Phone: (01227) 700306.

OAST HOUSES, KENT
(photograph courtesy of South East Tourist Board)

WHERE TO GO

Howletts Wild Animal Park
Bekesbourne, Canterbury.
Tel: (0227) 721286 - Open all year (except Christmas Day)

Big cats, Indian deer and antelope, gorillas, pongos, lemurs. Shops and cafeteria. Disabled visitors welcome.

Port Lympne Zoo Park, Mansion and Gardens
Lympne, Hythe.
Tel: (0303) 264646 - Open all year (except Christmas Day)

A large well-stocked zoo, specialising in breeding rare animals. Mansion with art gallery, exhibitions. Safari trailer journey. Restaurant, cafeteria, kiosks and barbecue in summer. Disabled visitors welcome. Free car park.

Dover Castle and Hellfire Corner
Dover, Kent.
Tel: (0304) 201628

One of the most powerful medieval fortresses in Western Europe St Mary in Castro Saxon Church, Roman lighthouse, Hellfire Corner. All the Queen's Men exhibition and Battle of Waterloo model.

Whitbread Hop Farm
Beltring Paddock Wood, Kent.
Tel: (0622) 872068

Largest collection of Victorian oasts in the world, rural museums, play area, animal village, birds of prey, pottery workshop. Whitbread shire horses. Hop story exhibition.

Powell Cotton Museum
Quex House and Gardens, Quex Park, Birchington, Kent.
Tel: (0843) 42168

Regency house with period furniture, Museum with ethnographic collections, diorama of African and Asian animal, weapons, archaeology and Chinese porcelain.

The Historic Dockyard
Chatham, Kent.
Tel: (0634) 812551

Historic 18th Century 80 acre dockyard, now living museum. Former HMS Gannet undergoing restoration. Sail and colour loft, ordnance mews, 'Wooden Walls' gallery.

OXFORDSHIRE

HOTELS & GUEST HOUSES

BAMPTON. 17th century Georgian building, traditional inn-restaurant just refurbished. 9 en-suite bedrooms. Quiet village location. Good food reputation. Chef proprietor. Well recommended. 3 nights £80, 7 nights £150 per couple. Brochures Phone: (0993) 850237. Romany Inn.

BAMPTON. Country pub close to Cotswolds, Vale of White Horse, Oxford. All rooms en-suite with tea, coffee and colour television. Double room for two people from £30 with breakfast. Special weekly rates. Phone: (0993) 850316.

WITNEY. Field View, Woodgreen. In quiet set-ting. Close to Witney town centre. Ideal for Cotswolds and Oxford. All rooms en-suite, with colour television and tea making facilities. ETB 2 crowns highly commended. Phone: Simpson (01993) 705485.

WOODSTOCK. Double and single rooms on ground floor. Family room, en-suite, shower, toilet and washbasin. First floor colour television and tea/coffee facilities in double and family rooms. 35 Wroslyn Road, Freeland, Oxon. Phone: (0993) 882003.

SELF-CATERING

COTSWOLDS

Personal service for quality cottages in Oxfordshire & Gloucestershire. Linen & towels, colour TV, well equipped. Free brochure: Manor Cottages, Village Farm, Little Barrington, Burford OX18 4TE. TEL: 01451 844643.

English Tourist Board
REGISTERED AGENCY

STEEPLE ASTON. Very comfortable flat in grounds. Small country house. Tasteful decor, exposed beams, fully equipped. Peaceful location. Convenient for Oxford, Warwick, Stratford, Cotswolds. Warm welcome guaranteed. ETB 4 key highly commended. Phone: (0869) 340238.

WHERE TO GO

Broughton Castle
Banbury, Oxfordshire.
Tel: (0295) 262624

Medieval moated house built in 1300 and enlarged between 1550 and 1600. The home of Lord and Lady Saye and Sele. Civil war connections.

Blenheim Palace
Woodstock, Oxforshire.
Tel: (0993) 811091

Birthplace of Sir Winston Churchill, designed by Vanbrugh with park designed by Capability Brown. Adventure play area, maze, butterfly house, garden centre and Churchill exhibition.

The Oxford Story
6 Broad Street, Oxford, Oxfordshire.
Tel: (0865) 728822

Heritage centre depicting 800 years of university history in sights, sounds, personalities and smells. Visitors are transported in moving desks with commentary of their choice.

Waterperry Gardens
Waterperry, Oxfordshire.
Tel: (0844) 339254

Ornamental gardens covering 6 acres of 83 acre 18th Century Waterperry House estate. Saxon village church, garden shop and tea shop.

Didcot Railway Centre
Great Western Railway, Didcot, Oxfordshire.
Tel: (0235) 817200

Living museum recreating the golden age of the Great Western Railway. Steam locomotives and trains, engine shed and small relics museum. Steam days and gala events.

Cotswold Wildlife Park
Burford, Oxfordshire.
Tel: (0993) 823006

180 acres of gardens and woodland, large and varied collection of animals from all over the world, reptile house, aquarium, bat exhibit, tropical house, picnicking areas, adventure playground and narrow-gauge railway.

SURREY

HOTELS & GUEST HOUSES

GATWICK
STAITH HOUSE

Accommodation close to Horley town and station. 6 minutes Gatwick airport. All rooms, colour TV, hot and cold, central heating, tea making facilities. Free courtesy transport available. Guest parking by arrangement.
Tariff from £17.50
Phone: (01293) 785170

REDHILL. Lynwood Guest House. Gatwick 10 minutes by train or car. 5 minutes to station, shops and leisure facilities. 30 minutes to London by train. Most rooms en-suite with colour television, tea facilities. Phone: (0737) 766894.

WHERE TO GO

Birdworld Bird Park, Gardens and Underworld
Holt Pound, Farnham, Surrey.
Tel: (0420) 22140

All kinds of birds ranging from penguins to ostriches. Underworld is a large aquarium of tropical fish. Shop, cafeterias, snack bar and picnic area. Disabled visitors welcome.

Chessington World of Adventures
Leatherhead Road, Chessington, Surrey.
Tel: (0372) 727227
About 480 animals located in a large section of this well-known theme park. Animals include wallaby's, monkeys, polar bears, big cats, sealions, camels, reptile house and children's zoo. Restaurant mother and baby room. Disabled visitors welcome.

Great Cockcrow Miniature Railway
Harwick Lan, Lyne.
Tel: (0932) 228950
There are steam and diesel locomotives on a fully signalled track. Refreshments available.

Guildford Cathedral
Guildford, Surrey
Tel: (0483) 65287
Anglican cathedral, foundation stone laid in 1963 and consecrated in 1961. Notable glass engravings, embroided kneelers, modern furnishings. Brass rubbing centre.

Thorpe Park
Staines Road, Chertsey, Surrey.
Tel: (0932) 562633
Over 100 rides and attractions especially for families with children 4-14 years. These include the Flying Fish family roller-coaster, Depth Charge, Carousel Kingdom, Loggers leap, Thunder river, Thorpe Farm and Fantasy Reef and playpools.

South of England Rare Breeds Centre
Highland Farm, Woodchurch, Nr. Ashford.
Tel: (0233) 861493
A collection of 55 rare farm breeds on a 90 acre working farm. There are pigs, sheep, goats, rabbits and cattle which may be touched in the kiddies corner, also farm trailer or horse-drawn cart rides and pony rides in the summer. Nature trails, a woodland walk and demonstrations of grooming milking and shearing.

BLUEBELLS
(photograph courtesy of South East England Tourist Board)

SUSSEX

HOTELS & GUEST HOUSES

ARUNDEL. Mill Lane House, Slindon BN18 ORP. In National Trust village. Views to coast. Rooms en-suite, excellent walking. Visit Arundel, Goodwood, Chichester. Good pubs walking distance. Evening meals by arrangement. Bed and breakfast £18. Phone: (01243) 814440.

BOGNOR REGIS. Selwood Lodge, 93 Victoria Drive. Small family hotel. Good food, bar, lounge, games room, television. Tea making facilities all rooms. No restrictions. Access, Visa welcomed. Phone: Mrs Bodle (0243) 865071.

BRIGHTON. Kimberley Hotel. Comfortable licensed hotel. 15 bedrooms with shower, colour television, central heating, tea making facilities. Some en-suite. Centrally situated. Near sea front. ETB, AA, RAC members. Terms from £15. 17 Atlingworth Street. Phone: (01273) 603504.

BRIGHTON MARINA HOUSE HOTEL

8 Charlotte Street, Marine Parade, Brighton BN2 1AG
Tel: (0273) 605349 and 679484. Fax: (0273) 605349
Your satisfaction is our first concern
Highly recommended, cosy, well-kept and equipped, elegantly furnished Victorian family hotel in conservation area in a quiet street. Comfortable, clean, caring, hospitable. Near sea, central for Palace Pier, Royal Pavilion, Lanes, Conference and Exhibition halls, tourist and business attractions and facilities. Few minutes to Marina. Single/Double/twin/triple/family/standard and en-suite rooms. Licensed restaurant; English breakfast; English, Chinese and Indian cuisine. Flexible breakfast time. 24-hour access/check in/out. Luggage storage. Cards accepted. Hen parties welcome. Best in price range – £13.50 to £31.
THE GUESTS WHO PASS THROUGH OUR DOORS ARE THE MOST IMPORTANT PEOPLE.

Les Routier **RAC** **AA**
ACCLAIMED QQQ

BRIGHTON. Chester Court, 7 Charlotte Street. Highly recommended with charm and character. Modern facilities and refurbishment. High standards. Proprietors eighteen years experience welcome new and old friends. Phone: (0273) 621750. Bed and breakfast from £17-£20.

BRIGHTON. Diana House. Friendly, traditional guest house close seafront, marina, conference centre and town. All rooms with shower, colour television, tea/coffee facilities, some en-suite. Well behaved pets welcome. Phone for details (0273) 605797.

BRIGHTON. Kimberley Hotel, licensed. Central- ly situated, one minute from seafront. 15 bedrooms with shower, television, tea making facilities. Bed and breakfast £15 to £20 per person per night. 17 Atlingworth Street, Brighton. Phone: (01273) 603504.

BRIGHTON. Chester Court, Charlotte Street BN2 1AG. Highly recommended. Maintaining its charm and character. Offering modern facilities and refurbishment to high standards. Best in bed and breakfast. Prices retained throughout year. £17 - £20 per person. Phone: (0273) 621750.

Please mention
Daltons Directory
when replying
to advertisements

BRIGHTON. Elegant hotel. Ideally situated near seafront, shops and entertainments. All rooms en-suite, bathrooms, television, teas making, hairdryers, phone, 4 poster bedrooms for romantics!!! Licensed bar, choice of breakfast. From £18, Andorra Hotel, Oriental Place. Phone: (0273) 321787.

BRIGHTON. Oak Hotel. 3 star AA/RAC. Modern comfortable, centrally located hotel just off the seafront. All rooms en-suite and television, tea/coffee making facilities. Close all Brighton amenities. Informal atmosphere. Bar and restaurant. Ideal short breaks. Phone: (01273) 220033.

BRIGHTON. Marina House Hotel. Highly recom- mended offers best best in Victorian and Regency Brighton. Situated in the heart of Kemptown. 1 minutes walk from seafront. All facilities. Near business/tourist amenities/attractions. Best in price range. Phone/fax: (0273) 605349.

EASTBOURNE. Small friendly family run hotel in central position. Heating, television, tea and coffee making facilities in all rooms, some en-suite. Choice of menu, separate tables. Licensed. Open all year. Cromwell Hotel. Phone: (01323) 725288.

EASTBOURNE. Edelweiss Hotel. Family-run hotel. 50 yards from seafront. Rooms with television and tea-making. Weekly bed and breakfast from £85, half board from £105. Limited en-suites. Peter & Sally Butler, 10-12 Elms Avenue, Eastbourne. Phone: (0323) 732071.

EASTBOURNE
BRACKEN GUEST HOUSE
Comfortable and friendly. Traditional home cooking. Beautifully decorated rooms, en-suite available. Close to seafront.
01323 725779

EASTBOURNE, "Lynmar". Family run, homely guest house. Television and tea-making in rooms. Near sea and shops. Moderate terms. Short breaks and mid week bookings available. No. 8 St. Aubyns Road, Phone: (0323) 732757.

Ambria House
Small and friendly family guest house. Choice of good home cooked food. Residential licence. Three minutes level walk to sea front, 10 minutes from our excellent shopping centre and theatres.

S.A.E. please to Amanda & Brian Bignell

85 Pevensey Road, Eastbourne,
East Sussex BN22 8AD
Telephone: (01323) 642303

EASTBOURNE. Sunningdale Guest House. High- ly recommended. Wholesome food. Separate tables. Tea-coffee making facilities. Television lounge. 3 minutes sea, shops. Bed and breakfast, evening dinner £85 to £99.50 according to season. Established 23 years. Sae 63 Pevensey Road. Phone: (0323) 723928.

EASTBOURNE. Non-smokers only. Close sea, centre, theatres. Family run. All rooms en-suite with colour television. Phone: Arden Hotel, 17 Burlington Place, (0323) 639639 for details.

EASTBOURNE. A 'Fawlty Towers' type hotel. Superb seafront location. Family owned. 'You come as a guest and leave as a friend'. (Basil) and (Sybil) (T.M. Cooper). Malvern House Private Hotel, 82 Royal Parade, Eastbourne, East Sussex. Phone: (01323) 721969.

EASTBOURNE. Cherry Tree Hotel. A small friendly family run hotel offering a high standard of service. Facilities, and cuisine. All rooms en-suite, with colour television, tea making facilities and telephone, 15 Silverdale Road. Phone: (01323) 722406.

EASTBOURNE. Bay Lodge Hotel. Ideal seafront location. 12 bedrooms, all doubles en-suite. 1 ground floor bedroom. Sun lounge. Non smokers lounge. Hospitality trays. Unrestricted street parking. AA 3 'Q' grading awarded. RAC 'acclaimed'. ETB 3 crowns commended. 61/62 Royal Parade. Phone: (01323) 732515.

EASTBOURNE. James Hotel. Off seafront, (2 minutes). Close theatres, Devonshire Park. En-suite, selection beverages, colour television, hair dryers all rooms. Fresh food daily. Quality, friendly small hotel. Phone: James (0323) 732503 for information pack.

EASTBOURNE. Cheriton Guest House. Family run, in quiet residential area. Close seafront. All rooms colour television and tea making facilities. Excellent home cooking served at separate tables. No parking restrictions. 34 Redoubt Road. Phone: (01323) 735446.

EASTBOURNE. Bisenden Private Hotel. 5 min- utes level walk from sea, shopping centre, rail - coach stations. Licensed. ETB 3 crown. Some en-suite bedrooms. Tea making facilities available. Special Christmas programme. Contact Joyce Bailey, 91 Pevensey Road. Phone: (01323) 723467.

HASSOCKS. Bed and breakfast in large coun- try house with beautiful views over the Weald. Ideal walking, cycling South Downs way. Only 15 minutes from Brighton. Colour television in rooms. Library. Parking. Always a warm welcome. Phone: (0273) 843363.

HASTINGS town centre. Holiday guest house. Close rail, bus stations and beach. All rooms with colour television, central heating, tea making. Some en-suite. Bed and breakfast £13 to £16. Steele, Amberlene, 12 Cambridge Gardens. Phone: (0424) 439447.

LANCING. Holiday accommodation close to sea. All rooms hot and cold, one en-suite, shower. Tea making facilities, television lounge. Bed and breakfast £12.50 daily, children reduced rates when sharing. Ford, 96 Penhill Road. Phone (0903) 767723.

LEWES, Bankside. Family bed and breakfast. En-suite, television, children welcome. Situated between historic Lewes and Newhaven Ferry on South Downs Way, close to Glyndebourne. This delightful village was once the home of Virginia Woolf. Phone: (0273) 477058.

LEWES. Bankside, Rodmell. Comfortable, friendly bed and breakfast. En-suite. Television. Situated in delightful village once the home of Virginia Woolf. Near Glyndebourne, Newhaven ferry and on South Downs way. A real home from home. Phone: (0273) 477058.

LITTLEHAMPTON, West Sussex. Sharoleen licensed Hotel. Smoking restricted. Small, comfortable, friendly. Good home cooking. Bed and breakfast from £10.00. Evening meals from £4.00. Some en-suites. Ideal touring. Near sandy beach, river, town. Brochure Phone: (0903) 713464.

LITTLEHAMPTON. Quayside guest house. Family run. All rooms en-suite with colour television, tea making facilities. 2 minutes from sea and town centre. Evening meals available. Access at all times. Children welcome. Overlooking harbour. Phone: (0903) 721958.

LITTLEHAMPTON. Victoria Hotel. Comfortable family run hotel. All rooms colour television, tea making facilities, hot and cold. Close to all amenities. Bed and breakfast or residential accommodation. 59 New Road. Phone: Littlehampton 717175.

LITTLEHAMPTON. Tudor Lodge. Family run guest house. Full English breakfast. Most rooms en-suite with colour television and tea making facilities. Family rooms. Pets welcome. Car parking access all times. Payphone for guests. Phone: (0903) 716203.

LITTLEHAMPTON. Licensed hotel overlooking the seafront. Short walk to river, leisure facilities and shops. All rooms have private toilet and shower, television, hairdryer, telephone and hospitality tray. Colbern Hotel, South Terrace. Phone: (01903) 714270, Fax: (01903) 730955.

PEVENSEY BAY. Driftwood. Comfortable fam- ily home. Full English breakfast. Television lounge. Television, tea-making, washbasins all bedrooms. Good local pub grub. Village centre. Two minutes from beach. £12.50 - £15. Parking. 36 Eastbourne Road. Phone: (0323) 768530.

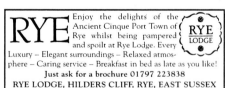
SEAFORD. 'Sunnyside', 23 Connaught Road. Comfortable family house. 120 yards from sea. Situated between Eastbourne and Brighton. 3 miles Newhaven Ferry and South Downs Way. Bed and breakfast only. Phone: Roberts (0323) 895850.

SELSEY. South of Chichester. St. Andrews Lodge Guest House. ETB three crowns commended. Licensed. Friendly, relaxed atmosphere. All rooms en-suite. Satellite television. Secluded garden. Ample parking. Reductions on short breaks and weekly bookings. Phone: (0243) 606899.

WADHURST. Dale Hill Hotel and Golf Club. High on the weald, our modern purpose built 4 star hotel offers every luxury. The restaurant overlooks our 18 hole golf course. Gastranomic cuisine. 30 bedrooms. Phone: (0580) 200112.

WEST CHILTINGTON. Newhouse Farm. Bed, breakfast. XVth century beamed farmhouse. Log fires in Winter. En-suite, television, beverage trays. Golf course 1/4 mile. Wildfowl reserve 3 miles, Gatwick 35 minutes. Steele, Pulborough RH20 2LA. Phone: (01798) 812215. ETB 2 crown commended. Historic area.

WINCHELSEA. The Strand House. 15th century house of charm and character with low beams and inglenooks. En-suite rooms. 4 poster available. Television and beverage facilities. Ample parking. Rural aspect. Good base for exploring. Phone: (0797) 226276.

BRACKLESHAM BAY (Chichester). Detached. One minute beach/launching ramp. Near shops. 2/3 bedrooms, big living room, dining kitchen. Automatic washing machine, dishwasher, video, cot. Secluded garden, 2-car parking. Phone: (0243) 670038, (0243) 670614 or (0952) 813864.

BRACKLESHAM BAY. Three bedroomed detached bungalow. 100 yards from beach. Large garden. Sleeps 6 to 8. Well equipped. Available from March. Chichester 7 miles. Local sailing, fishing, golf and many places of interest. Phone: (0243) 670613.

BRIGHTON, 12 miles (Cuckfield). Delightful single-storey cottage in an idyllic rural setting. Conveniently situated for historic houses and gardens, coast and London. Well equipped and highly recommended. Sleeps 2-4. For brochure please Phone: (0444) 451472.

BRIGHTON. Bodmin Court. Council approved. Modern spacious self-contained flats, 2-6 persons. Comfortably furnished, completely equipped, everything provided. Good residential area. Easy access shopping transportation, seafront, places of interest. Open all year. Free parking. Phone: (01273) 326963/720233.

WORTHING
NEW EVERSLEY HOTEL & RESTAURANT
Family run Victorian Hotel close Beach House Park & sea. Full licence á la carté or table d'hôte restaurant. En-suite rooms available. All rooms colour TV, phone, tea/coffee facilities. Ramped access to ground floor rooms for partially disabled. No steps.
PHONE: (01903) 239827

BRIGHTON SEAFRONT
SUPERB FULLY EQUIPPED PRIVATE HOLIDAY APARTMENTS LOCATED ABOVE THE RENOWNED 4-STAR HOTEL METROPOLE
Lifts to all hotel facilities including free use of indoor swimming pool.
Tourist Board Classification: 3 keys – Highly Commended.
For colour brochure telephone:
Harold or Valerie Williams on 01273 302431

BRIGHTON. 7 minutes walk from the sea, con-ference centre and many other attractions. Delightful, spacious, quietly situated 3 bedroom house with attractive views. Sleeps 6. Sun terrace overlooking park containing children's play area. Phone: 071 352 6799.

BRIGHTON. Seafront spacious 3rd floor flat. Lounge. Sea views. Kitchen. 2 bedrooms, bathroom, 2 toilets. Bed linen provided. Central heating, gas £1 meter. £175-£250 per week. Private parking. Phone: (0273) 687399.

BRIGHTON. Near seafront. Two well main-tained houses, sleep 4/10 with ground floor cloakrooms. Well fitted kitchens, microwave, etc., colour televisions, patios/gardens (small dogs allowed), parking. Also enquire Arts and Activity Holidays Phone: (0273) 304337/724862.

BRIGHTON. Penthouses. 1, 2 or 3 bedroomed, above the superb 4 star hotel Metropole. Panoramic sea and/or town views. Access by lifts to hotel facilities, free use of luxury heated indoor swimming pool. Also elegant Brighton marina apartment. Phone: (0273) 600503, Fax: (0273) 600560.

SELF-CATERING

ANGMERING-ON-SEA. Period cottage, sleeps two. Central heating, television, telephone. Adjacent sea and village. Summer/winter lets. Phone: (0903) 234144.

ARUNDEL. Self-contained ground floor annexe near sea and South Downs. Lounge, diner, kitchen, bathroom, shower, toilet, two bedrooms, sleeping four. Bed linen included. Parking space. For details and availability Phone: Mrs Bitten (01903) 883260.

ASHBURNHAM
NEAR BATTLE
SLIVERICKS FARM
Attractive fully equipped holiday cottage, on stud farm. Sleeps 4-6. In quiet countryside with spectacular views of sea and downs. Pets welcome. Reasonable rates. Linen included. Good base for touring, golf, fishing, riding.
Phone Mrs. Wheeler (0435) 830571

BEXHILL. Modern detached chalet style three bedroom house. Superior purpose built two bedroom flat. Adjacent seafront. Available holidays, short term tenancies. Central heating, colour television. Garden, garage and parking. Competitive rates. ETB three keys. Phone: (0424) 220060.

BRACKLESHAM BAY
3 bedroom bungalow with all facilities. Colour television, close to sea.
From £250-£300 per week
Phone: (0181) 397 2161

HOME *from* HOME
HOLIDAYS
Self-catering Cottages, Houses, Bungalows and Flats in West Sussex

Seaside and rural locations available throughout the year

BOGNOR REGIS TO BRIGHTON
1-4 weeks

For free Brochure Please Contact:
2-3 Churchill Court, 112 The Street, RUSTINGTON, West Sussex BN163DU Tel: 01903 787040 Fax: 774137

Association of Residential Letting Agents

Nationwide

BRIGHTON. Dolphin House Holiday Flats and Flatlets. Colour television, fridges. Reasonably priced. Near all amenities. Shops, seafront, sea and pier views. All flats with showers or baths. Cade, 24 Rock Garden. Phone: (0273) 696186.

BRIGHTON. Town house, North Laine. Near station. Kitchen/diner, utility room, lounge, 3 bedrooms (sleeps 7), bathroom, shower room. Comfortably furnished, television, video, microwave. July, August, September £195-£265 per week. Phone: Brian (01737) 354813 or Lindsey (01273) 620664.

BRIGHTON Marina Holiday Apartments. Luxury apartments. Beautifully furnished. Highest possible award from the ETB. Fully fitted kitchen. Free parking. Susan Wills, 5 Mariners Quay, Brighton Marina, Brighton, Sussex. Phone/Fax: (0273) 693569.

CHICHESTER. Two delightful, 2 bedroomed cottages. (10 minutes walk from city centre). Television, washing machine, telephone (incoming calls only). Gas central heating, and electricity included. Fully equipped. Pets by arrangement. Linen provided. Brochure Phone: (0243) 371370.

CROWBOROUGH. Comfortable, well equipped three bedroom bungalow. Fully fitted kitchen. Secluded garden, garage - parking. Sleeps 6/7. Walking distance Ashdown Forest. Good centre touring Sussex, Kent. Easy reach South coast. Details Phone: (0892) 661948.

CROWHURST, near Battle. Country cottage on dairy farm. Fully equipped, including bed linen, shower, colour television, woodburner. Riding, fishing, golf nearby. For short breaks and longer holidays Phone: Mrs Butler (0424) 852505 for brochure.

EASTBOURNE. Bungalows on Kings Park. Two bedrooms, lounge, kitchenette, bathroom. Easy parking. Level location. Also ground floor apartment. Three bedrooms, lounge, dining room, kitchen, two bathrooms. Phone: Mrs Thompson (0323) 728369.

EASTBOURNE. First floor self-contained re- decorated cosy flat. Two non-smoking adults. Edge South Downs. Ideal sightseeing base for famous beauty spots. Nearby walks, woods, tennis. Parking, bus routes. Weeks, breaks, all year. Phone: (0323) 646971.

EASTBOURNE. Lovely self-catering bungalows. Also luxury house. Open all year. Parking. Near amenities. Children, pets welcome. Quiet site. Close to marina, park, swimming pool, supermarket, restaurants. For brochure Phone: (0323) 764746 Chesterman.

EASTBOURNE (East Dean). Detached chalet/ bungalow, garage. 3 double bedrooms (1 ground floor with cloakroom), refrigerator, colour television, central heating. Superb sea and downland views. Available all year. Personally supervised and visitors met on arrival. Phone: 081 644 7271 or (0323) 422303.

EASTBOURNE. Seafront. Immaculate self-con- tained holiday flats for couples. Also nearby flats and 200 year old cottage for up to 4 persons. Fully equipped. Good rates and high standards. Open all year. Discounts April - May. Phone: (01323) 723248.

EASTBOURNE. Travancore holiday apartments. Self-contained. Colour television. Linen. Towels and hot water included. Excellent position opposite Congress Theatre. Winter Gardens. Just off seafront. Lift, car park. For brochure, Tang,Wilmington Gardens. Phone: (0323) 723770.

EASTBOURNE seafront. Large, comfortable ground floor flat. Between Princes Park and Redoubt. Sitting room, toilet/shower, kitchen/diner, twin bedroom. Central heating. Television. All amenities. Bed linen supplied. Unrestricted car parking. Vacancies June - September. £128. Phone: (0323) 734472 pm.

FAIRLIGHT, near Hastings. Large centrally heated house. Carpeted throughout. Sleeps 12. Suitable two families sharing. Panoramic views from lounge of sea and Downs. Games room. Large enclosed garden. Phone: 081 852 9062 or (0424) 813429.

FERRING-BY-SEA, Sussex. Georgian style house in delightful village. Situated between sea, downs. Peaceful setting near church. Five minutes shops, Chichester, Arundel, Brighton easy drive. Sleeps four. Central heating. Television. Garage. Pretty enclosed garden. Details Phone: (0727) 853136.

HENFIELD, Sussex. 3 holiday cottages. Quiet. On working farm. Open plan lounge, diner, kitchen. 2 or 3 bedrooms, bathroom. Fully equipped. Duvets, bed linen provided. Private gardens and parking. Phone: (0273) 492457.

LITTLEHAMPTON (seafront). Self-contained holiday flat. Private balcony. Lovely accommodation. Sleeps 2/5 persons. Also smaller flatlet. Both well equipped, overlooking sea. (En-suite bed and breakfast also available). Sae brochure: A. Wakefield, 86 South Terrace, Littlehampton, Sussex BN17 5LJ. Phone: (0903) 715092.

NEWICK, East Sussex. Large country house, sleeps 9. Fully equipped. Microwave, television, washing machine, dryer, cooker, dishwasher, telephone, linen. Large lawned garden, swimming pool. Places of interest nearby beautiful countryside views. Ample parking. Phone: (0825) 724135.

NEWICK, East Sussex. Small chalet bunga- low, sleeps 2-4. Fully equipped. Television, linen provided, heated swimming pool. Situated between 2 villages in quiet country lane. Beautiful countryside views. Various seaside resorts 30 minutes by car. Phone: (0825) 724135.

NORMANS BAY. Between Eastbourne and Bexhill. Ground floor self-contained holiday flat, beside quiet beach. Sleeps two. Colour television etc. Ideal touring centre. Sorry no pets. Rates from £60 per week. Details Phone: (0323) 763961.

NORMANS BAY. Particularly comfortable warm bungalow, sleeps four. Actually built on beach. Very quiet and peaceful in both winter and summer. Panoramic views of sea/South Downs. River/sea fishing. Regret no children/pets. Phone: (0273) 400511.

PEVENSEY BAY. Modern self-contained first floor flat with parking. Facilities: lounge, colour television, fitted kitchen, two bedrooms, toilet and bathroom, all electric. Please state dates. Four adults. No pets. Minute sea. Miss Pattison. Phone: (0903) 743334.

POLEGATE. On the edge of Arlington. Reser- voir, lakeside side bungalows. Sleeps 4-6. Lounge, dining area, bathroom, kitchen. Car essential, parking. Children, pets welcome. Open May to October. Weekly terms from £140. Mrs P. Boniface. Phone: (0323) 870111.

SELSEY. Charming detached bungalow, seclu- ded garden. Sleeps 6 plus cot. 5 minutes walk from quiet beach. Set in quiet unmade road, with little traffic. Ideal for young children. Pets welcome by arrangement. Phone: (0306) 631768.

ST LEONARDS. Spacious 1 bedroom flat with lift and communal garden. Very close to the sea. Quiet area. Non smokers. £125 to £150 per week. Phone: 071 483 2293.

WORTHING. Well furnished spacious flats, quietly situated elegant Edwardian house. 3 minutes level walk sea and shops. Sleep up to 4 persons. Torrington Holiday Flats, 60 Manor Road, Worthing. Phone: (01903) 238582, 814988 or (0860) 699268 Joyce Elsden.

CARAVANS, CHALETS & HOLIDAY PARKS

AMBERLEY, Arundel. Heart of South Downs, alongside River Arun. Fully serviced and equipped modern 6 berth caravans. Walkers' paradise. Four minutes main line Victoria. Regret no pets. Houghton Bridge Caravan Park, Amberley, Arundel, West Sussex BN18 9LP. Phone: (0798) 831558.

ARLINGTON. Farm holiday caravan, sleeps 6, 2 bedrooms plus bed settee. Full bathroom facilities, heating, microwave, linen included. Small outdoor pool. Between Brighton, Eastbourne. Hobden, Chilverbridge Farm, Arlington, Polegate, Sussex BN26 6SB. Phone: (0323) 870349.

BATTLE. Quiet detached chalet. Two bed- rooms, fully equipped, colour television, microwave. In grounds of lovely country hotel with all facilities available. Golf and horse riding nearby. Phone: 071-404 2674 day, (0424) 870866 evenings or weekends (Mr/Mrs) Jeffery.

BOGNOR REGIS riverside. Four berth caravan, fully equipped. All mains services. Clubhouse, swimming and paddling pools, childrens playground, shops etc. Television. Phone: Joel 081-441 1943.

BRACKLESHAM BAY. Luxury chalet, Sussex beach holiday village. Two bedrooms, sleeps 6. Fitted kitchen with microwave and freezer. Full size bathroom, all electric. Full entertainment programme, cabaret every evening. Linen included. Non-smokers preferred. Phone: (0243) 672705.

BRACKLESHAM BAY. Caravan to let, ideal for family holidays. Close to beach. Weekends/short breaks available. Golf and fishing nearby. 3 bedrooms (sleeps 6), kitchen, bathroom, lounge. Reasonable rates. Sorry no pets. Phone: (0737) 221155/(0243) 671387.

BRIGHTON AREA. Modern four berth caravan on dairy farm, near South Downs. Peaceful situation, wide views. Beach 5 miles. Shop, pub nearby. Good base for touring Sussex. Reasonable rates. For details Phone: (0273) 493157.

CAMBER SANDS Leisure Park. Four and six berth chalets to let on superb site. Indoor fun pools, nightly entertainment, kids club, amusements, restaurant, health club, water sports and golf nearby. Clean, sandy beach. Phone: 0268 523036.

CAMBER SANDS. Leisure Park. 6 berth chalet. Heated 4 indoor pools. Nightly entertainment. Colour television, microwave. Walking distance to the beach and local shops. No dogs. Families only. Phone: 071 733 6883. One open air swimming pool.

CAMBER SANDS, Sussex. 6 berth luxury caravan. Great local attractions. Day trips to France. Sandy beach, clubhouse, shops, pools, sauna, gym, restaurants. Families only. No pets. Non smokers. Discounts on 2 week bookings. Phone: (0734) 722779.

CAMBER SANDS. Camber Sands Leisure Park. 3 bedroom luxury 1993 caravan. Separate shower and toilet. Fully fitted kitchen. Lounge, gas fire, colour television. Families only. Sorry no dogs. Short breaks available. Phone: 081 402 1303 answer phone.

EASTBOURNE. Castle View, Pevensey Bay. Modern static caravans. 2 bedrooms, bathroom, colour televisions. All facilities for touring caravans, tents. On quiet privately owned family site, in countryside. Close by sea and Eastbourne. Brochures Phone: (0323) 763038.

GOLDEN CROSS, near Hailsham. 11 miles Eastbourne. Static luxury holiday caravans for sale on quiet country park. Near to South Downs. All services. Ideal for leisure pursuits. Touring caravans/motorised welcome. Static caravan for hire. Phone: (01825) 872532.

HASTINGS. Combe Haven Holiday Park. 8 berth caravan. Colour television, microwave. 3 bedrooms. 2 night clubs. Children allowed. Fun palace. Indoor and outdoor heated swimming pools. roller, disco, adventure playground. Phone: (0734) 416900.

HASTINGS. Privately owned 6-berth caravan on country site. Newly refurbished. Shower - wc. Gas, electricity, bed linen included. Colour television. On-site facilities include clubhouse, fishing lake. Beautiful scenery. Convenient for touring. Competitive rates. Phone: (0892) 535570.

HASTINGS. Luxury three bedroom caravan. Sleeps up to eight. Fully fitted. Situated on one of Havens top holiday parks. Free use of all excellent facilities including two swimming pools. Full entertainment programme. Phone: (0424) 219227.

HASTINGS. Combe Haven Holiday Park. Caravan, sleeps 7. Club, children's fun palace, indoor - outdoor pools, crown bowls (all weather) pitch and putt, all weather outdoor sports area. Launderette, shops. Private garden. Phone: (0634) 570807.

HASTINGS. Combe Haven Holiday Park. 7 berth caravan. Colour television, shower. Entertainment including night club, swimming pools, roller disco and much more for all the family. Gas, electric, hot water, entertainment free. Phone: 081 641 5974.

LITTLEHAMPTON. Ideal centre for exploring the South coast. Caravan leisure homes on pleasant park between seaside, Littlehampton and historic Arundel. Mains services. No dogs. Some for sale too. 'Brookside', Lyminster, Littlehampton, West Sussex BN17 7QE. Phone: (01903) 713292.

NEWHAVEN. One mile, quiet rural park. 4/6/8 berth caravans with electric, water, toilet. Pets welcome. From £85 to £160 all plots fenced. Two fishing lakes. Personal supervision. Resident owner. Small shop. Ansaphone days, Phone: (0273) 514950 evenings.

PAGHAM. Church Farm is one of 19 holiday parks coast to coast. Our luxury holiday homes, sleep 2-8 people. Prices start from £9 per person per night, based on 6 sharing. For a free colour brochure Phone: Lo-Call (0345) 508 508.

RYE BAY CARAVAN PARK
Winchelsea Beach, Sussex TN36 4NE
(Nr. Rye and Hastings)
4/6 berth caravans available. Ideal family holiday, adjoining beach, shop, licensed club, entertainment, games room, children's playground. Touring caravans welcome. Also new and secondhand caravans for sale on site.
For brochure phone:
RYE (0797) 226340

SELSEY, West Sands. Modern fully equipped 6 berth caravan. Shower, toilet, colour television. Well maintained. Indoor swimming pool, clubs, shops and entertainment on site. Reasonable rates. Phone: (0442) 243249.

SELSEY, West Sands, West Sussex. 4 - 6 and 8 berth, all mains. Caravans fully equipped and well maintained. Shower, toilet. Colour television. Clubs, entertainments, swimming pools. By the sea. Restaurant and supermarkets. Phone: (01734) 692859 and (01243) 607562.

WITTERINGS older style, large, mobile home with five rooms, on residential site, surrounded by fields. Fully furnished with two bedrooms, bathroom and television. Sleeps four. Five minutes' walk to sea and nearby shops. Phone: (0243) 779885.

WHERE TO GO

Tangmere Military Museum
Tangmere Airfield, Tangmere, Nr Chichester
Tel: (0243) 775223

A famous Battle of Britain airfield but now the home of a museum of the history of military aviation in West Sussex, with relics, maps, photos, medals and uniforms. There are working models and a flight simulator for children, also a Hawker Hunter jet fighter and a T33 american trainer. There is a new hanger, which contains full size aircraft and other displays. Souvenir shop and bookstall. Light refreshments, picnic area.

Amberley Museum
Houghton Bridge, Amberley, Nr Arundel
Tel: (0798) 831370

An exciting working museum set in the beautiful South Downs. Here you can visit our craftsmen and experience the sights, smells and sounds of their workshops, take a ride on a narrow gauge railway and sample the delights of the early motor bus. Many other exhibits include the village telephone exchange, the wheelwright's workshop and See board Electricity Hall.

Bignor Roman Villa
Bigmor, Nr Pulborough
Tel: (0798) 869259

The remains of a large villa in rural surroundings, containing some of the finest mosaic pavements discovered outside Italy and still wonderfully coloured including a 80 ft. long corridor of mosaic and hypercaust underground heating system. There are also various displays of Roman artefacts. Gift shop. Cafe for light snacks, picnic site.

Lannards Gallery
Okehurst Road, Billingshurst
Tel: (0403) 782692

A high standard of paintings and designer craft are displayed in the octagonal cedarwood and pine gallery, with views over Sussex Weald. There are also antique paintings and furniture.

St Clement's Caves, Hastings
Tel: (0424) 422964

Descend into the secret underground haunts of the Smugglers of Hastings. Embark on a journey through time, reliving the dangers and excitement that faced smugglers in times past. Set in a labyrinth of passages and secret chambers deep below ground, realistic recreations of past dark deeds and dramatically brought to life with scenic effects and spectacular sounds and lighting. A smuggling museum and exhibition, video theatre and adventure walk - press the buttons and be prepared for a few suprises!

The Bluebell Railway
Tel: (0825) 723777

Operates Vintage Steam Trains between Sheffield Park and Horsted Keynes, and extension (including tunnel). Situated on A275 between Lewes, and East Grinstead. Savour the age of the steam train. Visit the museum; collection of locomotives dating from 1872, buffet and shop at all Sheffield Park, picnic field at Horsted Keynes. Pullman dining trains (with optional overnight sleeping accommodation) run on certain dates, or charter.

Sheffield Park Garden
Tel: (0825) 790231/790655

Midway between Lewes and East Grinstead, east of A275. 100 acres of beautiful Capability Brown gardens and woodlands with 5 lakes on different levels joined by cascades and waterfalls. The 18C garden is carpeted with daffodils and bluebells in Spring followed by magnificent rhododendrons and azaleas. Its many rare trees turn into a blaze of red and gold in autumn. Tearoom and shop.

Brighton Sea Life Centre
Tel: (0273) 604234

Explore Europe's Biggest Underwater Tunnel and experience a completely uninterupted view of life beneath the waves as giant conger eels, stingrays and sensational British sharks glide silently overhead! A host of other spectacular multi-level viewing and innovative displays provide thrilling encounters! Explore perfectly recreated rockpools and enjoy Daily Talks and Feeding Displays. Other facilities include the fascinating Sea Lab, Ocean Film Theare, Restaurant and Themed Gift Shop.

The Royal Pavilion
Brighton
Tel: (0273) 603005

The former seaside Palace of King George IV is an oriental fantasy no visitor should miss. The completed restoration programme reveals the true magnificence of the Indian exterior. The interior is richly decorated in a lavish Chinese style. The adjacent Museum and Art Gallery feature many temporary exhibitions.

EAST OF ENGLAND

CAMBRIDGESHIRE • LINCOLNSHIRE • NORFOLK • SUFFOLK

This region, is of course, famed for its flat, expansive landscapes. But flat doesn't mean featureless! This is, after all, Constable country. So if, like me, you've marvelled at the magnificent paintings, why not experience first-hand the countryside that inspired them?

When I first visited this part of England it was, literally, a breath of fresh air. What more pleasant way to spend an afternoon than to sit outside a charming village pub, sipping a fine local ale and watching the wheat and rye field rippling in the afternoon sun? (Incidentally, the eastern counties tend to enjoy more sunshine than anywhere else in the British Isles, surely a recommendation in itself!)

And, once refreshed, you can set off to enjoy all the other attractions this locale has to offer. As well as featuring some of the most impressive Georgian streets in England, the area is rich in sites that reflect many other periods of history. At Flag Fen, the wooden walls of Bronze Age houses reveal what life was like 3,000 years ago; Colchester was the Roman capital of Britain and

will always be associated with Boadicea, East Anglia's own warrior queen; while the ruins of the Abbey at Bury St. Edmunds mark the spot where the Magna Carta was drawn up.

The capital of East Anglia is Norwich. Centuries of effort to reclaim the marshlands and cultivate the area have resulted in a huge network of drains, dikes and canalised rivers – today their attraction for the tourist includes boating and birdwatching holidays. It's interspersed with some of the richest farmland in the country. All of this is known as 'The Broads' and Norwich Cathedral stands out like a ruler surveying them.

The most easterly point in the whole of Britain is Lowestoft – holiday resort and fishing port. The south of the town is a modern resort with a sandy beach – the north is the old town complete with lighthouse. The Maritime Museum is well equipped with model ships and fishing tools.

Elsewhere, Felixstowe still prides itself on its 18th century Martello Tower, built to warn of invasion; and

Ipswich simply, and splendidly, oozes Saxon history. Add to this the charismatic cathedrals at Ely and Peterborough and the colleges of Cambridge, the university town that is virtually synonymous with English history and heritage.

History even caught up with me while in pursuit of one of my more forbidden pleasures. The first time I ever visited Newmarket, modern home of horseracing and breeding, a wise old native informed me that the town is also the original home of the sport, having been introduced there in the reign of James I.

Another part of the East that combines past and present in perfect harmony is Lincolnshire. Why not spend one day being enchanted by the Lincoln Cathedral's triple tower and by the town's Roman arch, the only one still used by modern traffic. Then spend the next day on the Lincolnshire coast – Skegness being the ideal family resort.

But, getting back to Newmarket... Okay, I'll admit it, all my horses lost! But I could still afford to sail on the Grand Union canal, the wonderful waterway that links London to the Midlands; and to visit Great Yarmouth, another of the great British seaside resorts. With its Maritime Museum and Kingdom of the Sea, sandy beaches and rollercoasters – what more could you want? Well, actually, there were the amusement arcades, where I also staked a few quid – and, yes, I lost again!

But – the odd bet aside – I'd be the first to say that this perfect part of England is a resounding winner for any holidaymaker!

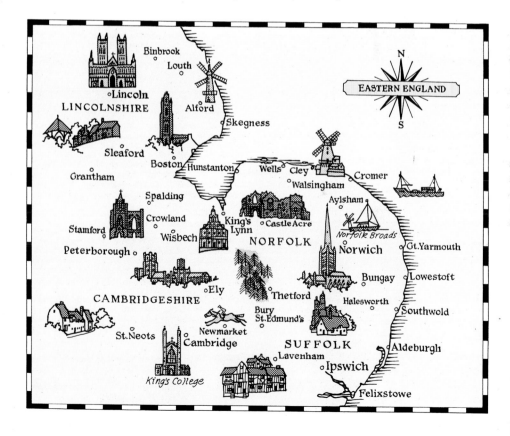

CAMBRIDGESHIRE

HOTELS & GUEST HOUSES

CAMBRIDGE. AA, QQQ, RC. Cristinais Guest House. ETB 2 crown. Quiet location. 15 minutes walk from city centre and colleges. Some rooms with private facilities, tea making facilities, television lounge, central heating. Private car park. Phone: (0223) 65855/327700.

CAMBRIDGE NEAR

Pretty period beamed cottage. Friendly and comfortable. Rural position. 2 acre gardens. Picturesque historic area. Nearby pub serves excellent food. Near Stanstead airport, Cambridge, Newmarket, Duxford Imperial War Museum. Coloured TV, tea making in bedrooms.

B&B from £17.50-£20 per person per night.

Phone: (0799) 599511

CAMBRIDGE. Hall Farm, Great Chishill, near Royston. Homely Georgian farmhouse in secluded gardens. 11 miles south of Cambridge. Beautiful views. Golf and riding nearby. Good local pubs. Phone or Fax: (01763) 838263.

2 persons £60 2 days
Weekly £130
for 2 persons
£260 for
6 persons
B&B £60
2 persons 2 days

Views of Ely Cathedral in **THE FENS**
01353 861972

SELF-CATERING

CAMBRIDGE. 7 bedroomed Victorian house next to park, 10 minutes walk from city centre. Colour television. All modern conveniences. Parking. Quiet road. Holiday let available July to end September. £250 per week. Phone: 081 502 1969.

ELY. Quaint cottage, sleeps 2-6. Stunning views of cathedral. Linen provided. No pets. No smoking. 2 persons (£30 daily) or (£130 weekly). 6 persons (£90 daily) or (£260 weekly). Central heating £1 meters. Phone: (01353) 861972.

WISBECH. A holiday with a difference! 2 delightfully converted Victorian railway carriages. All conveniences. Sleep 2 or 4. Rural setting. Each on separate sites. Set in own gardens. Parking. Pets welcome. Phone: (0945) 410680 after 6 pm.

WHERE TO GO

Anglesey Abbey
Lode, Cambridge
Tel: 0223 811200

13th century Abbey, later Tudor House with sumptuous furnishings, contains Fairhaven collection of paintings and furniture, 100 acre 20th century landscaped garden with outstanding flower gardens, exotic bees

Wimpole Hall and Home
Arrington, Cambridgeshire
Tel: 0223 207257

18th Century house in landscaped park. Folly and yellow drawing room in house, work of John Soane. Home farm - rare breeds centre. Museum, children's corner, adventure playground.

LINCOLNSHIRE

HOTELS & GUEST HOUSES

CHAPEL ST. LEOANRDS, near Skegness. Seaside holiday bungalows/chalets/caravans. Self-catering. Sandfield Holiday Centre booking office. For brochure Phone: (0754) 763815.

GAINSBOROUGH. Quiet village. Riverside walks from garden. Well behaved dogs welcome. Bed and breakfast in ivy covered cottage. En-suite available. Television and tea making facilities in rooms. Private parking. From £12.50. Phone: (0427) 811943.

LINCOLN 2 miles. Bed and breakfast, £32 double. Optional evening meal offered on dairy farm. Private facilities. Private lake, fishing included. Horse riding, golf and nature reserve nearby. Ground floor rooms. Phone: (0522) 527326.

THE LANCHESTER GUEST HOUSE
84 Harrowby Road, Grantham.
A warm and friendly Edwardian Guest House, with high standards and a professional service. Situated on a pleasant tree-lined road, 5 minutes to town centre. Single, twin & double en-suite rooms, with TV, tea/coffee facilities, lounge & dining room. B&B from £15.
RAC acclaimed ETB
PH.: (0476) 74169

LINCOLNSHIRE, near Wolds. Self-catering cottages in heart of the countryside. Clean, comfortable accommodation. Colour television. Bed linen provided. Children and pets welcome. Larger parties welcomed. English Tourist Board registered. Apply Mrs Allen Phone: (0526) 388328.

STAMFORD, Abbey House, Maxey. ETB two crowns commended. Former vicarage dating in part from 1190. Quiet village location. Ideal for fishing, golf and touring Eastern Shires, visiting stately homes, castles and cathedrals. Phone: (0778) 344642.

SELF-CATERING

ALFORD. Luxury log cabins with central heating, double glazing in woodland. Suitable disabled. Cottages centrally heated on private road, all one mile from village, six miles from the coast. Park Farm, Withern, Lincolnshire LN13 0DF. Phone: (01507) 450331.

LINCOLNSHIRE WOLDS, Saltonby. Two bedroom cottages in old barn conversion. Centrally heated and fully equipped. Trout and coarse fishing in own grounds. Child's play area. Pets welcome. Open all year. For brochure Phone: (0790) 753187.

LINCOLNSHIRE COAST. Country village. Ground floor flat. One bedroom en-suite, fully equipped, colour television. Garden with summerhouse. Nature reserves, beaches, market towns, historic Lincoln, Racecourse. Phone: (0472) 388621.

LOUTH, Lincolnshire Wolds. Lovely Georgian market town. Three high quality, self-catering homes, set in two acres with coarse fishing lake. Discount OAPs. All no smoking. Phone: (0507) 609295 for details. Come to see our kingfisher.

SKEGNESS 5 miles, cottages in pretty village of Burgh-le-Marsh. Quiet location with all amenities nearby. Come and explore Lincolnshire and its old market towns. For brochure write Janet and Jim Dodsworth, The Hollies, West End. Phone: (0754) 810866.

WOODTHORPE HALL COUNTRY COTTAGES

Very well-appointed luxury one- and three-bedroomed cottages, overlooking the golf course, all with central heating, colour TV and microwave. Woodthorpe is situated approx six miles from the coastal resort of Mablethorpe and offers easy access to the picturesque Lincolnshire Wolds. Adjacent facilities include golf, fishing, garden centre, aquatic centre, snooker, pool and restaurant with bar and family room.

For Further Details contact:
**Woodthorpe Hall,
Woodthorpe,
Nr. Alford, Lincs. LN13 0DD
Telephone (0507) 450294**

SKEGNESS 4.5 miles. Mews holiday cottage. Centre Burgh Le Marsh village. Sleeps 6. Near restaurants, inns, shops, fishing, beach and golf. Ideal touring centre. Brochure sae or Phone: Mrs Mary Boulton, 10 West End, Burgh Le Marsh, Skegness PE24 5EA. 01754 810266.

WOODALL SPA. Lincolnshire. Holiday bunga-low, secluded area. 2 bedrooms. All amenities. Large garden, conservatory. Near fishing, golf and leisure centre. All pets welcome. Phone: 081 200 0707.

CARAVANS, CHALETS & HOLIDAY PARKS

LINCOLN 2 miles. 8 berth caravan on dairy farm. All services. Colour television. Private lake, fishing included. Horse riding and golf nearby. Pets accepted. £85 to £110 per week. Phone: (0522) 527326.

NORTH SOMERCOTES. 6 berth, 2 bedroom lux-ury caravan. Fully equipped, shower, microwave, television. Beautiful quiet woodland site with large fishing lake. Full amenities. Pool, club, supermarket. Families and couples only, no pets. Details Phone: (0673) 843075.

WHERE TO GO

Mablethorpe's Animal Gardens
North End, Mablethorpe.
Tel: (0507) 473346

Over 200 animals in gardens and natural dunes, breeding small mammals and birds such as gents, raccoons, also monkeys and parrots, seals and owls. Wildlife hospital. Tea gardens. Disabled visitors welcome.

Natureland Seal Sanctuary
North Parade, The Promenade, Skegness.
Tel: (0754) 764345

Tropical house, aquarium, pets corner, floral palace, seal sanctuary. Tropical butterflies. Animals brass rubbing, gift shop, refreshments kiosk.

Lincoln Cathedral

Lincoln, Lincolnshire.
Tel: (0522) 544544

Triple-towered cathedral founded 1072, with Norman west front 12th Century work. Angel Choir of 1280. Wren library of 1674. Treasury Regular services.

Heckington Windmill
Hale Road, Heckington, Lincolnshire.
Tel: (0529) 60765

Unique 8-sailed tower mill built 1830 and restored to full order. Milling at weekends (wind permitting). Wholemeal flour on sale.

TRAVELLING BY COACH OR RAIL?

TURN TO THE BACK OF THIS GUIDE FOR USEFUL TELEPHONE NUMBERS

NORFOLK

HOTELS & GUEST HOUSES

BACTON. Family run hotel. Ideal for touring or seaside. All rooms have colour television, tea makers, hairdryers, hot and cold. Some en-suite. Licensed. ETB 3 crown approved. From £15 per night. Sheila Cavaliero, Seacroft, Bacton. Phone: (0692) 650302.

FELTWELL. Shortlands 17th century guest house bed and breakfast. Televisions, tea, coffee all rooms. Some en-suite. Television lounge. Ideal location for touring East Anglia. OAPs welcome. Local golf course, fishing, forest walks. Phone: (0842) 828429.

GORLESTON-ON-SEA

HARBOUR HOTEL

The only private hotel/guest house with a level walk to the lovely clean Gorleston beach and amenities, 1 minute away. En-suite rooms available. Sea and harbour views. No restrictions. Ample parking. Daily and weekly rates. Free brochure.

Phone: (01493) 661031

GORLESTON-ON-SEA. Look Squirrels Nest offers all en-suite rooms with sea views. Great food, bar. Car park. Special offers. Bed and breakfast from only £15. Children free. ETB 2 crown. AA, RAC acclaimed. Colour brochure. Phone: Irene (0493) 662746.

CONCORDE HOTEL

84 NORTHDENE ROAD, GREAT YARMOUTH

Family run hotel, open all year, 300 yards beach, close to all amenities, licensed bar, baby listening, car parking, tea/coffee making all rooms, some rooms en-suite. All rooms colour TV. Weekend and midweek bookings. Pets by arrangement. Choice of menu. Special 4 day Christmas Break.
Send for brochure and tariff or phone:
(0493) 843709

GREAT YARMOUTH. Lea-hurst Guest House. Bed, breakfast, evening meal. From £75.00 per week. Good food, tea making facilities and satellite colour television each room. Some en-suites, licensed. Home from home. 117 Wellesley Road. Phone: (0493) 843063.

SHREWSBURY HOUSE

9 TRAFALGAR ROAD, GREAT YARMOUTH NR30 2LD

Centrally situated between town and seafront. All bedrooms have colour televisions and tea/coffee facilities. Choose between standard rooms, rooms with shower or en-suite bedrooms. Bed, breakfast and evening meal is available; enjoy the good home cooking we offer. Special low cost weekly rates in May and June. For details please contact Pam Eady.

01493 844788

GREAT YARMOUTH. Guest house. Home cook- ing, tea making facilities. Licensed bar. 2 minutes sea and town centre. Fire certificate, hygiene certificate. Friendly hosts. Phone: Christine (0493) 844091 for details.

GREAT YARMOUTH. Siesta Lodge Guest House. Licensed, good home cooking. 80 yards beach and marina leisure centre. Duvets all beds. Own key. Colour television with satellite, all rooms. Phone: Jan Brown (0493) 843207.

GREAT YARMOUTH. Offering one of the best locations. Highly recommended. Some en-suite rooms with television and tea-making facilities. Games room, bar. Personal attention, friendly atmosphere. Situated one minute sea front and shops. Established 10 years. 18 Princes Road. Sae or Phone: (0493) 842515.

GREAT YARMOUTH CHARRON HOUSE

Highly recommended licensed guesthouse. Home cooking with varied menu. Bedrooms available with shower and toilet. Colour TV and tea/coffee all rooms. No restrictions – "come and go as you please."

Write or phone for colour brochure
Pat and Graham Bidewell.

151 Nelson Road Central, Great Yarmouth Norfolk NR30 2HZ
PH: (01493) 843177

GREAT YARMOUTH. Quinton House. 2 minutes central seafront. Full central heating, tea making facilities, television in all rooms. Bed and breakfast, evening meal optional. Plenty of good food. Minton, 35-36 Rodney Road, NR30 2LH. Phone: (0493) 844106.

GREAT YARMOUTH. Family run Guest House offering good clean accommodation. Good home cooked food, separate tables. Family rooms available. Ample parking. Low season prices for OAP. On main bus route, close beach and town. Phone: (0493) 842997.

GREAT YARMOUTH. 'Armani'. Bed and break- fast and evening meal. Good situation between Britannia/Wellington piers and Pleasure Beach. 1 minute from beach and amusements. Open all year. Sky television. Gas heating. Own keys. Reduction for children. Phone: (0493) 850230.

* Three minutes from beach and Venetian Waterways
* Free car parking
* Colour television and tea making facilities in all rooms
* Colour television guest lounge
* Excellent home cooked food
* Special reductions for senior citizens and children
* Own keys
* Cleanliness and comfort assured
* Open all year including Christmas
We wish all our guests a Happy Holiday

Resident Proprietress
Miss Tracey Dunn
82 NORTH DENES ROAD
GREAT YARMOUTH
NORFOLK, NR30 4LW
Telephone: (01493) 844092

GREAT YARMOUTH
SUNNYSIDE
GUEST HOUSE
10 WELLESLEY ROAD
NR30 2AR

Highly recommended for cleanliness and good food. Food hygiene certificate granted. TV lounge. 2 minutes from beach. Britannia Pier, shows and shops, also large car park/coach station. Free colour, Sky TV and teamaking facilities all rooms. Bed and Breakfast and 3 course substantial evening meal from £63 p.w. Choice of menu.

Write or telephone for brochure.
Mrs. Stidworthy
(01493) 844013. (01493) 722035.

GREAT YARMOUTH. Dene House. Bed, break-fast and evening dinner. Renowned for good food and cleanliness. Car parking on premises. Beach 3 minutes. Established 22 years. Brochure Phone: Mrs Elmer (01493) 844181. 89 North Denes Road.

GREAT YARMOUTH. Private hotel, close beach and shops. Bar, video and television lounge. Friendly atmosphere. Owner golf club member. Tea making facilities, wash basins all rooms, some en-suite. Competitive rates. For brochure Phone: (0493) 844680.

GREAT YARMOUTH. Dacona Guest House, 120 Wellesley Road NR30 2AP. Bed and breakfast guest house. Very close seafront and town centre. Warm welcome for overnight or longer stay guests. Clean and comfortable. Phone: (0493) 856863.

GREAT YARMOUTH. Family run hotel. Central town/seafront. Some en-suite rooms. Television and tea/coffee making in rooms. Licensed bar. Central heating. Highly recommended for food, comfort and friendliness. 18 Princes Road. Phone: (01493) 842515.

GREAT YARMOUTH. Janic House. Homely guest house. Close to Britannia Pier. Home cooking and friendly atmosphere with television and tea making facilities all rooms. Children welcome. Open all year. Phone: Janet (0493) 851955.

GREAT YARMOUTH. 'Nomarno'. Friendly, family run hotel. Some sea views. Open all year including Christmas. Hospitality tray in rooms. Choice menu. Residential licence. Children welcome. Close to amenities. Short or long breaks. Phone: Ann (01493) 843897.

GREAT YARMOUTH. Royston Hotel. Com-fortable, licensed private hotel. 125 yards from beach. Central for all attractions. Excellent menu, choices each course (except Saturday). Television some rooms, Sky television in bar. En-suite available. Phone: (01493) 844680.

GREAT YARMOUTH, Kismet House. Licensed. Very central. 2 minutes sea and shops. A friendly welcome and good food. 1 week's bed, breakfast and evening meal, low season £78. High season £110. For brochure Phone: (0493) 859478.

HAPPISBURGH. Cliff House Guest house and tea shop. Views over sea and lighthouse. Home baked bread. Licensed. Central heating, television, tea/coffee making facilities all rooms. Bed and breakfast £14.50. Concessions children/OAP's. Phone: (01692) 650775.

HORSEY CORNER. The Old Chapel. Tranquil National Trust location. Beach and Broads a short stroll. Quality bed and breakfast from £15. Family, double and twin rooms. En-suite option. ETB commended. Phone: (0493) 393498 for brochure, reservations.

HUNSTANTON. Small friendly guest house. Bed and breakfast, optional dinner. Televisions, tea making all rooms. Children and pets welcome. Reasonable prices. Phone: (0485) 534320.

HUNSTANTON. 'Coralyn' Guest House. All bed-rooms provided with television, tea and coffee making facilities. Full central heating. Guests are supplied with own key for unlimited access. Jenny and Arthur Chapman, 12 Glebe Avenue. Phone: (01485) 534672.

KING'S LYNN. Ffolkes Arms Hotel. 2 miles from Sandringham A148. All rooms en-suite, colour television, tea/coffee. Rural setting with landscaped gardens. Carvery restaurant, bar meals. Snooker, pool, barbecues, Sky television. Ideal location. Children welcome. Phone: (0485) 600210.

NORWICH. Fuchsias Guest House. Friendly, family run. Good value. Convenient for city and surrounding countryside. Central heating. All rooms with washbasin. Colour televisions. Special diets available. Personal keys. Leisure facilities, archery to zoology nearby. ETB listed, commended. Phone: (0603) 51410.

NORWICH. Earlham Guest House. Elegant Victorian residence. Close city centre. AA listed 3 crowns commended. ETB. 7 lovely rooms, most non-smoking, some en-suite. Vegetarian breakfasts if preferred. Handy parking. 147 Earlham Road. Phone/Fax: (01603) 454169.

OLD HUNSTANTON. Linksway Country House Hotel. Adjacent to golf club. Sandy beach 2 minutes. All rooms en-suite, colour television. Indoor swimming pool, licensed. Sandringham 8 miles. Bird reserves close by. Phone: (0485) 532209 for colour brochure.

WELLS. Norfolk - Scarborough House Hotel. 3 crown commended. AA, RAC 1 star. All en-suite. Parking, restaurant, bar. Television, tea and coffee all rooms. Open all year. Dogs welcome. Phone: (01328) 710309 for brochure.

WELNEY. Welney House. Classic Georgian farmhouse. 2 twin bedrooms. Colour television and tea making facilities. Within easy reach of Ely, Cambridge and King's Lynn. Also Welney Wildfowl Centre. Bed and breakfast £17 per person. Phone: Gerrard-Wright (0354) 71207.

WISBECH. Homeleigh Guest House. Victorian house built in 1800s. Close historic towns of King's Lynn and Wisbech. Licensed bar, restaurant. Television all rooms, tea, coffee making facilities. Bed and breakfast £15 per person. Phone: (0945) 582356, Fax: 587006.

WROXHAM. Broads Hotel. 4 crown ETB. All rooms en-suite. Convenient coast and historic Norwich. In centre Broadland. Bars, Excellent restaurant. Close boating, fishing, golf. Family run. Address: Station Road, Wroxham, Norwich, Norfolk. Phone: (0603) 782869, Fax: (0603) 784066.

SELF-CATERING

BACTON, North Norfolk coast. Well equipped family cottage near sandy beaches. Four bedrooms, sleeping seven plus cot. Washing machine, microwave. Private parking. Electricity, gas1 central heating and linen all included in the price. Phone: (01692) 650012.

BLAKENEY 3 miles. Superb listed cottage. Beams, log fire. Available all year. Night storage heating. Garden, parking. Two double bedrooms. Very well equipped. Owner supervised. Phone: (0328) 830213.

BRISTON, North Norfolk. Comfortable mod-ernised cottage. Owner supervised. Sleeps four. Cot. Oil central heating. Large rear garden. Good touring area. Parking. Phone: Griffiths (0263) 860417.

BRUNDALL, Norfolk Broads. Riverside bunga-
low, sleeps 4. Fully equipped bathroom/shower, kitchen, lounge and verandah, overlooking river. 40 feet river frontage and slipway. Parking, rowing, dinghy and life-jackets provided. Bed linen included, secluded garden with lawn. Garden furniture provided. Phone: (0394) 274231.

BURNHAM THORPE. Lord Nelson's birthplace.
A quiet village near coast. Choice of detached bunga-low or cottage with secluded gardens. Off road parking. Colour television. Sandy beaches, nature reserves, wildlife walks, all within easy reach. Phone: (0553) 673302.

CAISTER BEACH. Seafront bungalows, cara-
vans. Detached 3 bedroom bungalows, parklands Hemsby village. Bungalows, chalets, near beach, Hemsby. Small family discounts. Pets welcome. Springtime short breaks. Colour brochure: D. Witheridge, Blue Riband Holidays, Hemsby, Great Yarmouth. Phone: (0493) 730445.

CASTLE ACRE. Picturesque character cottage
in idyllic location. Fully equipped, sleeps 4 plus cot. Secure secluded garden. Pets welcome. Reasonable rates include linen, towels, electricity and logs. Open all year. Leaflet available. Phone: (0883) 717689.

CASTLE ACRE. Cosy holiday cottage, sleeps 4
plus cot. Log fire. Garden, garage. Picturesque village. Good walking, real ale inns. Ideal touring base for North Norfolk coast and Sandringham. Weekend breaks available. Phone: (0760) 722455.

CATFIELD. 4 miles from North Norfolk coast,
in heart of Broadland village. Quiet, comfortable cot-tage, sleeps 4 plus. Ideal for sailing, walking, fishing, bird watching and taking life easy. Phone: (0692) 582039.

CONGHAM. Two bedroom barn conversion.
Quiet location in grounds of old manor house, also near Sandringham and the sea. Phone: (0485) 600148.

CORPUSTY. 6 miles Holt. Village cottage.
Sleeps 3, 1 double, 1 single, equipped to high standard. No smoking. No pets. Reasonable rates. Phone: (0405) 860980 evenings.

CROMER. Norfolk. Luxury chalets, landscaped
park. Well equipped kitchen, sleeps 4 plus. 2 bedrooms, lounge/diner. Good parking. Beautiful cliff and wood-land walks. Modified chalet for disabled, close to ameni-ties. For brochure contact Joan. Phone: (0530) 260420.

CROMER (near). Quiet village. Luxury self-
contained flat, sleeps two. Patio door, very large pretty garden. Colour television, cooker, microwave. Pets wel-come. Secluded position. Car space. Reasonable prices. Phone: (0263) 833357.

CROMER. 2 miles West Runton. Comfortable
house. Quiet location. Centre seaside village. Beach few minutes walk. Well equipped, sleeps 7. Mrs Hack, 1 Abbey Road, Sheringham, Norfolk NR26 8HH. Phone: (0263) 824729.

CROMER. 17th century converted barn, close
to all amenities, yet set in beautiful surroundings. Ponds and waterfalls. Sleeps two. En-suite, colour television, video. Conservatory, car parking. Regret no pets. For details Phone: (0263) 512910.

EARSHAM, Norfolk, Waveney Valley. Rural set-
ing, semi-detached cottage, sleeps 2 plus 2. Fully equipped, all linen provided. Close to golf, fishing, swimming pool, own snooker table. Open all year. Phone: (0986) 892434.

ECCLES ON SEA, near Happisburgh. Secluded
shiplap bungalow in 1/3 acre. Sheltered by sand dunes. Overlooking farmland. Sleeps 5/6. Large, light living room, spacious kitchen, bath with shower, separate toi-let. Colour television. Carpeted throughout. Peaceful. Phone: (0865) 242176.

ECCLES ON SEA. Detached older style holiday
bungalow backing sandunes to beach. Sleeps up to 8. Large garden. Ample parking. Details from Potter, 2 Prince of Wales Road, Norwich, Norfolk. Phone: (0603) 627201.

FAKENHAM. Little Snoring. Modern well
equipped house in cul-de-sac. Sleeps 7 adults, cot avail-able. Extra bed downstairs optional, central heating and open fire. Lawned gardens enclosed, off-road parking for 3 cars. Colour television, linen. Phone: (0263) 821548.

FILBY, Great Yarmouth. Quiet, comfortable
farm cottage. Situated in riding school yard. Sleeps 4/5 plus cot. Close to coast, broads for fishing. Riding lessons available. No pets. Further details Phone: (0493) 369482.

GARBOLDISHAM. 'Squirrels'. Modern 2 bed-
room, 4 plus 1 well appointed wing of family run guest house. 10 acres wooded, streamside walk. Country loca-tion. Electric oven, microwave, fridge freezer, auto washer dryer, central heating, colour television. Brochure Phone: (01953) 681541.

GREAT YARMOUTH. (Hemsby). Detached sea-
side holiday homes. Comfortably furnished. Adjacent valley, dunes and beach. Mains services. Own gardens. Colour television. Details from Estate Office, Long Beach, Hemsby, Great Yarmouth, Norfolk NR29 4JD. Phone: (0493) 730023.

GREAT YARMOUTH. Spacious self-contained
holiday flats. 2 bedrooms, lounge, kitchen, bathroom. 2 minutes walk seafont and town centre. Ideal location. Mr Brown, 62 Albion Road, Great Yarmouth NR30 2JD. Phone: (0493) 844797.

GREAT YARMOUTH, California Sands. Luxury
chalets, equipped 6 people. Self-catering. Free entry clubs. Indoor heated swimming pool. Dogs welcomed. Free Brochure: 'Oakleigh', 35 Upper Grange Crescent, Caister-on-Sea, Great Yarmouth, Norfolk NR30 5AU. Enclose sae. Phone: (0493) 720330.

GREAT YARMOUTH, California Sands. Superb brick chalets. Fully equipped. Licensed clubs, indoor swimming pool. Near beach also Norfolk Broads. Highly recommended. Colour brochure. Woolston Holidays, 99a Yarmouth Road, Ormesby, Great Yarmouth, Norfolk NR29 3QF. Phone: (0493) 732916.

GREAT YARMOUTH. Quinton House Flats. 1 minute central seafront. Fully equipped. 2-6 people. Own toilet and shower. Linen provided. Colour television, fridge. Very clean. Minton, 35-36 Rodney Road, NR30 2LH. Phone: (0493) 844106. Sae please.

HAPPISBURGH. Comfortable self-contained flats in large thatched house. Sleep 6/4/2. Central heating. Garden. Attractive village. 5 minutes safe, sandy beach. Children and dogs welcome. £115 - £195 per week. Off season breaks from £85. Phone: (01692) 650775.

HAPPISBURGH
COMFORTABLE COTTAGE BY COAST
Enclosed private gardens. Comfortably sleeps 6-7, fully equipped with washing machine, microwave, freezer, etc. TV, video, open-fire for cosy winters. Full central heating inclusive. Ample parking, swings and sandpit. BBQ. Children and pets welcome.
SPECIAL BARGAIN BREAKS OUT OF SEASON AND WEEKENDS
Telephone 01692 651494

HEMSBY, Great Yarmouth. Self-catering luxury holiday chalets, sleep 6. Colour television. Heated swimming pool, supermarket, shops, club, restaurant, sauna. Near beach. No pets. Phone: 081 803 3615.

HEMSBY near, Longbeach, Great Yarmouth. Cosy, modern bungalow. Adjacent valley and sea. All modern conveniences. Conservatory, garage, garden. Enclosed plot. Phone: Mrs K. Browne, Norwich, Norfolk (0603) 898500.

HOLME-NEXT-SEA. Bungalow, spacious and secluded, fully equipped, three bedrooms. Adjacent lovely sandy beaches, bird reserves, golf, horse riding. ETB three keys commended. Ample parking. Phone: (0733) 66696.

HOLME-NEXT-SEA. 'Marshside Corner' cottage. ETB highly commended, 5 keys. Sleeps 10 plus cot. Caravan park. ETB 4 ticks. Mains services. Also 2 bedroom cottage available from Easter. For further details Phone/Fax: (01485) 525381.

HOLT. Comfortable and well-equipped tradi- tional flint stone cottage near town centre. Ideal base to tour Norfolk. Sleeps four to six. Central heating. Available all year. Pets by arrangement. Phone: (0708) 226259 after 6 p.m.

HOLT FARM. Guest House and bungalow. Open all year. 4 miles sea. Sleeps 2-8 people. Central heating, colour television. Private car parking. Rudd, Far End, Vale Road, High Kelling, Holt, Norfolk NR25 6RA. Phone: (0263) 713342.

HORNING. Picturesque riverside village, heart of the Broads. Comfortable, individual homes with waterside lawns, private fishing and launch hire. Pets welcome. Ideal for quiet, relaxing holiday exploring Norfolk and the Broads. Illustrated brochure, Phone: (0692) 630177.

HORNING. The centre of Norfolk Broadland. Waterside flat. Three bedrooms, kitchen, diner, lounge, bathroom, sun deck. Garden, parking, fishing. Launches for hire. Entirely detached. Full details and brochure Phone: (0692) 630428.

HORNING, Norfolk. Queen of the Broads. Luxurious three bedroomed brick house. Almost water's edge, river views. Full gas central heating, fitted carpets. Garage. Extremely reasonable rates off peak. Celebrate Christmas away too. Satisfaction guaranteed. Phone: (0777) 818544.

HUNSTANTON, coast and countryside. Large, small, modern or traditional. Over 50 fully furnished self-catering holiday homes. Close to beaches and holiday interests. Free colour brochure. Contact Sandra Hohol at Norfolk Holiday Homes. Phone: (0485) 534267.

KNAPTON, near Mundesley. Traditional old flint cottage. Modernised but retaining lots of original features. Sleeps 6 in 3 bedrooms (one has bunk beds). Log fire. Quiet village, overlooking countryside, near sea and Broads. Phone: 081 444 7678.

KNAPTON, near Mundesley. Charming, spa- cious character home. Beams and inglenook. 4 bedrooms with fitted basins, two have en-suite showers. Lovely garden. Quiet village overlooking countryside. Near sea and Broads. Luxury kitchen. Phone: 081 444 7678.

LUDHAM. Pretty cottage, furnished to a high standard. All modern amenities. Own private courtyard. Day boats for fishing, relaxing. Available at Womack Staithe. Opposite cottage, sleeps four. Children, pets welcome. Brochure Phone: (0602) 252255 or (0692) 678020.

MARTHAM. Free excellent bream, pike fishing from garden. River Thurne. Bungalow, sleeps 4/6. Sand dunes, beach 10 minutes. Excellent sailing. Surrounded by farmland. Good pets welcome. £99 - £300 per week. Short breaks. Leaflet Phone: (0273) 305277.

MUNDESLEY. Barn cottages. Furnished and equipped to high standard. Large garden with patio, table, chairs, barbeque. Parking. Sleeps 6. 1 1/2 miles sea. Convenient for Broads, Norwich, many historic houses and places of interest. Reasonable charges. Phone: (0263) 721344.

MUNDESLEY, near North Norfolk. Cottage wing. Regency hall, three bedrooms, two bathrooms, lounge, kitchen - diner. Use swimming pool, own garden. Bargain breaks available. From £100 - £325. Electricity and central heating included. Phone: (0263) 721800.

MUNDESLEY. Cottage with sea view and pri- vate parking. Near shops, beach, cliffs. Two bedrooms each with twin beds. Lounge, colour television, dining room, kitchen. Central heating available. Pets welcome. Enclosed garden. OAPs reduction. Phone: (0263) 720806.

MUNDESLEY. Brick and cobble cottage in quiet seaside village. 400 yards golden sandy beaches. Excellent local shops, parks, golf course. Easy reach Norwich, Broads. Sleeps 2/3. Colour television, gas, electricity inclusive. Phone: (0732) 460235.

MUNDESLEY. Detached 2 bedroomed bunga- low, sleeps 4-6. Tastefully converted. Farm/stable building. 10 minutes walk European Community standard beach. 1994 'Keep Britain Tidy' winner. Television, video, microwave. Night storage heaters. Patio. Rural views. Horse riding. Phone: (0263) 721060.

NORFOLK BROADS. Near Potter-Heigham. 10 units in 1 1/2 acre gardens, consisting thatched cottages, bungalows, apartments. Heated swimming pool in season. 100 yards from river. Public mooring for own boat. Owners in residence. Phone: (01692) 670320.

NORFOLK BROADS, Wroxham. Studio apart- ment, sleeps two. Swimming pool, heated from May until September. Quiet position. Bus and rail station. Boating, fishing, golf nearby. Open all year. Phone: (0603) 783778 for details.

NORFOLK BROADS. Private, detached river- side bungalow with fishing from own riverbank. Rowing, dinghy lifejackets, bicycles, boathouse/games room. Colour television. Garage. Sleeps 2/8 comfortably. Near sea. Wonderful holiday. Recommended. Early booking essential. Details Phone: (0442) 822919.

NORFOLK BROADS. Thurne. Idyllic country village. 7 bedroomed farmhouse. 10 spacious bungalows. Lovely peaceful gardens. Heated pool. Games room. Private fishing, River Thurne, boating. Easy access all Norfolk beauty spots. Phone: (01692) 670242, (01493) 844568.

NORFOLK BROADS. Fish from your own lawn. Forty private riverside bungalows. Fully equipped with televisions and linen provided. Boats available. Riverside Holidays, Potter Heigham. Free brochure Phone: (0692) 580496.

NORFOLK BROADS. Womack Water, Ludham. Beautiful, modern detached riverside bungalow. Central heating. Close to village, shops. Ideal touring, boating, relaxing, private fishing from own large garden. Mooring available. Children and pets welcome. Brochure Phone: (0602) 252255 or (0692) 678020.

NORFOLK BROADS. Neatishead. Quiet village. 6 miles coast, 10 miles Norwich. Charming cottage. High standard equipment includes microwave/video. Special facilities for disabled. 4 bedrooms, 2 bathrooms. Sleeps 6 plus cot. Small patio, garden. Yards walk village. Post office and pub. Phone: (01692) 630233.

NORFOLK BROADS, Martham. Part thatched cottage. Overlooking village green. 3 upstairs bedrooms, sleeps 7. Convenient sandy beaches and broads. Great Yarmouth 10 miles, Norwich 18 miles. Washing machine, microwave, shower, colour television. No pets. Phone: (0493) 740375.

NORFOLK BROADS. Thurne. Idyllic country village, adjacent river. 7 bedroomed farmhouse, spacious bungalows. Lovely peaceful gardens, outdoor heated pool. Games room. Boating, private fishing River Thurne. Easy access all Norfolk beauty spots. Phone: (0692) 670242, (0493) 844568.

NORWICH and Norfolk holiday homes offer houses, flats and cottages, some 5 key rated, in the beautiful 'fine' historic city of Norwich. Explore our delightful countryside and coastline. Tourist board 'registered' agency. Free brochure Phone: (0603) 503389.

PULHAM MARKET. Detached cottage in pretty village. Good location for touring Norfolk and Suffolk. Sleeps 5 plus cot. Electricity, linen and towels, baby equipment. Pets at no additional charge. Children and pets welcome. Phone: (0508) 578576.

SHERINGHAM. Town centre. Flint modern cottage, sleeps four plus baby. Two bedrooms, bathroom with shower. Fully furnished, equipped. Ideal for beach, town. Full central heating, double glazed, colour television. Open year round. No pets. Phone: (0949) 50021.

SHERINGHAM, North Norfolk. Bungalow, quiet area, 5 minutes walk shops or sea. Comfortable, colour television, fridge, cooker, microwave. Sleep 4/5. All floors level, with easy access. Central heating. Parking, large garden. Phone: (0263) 823586.

SHERINGHAM, Norfolk. Large four bedroomed maisonette, sleeps two/eight plus cot. Colour television. Low season £95 per week. High season £235 per week. Phone: (0263) 712688 after 3pm.

SNETTISHAM, North Norfolk. In pretty village. Cosy terraced cottage sleeps 4. Superbly equipped and furnished. Beams, log fire, private garden. Ideal for peaceful holiday. Bird sanctuaries. Hunstanton 5 miles, Sandringham 3 miles. Pets welcome. Phone: (0742) 303370.

STIFFKEY, near Blakeney. Charming beamed cottage in lovely village setting. Log fire in sitting room. Parking. Enclosed garden. Glorious views. Sleeps 4 in 2 pretty bedrooms. Walking distance of salt marshes and sea. Phone: (0263) 711029.

SWAFFHAM 4 miles. Five comfortable, well equipped cottages within rural 17th century barn in five acre grounds. 1/4 mile local pub. 1-3 bedrooms. No children. Pets by arrangement. Phone: (01366) 328794.

TEN MILE BANK in West Norfolk. Self-catering cottage, sleeps 5. Overlooking River Ouse. Excellent location for fishing. Ideal base for touring. Good location for bird watchers. Pets by arrangement. Phone: (0366) 383995 anytime.

TRIMINGHAM, near Cromer. Large self-contained private and well equipped wing of Georgian farmhouse. Peaceful setting opposite church. Sleeps 4 plus 1, cot. No pets. ETB 4 key commended status. Brochure Phone: (0263) 833269.

WELLS-NEXT-SEA. Spacious furnished cottage. 3 double bedrooms, cot, central heating. Garage, enclosed garden. Quiet yet near harbour, shops. Open all year. Phone: (0992) 583186.

WELLS-NEXT-THE-SEA. Attractive, spacious, well equipped cottage, sleeping 4. Quiet, convenient location with small secluded garden. Central heating all rooms. Colour television, telephone, washing machine etc. Short breaks available. No pets. Phone: (0279) 755451.

WYMONDHAM. Historic town centre Norfolk. Superb three bedroomed house, sleeps six plus cot. Microwave, dishwasher, washing machine, tumble dryer. Central for Norwich, broads, coast, Suffolk. Thirty golf courses. Available all year. Winter breaks £90. Phone: (01953) 602877.

CARAVANS, CHALETS & HOLIDAY PARKS

BACTON. Self-catering chalets, caravans and flats on small coastal site. Some accommodation with sea view. Ideal location for fishing, touring North Norfolk and the Broads. Licensed bar. Dogs welcome. Open March to January. Phone: (0692) 650815.

CAISTER. Haven site. Fully equipped luxury 8 berth caravan for hire. All entertainment. Gas and electric included in price. For details Phone: (0473) 713523 or (0473) 713584.

CAISTER, California Cliffs. 8 berth caravan. 3 bedrooms, shower, separate toilet. Colour television. Club with entertainment. Swimming pool. Restaurant, fish shop, supermarket, hairdressers, hire shop. Amusements, adventure park. Close to beach. Phone: 081 556 0953 or 081 558 1247.

CALIFORNIA CLIFFS. Haven site. Six berth, super luxury caravan. Constant hot and cold water, shower, gas fire, television, fridge freezer, microwave, free gas, electricity. Entertainment, children's club, swimming pool. No pets. Phone: (0992) 522268.

CALIFORNIA SANDS, Scatby, Great Yarmouth. Family chalet, sleeps 6. Television (colour), free entry to indoor pool and two clubhouses. 500 yards to beach. Phone: (0462) 730308.

CALIFORNIA SANDS, Great Yarmouth. Well maintained, fully equipped chalets, sleeps to six. All prices include club and indoor swimming pool fees, plus electricity. Cots available free if required. Only 400 yards from beach. Details Phone: (0493) 651299.

CROMER. Chalet, sleeps 6. Delightful views of town and sea. Walking distance, beach, golf course. Fully equipped kitchen, bathroom, separate toilet. Television. Phone: Gascoyne (0603) 51885.

GREAT YARMOUTH. Six berth caravan on Blue Sky Caravan Park. Leisure pool, club amusements, take-away, supermarket etc. Prices from £60 per week. Phone: (0485) 571639.

GREAT YARMOUTH. California Sands, Scratby. 6 berth, two bedroom, heated chalet. Colour television. Fully equipped. Apply Stockwell, 33 Eadie Street, Stockingford, Nuneaton, Warwickshire CV10 8JB. Sae please. Phone: (01203) 385201.

GREAT YARMOUTH, California Cliffs. Haven Park. Luxury private caravans. Wc, shower, cooker, fridge, colour television. Free gas, electricity. Heated pool, adult bars, family bar, children's clubs, shops, restaurant. Near beach. From £100 per week. Phone: (0992) 561424.

GREAT YARMOUTH, California Sands. Family owned chalet, sleeps 6. Well equipped. Free bed linen, colour television, microwave. Very clean. Free club, children's club, indoor heated pool. Close to sandy beach. Mrs Annette Terry, Phone: (0493) 700700.

GREAT YARMOUTH Caravans, South Denes and Caister beach, cottage, flats, bungalow in and around Great Yarmouth. Self addressed envelope please K.E. Knights, Ki-Te-Ke, 32 Sun Lane, Bradwell, Great Yarmouth. Phone: (01493) 663594.

GREAT YARMOUTH. Haven Holiday Centres (Caister, California Cliffs and Seashore). Luxury privately owned caravans. Available Easter to October. Free entertainment, gas and electricity. All amenities. Linda Hedges, Kittiwake Caravan Holidays. Phone: (0708) 222673.

GREAT YARMOUTH, California Cliffs. (Haven site near beach). Privately owned luxury 3 bedroomed caravan (no pets or children under 5) families only. Full entertainment. Indoor and outdoor swimming pool complex with flume. Phone: (0245) 353065.

HEMSBY. Privately owned chalets, sleep 4-6 or 6-8, on well-run site (with clubroom, swimming pool, shops). Fully equipped. Close Yarmouth, sea, Broads. Available from March to 31 October. Phone: (0493) 488613 or (0727) 863550.

HEMSBY, near Great Yarmouth. Brick chalets
fully equipped for up to 6 people. Licensed club, close
swimming pool, 500 yards beach. Cheap early season
breaks. Details 'Miclin', Low Road, Martham, Norfolk
NR29 4RE. Phone: (0493) 748350 or (0493) 740987.

HEMSBY. Chalet, sleeps six. All modern con-
veniences. Colour television. Club on site with children's
room, picturesque village and beach nearby with various amenities, for families. June to September. Sparrow,
343 High Road. Phone: 081 995 1120.

HEMSBY. Self-catering 2 bedroom luxury
chalets. Superbly equipped, television, fridge - freezer,
bed linen. Privately owned on Sundowner Park.
Amenities. Club, swimming pool, shop, amusements.
Short breaks. Highly recommended. Terms from £30.
Phone: (0502) 740389.

HEMSBY. Comfortable, fully equipped two and
three bedroomed chalets at popular holiday centre.
Near sandy beaches. Our hard-to-beat prices include
family club membership and use of heated indoor pool.
No pets. Phone: (0582) 460315.

HOPTON is one of 19 holiday parks coast
to coast. Our luxury holiday homes, sleep 2-8 people.
Prices start from £9 per person per night, based on 6
sharing. For a free colour brochure Phone: Lo-Call (0345)
508 508.

KELLING HEATH. Near Sheringham. Luxury
two bedroomed caravan, 35 feet by 12 feet. All amenities including colour television. Situated near coast and
countryside on prestigious 4 star site. Ideal for all the
family. No dogs. Phone: (0953) 498516.

MUNDESLEY, Norfolk. Luxury brick chalets
on a choice of 3 small sites. Close to beautiful sandy
beach. Children and pets welcome. Discount for OAP.
Colour brochure Gray Holiday Properties, 6a Paston
Road, Mundesley, Norwich NR11 8BN. Phone: (01263)
720719 or 721414.

NORTH WALSHAM. Woodland setting. Fully
equipped, all mains Caravan, 2 bedrooms, shower, heating, colour television. Barbecue, own garden with furniture. Superb quiet location yet close to coast and
Broads. Plenty of local amenities. Phone: (0692) 500350.

SEA PALLING. Very comfortable 6/8 berth caravans. On well organised select site. Near sea. containing fridge, television, toilet, hot and cold showers. Ideal touring area. Midway Yarmouth, Cromer, near Broads. Wilson, 25 Mountfield Avenue, Norwich. Phone: (0603) 401544/(0362) 688364.

THETFORD FOREST, Norfolk. Static caravan, sleeps 6, 2 bedrooms, colour television, full size cooker, bathroom. Private site. Free electricity, gas. Bring own bed linen. Sorry no animals. Phone: (0842) 890247.

WINTERTON ON SEA. Chalets with sea views, adjoining beach on quiet, spacious estate. Fully equipped. All electric. Colour television, microwave. Clubhouse. Shop. Children's play areas. Sleeps 4/6. Near Broads. Fishing. Anglia Coastal Holidays. Phone: (01708) 723063.

HOLIDAYS AFLOAT

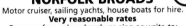
WHERE TO GO

Kingdom of the Sea
Southern Promenade, Hunstanton, Norfolk.
Tel: (0485) 533576
Watch sea life on a breathtaking scale in over 20 natural settings and come face to face with creatures of the deep.

Great Yarmouth Pleasure Beach
South Beach Parade, Great Yarmouth, Norfolk.
Tel: (0493) 844585
Condor, rollercoaster log flume, looping star, dodgems, go-karts, Caterpillar, toboggan.

Dragon Hall
115-123 King Street, Norfolk
Tel: 0603 6633922
Dragon Hall is a magnificent medieval merchant's hall, described as 'One of the most exciting 15th century buildings in England'. Timber-framed great hall, outstanding crown-post roof, intricately carved dragon, screens passage, vaulted undercroft. A legacy of medieval craftsmanship and mercantile trade.

Norfolk Lavender Ltd
Caley Mill, Heacham, Norfolk
Tel: 0485 70384
Lavender is distilled from the flowers and the oil made into a wide range of gifts.

Sandringham
Sandringham, Norfolk
Tel: 0553 772675
The country retreat of H.M. The Queen. Set in 60 acres of beautiful grounds and lakes, Sandringham is complemented by a museum of Royal Vehicles and memorabilia. House and grounds are surrounded by 600 acres of country park with visitor centre and shop.

Bygone Heritage Village Ltd
Burgh St Margaret, Fleggburgh
Tel: 0493 369770
A reconstruction of a 19th Century village set in over 30 acres of parkland. Traction engines. Working steam exhibits, classic vehicles, Victorian Gallopers, railway, fairground, adventure playground, bygone collections and working craft units. Meals and snacks available. Picnic areas.

SUFFOLK

HOTELS & GUEST HOUSES

ALDERTON. 14th century village Inn near sea and river. Offers chalet accommodation, showers, television, tea/coffee making facilities. Excellent cuisine and fine ales. Swan Inn, Alderton, Woodbridge, Suffolk. Phone: (0394) 411366.

FELIXSTOWE, near. Detached bungalow only 3 miles from Felixstowe. Sleeps 4 to 6. Fully equipped. Central heating. Enclosed garden with trees, shrubs. Send for brochure to Mrs D. Knights, 308 High Street, Felixstowe, Suffolk. Phone: (0394) 277730.

HITCHAM. Mill House. Large house in exten- sive grounds. Tennis court. All rooms have colour television and tea making facilities. Six miles from Lavenham on B1115. Central for villages and Constable country. Phone: Mrs White (0449) 740315.

LOWESTOFT, Suffolk. Fairways Guest House. Fully licensed. Most rooms en-suite. Colour television. Tea, coffee making facilities. 5 minutes beautiful beach, Blue Flag. 1 mile town centre and railway station. 398 London Road South. Phone: (01502) 572659.

SOUTHWOLD. Saxon House. Comfortable guest house. 100 metres beach. All rooms sea view. Radio and wash basin. 2 en-suite. Television, lounge. Children and pets welcome. Parking. No smoking. Enquiries Linda Whiting, 86 Pier Avenue. ETB 2 crown. Phone: (01502) 723651.

SELF-CATERING

BECCLES near. Teacher's cosy self-contained purpose built country cottage annexe. 'Home from home'. Colour television, electric blankets. Coast, reserves, historic towns nearby. 2 adults. Pets welcome. From £75 per week, inclusive sheets, electricity. Phone: (0502) 677453.

BURY ST. EDMUNDS. 16th century farmhouse and cottages. 1/2 mile from A14. 10 miles east of Bury. Sleeps 2-6. Set in 3/4 acre grounds with duck pond. Ideally situated for Cambridge, Lavenham, Suffolk countryside and coast. Brochure Phone: (0359) 242732.

CLARE
SUFFOLK
Self catering chalets from £12 per night. Delightful picturesque setting. Par 3 9-hole golf course. 4-acre fishing lake. Tennis court. Small camping/caravan area. Clubhouse and bar.
Telephone: 01787 278693

CORTON. Fully equipped houses and bunga- lows. Many overlook sea. Licensed club. Full entertainment. Large outside pool. Ideally situated for local attractions including theme park. Corton Beach Holiday Village, The Street, Corton, Lowestoft NR32 5HS. Phone: (0502) 730200.

DUNWICH. Cliff House, Minsmere Road. Self-catering flats, bungalows, caravans. Sleep 2/8. 30 acres. Beach frontage heritage coast, adjoins bird sanctuary and heathland. Central heating, colour television, microwaves. Touring caravans and tents welcome. Phone: (01728) 648282.

FELIXSTOWE, Suffolk. Seaview holiday flat. near seafront. First floor self-contained, fully equipped. Sleeps 6. Lounge, kitchen, bathroom/shower, games room, balcony, colour television, microwave, private garage. Close to bus station. Linen hire available. 4 key commended. Phone: (0394) 274231.

FINNINGHAM. Jasmine cottage. Unspoilt rural setting between Bury St Edmunds and Norwich. Sleeps four. All modern conveniences. Linen provided. Use of garden and garden furniture. Excellent food at local pub. Further details Phone: (0449) 781483.

FRAMLINGHAM 2 miles. Character cottage sur- rounded by open countryside. 3 bedrooms - sleeps 6, plus cot. Central heating, inglenook with log burning stove, colour television, washing machine, microwave. Garden furniture, barbecue. Children welcome. Phone: (0727) 827162.

HALESWORTH AREA. Personally supervised country cottage. Sleeps 4/5. Pets welcome. Garden and patio. Full linen. Heritage coast 12 miles. Prices £100 - £230. Short breaks and discounts available. Mrs Hammond, South Lodge, Redisham Hall, Beccles, Suffolk. Phone: (0502) 575894.

KESSINGLAND
SUFFOLK
Holiday bungalows on peaceful site next to beach. 2 bedrooms, sleeps 4/6. Fully equipped including colour TV. Ideal for all the family. Easy access to A12 and Broadlands. Open March to January.

Alandale, Bethel Drive
Kessingland NR33 7SD
Tel/Fax: 01502 740610

KESSINGLAND. Chalet bungalow overlooking the sea on prime position. Fully double glazed. Equipped to a very high standard. Very clean, warm, comfortable. Colour television, telephone. More suitable for mature persons. Quiet seafront site. Details Phone: (0922) 34398.

LOWESTOFT. Pakefield. Bungalow, sleeps four. Two bedrooms, colour television, garden, garage. Available all year round. Ideally situated for sea and Broads. Sanders, 5 Parkers Place, Ipswich IP5 7UX. Phone: (0473) 610485 after 6 pm.

PEASENHALL. Fully equipped bungalow in vil- lage. Sleep 2/4. Off road parking. No pets. Also well equipped bungalow in quiet, secluded situation at Ubbeston. Large garden. Sleeps 6. Heritage Coast 15 minutes. Phone: (0728) 660308/660201.

REDGRAVE. Recently renovated cottage. Sleeps two. Television, microwave. Garden. Rural conservation. Village pub, shop. Convenient Norwich, Bury, Thetford. Horse riding nearby, swimming, golf, gym, snooker at Diss. Weekends available. Linen provided. Phone for brochure (0379) 898259.

SOUTHWOLD. Walberswick, Westleton and other surrounding villages. Self-catering holiday homes. Apply H.A. Adnams, 98 High Street, Southwold, Suffolk IP18 6DP. Phone: (0502) 723292 or send sae for brochure.

SOUTHWOLD. H. A. Adnams self-contained holiday homes. Situated Southwold, Walberswick, Westleton and other surrounding villages. Apply 98 High Street, Southwold IP18 6DP. Phone: (0502) 723292.

SOUTHWOLD. Second floor apartment in Grade 2 listed building. 2 twin rooms. Town centre. Blue Flag beach 5 minutes. Sailing, golf, walks, birdwatching. Television. Parking. No pets. Available year round. Short breaks. Phone: (01502) 722002.

ST MICHAEL. 16th century country cottage adjoining farmhouse. Beams, inglenook fireplace with woodburner (logs available). Southwold 13 miles. Golf, fishing, swimming all nearby. Pub with food 1 1/2 miles. Available short breaks, full weeks. Phone: (0986) 782327.

WALDRINGFIELD. Estuary House. 100 yards beach, sailclub. 4 doubles, large attic playroom. Freezer, dishwasher. Climbframe, swing, toys. Enclosed garden, patio, barbeque. £200 till mid-July and September £300 August. Sailboards, rowing boats. Electricity, linens included. Phone: (0394) 382740.

WRENTHAM. Southwold five miles, coast one mile. Well equipped village cottage. Including colour television, microwave, telephone. Two bedrooms, sleeps four. Private garden and parking. Ideal angling, bird-watching, walking, sailing. Details including photo-graph Phone: (0502) 675692.

YOXFORD. 17th century granary providing comfortable facilities whilst retaining its unusual rustic charm. Ideally situated for exploring coast and local attractions. Sleeps 4. 1 double, 2 singles. Saturday - Saturday, weekend lets available out of season. Phone: (01728) 668459.

CARAVANS, CHALETS & HOLIDAY PARKS

KESSINGLAND. 4/6 berth quality holiday bungalows for hire and sale. Next to award winning beach. North end, Suffolk heritage coast. Many places of interest nearby. Linen provided. Clean, well main-tained. Alandale Holiday Estate, Lowestoft. Phone: (0502) 740610.

WHERE TO GO

Suffolk Wildlife and Rare Breeds Park
Kessingland, Lowestoft.
Tel: (0502) 740291

Lions, tigers, monkeys, chimpanzees, cattle, miniature American horses, childrens farmyard corner where animals can be stroked and fed, safari Road-Train. Various entertainments, Childrens play area, Cafeteria and gift shop.

Somerleyton Hall
Suffolk
Tel: 0502 730224

Rebuilt in Ango-Italian style 1840's. Fine state rooms, period furnishing and paintings superb gardens with famous maze. Deer park, tea room and picnic area.

Brandon Country Park
Suffolk
Tel: 0842 810785

30 acre-landscaped parkland with lake. Tree trail, forest walks and wayfaring course.

The Otter Trust
Bungay, Suffolk
Tel: 0986 893470

A unique wonderland of waterfowl, otters, night herons and muntjac deer on the banks of the River Waveney. World's largest collection of otters in natural enclosures where the British Otter is bred for introduction to the wild.

CENTRAL ENGLAND

DERBYSHIRE • GLOUCESTERSHIRE • HEREFORD &
WORCESTER • LEICESTERSHIRE • NORTHAMPTONSHIRE
NOTTINGHAMSHIRE • SHROPSHIRE • STAFFORDSHIRE
WARWICKSHIRE • WEST MIDLANDS

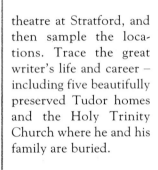

It's known as "The Heart of England", and it isn't just for the obvious, geographical, reason. On the contrary, this terrain is synonymous with characters – like Robin Hood and William Shakespeare – who are themselves the personification of a proud English heritage. You can't hope to understand the "essence" of Englishness until you visit the fine landmarks of this location.

It's true that Sherwood Forest is not as large today as it was in Robin Hood's time, but it still remains a fascinating place to visit, with its interpretative exhibition, adventure park and week-long Robin Hood Festival. You can also step back in time by soaking up the atmosphere of "Shakespeare Country". This encompasses such towns as Stratford-upon-Avon, Warwick and Kenilworth, as well as the city of Coventry and the famed Forest of Arden. Thrill to the plays themselves at the Royal Shakespeare Company theatre at Stratford, and then sample the locations. Trace the great writer's life and career – including five beautifully preserved Tudor homes and the Holy Trinity Church where he and his family are buried.

Indeed, "The Heart of England" resonates with the memory of many a renowned historical figure. Visit Royal Leamington Spa alone and you will be following in the footsteps of Queen Victoria, the Duke of Wellington, Brunel, Dickens, Churchill and many others who refreshed themselves in its splendid baths; while the distinguished Newstead Abbey was once home to Lord Byron.

Of course, this part of England was also the world's Cradle of Industry – and this rich heritage is celebrated in such attractions as the Royal Crown Derby factory; the city of Nottingham's Lace Hall; the Severn Valley Railway; and the Ironbridge Gorge

Museum which brings Victorian times to life in a reconstructed 19th century village. Indeed the Industrial Revolution of the 19th century gave us the capital of Central England, and after London – Britain's second largest city Birmingham. Birmingham was the 'City of a Thousand Trades' – its prosperity based on factories, workshops, and a huge network of canals. Today these are continually being restored and upgraded. Canal boating and walking isn't just for the countryside. Take the Birmingham and Fazeley Canal. From the city's centre it heads downhill through thirteen locks in its first one and a half miles – a great experience if you're not in a hurry! If that's not for you, marvel at the old factories and warehouses from revamped towpaths – certainly it's easier!

Other fine landmarks that I've enjoyed and would recommend include the lovely spa town of Buxton with its noble Opera House, and Chesterfield cathedral with its charming crooked spire. Add to this a day out at Alton Towers or Twycross Zoo; motor racing at Donnington Park or jousting tournaments at Belvoir Castle – and you've got the makings of a fabulous family holiday.

Or, if you really want to feel the "best" of the Heart Of England, why not simply enjoy its green, rolling pastureland? You might go walking the limestone hills and wooded dales of the Derbyshire Peak District, or ramble through the Forest of Dean and across the Malvern Hills. Not to mention the Cotswolds: spread over several counties, and a delight in every one...

DERBYSHIRE

HOTELS & GUEST HOUSES

AMBERGATE. Lawn Farm. Working family farm on quiet country lane. Ideal for visiting stately homes, Alton Towers, Carsington Water or walking in the peaks. Double en-suite family room. ETB 1 crown. Terms from £15. Phone: (0773) 852352.

ASHBOURNE. Farmhouse bed and breakfast. One twin or family room £15 per person. Cot and child rates available. Convenient for Alton Towers, walking and sightseeing in Peak Park, Chatsworth, Jodrell Bank. Phone: Church Farm (0335) 300659.

THROWLEY HALL FARM

English Tourist Board

COMMENDED

This Georgian farmhouse is situated in the peaceful Peak District countryside. Ideal for walking. Some rooms en-suite. All rooms are centrally heated with tea and coffee-making facilities and wash basins.
Also self-catering in a farmhouse and cottage sleeping 12 and 7. E.T.B. 4-keys commended.

Throwley Hall, Ilam, Ashbourne, Derbyshire DE6 2BB. Tel: 01538 308202

ASHBOURNE. Stone cottage. ETB listed, com- mended guest house. Charming 19th century cottage nestling in the Derbyshire Dales. Near Dovedale, Chatsworth, Alton Towers. Rooms with en-suite facilities, colour television/tea making. Excellent cuisine. Phone: Mrs A. Whittle (0335) 343377.

BRASSINGTON. Private house in the heart of Derbyshire. En-suite rooms, colour television, tea/coffee making facilities. Countryside views. Friendly family atmosphere. Non-smokers only. Phone: Sadie (0629) 540395 available all year. Bed and breakfast per person from £13.00.

BUXTON, DEVONSHIRE LODGE

Comfortable, affordable accommodation in family run guest house having full facilities. Central for walking in Peak District. 3 minutes from Pavilion Gardens and Opera House. B.&B. from £13.50 daily. Special rates for 4 and 5 day breaks. E.M.T.B. inspected and approved.
PH.: 01298 71487

HEATH FARM

Farm in Peak District National Park. 4½ miles from Buxton. Quiet location, many activities locally. Cot and babysitting available. Bed and breakfast from £13.50. Reductions children and weekly stays. All rooms TV's. Car essential, pets welcome. East Midlands Tourist Board Listed.
Mrs. L. P. Fearns, Heath Farm, Smalldale, Buxton SK17 8EB. Tel: (01298) 24431

DERBYSHIRE DALES. Recently renovated Georgian country house, maintaining many original features. Log fires and flagstone floors. Beautiful rural location. Ideal for walking, cycling and touring. Open all year. Dogs welcome. Non smoking. Phone: (0298) 84709.

MATLOCK BATH. Bed and breakfast accommo- dation. Large Victorian house with lovely views. Quiet location; close to shops and railway station. Families welcome. Evening meals, including vegetarian, by arrangement. Mrs Free, 2 Greenbank, Holme Road. Phone: (0629) 56615.

MATLOCK. Traditional family farm in Peak District. Beautiful views, peace and quiet. Ideally situated in the heart of Derbyshire for all main attractions. Television lounge, tea making facilities. All ages welcome. ETB. Phone: (0629) 650648.

MATLOCK BATH. Cliffside is a friendly family run guest house with spectacular views. Luxury en-suites and excellent cuisine. Children welcome. Colour televisions, tea making in rooms. Dogs welcome, babysitting by arrangement. Non smoking only. Phone: (0629) 56981.

MATLOCK. The centrally located 'Friendly hotel'. Above the shops that caters for all your needs to make your stay a happy one. 2 minutes walk from railway station. Television in all rooms. Fire certificate held. Phone: (0629) 582677.

THE PEAK
DISTRICT

Visit Chatsworth, Haddon and Hardwick Hall in one weekend. Our short breaks include a ticket to Chatsworth. Comfortable small hotel with excellent food.

DBB 2 nts from £71.50

Abbeydale Hotel
Cross Street, Chesterfield, Derbyshire S40 4TD
Tel: 0246 277849

THE PERFECT CENTRE FOR THE DERBYSHIRE DALES

STADEN GRANGE COUNTRY HOUSE

★ Surrounded by the beautiful countryside of the Peak National Park. 1.5 miles from Buxton.
★ All bedrooms en-suite with tea/coffee making facilities and colour TV, some ground floor.
★ Self catering apartments available.
★ Licensed. ★ Ample parking.
★ Sauna, Jacuzzi, Beauty Therapist.

SPECIAL OFFERS

Brochure and Tariff from Duncan and Mary Mackenzie
Staden Grange, Staden Lane, Buxton, Derbyshire SK17 9RZ. Tel: (01298) 24965

𝖂𝖔𝖔𝖉𝖘𝖎𝖉𝖊

Stanton Lees, Matlock

When visiting the Peak District/Derbyshire Dales enjoy a friendly welcoming B&B in a rural Peakland village with panoramic views. Ideal for walking/sightseeing. Ensuite or own bathroom in each bedroom, TV, tea/coffee facilities. E.M. available. Chatsworth/Bakewell/Matlock 4½ miles.

Tel. Matlock (01629) 734320.

PEAK DISTRICT. Country Inn. Between Buxton and Bakewell. Offers bed and breakfast. 2 rooms. Also used as holiday flat with self-catering kitchen. Ideal base for walking and touring Peak District. Enquiries Phone: (0298) 83348.

SELF-CATERING

ASHBOURNE/CLIFTON: Two charming, mod-ernised, three hundred year old cottages, each sleeping four. In peaceful village. Convenient for Alton Towers, Chatsworth, Carsington Water, Peak District. Details M.J. Davies, Clifton Hall, Ashbourne, Derbyshire DE6 2GL. Phone: (01335) 342265.

ASHBOURNE (2 miles). Luxury barn. Microwave, colour television, linen, gas, electricity included. 1 bedroom, sleeps 4. Walking, cycling, Alton Towers, Chatsworth, Dovedale, Carsington. (Short or long breaks). Phone: (0335) 300087.

ASHBOURNE, near. Waterkeepers' Cottage. In peaceful village of Mappleton. Gentle walks to Dovedale. Alton Towers nearby. 1.5 miles from Ashbourne. Cycle hire. Open all year including Christmas. Evening meal by arrangement when booking for 4 persons. Phone: Ashbourne 350444.

BAGSHAW. Peak District. Detached stone cot-tage with oak beams and open fire. Overlooking Chapel-en-Le-Frith with wonderful views. This is an ideal base for walking/touring. Sleeps up to 6/cot. Children/pets welcome. Phone: (0298) 813294.

BAKEWELL. Bolehill Farm holiday cottages. 8 charming stone cottages in attractive courtyard setting, overlooking Lathkill Dale. Bakewell 2 miles. Games room, sauna, solarium. Winners of EMTB self-catering holiday of year award. Colour brochure Phone: (0629) 812359.

DERBYSHIRE COUNTRYSIDE
(photograph courtesy of East Midlands Tourist Board)

BLORE. Blore Hall. Beautiful peakland location for our courtyard of cottages plus four poster and en-suites in old hall. Heated indoor pool, sauna, games barn, restaurant, bar, play areas and fishing! Alton Towers eight miles. Phone: (0335) 350525.

BONSALL, near Matlock. Attractive comfort-ably furnished country cottage. Centrally heated. Situated in old world village. Very well equipped. Registered with ETB. Use of garden. Central for beauty spots. Beautiful walking country. Terms £120 - £250. Phone: (0629) 823162.

BUXTON, near. Derbyshire. Newly furnished stone cottage, sleeps 6 plus cot. English Tourist Board approved 4 key. Brochure Phone: (0663) 746312.

A COUNTRY RETREAT IN THE PEAK DISTRICT

Charming limestone cottage in the village of Litton. Quality accommodation, owner maintained. Sleeps 2/3. Non-smokers only. No pets. £130-£210 weekly.

Mrs. Maxted, Ashleigh, Litton, near Buxton, Derbyshire SK17 8QU. Phone: 01298 872505 after 6pm.

CARSINGTON. Knockerdown Farm, Dalebreaks Cottages. Leisure facilities, indoor pool, games/exercise rooms, playground, bar. Watersports/cycling/fishing nearby. Central location Derbyshire Dales and Peaks. ETB 4 key highly commended. For full colour brochure Phone: (0629) 540525 anytime.

CARSINGTON WATER. Luxury cottages in breathtaking lakeside setting. Windsurfing, canoeing, sailing, fishing, walking, cycling, birdwatching available nearby. Close Alton Towers, Chatsworth and Peak District. Ashbourne and Matlock 8 miles. Cottages sleep 2-8 persons. Phone: (0335) 370282.

CARSINGTON WATER views. Peak District. Splendidly converted barns. Derbyshire, Dales, Alton Towers, Chatsworth. Excellent walking, water sports, cycling, golf. 2/3 bathrooms. Linen. Sleeps 6/12. Bungalows 4/5. Wheelchair access. Play area. Pets. Phone: (0629) 540625.

CHAPEL-EN-LE-FRITH. Luxury cottage. ETB 4 keys commended. Sleeps 4 plus cot. Fuel, towels, bed linen included. Well situated for all attractions in and around the Peak District. Brochure Phone: (0298) 814865, 812638.

CRESSBROOK. By Monsal Dale. Heart of Peak Park. Charmingly furnished Victorian cottage. Fully equipped 3/5. Lovely situation. Beautiful views. Phone: (0298) 871633.

CURBAR. Delightful detached cottage in quiet village. Clean, comfortable and well equipped. Large garden. Lovely views. Sleeps 6. Ideal for walking, touring. Within easy reach of all main attractions. Regret no pets. Phone: (0433) 631838/631154.

CUTTHORPE. Cosy one and two bedroom cot-tages, recently converted from stone barns. Picturesque rural setting. Ideal base for touring Peak Park. Close to several historic houses. Ward, Birley Grange Farm. Phone: (0246) 583292.

DERBYSHIRE DALES, near Matlock (Alton Towers .5 hour). Stone period cottages. Conservation area. Panoramic views. Sleeps 2 to 14. All facilities. Short breaks. Also quality cottage near York available (sleeps 2 to 6). Phone: (0773) 833007 for details/brochure.

DERBYSHIRE DALES. Newly converted large oak beamed early 19th century listed limestone cottage, sleeps 4. Beautiful rural location. Ideal for walking, cycling and touring. Dogs welcome. Non smokers only. Available all year. Phone: (0298) 84709.

HATHERSAGE. 17th century sheep farm in an idyllic setting off the beaten track. The comfortably converted farmhouse wing sleeps 5 and is ideal for visiting Chatsworth, Matlock, Bath and Castleton. Lovely walks from farm. Phone: (0433) 650494.

ILAM. Farmhouse and cottage, sleeping 12 and 7. Rural setting in Peak District. Well equipped with freezer, microwave and the option of open fires. Garden. ETB 4 keys commended. Phone: (01538) 308202.

KNIVETON. Rowfields Hall Farm. Down a country lane overlooking Peak National Park. One double/one single bedroom. 2 miles Ashbourne Market Town. Car essential. £200 per week. May/October. Tourist Board 3 keys. Phone: (0335) 342805.

LEA, near Matlock. Spacious luxury stone cot- tage, beamed ceilings. Three bedrooms, separate shower room and bathroom. Two toilets. Full gas central heating. Quiet village, secluded garden. Private parking. Ideal base for walking and touring. Phone: (0629) 534546.

MATLOCK. Primrose Cottage. Early 19th cen- tury cottage, set in terraced gardens within the River Derwent conservation area. Five minutes walking distance of Matlock with good restaurants, real ale inns, lawn tennis. Sleeps 2/4. Phone: (0773) 742276.

MATLOCK. Tansley village, Luxurious det- ached house, sleeps 10. Five bedrooms, lounge, dining room, fully fitted kitchen. Garages. Central heating, double glazed. Open year round. Ideal base for Derbyshire Peaks and Dales. No pets. Phone: (0949) 50021.

MATLOCK. Bath in beautiful Peak District. Large comfortable 2/3 bedroom flats. Spectacular views. Sleeps 2-18. Close to theme parks and stately homes. If you wish to bring your horse, quality stabling available on farm. Phone: (01629) 584460.

MATLOCK area. Terraced cottage, 2 bed- rooms sleeps 3 plus baby. Linen provided. Garden. No pets. Quiet village but good centre for walking, stately homes etc. ETB 3 keys commended. Phone: (0629) 823493 or (0629) 826230.

MATLOCK. Cosy centrally heated cottage adjoining owners' Victorian house in spectacular Matlock Dale. Two bedrooms, sleeps four. Private parking. Non-smokers only please. No pets. Weekly £135 to £195. Winter weekends available. Phone: (0629) 583878.

MIDDLETON, near Matlock, in the Peak District. Cosy modernised cottage. Sleeps 2. Bakewell, Chatsworth, High Peak trail nearby. Pets welcome. April to October. £130 per week. Brochure Phone: (0923) 774873.

MONYASH, near Bakewell. Heart of the Peak Park district. Very comfortable modernised 18th century traditional stone cottage. Overlooking village green. Enclosed garden. Dishwasher, microwave, fridge/freezer, washing machine etc. 3 double bedrooms, sleeps 6. Phone: (0462) 456869.

PEAK DISTRICT. Stone built bungalow, sleeps 5. Located on farm. Surrounded by field. Bed linen and towel included. Pets welcome. Ring for availability. Phone: (01246) 864370.

PEAK DISTRICT. Hope. Twitchill Cottages. Panoramic views surround these four stone built cottages. Extremely well equipped. ETB 4 keys, highly commended. Superb walking. Larger, sleeps 2-8. Smaller, sleeps 2-6. Golfing, horse riding nearby. Contact Mrs Atkin. Phone: (0433) 621426.

PEAK DISTRICT, Derbyshire. Attractive stone cottages, near Buxton. Comfortably, furnished. Sleep 4 to 5. Private parking, extensive grounds. Children welcome. Close to shops. Ideal centre. Linen hire. Phone: (0298) 813355.

PEAK DISTRICT, Bakewell. ETB 4 keys, highly commended. 3 bedroom barn, en-suite, shower. Large garden. Also 1 bedroom farmhouse apartment with 4 poster. Both equipped with dishwasher, video, microwave etc. Brochure Phone: Jo Read (0298) 871653.

PEAK DISTRICT. Two bedroomed detached bungalow. Sleeps four plus a cot. Gas central heating. Garden, patio. Parking for two cars. Foolow near Eyam. For information for fully equipped comfortable good views Phone: (0298) 871751.

PEAK NATIONAL PARK, Tideswell, near Bakewell. Cottage, sleeps 4. Central heating, colour television, automatic washer, fridge/freezer, outside parking. Excellent reputation. Heating and linen included. Very competitive rates. West, 'Westcliff', Church Lane, Derbyshire. Phone: (0298) 871272.

PEAK DISTRICT. Manor barn, Wetton. Con- verted barn, sleeps 6. Central heating, dishwasher, microwave. Very comfortable, beautiful walking country. Cot and high chair. Electricity included. £250 per week. For brochure Phone: 033 527 223.

PEAK DISTRICT, Buxton. Converted farmhouse. Near Longnor. Comfortably sleeps maximum 8. With bathroom and shower room. Reductions for small parties with low season rates also. Beautiful holiday location. Within 30 minutes of Alton Towers. Details Phone: (0298) 83583.

PEAK DISTRICT, Buxton (near). Delightful fully equipped beamed cottage situated in small quiet village near Manifold Valley and Dovedale. Sleeps 2/3 plus cot. Mrs Lawrenson, Hall Bank, Hartington, Buxton, Derbyshire SK17 0AT. Phone: (0298) 84223.

WARDLOW. 16th century barn conversion cot- tages on a working farm. Large garden. Play area, small children's pool. Five minutes Monsal Dale. Close Bakewell, Chatsworth. Short breaks from January, April, September, December. For brochure Phone: (0298) 871283.

WINSTER. Recently renovated two bedroomed listed period stone cottage, set in a quiet part of the historic village of Winster. Close to shops, pubs and restaurants. Pets accepted. Great place to stay. For brochure Phone: (0629) 650431.

CARAVANS, CHALETS & HOLIDAY PARKS

ASHBOURNE. 4 berth caravan individually located in secluded rural setting. Convenient for Ashbourne, picturesque Dales, Alton Towers, Matlock. Watersports nearby. Two bedrooms, shower, flush toilet, colour television. Cleanliness assured. Reasonable terms. Fully inclusive electricity. Phone: (0335) 344721.

CALLOW TOP HOLIDAY PARK
BUXTON ROAD, ASHBOURNE, DERBYSHIRE

Two beautiful Holiday Cottages and 1 Luxury Mobile Home. From £150 per week.
Heated Swimming Pool. Pub serving real ale and good pub food. Games Room: Pool Tables, Table Tennis, Games Machines. Playground. Alton Towers 20 minutes. Discount tickets available. Situated in the Derbyshire Dales with beautiful views. Cycle hire and access to the Tissington Trail Cycle Path. Market town of Ashbourne 1 mile. Carsington Reservoir: Watersports etc. 10 minutes.

Telephone 0335 344020
for free brochure and booking information

BAKEWELL. Modern static caravans for hire on a small quiet rural site with superb panoramic views of surrounding countryside. All have 2 bedrooms, bathroom with shower, television. Free brochure, Peakland Caravans, Stoney Middleton S30 1TL. Phone: (0433) 631414.

BAKEWELL. Peak District. Large 6 berth static caravan on working farm. Fully equipped, electric, gas, toilet, shower etc. Phone: (0629) 814195.

DERBYSHIRE DALES
Caravan and Camping on working farm near Matlock, new toilet block, play area. Close Tramway Museum, Chatsworth, Riben Fauna Reserve, Gullivers Kingdom, Cable Cars, American Adventure. **ALSO** Farmhouse accommodation. Homely 17th Century Farmhouse with 20th Century comfort. All rooms hot and cold, central heating. Ample parking. Fire Cert. Barn converted holiday cottages also available.
Phone: Matlock (01629) 582967

WHERE TO GO

Riber Castle Wildlife Park
Riber Castle, Matlock.
Tel: (0629) 582073
Collection of wildlife, including rare and endangered species, Comprehensive lynx collection. Gift shop, children's playground. Cafeteria and bar. Disabled visitors welcome.

American Adventure
Pit Land. Ilkeston, Derbyshire.
Tel: (0773) 531521
American theme park with more then 100 rides including Great Niagara Rapids Ride, The Missile Cherokee Falls, log flumes and many other attractions. Shoot-out and shows daily.

Chatsworth House, Farmyard and Adventure Playground
Bakewell, Derbyshire.
Tel: (0246) 582204
Built 1687-1707. collection of fine pictures,books, drawings and furniture. Garden laid out by Capability Brown with fountains cascade. Farmyard and adventure playground.

Midland Railway Centre
Butterley Station, Ripley, Derbyshire.
Tel: (0773) 747674
Over 25 locomotives and over 80 items of historic rolling stock of Midlands and LMS origin. Steam-hauled passenger service. Museum site. Country park.

The Heights of Abraham
Matlock, Bath, Derbyshire.
Tel: (0629) 582365
Cable car ride across Derwent Valley gives access to Alpine Centre with refreshments, superb views, woodlands, prospect tower and show caves.

Gullivers Kingdom
Temple Walk, Matlock Bath, Derbyshire.
Tel: (0629) 580540
Log flumes, chair lift, junior coaster, mine tour, dodgem cars, dancing water show, carousel, children's rides cycle monorail shops and catering .

PLEASE MENTION

DALTONS DIRECTORY

WHEN BOOKING YOUR HOLIDAY

GLOUCESTERSHIRE

HOTELS & GUEST HOUSES

BOURTON ON THE WATER. Come and share Farncombe's peace, tranquillity and superb views. Eat and sleep. Smoke free in Clapton, 2 miles from Bourton. 2 doubles with showers, 1 twin en-suite. Brochure Phone: Wright (01451) 820120.

BROADWAY, Cotswolds. Large Edwardian house on outskirts of beautiful Cotswold village of Broadway. Lovely views and garden. Good parking. All rooms private bathrooms, television, tea making. Super breakfasts. Bed and breakfast from £16.00. For brochure Phone: (0386) 858437.

CHALFORD, near Cirencester. Whitegates, peaceful hillside farmhouse with 16 acres. Lovely views. Good walking, central for touring. Holiday stabling. ETB 2 crowns. En-suites, tea/coffee, television. Non-smoking. Open all year. Brochure Phone: Cirencester (0285) 760758.

COTSWOLDS, Laverton. Near broadway. Non-smoking bed and breakfast, ETB listed (commended). Homely accommodation and a wonderful breakfast in peaceful backwater. Sorry, no pets. From £16 per person. Discount 3 nights or more. Phone/Fax (0386) 584280.

COTSWOLDS. Farmhouse bed and breakfast. Timber beamed rooms. Dated 1628 in unspoilt countryside. Breakfast in farmhouse kitchen. £14 per person per night, sharing £16 single. ETB commended. Hopkins, Bengrove Farm, Teddington, Tewkesbury, Gloucestershire. Phone: (0242) 620332.

COTSWOLDS. Crown Inn. Church Enstone near Oxford, Stratford, Warwick, Blenheim. En-suite rooms. Tea, coffee, television, restaurant. 17th century circa. Winter breaks available. Phone: (0608) 677262.

COTSWOLDS, Broadway and Evesham, near. Willowcroft. Comfortable accommodation. All rooms with en-suites, television, tea - coffee facilities. Pleasant gardens with patio. Bed and breakfast £14 per night. Phone: (0386) 832036.

FOREST OF DEAN, Coleford. A warm welcome awaits you at Allary Guest House. Enjoy a break anytime of year. Wonderful walks and scenery. Warm and cosy. En-suite, tea, coffee facilities, dinner available. Phone: (01594) 835206.

FOREST OF DEAN, Wye Valley. Whether pass-ing through or stopping longer, stay at Oak Farm. Warm and friendly welcome assured. Evening meal available, vegetarian and vegan catered for. Beautiful countryside all around. Phone: (01594) 860606.

FOREST OF DEAN. Ferndale House. Friendly, family bed and breakfast. En-suite. Comfortable accommodation. Evening meals with vegetarian menu available. Log fire, lounge. Attractions include walking, fishing, cycling. Wonderful views. Children/dogs most welcome. Phone: (0594) 861294.

GLOUCESTER near. Severn Bank. Fine riverside country house in 6 acres. Large en-suite non-smoking bedrooms, superb views, colour television, tea making facilities, central heating. Ample parking. Recommended viewpoint Severn bore tidal wave. ETB 2 crown. Carter. Phone: (01452) 750357.

KEMPLEY. Warm welcome on dairy farm. Superb food. Idyllic countryside. Many animals, play area. Many attractions locally. Easy access Wye Valley, Forest of Dean and Cotswolds. Bed and breakfast and self-catering. Phone: (0531) 890301.

MORETON-IN-MARSH. Tastefully converted country cottage guest house. ETB 2 crowns. All rooms en-suite, colour television, complimentary tea - coffee. Heated outdoor pool, garden, parking. Convenient for Cotswolds and Stratford. Brochure: Newton, Staddle Stones Guest House, Stretton-on-Fosse. Phone: (0608) 662774.

MORETON IN MARSH. Bed and breakfast in 17th century Cotswolds stone house. Extensive views. Oak beamed, bedrooms en-suite, private bathrooms, comfortable dining room with inglenook, roaring fires in Winter. Superb breakfasts, evening meals by arrangement. 'Roosters'. Phone: (0608) 650645.

NAILSWORTH. Ideal centre for touring the Cotswolds. Comfortable accommodation. Well equipped bedrooms. Luxurious private/en-suite bathrooms. In an area of outstanding natural beauty with wonderful panoramic views of surrounding countryside. Bed, breakfast from £11. Phone: (01453) 833626.

PAINSWICK. Bed and breakfast in 18th century cloth mill by stream in rural setting. Log fires. Old beams. Ideal walking. Horse riding nearby. Non smokers only please. ETB 2 Crown. Marden, Upper Doreys Mill, Phone: (0452) 812459.

ROYAL FOREST OF DEAN. Symonds Yat Rock Motel. In beautiful quiet setting. Family run. Rooms en-suites with colour televison, tea making facilities, central heating. Ideal touring and walking centre. Licensed restaurant. Dogs welcome. Phone: (0594) 836191.

STOW-ON-THE WOLD, The Lime, Evesham Road. Large Victorian AA/RAC house. Overlooking fields. 4 minutes town. 4 posters, double, twin, family rooms. Wash basins, televisions, tea - coffee facilities. Some en-suite. Parking. Attractive garden with ornamental pool. Phone: (01451) 830034.

STROUD. Heart of Cotswolds. Family run hotel. All rooms en-suite with full facilities. Garden to Stroudwater canal. Superb cuisine. Restaurant, bar, snacks, fully licensed. Ideal location for golf, walking, touring. Bell Hotel, Phone: (0453) 763556.

TEWKESBURY. Early eighteenth century Guest House overlooking river. Central heating, television, tea making, hair dryers all rooms. Comfortable, friendly. Excellent food. Lovely area, ideal centre. Bed and breakfast from £15. Pets welcome. 2 - 3 day breaks. Phone: (0684) 298935.

WYE VALLEY/Forest of Dean, near Symonds Yat. 15th century farm cottages for 2 or 4 plus persons. Ideal walking area from farm. All inclusive charges. 3 keys commended. Rates from £120 to £230 per week. Phone: (0594) 860072.

SELF-CATERING

BOURTON ON THE WATER. Traditional Cots- wold stone cottage. Secluded but central. Sleeps 6. One bedroom with en-suite facilities. 2 lavatories. Central heating, open fire. Secure walled garden. Private parking. Washing machine. Cot, television. Brochure Phone: (0359) 230125.

BREDON. 17th century barn recently converted. Fully equipped, 3 bedrooms, double en-suite, 2 twins, cot, bathroom, central heating. Tastefully furnished garden, play area. Coarse fishing, 2 rods. ETB 5 keys highly commended. Phone: (0684) 295556.

CHELTENHAM. Comfortable architect rede- signed terraced house, 3 double bedrooms, 2 bathrooms, twin garage. Overlooking Cheltenham boys college playing fields. Washing machine. Available July - August. £220 per week, inclusive of gas and electricity. Phone: (0452) 712106.

CHELTENHAM. Comfortable detached cottage in small village close to Cheltenham, Gloucester and Tewkesbury. Sleeps six. Bed linen provided. Gas central heating. Parking for three cars. Garden. ETB 4 keys commended. Phone: (0242) 680511.

CHIPPING CAMPDEN 2 miles. Luxury modern barn conversion. Sleeps 6. En-suite master bedroom. 200 metres high on Cotswolds Escarpment. Views walks. Good garden plus patio. Beams throughout. Quiet location. Large lounge feature fireplace. Dishwasher, fridge,freezer. Brochure Phone: (0235) 766802.

CIRENCESTER. Modern house, sleeping four. Furnished to high standard. Central heating, electricity, bed linen, towels included. Television, microwave, fridge, freezer, wash-dryer, telephone, garden, patio furniture. Ideal touring, walking Cotswolds. Pets. ETB. Open all year. Phone: (0285) 658056.

COTSWOLDS South. Comfortable country cot- tage, between Wotton-U-Edge and Dursley. Sleeps 6 plus cot. Large garden. Linen supplied. Pets welcome. Close proximity to many places of interest, Slimbridge Wildfowl Trust, Berkeley Castle etc. Phone: (0453) 542824.

COTSWOLDS. Lovely cosy thatched Tudor cottage. Inglenook fireplace for log fires. Carpeted throughout. Colour television. Spring interior mattresses. Very comfortable. 2 bedrooms. Sleeps 3. Garden and large private parking area. Phone: 081 859 1432 evenings and weekends.

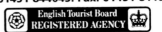
COTSWOLDS. Attractive detached 2 bed- roomed stone cottage. Central heating, large lounge, colour television, separate dining room, fitted kitchen, cooker, microwave, automatic washer, refrigerator. Enclosed garden. Parking. Ideal tourist location. Part weeks considered. No pets. Phone: (0453) 763938.

COTSWOLDS, Cirencester near. Period cottage in pretty village location with good amenities. Fully equipped, 3 bedrooms, sleeps 2 - 5. Linen provided. Colour television. Brochure Phone: (0452) 770072.

COTSWOLDS, Bourton-on-the-Water, Cots- wolds Comfortable detached house. 3 bedrooms, sleeps 5 plus child. Colour television, central heating. Garden with parking. In attractive village, good centre for exploring Cotswolds. Phone: Williams (0785) 760613.

FOREST OF DEAN, Wye Valley. Self-catering holiday flat. All modern conveniences. Sleeps 2 - 4 persons, bed linen optional. Pets. Shopping centre 10 minutes. Horse riding, golf nearby. Phone: Mrs Rogers (01594) 833718.

FOREST OF DEAN, Newnham. Delightful fully restored, equipped 17th century cottage. Sleeps 4-6. Centre village but quiet location. 5 minutes walk River Severn. Easy touring distance Cotswolds, Wye Valley, Welsh border, Cheltenham. For details, brochure Phone: (0285) 810001.

FOREST OF DEAN, Cinderford. Twixt Severn and Wye, cosy three bedroomed house. Five minutes town, three minutes woodlands. Television, central heating. Sleeps five. Phone: (0594) 825194.

FOREST OF DEAN. Old beamed cottage. Sleeps 4, on smallholding. Indoor heated swimming pool, tennis court. Colour television, log fire, centrally heated. Furnished to high standard. Pets welcome. Wonderful views. Good walking area. Quiet location. Phone: (0452) 760751.

FOREST OF DEAN. Two spacious apartments in listed coach house with games room and garden with excellent views. Sleeps 4 & 5. HETB 4 key commended. £80-£195 weekly. Phone for brochure (0594) 842339.

FOREST OF DEAN. Attractive detached bunga- low in quiet countryside. Comfortable, fully equipped accommodation. Sleeps 4/6 and baby. Available all year. From £110 per week, including electricity, linen. Phone: Mrs M. Andrews (01452) 760210.

NEWNHAM ON SEVERN, Forest of Dean. Fully equipped country cottage, sleeps 2 plus. Wood burner, central heating. Private parking, lovely gardens. All linen, gas, wood supplied. Ideal walking and touring. Short breaks welcome. Phone: (0452) 760436.

NEWNHAM-ON-SEVERN. Pretty character cot- tages, converted barns belonging to 17 century farm-house. Newly renovated to high standard and well equipped with private gardens. Granary cottage, sleeps 2/3. The Apple barn, sleeps 4/6. Phone: (0452) 760243.

STOW ON THE WOLD five miles. Two bed- roomed Cotswold cottage, overlooking green in pic-turesque village of Kingham, featured in Channel Four's 'The Rector's Wife'. Sleeps four. From £100 per week including central heating. Phone: (0608) 658596.

TEWKESBURY. Luxury 2 bedroom converted milking parlour, on edge of village between Cotswolds and Malvern Hills. Tennis court (shared with owners). Membership of local golf and country club with swim-ming pool, sauna, jacuzzi etc. Phone: (0684) 290808.

UPLEADON. Spacious barn conversion, sleeps 2/3 in beautiful Leadon Valley. Central for Malvern, Ledbury, Forest of Dean, Cotswolds. Phone: (0531) 822630.

WINCHCOMBE, Cotswolds. Four superb, fully equipped cottages in courtyard setting. Renovated by owners who live close by, from two stone barns. ETB approved five keys highly commended. Sorry no pets. Free colour brochure phone: (0242) 603855.

WYE VALLEY. Close to Black Mountains and Brecon Beacons. Ideal centre for sporting or relaxed hol-iday. Three studio apartments in 16th century farm-house. Coarse fishing pools on site. Mrs Eckley. Phone: (0874) 754224.

WYE VALLEY, Forest of Dean. Quiet country cottage. Sleeps 6/8 plus cot. Fully equipped. Ideal tour-ing centre for Malvern Hills, Cotswolds, Black Mountains. 6 miles from Ross on Wye. Winter short breaks available. Phone: (0708) 763438.

WHERE TO GO

Robert Opie Collection
Gloucester Docks, Gloucester.
Tel: (0452) 302309

Steeped in nostalgia, the Robert Opie collection of packaging and advertising brings over 100 years of shopping basket history vividly to life.

Keith Harding's World of Mechanical Music
Northleach, Gloucestershire.
Tel: (0451) 60181

17th century wood merchant's house, antique clock, musical boxes, automata and mechanical musical instruments present as an entertainment. A unique experience of sound.

St Augustine's Farm
Gloucester
Tel: 0452 740277

A working 124 acre farm situated at the horseshoe bend of the River Severn. Pigs, sheep, ducks, hens, calves, goats and other animals. Watch the cows being milked and wander through the fields and get close to the animals. Also a collection of bygone machinery in use today, farm trail, teas, gift shop and picnic play area.

Birdland
Rissington Road, Bourton-on-the-Water,
Gloucestershire.
Tel: 0451 820480

Bird garden on the banks of the river Windrush. Penguins, waterfowl and tropical birds, many at liberty.

HEREFORD & WORCESTER

HOTELS & GUEST HOUSES

BROADWAY. Whiteacres Guest House. Spacious Victorian house. ETB two crowns commended. 6 rooms en-suite, 4 poster beds available. Off-road parking. Free brochure on request. Reductions for 2 or more nights. Richardson, Station Road. Phone: (01386) 852320.

HEREFORD, near. Church Farm, Rowlstone Farmhouse. Bed and breakfast. May to September. Quiet location, unspoilt countryside for naturalists, walkers and history lovers. Near Welsh border, castles. 1 double bedroom, en-suite, shower and toilet. Phone: (0981) 240708.

THE OLD MILL, Hoarwithy

AA LISTED
COMMENDED

4 miles from Ross-on-Wye and 8 miles from Hereford. Situated in small unspolit village. 18th century Farmhouse with oak-beamed lounge and log fireplace, beamed dining room. Home cooking a speciality. Friendly atmosphere. Ideal for walking/touring Wye Valley, Welsh Border, Malverns etc.

Holiday cottage also available.

Write or phone: **CAROL PROBERT**
The Old Mill, Hoarwithy, Hereford HR2 6QH. Tel: (0432) 840602

HEREFORD 2 miles. Hotel set in 3.5 acres. All rooms en-suite, tea making facilities, television. Bar food. Parking for 100 cars. Golf nearby. Fishing, country walks. A-la-carte restaurant, traditional Sunday lunch. Run by resident owner. Phone: (0432) 760264

CWM CRAIG FARM
Little Dewchurch, Hereford
Herefordshire HR2 6PS
Georgian farmhouse, midway between Hereford and Ross-on-Wye. Edge of the Wye Valley. Three spacious bedrooms, one en-suite. Regret no pets. Excellent eating-out inns within the vicinity.
Mrs. G. Lee. Phone: Carey (01432) 840250

HEREFORD, Upper Newton Farmhouse, Kinnersley. Phone: (0544) 327727. 17th century, characterful home. Fluffy towels, flowers and exceptional hospitality on this working farm. Four poster, extensive garden. Peaceful. Centrally situated for touring, academic and physical activities. Pearl Taylor.

MALVERN area. Comfortable farmhouse accommodation, between hills and River Severn. Ideal touring, walking centre. Showers, colour television, tea - coffee making facilities. Evening meals by request. Home Cooking. Children welcome. Dogs by arrangement. Phone: Margaret (0684) 592193.

ROSS-ON-WYE. Brook House. Queen Anne Grade II listed house, offering comfortable en-suite rooms with television and tea making facilities. Home made muffins a speciality! ETB 2 crowns. Rates from £15.50. Non smokers preferred. Phone: (0989) 750710.

TENBURY WELLS. Cadmore Lodge. Hotel and country club. 3 crowns. ** AA. Idyllic lakeside setting. Excellent cuisine. Warm welcome. En-suite bedrooms. 9 hole golf course. Trout, coarse fishing, bowls, tennis. Special breaks. Phone: (0584) 810044.

WICKHAMFORD. Bed and breakfast in 16th century manor connected with George Washington, U.S.A. Excellent hospitality. Tennis, fishing, golf, riding nearby. Also self-catering cottages. Broadway. Sleeping 6-8. Well appointed. Children, pets welcome. June Ryan-Bell, Phone: (0386) 830296.

WORCESTER. Charming cottage in quiet vil-lage, four miles north west of city. En-suite bed and breakfast, ETB two crowns commended. Non smoking. Good local inns for evening meals. For details Phone: Helen Rendle (0905) 641123.

WORCESTER (nearby). Old Schoolhouse Hotel. Cosy accommodation in 17th century farmhouse/ Victorian school. Popular restaurant. Wonderful views. Gardens. Easy parking. Golf, clay pigeon shooting nearby, riverside walks. Phone: (01905) 371368

WORCESTER, Malvern. Croft Guest House, Bransford. 16-18th century country house. AA listed. ETB 2 crowns. Comfortable family run with en-suite rooms, central heating, sauna, jacuzzi. Licensed. Dinners inclusive. Short breaks. Golf locally. Children, dogs welcome. Phone: (01886) 832227.

WYE VALLEY, Ross-on-Wye. Superb 17th cen-tury character properties. Delightful village location. Sleeps 2-14. Owner supervised. Self-catering; bed and breakfast from £10. Brass 4 poster bed, en-suite, jacuzzi. Children, dogs welcome. H. Smith, Old Kilns, Howle Hill, Ross-on-Wye. Phone: (0989) 562051.

SELF-CATERING

BOLSTONE. 'Owls Hoot' is a modern bungalow in 3 1/2 acres of meadow land with wildlife pond. Adjacent to woodland with deer. Comfortable double or twin en-suite room with colour television and tea making facilities. Phone: (0432) 870616.

BROADWAY. Small cottage for two in quiet Cotswold village (Laverton). 20% of rentals donated to 'Crohn's in Childhood Research Association'. Ideal touring base. Sorry, no pets. Own garden and parking. Colour leaflet Phone/Fax: (0386) 584280.

BROMYARD. 16th century farmhouse wing. Comfortable accommodation with colour television. Dairy, sheep, donkeys, woodland walks. Sleeps 4 plus cot. Golf course 3 miles. Phone: (0885) 483287.

HAY-ON-WYE
DETACHED COTTAGE
On the slopes above the Wye Valley. Set in 35 acres of countryside and woodlands. Large garden for your private use. Close to the town of Books. Off street parking. Sleeps 2. Cot. Pets allowed.
Tel: 0497 820766

HEREFORD/WELSH BORDER. Spacious cottage in small village away from main roads. Very well equipped, open fires, 4 bedrooms, sleeps 7. Garden, shop, pub, village cricket. Lovely views of Black Mountains. Ideal all year. Phone: 021-472 3700.

HEREFORD. Buttercup Cottage. Recently con-verted barn, forming 3 bedroomed rural cottage. ETB 3 keys commended. Farmhouse, dining kitchen, autowasher, microwave. Living room, patio doors, colour television. Master bedroom en-suite. Central heating. Short breaks. Brochure Phone: (0742) 364357.

150 HEREFORD & WORCESTER Self-Catering

NORTH HEREFORDSHIRE

Stone Cottage, sleeps 5/6 in tranquil setting between Hereford-Leominster-Bromyard.
Black and white beamed cottage, sleeps 5/6 in peaceful village twixt Leominster-Ludlow. Pets welcome.
Tel: (01432) 820366 brochure.

HEREFORD. Historic city fringe. Much praised self-contained wing of owners' detached house, sleeps 3. ETB 4 keys commended. Country views. Services nearby. Car parking in pretty garden. Non smokers only. Sae brochure. Phone: (0432) 273380.

HEREFORD. A spacious cottage on a working dairy farm in rural countryside. Sleeps 8 plus cot. Large enclosed garden. From £140 to £240 per week. Sae Monkton Farm, Ocle Pychard, Hereford HR1 3QQ or Phone: (0432) 820217.

HEREFORD, near, 17th century listed building conversions. 9 only cottages and apartments. On site 40ft. indoor swimming pool. Saunas, snooker, carp lake. Cosy bar and restaurant. Beautiful countryside with nearby golf courses and riding stables. Brochure Phone: (0432) 761202.

HEREFORD. Delightfully converted farm cot-tages. Heated indoor swimming pool, sauna, solarium, games room. Coarse fishing. Large garden. Dogs welcome. Walks, golf. Colour televisions. Ideal touring. Poolspringe Farm Cottages, Much Birch, Hereford HR2 8JJ. Phone: (0981) 540355.

HEREFORD. One bedroom holiday cottage. Is a converted Cider Mill attached to the family house. Is in a quiet rural location by a stream, on a small holding. Phone: (0981) 540 237.

HEREFORD near. Small development. Character apartments in converted 17th century buildings. 40 feet indoor pool, saunas. Bar, restaurant. Carp lake. Snooker room. Lovely setting. Golf, riding 5 minutes. White House Farm, Brinsop. Brochure Phone: (0432) 761202.

KINGSLAND, Leominster. Peace and quiet rural location. 2 bedroom centrally heated barn. En-suite facilities. Sleeps 4. Disabled access, ground floor with toilet. Ideal for touring, walking, cycling, Shropshire, Wales, observing birds, wildlife. Phone: (0568) 708941.

KINGTON. (Huntington). Detached cottage, sleeps 5. Ample parking. Scenic walks over Welsh border - hills. Peaceful, unspoiled countryside of mid Wales. Ideal bird watching. (Red Kite Bussards). Pets welcome. Phone: (0544) 22289.

LEDBURY, near. Barn conversion on organic fruit farm and woodlands. For holiday let. Overlooking Malvern Hills. Sleeps 5. Hereford 10 miles, Ledbury 5 miles. Unspoilt countryside. Woodburning stove and central heating. Beautiful walks. Phone: (0531) 670511.

LEOMINSTER. Cottages. Camping. M. Brooke, Nicholson Farm, Leominster HR6 0SL. Phone: (0568) 760269. April 16th 1995 onwards. Phone: 01-568 760269.

LEOMINSTER near. Charming stone cottage. Inglenook log-burner, central heating. Beautiful views in own valley. Paddock, stream. Sleeps 6. Television, oak beams. Renovated warm comfortable accommodation. Golf, fishing, horse-riding. Black and white village. Good pub grub. Phone: (01568) 614555.

MALVERN. Award winning cottages converted from 17th century farm buildings in 9 acres. Exceptionally clean. ETB highly commended. Open all year. Dogs welcome. Winter short breaks. Phone/Fax: (01886) 880607, colour brochure. Whitewells Farm Cottages.

MALVERN. Holiday bungalow, 4 miles north of Malvern in a secluded valley in the middle of a fruit farm. Sleeps 4/6. Fully furnished. From £89 per week. 4 keys. No pets. Open all year. Brochure Phone: (0886) 884410.

MALVERN. Well equipped modern house. Double, twin, single bedrooms, sleeping 2-5. Holidays, short breaks from April 29th. Reasonable rates inclusive of gas and electricity. Beautiful walking and touring area. For further details Phone: (0684) 560912.

MALVERN HILLS. Coach-house and cottage apartments for 2 and 4/6 on Elgar's magnificent hills. Extensive grounds. Electricity £5, gas/linen included. Central heating. Dogs welcome. Excellent walking. Convenient Stratford, Cotswolds, Wye Valley. 4 key commended. Phone: Knight (0684) 564448.

MARTLEY, Teme Valley. Nestle in nostal-gia, inglenook and log fires in enchanting, beamed, 1750, detached cottage for three. All modern comforts. Village shop, church and inn, just a totter away. An unforgettable experience! Brochure Phone: (0564) 782748.

PEMBRIDGE, Near Leominster. Self-contained wing of black and white farmhouse on working farm. Near Welsh border, half mile from village of Pembridge. ETB 3 keys approved. Weekly or short breaks available. Sleeps 6. No pets. Phone: (0544) 388569.

ROSS-ON-WYE, Ledbury, Hereford. All within 10 miles. Very peaceful country cottage with outstanding views, sleeps 4. Extremely comfortably furnished, linen provided. Central heating, colour television. Private woodland, well behaved dogs welcome. Ideal for walking and touring. Phone: (0989) 86248.

ROSS ON WYE. Easy access Wye Valley and Forest Dean. Superior self-contained accommodation. 2/4. Quiet location, edge of village. Breathtaking country views. Cosy, tastefully furnished. All modern conveniences. Excellent for walking and touring. Phone: (01989) 720766.

ROSS-ON-WYE. Comfortable modern bunga-low. Quiet location with extensive views of the beautiful Wye Valley. En-suite, tea making facilities. Bed, breakfast, optional evening meal. Centre for touring, walking, fishing. Williams Wailea, Ballingham, Hereford. Phone: (0432) 840255.

TENBURY WELLS. 2.5 miles in peaceful coun-tryside. Modernised and extended semi-detached 19th century farm workers cottage. Providing comfortable, well equipped accommodation. Sleeps 5 plus cot. Double twin, single. Children, pets welcome. Owner supervised. Phone: (01568) 750255.

WYE VALLEY. Equidistant Ross, Symonds Yat and Forest of Dean. Sunny detached traditional stone cottage overlooking river. Refurbished to highest five-key ETB standards including 2 bathrooms. Sleeps 6 in 3 bedrooms. Phone: Mrs Jennings (01527) 833880.

WYE VALLEY. 17th century character cottages Superb views. Sleeps 2-14. Owner supervised. Equipped to high standard. Children, pets welcome. Also bed, breakfast from £10. Four poster bed. Jacuzzi en-suite. Smith, Old Kilns, Howle Hill, Ross-On-Wye. Phone: (0989) 562051.

CARAVANS, CHALETS & HOLIDAY PARKS

KINGTON, Herefordshire. Caravan, sleep 6/8, on small secluded family run site. Conveniently situated in Welsh border market town. Good centre for walking, (on Offas Dyke footpath), touring, fishing etc. From £80 per week. Phone: (0544) 230653/230220.

WYE VALLEY, Herefordshire. Two only, 6 berth caravans. Quiet country site, lovely views over Wye Valley and Forest of Dean. Amenities, mains water and electricity. Colour televisions, showers, fridges, all bed linen provided. Wilkes. Phone: (0989) 770473.

VALE OF EVESHAM
MANOR FARM LEISURE
FISHING AND FARM CARAVAN HOLIDAYS
Small family run site at Harvington, near Evesham, with personal service given. Excellent fishing (Warks Avon and Lake). Ideally situated for Cotswolds and Stratford. Statics for hire. Tourers welcome.
For brochure phone Wendy or David on
(0386) 870039

WHERE TO GO

The Lost Street Museum
27 Brookend Street, Ross-on-Wye, Hertfordshire.
Tel: (0989) 62752

Complete Edwardian street of shops including tobacconist, glassware, grocer, chemist, clothes store, pub and many others.

Severn Valley Railway
The Railway Station, Bewdley, Worcestershire.
Tel: (0299) 403816

Preserved standard gauge steam railway running 16 miles between Kidderminster, Bewley and Bridgnorth. collection of locomotives and passengers coaches.

Jubilee Maze and Museum of Mazes
Symonds Yat, Hertfordshire.
Tel: (0600) 890360

A traditional hedge maze with carved stone temple centrepieces, created to celebrate Queen Elizabeth's Jubilee in 1977. World's only 'hands-on interactive' Museum of Mazes.

The Commandery
Sidbury, Worcester, Worcestershire.
Tel: (0905) 355071

15th Century timber-framed building with great hall and panelled rooms. Civil War audio visual show and exhibition. Display on Worcester's working past.

Broadfield Gardens & Vineyards
Bodenham, Herefordshire
Tel: 056884 483

Tours and wine tasting, lunches, suppers and light refreshments to appointment, with wine purchase on the premises.

West Midlands Safari And Leisure Park
Spring Grove, Worcestershire
Tel: 0299 402114

The animal reserves, home to a variety of rare and exotic species - lions, tigers, giraffes, rhino, monkeys. Admission includes: Safari, pet corner, sealion show, animal encounter, reptile house, train ride to extensive amusement area.

LEICESTERSHIRE

HOTELS & GUEST HOUSES

UPPINGHAM
Bed and breakfast. Comfortable Victorian country house and converted coach house in 14 acres overlooking Eye Brook Valley. Double/twin/single and family en-suite rooms with TV's, tea/coffee. Edge of conservation village, ideal for touring, cycling, walking, riding, Watersports.

Old Rectory, Belton-in-Rutland, LE15 9LE
Tel: 01572 717279

CARAVANS, CHALETS & HOLIDAY PARKS

BELTON-IN-RUTLAND. ETB 3 key commended. Overlooking Eye Brook Valley and rolling Rutland countryside. Flat sleeps 2/6. Quiet location on edge of conservation village. With pub and shops. 10 minutes Rutland Water, Rockingham Castle. Phone: (01572) 717279.

WHERE TO GO

Twycross Zoo
Atherstone.
Tel: (0827) 880250/880440 - Open April to October

Gorillas, orang-utans, modern gibbon complex, elephant, giraffes, sealions, pets corner, aviaries, reptiles. First ever Bonobo chimps in British Isles. Special summer events, shops, playground. disabled visitors welcome.

Snibstone Discovery Park
Ashby Road, Coalville, Leicestershire.
Tel: (0530) 510851

Science and industry museum. colliery trail, indoor and outdoor science discovery centres. 1742 wheelwright's workshop, nature reserve, fishing lakes, picnic areas, gift shop and cafe. Free car parking.

Snibston Discovery Park
Ashby Road, Coalville
Tel: 0503 510851

New museum within a 100 acre former colliery, showing the history of the local textile, transport, engineering and extractive industries. 'Hands On' centre, nature trail, events area and fishing. Picnic and 250 year old wheelwright's workshop.

Stanford Hall and Motor Cycle Museum
Lutterworth
Tel: 0788 860250

William and Mary House. Family costumes/furniture, pictures. Replica 1898 flying machine. Motorcycle museum, rose garden and nature trail.

NOTTINGHAMSHIRE

HOTELS & GUEST HOUSES

BURTON JOYCE. Willow House. Quiet village location near beautiful River Trent. 15 minutes Nottingham centre. Sunny, comfortable rooms. Tea making facilities, colour televisions. From £16. Please ring for directions. Baker, 12 Willow Wong. Phone: Nottingham 312070.

SELF-CATERING

TEVERSAL. Old Manor. 16th century. Terraced gardens accommodation or self-catering. Get away from it all. Celebrations, weddings, business functions. Splendid manorial setting. Close to M1. Phone: (0623) 554569.

WHERE TO GO

The Tales of Robin Hood
Nottingham, Nottinghamshire.
Tel: (0602) 414414
Join the world's greatest medieval adventure and hide out in the Sheriff's eerie cave. Ride through the magical Greenwood and play the Silver Arrow game.
Rufford Country Park and Craft Centre
Ollerton, Nottinghamshire.
Tel: (0623) 824153
Parkland and 25 acre lake with ruins of Cistercian abbey. Woodlands walks, formal gardens sculpture garden. Craft centre with exhibitions of British craftsmanship.
White Post Modern Farm Centre
Farnsfield, Nr Newark, Nottinghamshire.
Tel: (0623) 882977
Working farm with llama, ostriches, egg incubator, free-range hens, lakes, picnic areas and tea gardens.
Millgate Museum of Social and Folk Life
Newark, Nottinghamshire.
Tel: (0636) 79403
Museum portraying local social and folk life. Series of street scenes with period shops. Mezzanine gallery with regular programme of temporary exhibitions.

SHROPSHIRE

HOTELS & GUEST HOUSES

ABDON, Shropshire. Magnificent country house. Panoramic views. Offering bed and breakfast and gourmet evening meal. Set in area of outstanding natural beauty. Perfect for rambling and historic sight-seeing. ETB highly commended. Phone: (0746) 34551.

CHURCH STRETTON. Belvedere Guest House. Comfortable, licensed guest house. Situated 200 metres from 6,000 acres of National Trust hill country. 12 rooms - 6 en-suite. Evening meals. AA, RAC, ETB commended. Rogers, Burway Road. Phone: (01694) 722232.

CLEOBURY MORTIMER. Kings Arms Hotel. Picturesque country inn. Scenic area. Superb cuisine. Excellent, well equipped rooms. Colour televisions, tea and coffee making facilities. 2 nights bed and breakfast, dinner £55 per person. Warmest welcome assured. Phone: (0299) 270252.

CLEOBURY MORTIMER. Unique 16th century coaching inn. Centre picturesque village. Famous superb cuisine. Bed and breakfast from £18. 2 night bed and breakfast and dinner from £55. Close golf, fishing. Excellent touring area. Excellent, well equipped rooms. Phone: (0299) 270252.

SHREWSBURY. If you're on the Cadfael trail and require bed and breakfast at £13, then please Phone Geoff, Anita on (0743) 367068. We are situated near Cadfael's Abbey.

SELF-CATERING

COLEMERE, near Ellesmere. Peaceful location. 6 self-catering country cottages for 2 to 6. All ETB three key commended. Colour television. Pets welcome. Brochure: Write Clarke, Colemere Farm, Ellesmere SY12 0QL or Ansafone (01691) 623420.

IRONBRIDGE. Cottage holidays. Superb lake-side houses. Lounge and balcony, overlooking lake. Conservatory, garage. Excellent facilities. ETB 5 key highly commended. Free brochure. 45 Newbridge Road, Ironbridge, Telford, Shropshire TF8 7BA. Phone: (01952) 433061.

LUDLOW. Detached holiday cottage in area of outstanding natural beauty. Sleeps 2/4. Well equipped and maintained. Garden area, terrace, parking. Bath/shower, microwave, fridge freezer. Well behaved pet and children by arrangement. Phone: (0584) 890146.

LUDLOW 6 miles. Self-contained ground floor, no internal steps. Working farm. Quiet village. Kitchen, bathroom, large lounge with double bed plus 1. Open all year. Sunny patio. 1 dog. 3 keys commended HETB. Brochure Phone: (056886) 243.

CARAVANS, CHALETS & HOLIDAY PARKS

CLUN VALLEY. Highly recommended mobile home on working farm. In beautiful peaceful surroundings, magnificent views. Central heating, television. From £90 weekly. Sorry no pets. Brochure Sue Wheeler, Brynmawr, Newcastle, Craven Arms, Shropshire. Phone: (0588) 640298 - (0588) 640339.

CLUN, near. South Shropshire. Caravan, large, comfortable, situated in peaceful spot near stream. Double bedroom, bed settee in lounge. All amenities, fully equipped. Linen supplied. Large parking area. Easily accessible. Brochure available. Television point. Phone: (0686) 670214.

WHERE TO GO

Telford Wonderland
Telford Town Park, Telford.
Tel: (0952) 591633
Theme Park based on nursery rhymes and fairy stories,

Ironbridge Gorge Museum
Ironbridge, Shropshire.
Tel: (0952) 433522
World's first cast iron bridge, Museum of the River and visitor centre, tar tunnel, Jackfield tile Museum, Coalport china Museum, rosehill and Blists Hill Museum.

Forestry Enterprise Bury Ditches Hill Fort And Woods
Clunton, Shropshire
Tel: (0970) 612367
Well preserved hill fort, with panoramic views of Shropshire and 3 waymarked forest walks. Car park and picnic site.

Corbet Wood
Corbet Wood, Grinshill, Shrewsbury.
Tel (0743) 254004
23 acres of woodland on steep hillside within nature trail. Main features are the view, disused quarry workings and a fine Scots Pine Wood.

STAFFORDSHIRE

HOTELS & GUEST HOUSES

12 *GOOD REASONS TO STAY*

Church Grange

Bradley, Alton, Staffs. ST10 4DF

- Just 2 miles from ALTON TOWERS
- A Warm Welcome Awaits You
- Tranquil Setting with Splendid Views
- Large, Comfortable Family Rooms
- Mouth-watering Home Cooking
- Vegetarian Dishes/Special Diets
- Ground Floor Bedroom for Disabled
- Close to the Beautiful Peak Distict
- BBQs & Afternoon Tea in the Garden
- Special Interest Breaks including Golf, Gourmet Eating, Rambling, Cycling
- High Standards of Comfort & Service
- Self-catering Cottage also available

PLEASE TELEPHONE FOR OUR
BROCHURE

0889 26507

LEEK. Convenient to Alton Towers, Moorlands Peak Park and Pottery towns. Working stock farm. 2 cottages, sleeping 3. Wheelchair friendly, fully equipped. Josephine Edwards, 'Milestones', Ashbourne Road, Bottomhouse, near Leek, Staffordshire ST13 7NZ. Phone: (0538) 304548.

LEEK near. Middle Farm Guest House. A 100 acre farm within easy reach of Alton Towers, Leek town centre and Peak District National Park. Full en-suite. Tea, coffee facilities all rooms. Special rates for families. Phone: (0538) 382839.

White Gables Hotel

PROPRIETORS: Robert & Susan Worrall
TRENTHAM RD., BLURTON, STOKE ON TRENT, STAFFS.
TELEPHONE (0782) 324882

Beautiful 18th Century Hotel. 1 mile Wedgwood. 10 miles to Alton Towers. Facilities inc.: Table Tennis, Tennis, Pool Table, Videos (all free). Large gardens. Car park. All rooms hot and cold. TV. Tea/coffee making facilities. Families welcome.

SELF-CATERING

HORTON GOWER COAST

Peaceful seaside cottage, walking distance to safe sandy beach. Beams, inglenook fireplace, double glazing and night storage throughout. Games room with table tennis, darts and snooker. Dishwasher, washing machine and microwave. Colour TV, sleeps 7 plus Cot.
MESSAGE SERVICE.
Phone: 0941 106304

IPSTONES, Staffordshire moorlands. Holiday cottages. Self-catering. Panoramic views over open countryside. Convenient for Peak District, Alton Towers, Chatsworth, Churnet Valley and the Potteries. Village shops and pubs five minute walk. Ample parking. Phone: (0538) 266465.

PEAK DISTRICT, Staffordshire Moorlands. Beautiful farm cottage. ETB 4 keys commended. Set in a superb position with magnificent views. Full central heating. Cot and high chair available. Close to Alton Towers (3 miles, Peak District and Potteries). Phone: (0538) 266243.

UTTOXETER. Flat, convenient, clean, comfort- able. Sleeps 4, central heating, television. Parking. Near Alton Towers, Peak District. Available all year round. Short lets. Details Phone: (0889) 564086.

CARAVANS, CHALETS & HOLIDAY PARKS

LEEK. Three berth 14 foot caravan to let on static pitch. Very quiet site with scenic view and good walking. Hot showers and electric hook up. Steam boat, steam railway, nearby. From £20 per week. Phone: (0663) 764026.

WHERE TO GO

Drayton Manor Park and Zoo
Tamworth.
Tel: (0827) 287979
Predominantly a leisure park, though incorporating a small well-stocked zoo. Log flumes, giant wheel, pirate adventure ride, jungle cruise, tea cup ride. Splash Canyon. Cafeteria, shop and garden centre. Disabled visitors welcome.

Alton Towers Theme Park
Alton, Staffordshire.
Tel: (0538) 702200
Over 125 rides and attractions including Haunted House, Runaway Mine Train, Congo River Rapids, Log Flume, New Beast, Corkscrew and Thunderlooper.

Tamworth Castle and Museum Service
Tamworth, Staffordshire.
Tel: (0827) 63563
Norman moat and bailey castle shell keep and Norman tower. Late medieval great hall, tudor stairs, Jacobean state apartments. Local history museum.

Chatterley Whitfield Mining Museum
Tunstall, Stoke-on-Trent, Stafforshire.
Tel: (0782) 813337
Underground guided tour, British Coal Collection, energy hall, winding engine, pit ponies, underground and surface locomotives.

Bass Museum, Visitors Centre and Shire House Stables
Horninglow Street, Burton-upon-Trent, Staffordshire.
Tel: (0283) 42031
First major museum of brewing industry. Story of different methods of transporting beer since the early 1800's.

WARWICKSHIRE

HOTELS & GUEST HOUSES

COVENTRY near. Country guest house, offering peace and tranquillity. Tourist Board 3 crowns. Luxury en-suite rooms - chalets. Colour television. Twin £45; double £40; single occupancy £25. No smoking. Private parking. Near Coventry, Forest of Arden, Belfry. NEC. Phone: (01676) 541898.

KENILWORTH. Clarendon House Hotel. 4 crown historic Inn. Egon Ronay Bistro restaurant. Real ale bar. Rooms en-suite. £25 per person. Minimum 2 nights, Friday - Sunday. Ideal for Warwick and Stratford. Phone: (0800) 616883.

STRATFORD-UPON-AVON. Newbold Nurseries, Newbold-on-Stour. Modern farmhouse and hydroponic tomato nursery. Comfortable rooms with television, tea/coffee. Pets welcome. Central for Cotswolds, Hidcote Gardens, Warwick. Horse riding and fishing nearby. En-suite available. From £14.50 nightly. Phone: (0789) 450285.

STRATFORD ON AVON. Nolands Farm and restaurant. Bedrooms in converted stables. All en-suite, modern conveniences, 4 posters. Licensed restaurant. Fishing, clay pigeon shooting, bicycles, riding. Peaceful and quiet. Prices from £15 to £20 person. AA selected, RAC commended. ETB 3. Ground floor bedrooms. Phone: (01926) 640309

WARWICKSHIRE COOPERAGE FARM

Bed/breakfast is a 300-year-old listed farmhouse situated in the heart of England in the village of Meriden. Friendly family run establishment. Tea/coffee facilities, central heating. Transport available. En-suite rooms.

English Tourist Board

Tel: 01676 523493

WARWICK near. Comfortable house with ex-tensive country views. Garden. Woodland. Wildlife. Open fire. Full central heating. All rooms tea facilities, hot, cold basins. Television lounge. Dogs, cats. Handy Warwick, Stratford. Bromilow, Woodside, Langley Road, Claverdon. Phone: (0926) 842446.

WOOLATON HALL,
NOTTINGHAMSHIRE
(photograph courtesy of East Midlands Tourist Board)

SELF-CATERING

BIDFORD ON AVON. Self-catered spacious wing of farmhouse. Suitably equipped for 2 people. Set in Shakespeare countryside. Easy reach to Stratford and the Cotswolds. Wheeler, Homelands, Marlcliff, Bidford. Phone: (0789) 772204.

COVENTRY outskirts. Country Guest House. 3 crowns - Tourist board recommended. Peace and tranquillity. Open countryside. Single room from £17; double £40; twin £45. All en-suite - colour television including full English breakfast. Near NEC/Belfry. Phone: Fillongley (01676) 541898.

STRATFORD ON AVON, Shakespeare country. Gateway to Cotswolds. Self-catering holiday house. Sleeps one double, two singles. All modern conveniences. Easy walking distance town centre, theatre etc. Open all year round. Brochure Phone: (01789) 750237.

WHERE TO GO

Warwick Castle
Warwick Castle, Warwickshire.
Tel: (0926) 495421

Set in 60 acres of grounds and gardens. State room, armoury, dungeon, torture chamber, clock tower. 'A Royal Weekend Party 1898' by Madam Tussards Medieval banquets.

Shakespeare's Birthplace
Stratford-upon-Avon, Warwickshire.
Tel: (0789) 204016

Half-timbered building furnished in period style, containing many fascinating books, manuscripts and objects, BBC TV Shakespeare costume exhibition.

Hatton Country World
Hatton, Warwickshire.
Tel: (0926) 842436

A 100 acre haven of rural attractions including over 40 breeds of rare farm animals. Craft centre.

Wellesbourne Watermill
Mill Farm, Kineton Road, Wellesbourne, Warwickshire.
Tel: (0926) 470237

Dramatic wooden waterwheel powering impressive machinery. Stoneground flour, conservation work, millpond, farm animals, local crafts and exhibitions.

Edgehill Battle Museum
The Estate Yard, Farnborough Hall, Nr Banbury, Warwickshire

Tel: 0295 89593 or 0926 332213
Museum containing some dramatic displays of Arms & Armour, costumes, models, dioramas and maps of the Battle on 23rd October, 1642. Battlefield tours and AV for groups by prior arrangement.

Heritage Motor Centre
Gaydon, Warwickshire
Tel: 0926 641188

Worlds largest collection of historic British cars. Lucas and Corgi museum collections. Computer-controlled audio/visual presentation. Themed exhibitions and displays. 4-wheel-drive circuit. Children's playground. Land Rover shuttle ride. Picnic area and nature reserve.

TISSINGTON, DERBYSHIRE
(photograph courtesy of East Midlands Tourist Board)

NORTH WEST ENGLAND

CHESHIRE • CUMBRIA • GREATER MANCHESTER
ISLE OF MAN • LANCASHIRE • MERSEYSIDE

As my first television job in England was based in Manchester, I was lucky enough to be able to explore at first hand the wonderful corner of England that is the North West. A region as famed for sport and the arts as it is for scenery.

Liverpool boast colourful Chinatown districts; the Fylde coast features Dutch style windmills and waterways, and for something that little bit different there are the Japanese gardens at Tatton Park.

There are the sporting achievements of Manchester United, Liverpool and Wigan's Rugby League team to name but three of the top teams clustered here. Who hasn't swooned to the sound of the Beatles? Who hasn't laughed at the great comedian who took his name from his home town – Eric Morecambe? And you can't have holidayed here without sampling Kendal mint cake and Blackpool rock. But the North West has a special resonance that extends beyond its boundaries, the real treat is to experience those pleasures for yourself. And, as befits a region that pioneered trading links with the rest of the world, the North West is a remarkably cosmopolitan location. Manchester and

The North West's distinguished industrial and trading past is a source of great pride, and many of yesterday's workhouses are today's museums, galleries and hotels. The past is brought to life at such attractions as the Rochdale Canal which has linked the industrial centres of Lancashire and Yorkshire for over 200 years; and Lancaster's Georgian Quay, where you can almost still smell the rum and sugar cargoes of old. Not forgetting the Ellesmere Port Boat Museum, the world's largest collection of traditional canal boats; and the Merseyside Maritime Museum, which chronicles the past glory of the region's shipbuilding history.

For cultural pleasures, the phrase 'spoilt for choice' springs to mind.

Take the largest collection of fine art outside London at Liverpool's Walker Art Gallery, and the world's largest L.S. Lowry collection at Salford Art Gallery. If you are a music lover, hear for yourself why Manchester's Halle Orchestra is renowned worldwide; or be entranced by WOMAD, Morecambe's annual world-music festival, sponsored by Peter Gabriel.

The words 'family holiday' and 'Blackpool' are almost synonymous. It's easy to see why: Pleasure Beach, spectacular illuminations, the world's tallest and fastest rollercoaster rides and, of course, the famous Blackpool Tower, now in its second century.If you want to calm down from the thrills and spills of the rollercoaster, you don't have far to travel. A walk along the coast's miles of beaches soon brings the pulse rate back to normal ! I always found a sightseeing trip to the noble Roman towns of Carlisle and Chester made me feel less guilty about indulging in amusement arcades and 'Kiss Me Quick' hats. Though a ramble through the hills and woods of the Lake District is surely the supreme way of 'getting back to nature'. This is, after all, Wordsworth country – Britain's finest poet of the senses and seasons.In the unlikely event that you run out of things to see and do on the mainland there's always a boat or plane trip to the Isle of Man – another jewel in the North West's charismatic crown.

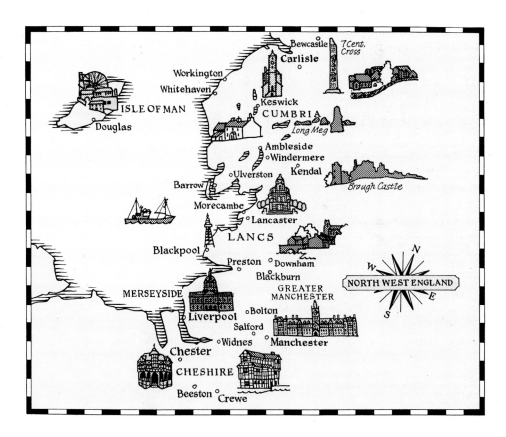

CHESHIRE

CUMBRIA

SELF-CATERING

RUSHTON SPENCER. Detached stone farm cot-tage. Pennines Foothills. ETB five keys. Ground floor double, shower, en-suite. Twin plus single. Alton Towers, Chatsworth, Dovedale. Granada studios. Central heating. Very well equipped. Phone: Mrs Goodwin (0260) 226397.

Merseyside Holiday Homes

Victorian cottages in Bebington, sleep up to 6. £85-£140 pw. Details from:

**Proprietor:
11, West Drive,
High Wycombe,
Bucks, HP13 6JT
☎ 04944 38888 (after 4.30pm)**

WHERE TO GO

Chester Zoo
Upton-by-Chester, Chester, Cheshire.
Tel: (0244) 380280

Penguin pool with underwater views, tropical house, spectacular displays of spring and summer bedding plants. Chimpanzee house and outdoor enclosure. New monorail.

Lyme Park
Disley, Stockport, Cheshire.
Tel: (0663) 762023

Nature trails and herds of red and fallow deer in 1377 acres of moorland, woodland and park. State rooms, period furniture, tapestry, Grinling Gibbons carvings in hall and clock collection.

The Railway Age
Crewe Heritage Centre, Vernon Way, Crewe, Cheshire.
Tel: (0270) 212130

'The Railway Age' provides a fasinating insight into Crewe's place in railway history. Featuring miniature and standard guage railways, three working signal boxes, stored diesel and steam engines, weekend rides behind steam locomotives prepared in the Centre's sidings.

HOTELS & GUEST HOUSES

ALLONBY. Peaceful Cumbrian coastal village. Well equipped. Comfortable cosy chalet. 3 bedrooms, 2 single, 1 double, lounge, loggia kitchen. Indoor toilet, basin, shower. Ideal lakes, borders, Roman wall, historical Carlisle, wind surfing, horse riding. Phone: 051 625 7668.

Buckle Yeat
Guest House

VISA   Access

This old cottage illustrated in many of Beatrix Potter's books has been tastefully furnished for your comfort, having a large lounge with log fire, colour TV and central heating throughout. All rooms are en-suite and have tea and coffee making facilities and colour TV's. The cottage is situated in the village of Near Sawrey close to Hawkshead, Ambleside and Windermere.

 AA
INSPECTED

 English Tourist Board
COMMENDED

**Mrs. Helen Kirby, Buckle Yeat, Sawrey,
Ambleside, Cumbria.
Tel & Fax: (015394) 36446 or
Tel: (015394) 36538**

ALSTON, North Pennines. Magnificent location overlooking quiet valley. Licensed country house hotel with beautiful views. Bed and breakfast £18.50, dinner, bed and breakfast £26. Children welcome. Also modern, well equipped, self-catering apartments available. Phone: (0434) 381978.

ALSTON, North Pennines. Tastefully furnish-ed two crown commended farmhouse, superb views, en-suite rooms, good home cooking including bread. Bed and breakfast weekly £105. Dinner £9. Reduction children. Mrs Dent, Middle Bayles Farm, Alston. Phone: (01434) 381383.

BOWNESS ON WINDERMERE. Ideally situated Guest House, overlooking lake. Close to shops. With ample parking facilities. Quiet location. Centrally located. All rooms with colour televisions, tea and coffee making, central heating. Fallbarrow Road. Phone: (05394) 43558.

COCKERMOUTH. 15 acre small holding with sheep and horses. Lovely views. Good home cooking with fresh produce. Children welcome all ages, reduced rates. Bed and breakfast, optional evening meal. Warm welcome. Mrs D. Richardson, Pardshaw Hall, Cockermouth. Phone: (0900) 822607.

CONISTON TORVER. Old railway booking office self-catering, two people. Comfortable cottage, modernised. Quiet situation. Inn next property. Walking, fishing, horse riding. Reasonable tarrif. Wilkinson Station House. Sorry no smokers - pets. Private parking. Sae Phone: (05394) 41392.

KENDAL. Lake District. Farmhouse bed and breakfast. Working dairy farm, 16th century. Friendly and comfortable accommodation. En-suite 3 rooms. English breakfast. Ideal base to explore Lakeland. Phone: (0539) 721122. Gardner, Natland Millbeck, Kendal. Also self-catering cottage, sleeps 4.

KENDAL. Patton Hall Farm, Kendal LA8 9DT. Guests welcome, friendly home working farm overlooking Kendal. Good food and comfort assured. Easy reach lakes, dales, river, fishing. Bed and breakfast, evening meal. Sae for brochure. Margaret Hodgson, Phone: (0539) 721590.

KENDAL. 'Higher House Farm', Oxenholme Lane, Natland, Kendal, Cumbria LA9 7QH. 17th century beamed farmhouse in tranquil village of Natland, South Kendal, overlooking Lakeland Fells near M6, Junction 36. All rooms en-suite, 4 poster. Delicious cuisine. Pets welcome.

KENDAL, Lake District. AA, RAC acclaimed farmhouse on large farm situated between Kendal/Windermere. All bedrooms have colour television, tea making facilities. Most en-suite. Also cottage sleeps 9. Both lovely views. Beaty, Garnett House, Burneside, Kendal. Phone: (01539) 724542.

KESWICK. No stars or crowns, just good value bed and breakfast from £14 per person, per night. Optional dinner £9. Mountain views from some rooms, colour television, tea, coffee makers, hair dryers. Some en-suite. Phone: (07687) 73261.

KESWICK. Lyndhurst Guest House. Small comfortable guest house, centrally situated. Close to town and lake. Good home cooking and a warm welcome. Phone: (07687) 72303.

KESWICK. 'Thelmlea'. Small country guest house with 1.75 acre grounds in Braithwaite village. Spectacular (mountain) views. Friendly, relaxed atmosphere. Full facilities. Ideal base for touring, walking. Within easy reach of all lakes, coast and Carlisle. Brochure Phone: (07687) 78305.

KESWICK. The Cartwheel. Non smoking family run guest house. Hot and cold. Colour televison. Tea and coffee in all rooms. Evening meals optional. 5 minutes from town centre. Home from home. Phone: (07687) 73182.

KESWICK. Country bungalow. Lovely views. Keswick 1 mile. Bed and breakfast, optional evening meal. Comfortable lounge. Tea and coffee making facilities. Ideal centre for touring lakes. Mrs Jean Ray, Littlethwaite, Thrushwood, Keswick CA12 4PG. Phone: (07687) 72608.

KIRKBY, LONSDALE. Mill Brow House, Carn-forth, Lancashire. LA6 2AT. Bed and breakfast and self-catering apartments. Delightful market town. Ideal centre for lakes and dales. Garden, parking. Beautiful views. Pets welcome. Details Pat Nicholson, Phone: (015242) 71615.

LAKE DISTRICT, fringe. Farmhouse bed and breakfast on working family farm. Guests sitting room, colour television, tea facilities all rooms. Children welcome. Double, single and family rooms. Also self-catering cottage, sleeps two. Phone: (0931) 715238.

LAKE DISTRICT, Borrowdale. Ashness Cottage. Beautiful views over Derwent Water. 200 yards Ashness bridge. Small friendly bed and breakfast cottage. Hot and cold, tea, coffee facilities all rooms. Hamilton Wright, Ashness, Borrowdale, Keswick, Cumbria. Phone: (07687) 77244.

LAKE DISTRICT. Penrith Park House, Farm Dalemain. Wake-up to wonderful views, peaceful, tranquillity, generous breakfasts. En-suite available. 1 crown. Find us behind Dalemain mansion, ignoring the no cars sign. 3 miles Ullswater. Phone: (017684) 86212.

LAKE DISTRICT, Near Sawrey, Little Eeswyke, Hawkshead. Set in beautiful gardens. Outstanding views of Esthwaite Water and surrounding fells. All rooms have private bathrooms, television, tea facilities. Guests lounge with open fire. Evening meal optional. Phone: (05394) 36335.

LAKE DISTRICT, North Pennines. Near Hadrian's Wall, Scottish border. 2 bedroomed cottage. Peaceful wooded location. Excellent walking, golf, fishing, birdwatching. Central heating, colour television. Children, pets welcome. Phone: (0228) 70428, (0228) 70592 for brochure.

LAKE DISTRICT, Windermere. Heatherbank Guest House. Quiet location yet only 5 minutes from rail and bus stations. Shops and restaurants nearby. En-suite rooms ˙with colour television, tea making facilities. Superb breakfasts. From £15 per person. Phone: (015394) 46503.

LANGDALE. Luxury country mews cottages, situated near the foot of Langdale Pikes. Cosy and warm with en-suite bedrooms. Super mountain views. Village shop, pubs 1 mile. Leisure club included. Garden. Enclosed parking. Resident owners. Phone: (015394) 37222.

PENRITH. Views of Skiddaw Fells make an ideal setting for the inn. Easy access A66. Between Penrith and Keswick. Good food, real ales. Bed and breakfast from £12.50. Horse Shoe Inn, Hutton Roof. Phone: (07684) 84354.

BRANDELHOW GUEST HOUSE
1 PORTLAND PLACE, PENRITH, CUMBRIA CA11 7QN
AA QQQ RECOMMENDED
Guest House offering a high standard of comfort and cleanliness. Five spacious bedrooms all having colour TV, tea/coffee making facilities, central heating and double glazing including superb family room for up to 5 persons. Daily, weekend breaks and weekly terms available.
For further details Tel: Mrs. Carole Tully
(0768) 64470

PENRITH, Westwood, Cliburn. Eden Valley/ Eastern Lakes. Comfortable, well equipped modern bungalow, open fire. Sleeps 8. Plus self-contained flat. Sleeps 2/4. Central heating both properties. Large garden. Fantastic views. Pets welcome. ETB 3 key commended. Phone: (0931) 713376.

RAVENSTONEDALE. Bed and breakfast. Newly converted comfortable, clean farmhouse. Tea making facilities. Beautiful dales village. 10 minutes M6. Ideal exploring lakes - dales or breaking journey south to north. Fell walking. Warm welcome. Reasonable terms. Phone: (05396) 23231.

TEBAY, Cumbria. Carmel House. Guest house situated in Lune Valley, close M6 junction 38. All rooms en-suite, tea, coffee, television. Ideal for walking, cycling, Howgills, Cumbrian Fells, Coast-to-coast. RAC, AA. Tourist Board. Marsden, Mount Pleasant CA10 3TH. Phone: (05396) 24651.

TROUTBECK, Windermere 2 miles. Superb king size and double luxury rooms. Peaceful lodge. Fantastic lake and mountain views. Walkers/motorists paradise. Fabulous breakfast from £17.50 per person. Gourmet pubs nearby. High Green Lodge. Phone: (05394) 33005.

WINDERMERE, Holly-Wood. Comfortable Victorian Guest House, RAC acclaimed. Ideal base for Lake District, Dales, Morecambe Bay. Traditional breakfasts, tea makers, central heating. Residents lounge, en-suites with television. Short breaks/weekly terms/low season breaks. Phone: (05394) 42219.

WINDERMERE. 'Haisthorpe' Guest House. Situated in a quiet location yet close to village centre. All rooms have colour television with satellite channel, tea/coffee making facilities. Most rooms en-suite. Private parking. Short break specials. Phone: (05394) 43445.

WINDERMERE. Gill and Barry offer friendly, comfortable accommodation and great breakfasts. Some en-suite rooms, all with tea-making and colour television. Conveniently located near to station, restaurants, shops. Ample public parking. AA listed, ETB 2 crown commended. Phone: (015394) 46532.

WINDERMERE, Lake District. Small, quiet, non- smoking guest house. Home cooking. ETB classification. 2 crowns commended. From £121 per week half board. Pensioners reductions. Acton House, 41 Craig Walk, Windermere, Cumbria LA23 2HB. Phone: (015394) 45340.

WINDERMERE. Quiet guest house with en-suite facilities, televisions. Non smoking. Parking. Near to lake. Collect from station. Silver setting dinner. High standards. Relaxed atmosphere. From £15. Langdale View, Graigwalk, Bowness, Windermere. Phone: (05394) 44076.

WINDERMERE. Blenheim Lodge Hotel. Set against National Trust woodlands at end of Dalesway footpath. Lake views. Quiet, peaceful yet close to lake and shops. En-suite. Parking. Home cooking. Brantfell Road, Bowness-on-Windermere. Phone: Jackie (015394) 43440.

WINDERMERE, near. Idyllic 14th century farm- house offers excellent bed and breakfast. En-suite. Set in beautiful countryside. This is a real working farm located in small picturesque village. Mrs Swindlehurst, Tranthwaite Hall, Underbarrow, Kendal LA8 8HG. Phone: (05395) 68285.

WINDERMERE, near. Quality bed and break- fast. Peaceful and secluded 17th century lakeland farmhouse. Hot and cold all rooms. Some en-suite. Tea, coffee making facilities. Full English breakfast, free-range eggs, home made preserves. Self catering available. Phone: (0539)568360.

WINDERMERE. Rockside. Superb accommoda- tion in Windermere village. Ideal for whole of Lake District. Most rooms en-suite with colour television, clock radio, telephone. Choice of breakfast. Private parking. ETB 2 crowns. RAC acclaimed. From £16.50. Phone: (015394) 45343.

WINDERMERE. Laurel Cottage. Bed and break- fast. Situated in village centre. Shops, restaurants, pubs, lake very near. Leisure club. Excellent en-suite rooms with colour television. Ideal touring centre. Private car park. St. Martin's Square, Bowness LA23 3EF. Phone/Fax: (015394) 45594.

WINDERMERE. Heart of the English Lake District. Traditional lakeland stone guest house. Single people, pets, children, everyone welcome. Bed and full English breakfast £14.50 or less per person per night. Warm, clean and very friendly. Phone: (015394) 45649.

SANDOWN
COMMENDED
Windermere, Lake District LA23 2JF
Member of South Lakeland Catering Association
Superb Bed and Breakfast accommodation, with own colour TV, Tea/Coffee making facilities. Situated 2 minutes from Lake Windermere. Shops and cafes nearby . . . many lovely walks. Plenty of parking space.
S.A.E. or telephone for further details
Prop: Irene and George Eastwood Tel: 015394 45275

SELF-CATERING

ALSTON MOOR. Pretty, traditional stone cottage. Garrigill, near Alston. Open fires, all modern conveniences, sleeps 4/6. Central for Lakes, Borders, Dales, Northumbria. Ideal walking, relaxing, touring holiday. Short breaks available. For more details Phone: (0434) 381688.

ALSTON. 17th century cottage. Set in secluded valley. Sleeps 4 to 6. Tastefully modernised, retaining original character. Ideal for wildlife and gardening enthusiasts. ETB three keys commended. Hartside Nursery Garden, Alston, Cumbria CA9 3BL. Phone: (0434) 381372/381428.

ALSTON. 17th century, 3 bedroomed farmhouse in beautiful unspoilt countryside. Sleeps 2/6. Ideal for walking, touring, golf, riding, cycling, fishing. Close to Lakes and borders. Open fired central heating, colour television, well equipped. Phone: (0434) 381794.

AMBLESIDE. Centre of Lake District. Ashtree Cottage, 17th century. Fully equipped. Garage available. 3 bedrooms, sleeps 5. Ideal for walking and touring. All bed linen provided. Armer, 3 Millans Terrace, Ambleside, Cumbria LA22 9AF. Phone: (05394) 32754.

HEART OF NATIONAL PARK GRASSMERE/ AMBLESIDE AREAS
OPEN ALL YEAR

Elegant, exclusive, furnished to a high standard for the discerning clientele.
Lodges and cottages in Grassmere and Ambleside areas from £200-£500 per week. Sleeps 4-8 persons. 2 minutes to shops, walks and touring.
For business executive personnel visiting on business in the Lake District.
Farm style breakfast if required
Tel for colour brochure and booking forms
Phone: 05394 31733

AMBLESIDE. Two comfortable houses. One sleeps eight, one sleeps six. Parking available at larger house only. Smaller house, street parking. Well furnished and equipped. Gardens. Within easy reach shops and Lake Windermere. Leaflet Phone: (0995) 671543.

APPLEBY-IN-WESTMORELAND. Comfortable, well furnished beamed cottage. Peaceful village. Sleeps 4. Wood burning stove. Attractive garden. Close to lakes and Dales. Ideal walking area. Friendly pub and shop in village. Regret no pets. Phone: (0509) 844099.

APPLEBY. Three bedroom stone end of terrace cottage in town overlooking river. Sleeps five. Colour television, cooker, washing machine, electric and gas heating. Rates £180 to £330 per week. Phone: 071 923 2299 or 081 363 2807.

APPLEBY. Beautifully beamed quality cottages in excellent locations for walking/touring lakes, borders, dales. All centrally heated. Microwaves, washing/drying facilities, dishwashers etc. Children/pets welcome. Short breaks available. Prices £130 - £300. Phone: (017683) 61867, (0836) 547130.

BEWCASTLE, Scottish borders. Why not leave everything and stay on a remote sheep farm, with a large indoor heated swimming pool. Snug in our pine board luxury chalet, sleeps six. Owston, Collin Bank, Bewcastle, Carlisle CA6 6PU. Phone: (06977) 48611.

BEWCASTLE – DELIGHTFUL STONE COTTAGE
on working Border farm with spectacular views over Kershope Forest and the Fells. Ideal for exploring Northern Lakes, Scottish Borders and Hadrian's Wall country. Superb game and coarse fishing locally. Woodburning stove, central heating, colour TV, sleeps 2/3.
Phone Catherine Leach 06977 48354

BOWNESS-ON-WINDERMERE. Spinnery cottage. Comfortable one/two bedroomed flats, situated in a 200 year old converted Spinnery. Central heating throughout. Close to village, yet quiet and secluded. Private parking. Dogs accepted. Leisure club facilities. Phone: (015394) 44884.

BROUGHTON IN FURNESS, South Cumbria. Comfortable cosy terraced cottage in interesting old market village. All facilities. Coal fire. Accommodates 4. Ideal hill walking, bird watching. Near Duddon Estuary, Coniston Lake. Enquiries Phone: 081 459 2427. Short winter breaks.

CALDBECK
Comfortable village house, sleeps 6/8. Ample secure parking. Excellent walks. Enclosed garden. Well equipped with central heating.
Mrs. D Helme (01799) 540627

CALDBECK. Monkhouse Hill. Superior cottages in courtyard setting in foothills of Caldbeck Fells. Sleep 2 to 8. Spectacular views. Ideally situated for lakes and borders. Open all year. Children and most dogs welcome. Brochure Phone: (016974) 76254.

CARLISLE. 7 miles. Self-contained part of farmhouse in small village. Storage heaters, sleeps 2/6, available all year. Ideal base for touring Lake District and Scottish Borders. £60-£120 weekly. Wharton, Stockdalewath, Dalston, Carlisle CA5 7DN. Phone: (06974) 76250.

CARLISLE, near Scottish Borders off the beaten track yet only 14 miles to M.6. Ideal touring, walking base. Well equipped courtyard. Cottages sleep 3 - 4. Lovely forestry setting. Pets very welcome. From £120. Phone: (0228) 577440.

CARTMEL. Historic village near lakes. Roomy house for five. Central heating. Log fires. Modern kitchen. Private parking and patio. Colour television. Many local attractions and charming pubs. Phone: Sue Strike (0229) 772174.

CARTMEL VALLEY COTTAGES
3 family run luxurious cottages set in charming historic villages in the Cartmel Valley. Oak beamed ceilings, log fires, 4 posters, lots of character and charm. These cottages are made for relaxation an

Colour brochure Telephone 05395 59100

CARTMEL/LAKES. Elegant Georgian house by ancient village. Quiet, sunny position. Lovely views. Walled garden. Games room. Log fire. Dogs welcome. Beautifully furnished and equipped. Sleeps 8, cosy enough for 2. Short winter breaks. Phone: 081 886 6269.

COCKERMOUTH. Comfortable well equipped end terraced cottage. Lovely views of Fells. Boating, fishing, golf and walking nearby. Close to all amenities of village. Personally cared for by owners. CTB approved. Sleeps 2-4. Phone: (07687) 76273.

CONISTON, Lake District. Self-contained flats, quiet situation. 1/5 people. Fire protected, clean, comfortable, well proportioned, carefully maintained by owners. 3 key ETB approved. Excellently priced. Phone: (05395) 31223.

CONISTON WATER 3 miles. Traditional lakeland cottage. Cosy atmosphere and many original features. Lovely riverside cottage garden. Views over picturesque countryside. Central heating, colour television, antique country furniture, linen included. Sleeps 4. Brochure Phone: (0229) 869418.

CONISTON, near. Comfortable holiday cottage. Sleeps 6. Peaceful setting. Close Coniston Water. Panoramic views. Well equipped comprising kitchen, living room with open fire. Ground floor bathroom, 3 bedrooms. Garden, patio, garage. Excellent walking, sightseeing. Brochure available, Phone: (0274) 833715.

CONISTON. Comfortable, well furnished, modern cottage. Sleeps 4/5. Electric cooker, fridge/freezer, washing machine, microwave, colour television, storage heating. Parking space. Convenient for shops, restaurants, lake steamer, pier and launching site. No pets. Phone: Heywood (0844) 342495.

CROSBY RAVENSWORTH. Four comfortable 18th century self-catering cottages. Ideal base for walking or touring the Lake District and Yorkshire Dales. Children and pets welcome. Colour brochure: Jennywell Hall, Crosby Ravensworth, Penrith CA10 3JP. Phone: (0931) 715288.

CUMBRIA
ENGLISH LAKES & EDEN VALLEY
Excellent Selection of S/C Flats, Cottages & Houses
For Free Brochure Contact
LOWTHER SCOTT-HARDEN. TEL: (01768) 64541 – 24 HRS

EDEN VALLEY/North Lakes. Olde-worlde luxury oak beamed cottage in idyllic hamlet. 5 minutes drive to Lake District National Park. Full of atmosphere and well equipped with all modern conveniences. Short winter breaks available. Phone: (0931) 712279.

EDEN VALLEY. Three centrally heated, well equipped self-catering cottages on working farm in peaceful village at foot of Pennines. Sleeps 2-5. Ideally situated for touring lakes. Borders Scotland. Child facilities. Resident owners. Phone: (0768) 881356.

GLENRIDDING. Bungalow with extensive views of mountains and Lake Ullswater, and associated sports. Sleeps 8. Central heating and open fire. Facilities for disabled. Pets allowed. Private grounds. Tourist Board commended. Matthews, Vicarage, Braithwaite, Keswick. Phone: (07687) 78243.

TRAVELLING BY COACH OR RAIL?
TURN TO THE INFORMATION SECTION AT THE BACK OF THIS GUIDE FOR USEFUL TELEPHONE NUMBERS

GRANGE OVER SANDS. Beautifully modernised cottage on family farm. Sleeps 2/6. Children's play area. Lovely situation with magnificent views over Morecambe Bay and Lakeland hills. ETB 2 key highly commended. Mrs Brocklebank, Spring Bank Farm. Phone: (05395) 32606.

KENDAL/WINDERMERE. 2 delightful holiday homes, (1 bungalow). Maintained to high standards/Cumbria Tourist Board up to 5 keys. Highly commended. Beautifully situated. 1 near Lake Windermere, the other in a quiet village near Kendal. Phone: Margaret and Barry Haslam (01539) 740170.

Fieldside Grange

English Tourist Board
COMMENDED
♈ ♈ ♈

Keswick, Cumbria
CA12 4RN
**Tel: Keswick
(017687) 74444**

Our comprehensively equipped self contained apartments, sleeping 2-6 persons offer the perfect self catering holiday. Converted from an old lakeland farm, standing in private grounds with magnificent views over Keswick and the surrounding hills. Open all year. Winter & Spring breaks available. Weekly terms from £135 to £380. Resident proprietors Jackie & Peter Werfel invite you to write or phone for brochure.

KESWICK. Cottage, Thornthwaite. 3 miles West Keswick alongside Combe Beck. Maintained by owner to high standard. Open all year. Reduced terms Winter. Linen supplied. Heating, electricity. ETB approved. Television. Contact Lawson, Beckside, Thornthwaite, Keswick after 7 pm. Phone: (07687) 78395.

KESWICK
5 MILES
Delightful 3 bedroom cottage. Sleeps 6. Nestling at the foot of Thornthwaite Forest, just off A66 overlooking Bassenthwaite` Lake and Mountains. Set in a large private garden with ample parking. Ideal for families. Regret no pets.
Phone: 01287 632630 evenings.

KESWICK. Central location. Self-catering houses. Modern, comfortable, fully equipped. Each sleeps 4. Central heating, washer/dryer, colour television. Off street parking. No pets. For brochure Phone: (01252) 722339.

KIRKBY LONSDALE. Close to both Lakes and Dales. Three luxury cottages in quiet rural setting. All modern conveniences. Sleep four to six persons. Phone: (05242) 71865 for descriptive brochure. Short breaks available. Dogs welcome. Phone: (05242) 71865

KIRKLINTON. Wake up to green fields and peace. A farm cottage with admirable blend of 'modern conveniences' and traditional charm. All inclusive. Open all year. Short breaks. Sleeps 4. No pets. Enjoy our Borderlands. Brochure Phone: (01228) 75650.

KIRKOSWALD. Pets welcome. Clean, cosy cottages adjacent private lakes. River land. Escape, relax, unwind. Good walking, wildlife, fishing. No silly rules! Brochure Phone: (0768) 898711 (24 hour), (0768) 896275 (8 am - 10 pm). Sae Crossfield, Kirkoswald, Cumbria CA10 1EU. Now is never too late.

LAKE DISTRICT, Cartmel. Luxury pine lodges in beautiful setting in South Lakes. Sleep 2/6. Beamed lounge, colour television, heating, fridge/freezer, microwave, corner bath/shower. Open March to January. Ideal walking, touring or just relaxing. Brochure Phone: (0327) 703761.

LAKE DISTRICT, Windermere. Lakelovers self-catering holiday homes. Attractive properties in good locations within Lake District National Park. Well equipped, Tourist Board inspected, personally managed by friendly staff. Detailed brochure highlighting many above average features. Freefone (0500) 131227.

LAKE DISTRICT, Windermere. Lakeland. House. situated in a quiet cul-de-sac off high street. Close to all village amenities. Ideal location for touring, walking, climbing etc. Private parking. Well equipped. Sleeps 7. 3 keys ETB. Phone: (05394) 42512.

LAKE DISTRICT. Quiet country cottage, sleeps 4/6. Children and pets welcome. Colour television. Linen and heating included. Easy access to lakes and Yorkshire Dales. Pub and shop 2 miles. Private parking. Reasonable rates. Phone: (05396) 24462.

LAKE DISTRICT, near Windermere. Idyllic cot-tage sleeps 4. Also secluded cottage studio apartment, sleeps 2. Set in small picturesque village. Immaculate accommodation. Beautiful views of Lakeland Fells. Private gardens and parking. Short breaks from £65, weekly from £125-£275. Phone: (015395) 68285.

LAKE DISTRICT. Bassenthwaite Lake 4 miles. Self-catering, 2 bedroom cottage, sleeps 4. Centrally heated, fully equipped kitchen, bathroom, lounge with coloured television and music centre. Rent includes electricity, coal and duvet bedding. Phone: (016973) 71304.

LANGDALE. Wheelwrights Holiday Cottages. High quality properties. Maintained with care. Family run. Set amongst magnificent mountain scenery. For brochure Phone: (015394) 37635. 24 hour answering service. Visa/Master Cards accepted.

LANGDALE. Chapel Style. 3 and 4 bed luxury houses. Membership of Langdale Country Club with swimming pool and squash courts included. Shop, pub and river nearby. Large garden with views of Fells. Phone: 061 904 9445.

LOWESWATER. Two holiday cottages on work-ing farm, sleeps 4/6. One with log fires. Ideal for walking or touring. Phone: Bell (0900) 85227.

MALLERSTANG VALLEY. Converted barn. Ground floor accommodation. Majestic and peaceful. Central to Lake District, Yorkshire Dales, Herriot country, Settle/Carlisle Railway. Walking, touring, waterfalls, castles, market towns, shows. Log fire. Bed and breakfast and dinner available. Phone: (07683) 72122.

NATLAND. 'Jasmine cottage'. Near Kendal. Comfortable cottage. Lovely views. Convenient for lakes and dales, Kendal 2 miles. Horse riding and Asda nearby. Central heating. Colour television. Bed linen supplied. Open all year. Phone: (05395) 60564.

NORTHERN LAKES. 2 cottages midway between Loweswater and Ennerdale Lakes. Standing in private grounds in tranquil surroundings. A warm welcome awaits you to this truly rural retreat. For further details Phone: Mrs Cook (01946) 861338.

RAVENSTONEDALE, Eden. Wide open spaces. Wonderful walks, welcoming pubs. Very comfortable cottages, linen included. Central to visit Lakes/Dales/Borders yet return to uncrowded peace. Bring dogs, horses. Locally fishing, mountain biking, golf etc. Phone: (05396) 23254.

SOUTH LAKELAND (Ulverston). Cottage in open countryside. Sleeps 5. Easy reach of local tourist attractions and lakes. Nicely furnished. Well equipped. Pets welcome. Owner maintained and cleaned. Reasonable prices. ETB approved. Phone: Mrs Atkinson (0229) 582012.

SOUTH LAKELAND, Beetham. Cosy detached 17th century cottage, sleeps 2. Tastefully renovated. Exposed beams, mullioned windows. Quiet rural setting. Convenient for lakes, dales. ETB rating 3 keys. Highly commended. Ensures quality. Phone: (05395) 62798.

SPARK BRIDGE, Southlakes. Four timber lodges set in secluded mature grounds. Flat and cottage as part of Georgian country house. Accommodation to tourist board 3 keys highly commended standard. Mrs Campbell. Phone: (01229) 861510.

WABERTHWAITE. Mill cottage, fully equipped and newly furnished. 3 bedrooms - sleeps 2 to 8 people. Pets are also welcome. Eskdale 15 minutes drive. Weekly/mid-week/weekend terms available. Details Phone: (0229) 717326.

WINDERMERE. Deloraine - secluded Edwardian mansion apartments/cottage, sleep 2-6. Large lawn and grounds, near lake, boats, shops. Offer quality, character, dramatic views. Wheelchairs welcome. ETB commended. £90 - £330 per week. Resident owners - Helm Road LA23 2HS. Phone: (015394) 45557.

CARAVANS, CHALETS & HOLIDAY PARKS

BEWCASTLE, Scottish borders. Why not leave everything and stay on a remote sheep farm, with a large swimming pool. Snug in our luxury mobile home. Mrs Owston, Collin Bank, Bewcastle, Carlisle CA6 6PU. Phone: (06977) 48611.

COCKERMOUTH near. The Beeches. Luxury caravans for hire on select country park. Excellent facilities include bar and bistro, shop, laundry room. Ideal base for touring north lakes. From £90 weekly. For brochure Phone: (06973) 21555.

CONISTON. Self-catering caravan, situated on a working lakeland farm, own car park space and garden with barbecue. Ideal for walking. Sleeps six, bedding included. Toilet, shower and television. Cooper, Bankend Cottage, Torver, Coniston. Phone: (05394) 41714.

EDEN VALLEY. Luxury fully equipped caravan on private site on working farm overlooks Carlisle. Settle railway and nature reserve. Ideal for lakes, Yorkshire Dales. £50, £130. Shardale Hall. 3 miles Kirkby Stephen. Phone: (07683) 71260.

EDEN VALLEY, Cumbria. Fully equipped cara- van on private site on working farm. Ideal for lakes, Yorkshire Dales. Nature reserve and walks. Phone: (07683) 71228.

GRANGE OVER SANDS, near. South Cumbria. Two bedroom, 36 ft. caravan, available June, July and August. Sited at Lakelands Caravan Park. Family entertainment nightly plus cabaret. Two heated swimming pools, tennis, horse riding. No pets. Phone: (0539) 727557.

KENDAL. Eight berth caravan on farm. 1 mile south of Kendal. Shower, wash basin and toilet. Full gas cooker, fridge, electric fire. Shops, golf and leisure centre one mile. Phone: (0539) 723977.

LAKE DISTRICT. Luxury static caravan on single working farm. 1 double, 1 twin bedroom. Linen provided. Fitted kitchen, bathroom, shower, hot and cold water. Colour television. Ideal centre for walking, fishing, touring, horse riding. Phone: (015395) 63274.

LAKELAND is one of 19 holiday parks coast to coast. Our luxury holiday homes, sleep 2-8 people. Prices start from £9 per person per night, based on 6 sharing. For a free colour brochure Phone: Lo-Call (0345) 508 508.

PENRITH. Beckses Caravan Camping Park, Penruddock, Penrith. Just off A66 Penrith to Keswick Road. Modern 6 berth caravans to let, fully equipped with hot water, showers, television etc. Tourers welcome. Electric available. Phone: (07684) 83224.

SILLOTH ON SOLWAY, Cumbria, Lake District. Static 6 berth caravan on large site. Indoor pool, 9 hole golf course, bars, disco, Bistro, entertainment. From £90. Gas, electric, bedding, towels, all free. Phone: (0539) 733725.

WINDERMERE 20 minutes, Kendal 5 minutes. 1994 luxury caravan, fully equipped. Own patio, beautiful views. Quiet rural setting. A lovely place to stay. Sorry no pets. Phone: (05395) 60351.

WINDERMERE. No phones, no traffic, no neighbours! Just perfect peace and quiet. Come and share the tranquillity of our Lakeland hill-farm. 2 comfortable caravans in separate secluded locations. Ideal walking and exploring Lakes. Phone: (05395) 68353.

WHERE TO GO

Lakeland Wildlife Oasis
Hale, Cumbria.
Tel: (05395) 63027
A wildlife exhibition where both living animals and animate 'hands on' displays are used to illustrate evolution in the animal kingdom. Gift shop.

Lowther Leisure Park
Hackthorpe, Cumbria.
Tel: (0931) 712523
Over 40 attractions including Stevensons Crown Circus, Lowther adventure fort, Tarzan trail, assault course and train rides.

Muncaster Castle, Gardens and Owl Centre
Ravenglass, Cumbria.
Tel: (0229) 717614
14th Century with 15th and 19th Century additions. Gardens with exceptional collection of rhododendrons and azaleas. Extensive collection of owls.

Carlise Castle
Carlise, Cumbria
Tel: (0228) 31777
Border stronghold - keep built 1092 on site of Roman fort. 12th Century keep with vaulted passages, chambers, staircases, towers and dungeon. 14th Century gate with portcullis.

The World of Beatrix Potter Exhibition
The Old Laundry, Crag Brow, Bowness-on-Windermere, Cumbria.
Tel: (05394) 88444
Exhibition interpreting the life and works of Beatrix Potter, comprising 9 screen video wall and film.

Windermere Steamboat Museum
Rayring Road, Bowness-on-Windermere, Cumbria.
Tel: (05394) 45565
Steamboats and other vintage craft, many afloat and steam launch trips. Model boat ponds, museum, shop and restaurant.

THE QUALITY Q IS YOUR

SURE SIGN

OF WHERE TO STAY

CARAVAN, CHALET AND CAMPING PARKS

Throughout Britain, the tourist boards now inspect over 1,200 holiday parks, every year, to help you find the ones that suit you best.

THE GRADES: 1-5 ✓s within the **Q**, for quality symbol tell you the quality standard of what is provided. The more ✓s, the higher the standard.

More detailed information on the **Quality Q** is given in free *SURE SIGN* leaflets, available from any Tourist Information Centre.

We've checked them out before you check in!

ISLE OF MAN

SELF-CATERING

ISLE OF MAN, Architect converted country chapel and secluded farmhouse, both in open countryside with beautiful views. Convenient for southern beaches, golf courses and walking. 212 Cromwell Tower, Barbican, London EC2Y 8DD. Phone: 071 628 0755.

ISLE OF MAN. Self-catering, detached Manx stone house. Situated near Ramsey in lovely countryside with extensive sea views. Own gardens. Car parking. Garage. Well equipped. Sleeps 2/7. Central heating. Mrs Desmond, 33 Rheast Mooar Lane, Ramsey. Phone: (0624) 812303.

LANCASHIRE

HOTELS & GUEST HOUSES

BLACKPOOL. Highbury Hotel. All rooms en-suite. Open all year. Bed and breakfast, colour television and tea making facilities all rooms. Adjacent to promenade. Close to all amenities. Tutton, 12 Shaw Road FY1 6HB. Phone: (01253) 404791.

BLACKPOOL
BELGRAVE GUEST HOUSE
Highly recommended home from home 3 minutes from promenade & pleasure beach, television lounge, own keys.
**Details: Mrs Watson – PHONE: (01253) 344048
60 Burlington Road, Blackpool FY4 1JR**

BLACKPOOL. Rosebank Villa Hotel. Central, close to promenade. Winter gardens tower. All rooms have colour televisions, tea making facilities, duvets, heating. No meters. New management since October 1993 and upgraded. For further details Phone: (0253) 24939.

BLACKPOOL
STAYMOR HOTEL
555 NEW SOUTH PROMENADE
Friendly family run licensed seafront hotel. En-suite available. Tea/coffee making all rooms. Choice of menu. Full central heating. Car park.
**Booking for illuminations
Short break specials
also booking Christmas
and New Year**
Phone: 0253 341487

BLACKPOOL. Lynwood, 38 Osborne Road, South Shore. Adjoining promenade, Pleasure Beach, Sandcastle. First class en-suite bed & breakfast. From £15. AA/RAC listed, ETB 3 crowns commended. Short stays welcome. Good food and hospitality guaranteed. Phone: (01253) 344628.

BLACKPOOL. Valdene Licensed Hotel. 2 min-utes from train station and promenade. Satellite television all rooms. Bed and breakfast from £11. May, June special half board £65. July, August £84. Clean friendly family run hotel. Phone: (0253) 291080.

BLACKPOOL
New Bolingbroke Hotel
36-38 Queens Promenade
Lancs. FY2 9RW

We are a family run hotel in a prominent enviable corner position on Queens Promenade. 50 en-suite bedrooms, 27 bathrooms, 23 showers and 40 with sea views. 2 lifts. TV, tea facilities all rooms. Large car park. Full C/H. Spacious dining room, separate tables. Choice of menu, vegetarian on request. Late bar, dance floor, seating 100 plus. Live entertainment. Games room. Season trips included.

Morning trip to Fleetwood Market (Tuesday).
Full day trip to the Lakes (Wednesday).

Senior citizens welcome

Also Grand National Trip
OPEN ALL YEAR
"Nice people come to meet nice people"
B&B & ED plus light lunch
Free brochure on request
Phone: 0253 351109

BLACKPOOL. Highfield Hotel. Overlooking select Queens Promenade. Licensed. Most rooms en-suite with televisions, tea makers, central heating. Refurbished 1995. Excellent food. Bed and breakfast from £15. June special, dinner, bed, breakfast, £110 weekly. Phone: freephone (0500) 657816.

HOTEL ST. GEORGE
BLACKPOOL
Fully licensed hotel close to giant roller coaster. 30 bedrooms, mostly en-suite. Choice of menu and separate tables. Top line cabaret in separate bar, lounge, large car park and coach parties welcome.
Reasonable rates
Phone: 0253 341514

BLACKPOOL, central. Roseheath Hotel, 110 Palatine Road. Centrally heated, clean and comfortable. Gutbusting meals, late bar, karaoke, games room, spabath, satellite televisions, morning cuppa. Babies and children welcome. Phone Lynda and John for best rates/dates. Phone: (01253) 27613.

BLACKPOOL. Sandalwood Hotel, 3 Gynn Avenue. 50 yards promenade. Good home cooking. Cleanliness assured. Small car park. Early season reduction senior citizens. Some en-suite bedrooms, tea - coffee, television, lounge. Book early, illuminations. Children welcome. Phone: (01253) 351795.

BLACKPOOL, North Shore. Willows Private Hotel near Gynn Gardens. Television lounge, tea, coffee facilities. Good home cooking. Reductions senior citizens and children. 3 King George Avenue. For details Phone: (01253) 351183.

BLACKPOOL. 'Kelvin', 98 Reads Avenue. Small private hotel. Car park. Tea/coffee facilities bedrooms. Plenty good food. Semi. residential area. Central. Bed and breakfast from £11. Evening dinner from £14. Long/short stays. Mrs Duckworth, Phone: (01253) 20293.

BROOKLYN LICENSED HOTEL
9 Kirby Road, Blackpool
Close to promenade, all shops and amenities. Adjacent coach and car park. TV lounge, central heating, tea making facilities all rooms.
★ Free child places when sharing ★
★ Weekend bookings available ★
★ Also open at New Year ★
Phone: 0253 22166

BLACKPOOL. Newholme Private Hotel. ETB three crowns approved. 30 yards north promenade, adjacent Imperial Hotel. Unrestricted parking. Licensed. All en-suite. Tea makers, colour televisions. Choice of menu. Short or long breaks. Brochure 2 Wilton Parade. Phone: (01253) 24010.

BLACKPOOL. Loreto Guest House. Licensed. Three minutes from sea. Near all facilities. Television, tea making and clock radios all rooms. Special diets catered for. Small pets welcome. Home from home atmosphere. Contact Jenny, Phone: (0253) 345803.

BLACKPOOL. Lindfield Hotel, near Pleasure Beach and Promenade. Small, friendly, family run hotel with the accent on food. Comfort and warm personal service. Welcome trays. Parking. Daily rates from £10. 14 Carlyle Avenue. Phone: (0253) 343538.

BLACKPOOL. Appalachian Hotel. Licensed bar, meals, home cooking. Cleanliness assured. Specials throughout the season. Bed and breakfast from £10. Tea facilities, heating to all rooms. Television lounges. Near shops, south promenade. Coaches welcome. Car park. Phone: (0253) 403428.

BLACKPOOL. Licensed, all en-suite. Tea-mak- ers. Friendly. Bed and breakfast from £12 or bed, breakfast, evening dinner. 1 minute promenade. Close bingo, clubs. Sun lounge. Open all year. Book early. 18 Shaw Road. Phone: (0253) 341340.

BLACKPOOL
DALTON HOUSE
Licensed Guest House. Tea makers and colour TV all rooms. Close to all amenities. Couples and families only. Prices on request.
Phone: Dave or Ruth (01253) 24321

BLACKPOOL. Homeleigh Guest House. Close all amenities. Family atmosphere. Friendliness assured. Tea making facilities all rooms. Tariffs from £10. Discounts for children and OAP's. Free babysitting. For more information Phone:Dale or Valerie on (0253) 695165.

BLACKPOOL. Glenburn Guest House. Satellite television and tea making facilities in all rooms. Traditional home cooking. Cleanliness and friendliness assured. Reductions for OAP's and children. Come as guests go home friends. Phone: Mary, Susan, (01253) 347493.

LYNTON HOUSE
24 St. Bedes Avenue
off Waterloo Road
Blackpool FY4 1AQ

OPEN ALL YEAR
2 minutes from shops and promenade, midway between south and central piers. Good home cooking. Full central heating. Satellite TV and tea makers in all rooms. Reductions for children and OAPs.
From £10 B.&B.
Evening meal £3 extra
Ph.: 01253 345784

LYTHAM ST. ANNES. Langcliffe Hotel and holiday apartments, seafront. Bars, restaurant, garden, patio. Wheelchair access. OAP's., families. Group bookings welcome. Ballroom. Car park. Every comfort. Business or pleasure. For brochure write 69-71 South Promenade, St. Annes-On-Sea. FY8 4LF. Phone: (0253) 724454. Fax: 726674.

SOUTHPORT. Windsor Lodge Hotel. Small, friendly, family run. Situated quiet residential area, only five minutes walk from most amenities. Ground floor en-suites available, suitable disabled. Phone Wendy or John for brochure and tariff, (0704) 530070.

Hotel Bel Air
236 WIGAN LANE, WIGAN WN1 2NU
The Bel-Air is an award winning Hotel situated in a leafy suburb, 3 miles junction 27 on A49. Twelve en-suite rooms. Elegant restaurant. Superb food. Convenient for Blackpool, The Lakes, Camelot, Southport and the famous Wigan pier.
Tel: 01942 41410. Fax: 01942 43967

SELF-CATERING

BLACKPOOL. Self-contained en-suite holiday flats. Just off promenade. Near Pleasure Beach and Sandcastle Leisure Centre. Nicely furnished and decorated, colour television. Each flat spacious accommodation. Secure enclosed, car park. Resident proprietors, 7 Dean Street. Phone: (0253) 346023.

BLACKPOOL. Select holiday flats 30 yards Prom north central. All with own shower and toilet. Comfort assured. Couples only, low season £90 a week, high season £110, any 3 nights £60. Phone: Hickman (0253) 20387.

BLACKPOOL. Illuminations. Promenade holi-day flats/flatlets with sea views. Completely self-contained with private bathroom and toilet. Coloured television, fridges etc. Maintained to a high standard. Between Blackpool Tower and Pleasure Beach. Phone: (0253) 343927.

BLACKPOOL, North San Remo. Luxury holiday flats, apartments and holiday bungalow. 30 yards promenade in select area. Car park. Sea views. Self-contained, fully equipped, colour television. Cleanliness assured. Phone: Mrs Crowe for brochure (01253) 353487.

BLACKPOOL. Sandalwood Holiday Flats. All flats with private shower, toilet facilities, television and central heating. All bedding supplied. Only 50 yards from pleasure beach and promenade. High standard of cleanliness with quality furnishings. Phone: (01253) 346512.

BLACKPOOL. Holiday flats. Central. Adjacent Winter Gardens, main shopping area, promenade. Special offers May, June. Illuminations. Small pets welcome. Please phone for brochure and quote (0253) 751069.

BLACKPOOL. Holiday flats. North Shore. Sleep 2/3 plus cot. Clean, comfortable. 2 minutes beach, shops. Colour television, bed linen provided. Bebbington, 26 Carshalton Road. Phone: (0253) 22635.

SELF CATERING FLATS
at Seaspray, 11 Shaw Road
Sleeps 2-6 persons. Close to promenade. Sky colour TV. Pets welcome. Some parking. Ground floor available.
From £7.50 per person per night reductions for children
Phone: Francis (0253) 341810

HAYWARD HOUSE
20 PALATINE ROAD, BLACKPOOL FY1 4BT
Superior, en-suite Holiday Flats. Near Tower and all amenities. Fully equipped, colour TV, bedding provided. Prices from £65 per week per flat. According to size and season. Open all year.
Phone: (01253) 751988

BLACKPOOL. En-suite holiday flats, 50 yards from promenade. Central. Fully equipped. Colour television, laundry room. Established 27 years. Highly recommended. Special early season reductions, from half price. Colour brochure, New Southdown, 13 - 15 Barton Avenue, FY1 6AP. Phone: (01253) 763112.

BLACKPOOL, North Shore. Adjacent promen-ade and Gynn Gardens. First floor, self-contained flat. Two bedrooms, separate lounge, kitchen, bathroom, toilet. In quiet area, convenient for buses and trams. Parking available. 34 Seafield Road. Phone: (0253) 358707.

BLACKPOOL. Carnival superflats. Top of the range holiday apartments. All en-suite with fitted kitchens and choice of 1 or 2 bedrooms. Contact Yvette Smith, 376/380 Lytham Road, Blackpool, FY4 1DW Phone: (0253) 403601 or (0253) 752970.

BLACKPOOL. New Aleda holiday flats. Fully self-contained. Private shower, toilet. Car park. Opposite Sandcastle, South Pier, Pleasure Beach. 14 Withnell Road. Phone: (01253) 343852.

CARNFORTH, Cumbria, Lancashire border. 3 self-catering cottages on working farm. Near Leighton Moss, bird reserve, nature trail and playground. Laundry facilities. Fishing, riding and golf nearby. ETB commended. Clarke, Brackenthwaite, Yealand, Redmayne. Phone: (05395) 63276.

DUNSOP BRIDGE. Keepers Cottage, Whitendale. Spacious family cottage at the heart of England. Enclosed garden next to small stream. Ideal base for walking/touring surrounding countryside. Fuel and power included. Sleeps 5. For brochure Phone: (0200) 448665.

LYTHAM ST. ANNES. Near Blackpool. Luxury detached residence overlooking golf course. Four bedrooms, three bathrooms. Private drive. Acre garden. Terrace, patio. Maid service. All enquiries welcome. Phone: Elaine Marie on (0253) 738901 or 724454.

MORECAMBE. Luxury fully self-contained apartments overlooking sea and Lakeland hills. Car park. Stair lift. Promenade position. Illuminations. August to October. Book early. Phone: Mrs Holmes (0524) 411858.

ST. ANNES, near Blackpool. Spacious holi-day apartments including ground floor. Private entrance lounge. Two bedrooms, dining room, modern kitchen, bathroom, central heating. Linen. Parking. Yards from beach and shops. Hotel facilities nearby. Phone: (0253) 738901/724454.

CARAVANS, CHALETS & HOLIDAY PARKS

BLACKPOOL. Holiday caravans, licensed club, swimming pool, green bowls, amusements, shops. Caravans have showers, toilets, colour television, free electric and gas. Reduced rates, early and late season. Wilsons Caravans, 32 The Avenue, Poulton-le-Fylde, Blackpool. Phone: (01253) 892192.

FLEETWOOD. Cala Gran is one of 19 holiday parks coast to coast. Our luxury holiday homes, sleep 2-8 people. Prices start from £9 per person per night, based on 6 sharing. For a free colour brochure Phone: Lo-Call (0345) 508 508.

WHERE TO GO

Blackpool Pleasure Beach
525 Promenade, Blackpool.
Tel: (0253) 341033

Europe's greatest amusement park with over 150 rides, Space Invader, Tokaydo Express, Avalanche, water chute, log flume , bug dipper, swamp buggies, Grand National, Beaver Creek water ride, funshineland for children, Sir Hiram Maxin flying machine, the Revolution, and much more. Restaurants. Disabled visitors welcome.

Blackpool Sea Life Centre
Blackpool. Lancashire.
Tel: (0253) 22445
Tropical sharks up to 8ft in length housed in 100,000 gallon display with underwater walk through tunnel.

Wigan Pier
Wallgate, Wigan, Lancashire.
Tel: (0942) 323666
Take a trip back in time to the year 1900, where you can experience life in a Victorian classroom, the pub the cottage, the coalmine and even journey to Blackpool - all without leaving Wigan.

Wildfowl and Wetland Centre
Martin Mere, Burscough, Lancashire.
Tel: (0704) 895181
45 acres of gardens with over 1,600 ducks, geese and swans of 120 different kinds. Two flocks of flamingoes 300-acre wild with 20 acre lake.

CITY WALLS, CHESTER
(photograph courtesy of North West Tourist Board)

NORTH EAST ENGLAND

CLEVELAND • DURHAM • HUMBERSIDE
NORTHUMBERLAND • TYNE & WEAR • YORKSHIRE

North East England can boast the only English Football team in the Scottish League! – Berwick Rangers! Berwick-upon-Tweed is just about as far North as you can go in a region with familiar names – great shopping towns like Newcastle and Leeds and miles and miles of open roads.

Where better to start than York? Still encircled by its ancient walls, York is host to such must-sees as the magnificent Minster, the largest Gothic church in England, and the mechanical magic of the Museum of Automata. And, when your sightseeing works up a healthy appetite, there's always Yorkshire pudding and the tastiest fish and chips in the world!

Equally steeped in history is Durham City with its 12th century cathedral and castles. Indeed, Northumbria as a whole boasts more castles and strong-holds than any other English region. And, of course, don't miss a pilgrimage to Hadrian's Wall – still the most resonant testament to Roman times.

It's reputed that the seaside town of Whitby may be haunted by the spirit of Count Dracula! What is certain is that Captain Cook, Britain's most celebrated traveller, learnt his trade here.

The North East is also buzzing with more modern pleasures, as befits the region that can claim the nation's newest city – Sunderland. The Metro Centre at Gateshead is Europe's largest indoor shopping complex while Doncaster Dome is Britain's biggest leisure centre under one roof. Bradford is home to the National Museum of Photography, Film and Television; I wonder if any of my programmes are in their archives? And theatregoers can choose between Hull Truck Theatre, West Yorkshire

Playhouse or the latest Ayckbourn at Scarborough. He's not only that town's favourite adopted son but the country's most prolific play-wright since Shakespeare! Scarborough really is a tale of two, if not exactly cities, then towns!

As well as the theatres, fine art gallery and the museums, there's everything one would associate with a good old fashioned British seaside resort par excellence – and more! Side by side with the town's Victorian grandeur is the sort of attraction today's visitor would normally only expect to marvel at in more exotic climes. It's the Sea-Life Centre – entertaining and educational where you can ogle at, and photograph, hundreds of oceanic species from the comfort of the Centre's underwater glass tunnels.

After you've followed in the windswept footsteps of Cathy and Heathcliffe, Yorkshire affords many other splendid terrains. Walk the dales and farms and hillsides and you remember that this is also the land of "The Railway Children", "Emmerdale" and even the Hovis commercials! Elsewhere, the rocky Northumberland coast is host to colonies of birds and seals; the heathery slopes of the Cleveland Hills attract many walkers and back-packers; and, for the serious hiker, the Pennine Way is a timeless, irresistible challenge.

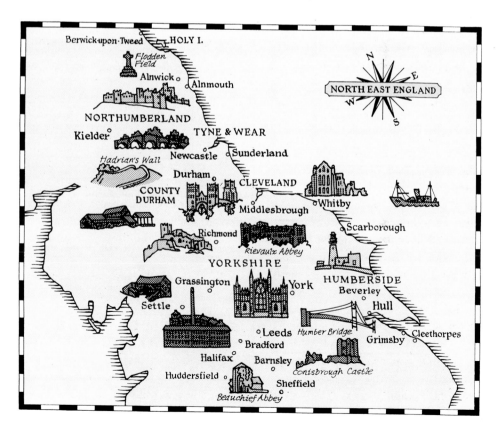

DURHAM

HOTELS & GUEST HOUSES

DURHAM. St. Aidan's College, Windmill Hill, Durham DH1 3LJ. En-suite and standard single/twin rooms, reasonable price during University vacations. Adjacent golf course, ample car parking, ETB listed. Phone: 0191 374 3269.

SELF-CATERING

WOLSINGHAM. Gateway to Weardale, land of the Prince Bishops. Tourist Board 1 key commended. 2 bedroomed, terraced cottage. Sleeps 4. Cosy living room with coal fire. Overlooking small village green. In old part of town. Phone: Gardiner (0388) 527538.

WHERE TO GO

Durham Castle
Palace Green, Durham City, Co Durham.
Tel: (091) 374 3863

Castle with fine bailey founded in 1072. Norman chapel dating from 1080, kitchens and great hall dating from 1499 and 128 respectively.

Beamish - The North of England Open Air Museum
Beamish, Co. Durham.
Tel: (0207) 231811

Open air museum of northern life around the turn of the century. Buildings re-erected to form a town with shops and houses. Colliery village, station and working farm.

Durham Cathedral
Durham City, Co. Durham.
Tel: (091) 3682367

Widley considered to be the finest example of Norman church architecture in England. Tombs of St. Cuthbert and the Venerable Bebe.

HUMBERSIDE

SELF-CATERING

BEVERLEY. Three bedroom converted barn, (1 (one en-suite. Snooker room, grass tennis court. Central heating. Linen and towels provided. Private parking. 5 key highly commended ETB. Contact Skinner, Carr Croft, Main Street, Tickton, North Humberside. Phone: (0964) 543857.

CARAVANS, CHALETS & HOLIDAY PARKS

HUMBERSTON. Thorpe Park is one of 19 holiday parks coast to coast. Our luxury holiday homes, sleep 2-8 people. Prices start from £9 per person per night, based on 6 sharing. For a free colour brochure Phone: Lo-Call (0345) 508 508.

WHERE TO GO

Sewerby Park Zoo
Bridlington.
Tel: (0262) 673769
Llamas, penguins, macaws, coatimundi, pheasants, flamingoes, deer, wallabys, avaries. Amy Johnson collection, Novel trains from park to Bridlington. Cafetertia. Disabled visitors welcome.

Bridlington Leisure World
The Promenade, Bridligton, Humberside.
Tel: (0262) 606715
Wave pool, adult and junior pools. Multi-purpose hall with indoor bowling area, entertainment centre, club, disco.

Museum of Army Transport
Beverley Humberside.
Tel: (0482) 860445
Army road, rail, sea and air exhibits excitingly displayed in two exhibition halls, plus the huge, last remaining, Blackburn Beverley aircraft Gulf exhibition.

Elsham Hall Country and Wildlife Park
Elsham, South Humberside.
Tel: (0652) 688698
Trout and carp lakes, wild butterfly garden walkways, animal farm, pets corner, adventure playground, new falcony centre, craft centre, art gallery and clock tower shop.

NORTHUMBERLAND

HOTELS & GUEST HOUSES

BERWICK UPON TWEED. Opposite Holy Island. Large detached cottage, sleeps six. All amenities. Gardens front and rear. Golf and horse riding nearby. Not suitable for under fives. Phone: 091 281 6467.

HEXHAM/CORBRIDGE. Corbridge Guest House (bed and breakfast) and three self-catering cottages and flat. Each sleeps 5 persons. Car parking. Enquiries The Hayes, Newcastle Road, Corbridge NE45. Phone: (01434) 632010.

HEXHAM, Rye Hill Farm, Slaley. Small working livestock farm. Magnificent rural setting. All rooms en-suite. Colour televisions, tea/coffee facilities. Real home-made evening meals. Pets, children welcome. ETB 3 crowns commended. Phone: Mrs Courage (01434) 673259.

SELF-CATERING

ALNWICK. Titlington Hall Farm. 3 lovely country cottages. All are centrally heated, spacious and very well equipped. Sleeping up to ten (10). All linen included. Children and pets welcome. Phone: (0665) 578253.

HALTWHISTLE. Ald Whitecraig Farm, near Hadrian's Wall. Superior self-catering holiday homes. Moorland peace and quiet. Walking, golf, birdwatching yet under 1 hour Durham, Metro-Centre, Scotland, Lakes, North Pennines. 'A countryside for connoisseurs'. Brochure Phone: (0434) 320565.

CARAVANS, CHALETS & HOLIDAY PARKS

BERWICK is one of 19 holiday parks parks coast to coast. Our luxury holiday homes, sleep 2-8 people. Prices start from £9 per person per night, based on 6 sharing. For a free colour brochure Phone: Lo-Call (0345) 508 508.

YORKSHIRE

HOTELS & GUEST HOUSES

AIRTON, Malhamdale. Comfortable, spacious, semi-detached cottage in picturesque Dales village. 3 bedrooms, bathroom and shower room. Central heating, open fire. Exposed beams. Open all year. ETB 4 keys commended. Phone: (01729) 830253 for brochure.

AMPLEFORTH. Carr House. 18 miles from York. Internationally recommended. Idyllic 16th century farmhouse accommodation. Romantic four poster bedrooms, en-suite. ETB 2 crowns. Picturesque countryside. Good access moors, dales, historical area. Informal atmosphere. No smoking. Brochure Phone: (0347) 868526.

BUCKDEN, Yorkshire Dales. A warm welcome awaits you in our Wharfedale converted barn. Log fires, television, tea, coffee making facilities. Ideal walking, cycling, sight-seeing or just relaxing. Bed and breakfast £15 per person per night, dinner optional, £10. Phone: (0756) 760305.

GARGRAVE. Kirksyke Hotel. En-suite rooms, colour television, some ground floor. Handy for Bronte, Herriot, Emmerdale areas and Carlisle Settle railway. Car park. Quiet village. Bed and breakfast £42 double, £29 single. Licensed. Home cooking. Phone: (01756) 749356.

GIGGLESWICK, Settle. Bed and breakfast. All rooms en-suite with colour television, tea and coffee making facilities. 250 year old residence. Within easy reach of all amenities. Mount View, Phone: Belle Hill (0729) 822953.

FOURPOSTER LODGE HOTEL
68/70 Heslington Road,
Off Barbican Road, York YO1 5AU
Telephone: 01904 651170

Your hosts Peter and Judith Jones, welcome you to their Victorian Villa restored and furnished for your comfort: Fourposter en-suite bedrooms include: Colour TV, Radio, Hairdryer and Hospitality Tray. Start your day with a hearty English breakfast. Then take a leisurely stroll to Yorks historic centre.
The University and Barbican Leisure Centre are both close by. Our other amenities include a private car park and residents licence.

RAC
ACCLAIMED

AA
QQQ

COMMENDED

LASKILL FARM

HAWNBY, NR HELMSLEY, YORKSHIRE YO6 5NB
TEL: 01439 798268

Charming old stone-built farmhouse with its own lake. Situated in the North York Moors National Park. A walkers paradise, with numerous walks and nature trails nearby. Peace and tranquillity. All rooms well equipped. Tea and coffee making facilities in all rooms. Colour TV in all rooms. Generous cuisine of high standard.

Bed and Breakfast – Evening Meal by arrangement
We are recommended in Elizabeth Gundrey's
"Staying off the beaten track"

HARROGATE. High Winsley Farm. Situated in peaceful countryside, seven miles north of Harrogate. Excellent base for touring the Yorkshire Dales. Comfortable, spacious rooms with washbasins, tea, coffee. Guests bathroom, television lounge. Excellent food. Phone: (0423) 770376.

HOLMFIRTH. Last of the Summer Wine. Small friendly guest house with hearty traditional or vegetarian breakfast. All rooms central heating, hot and cold, tea and coffee. En-suites available. On local bus route. Pets welcome. Phone: (0484) 681643.

HUSTHWAITE, York. Throstle Nest is situated about 1.5 miles just off the A19, between Easingwold and Thirsk. Ideal for touring moors and dales also East Coast and York. 2 double rooms from £12. Phone: Mrs Clark (0347) 821291.

Set high up on the hillside with panoramic views over the Calder Valley, near Halifax, The Hobbit is renowed for providing excellent food and drink at reasonable prices.

The Hobbit
Hob Lane, Norland, Sowerby Bridge
Tel: 0422 832202

ASK FOR OUR SPECIAL "Murder Mystery" THEME BREAK BROCHURE

- 22 ensuite bedrooms with all facilities
- Golf & horse riding nearby
- Ideally situated for Calderdale's wealth of tourist attractions including Eureka! Childrens Museum, Piece Hall and Hebden Bridge
- 2am licence Mon.-Sat.
- Good entertainment programme
- Exits 22 and 24 from M62 nearby

COMMENDED

INGLETON. Gatehouse, Far Westhouse. Working farm in elevated position. Enjoying panoramic views. Guest dining room, lounge with colour television. Bedrooms with private facilities and tea trays. 15 miles exit 34 M6. Ordinance map reference SD 678 737. Phone: (015242) 41458.

INGLETON. 'Langber' Guest House. Yorkshire Dales Three Peaks area. Good centre. Panoramic views. Comfortable accommodation, some en-suite. Phone: Mrs Bell (015242) 41587, LA6 3DT.

KNARESBOROUGH. Ebor Mount Guest House. Charming 18th century town house. All en-suite rooms. Non-smoking. Private car park. Picturesque market town. Central for Dales and York. Double room £35 - £38. York Place, HG5 0AA. Phone: (01423) 863315.

MALTON. Oakdene Country House Hotel, between York and coast. In 1 acre of beautiful gardens. All bedrooms en-suite. Residents bar, home cooking & personally run by owners Tom & Elaine Harland, 29 Middlecave Rd., Malton, N. Yorks. YO17 0NE. Phone: (0653) 693363.

RAVENSCAR. Smugglers Rock Country Guest House. Twixt Whitby and Scarborough with panoramic views over the surrounding National Park and sea. Reputedly a smugglers haven. All rooms en-suite. Homely atmosphere. Ideal for touring and walking. Phone: (0723) 870044.

RIPON. Stay on a working farm in our 17th Century farmhouse, offering bed and breakfast accommodation. Oak beamed lounge with Inglenook. Tea and coffee facilities all rooms. Fountains Abbey two miles. Phone: Mrs Watson (0765) 620217.

SCARBOROUGH – NORTH BAY
HOTEL ALMAR
116 Colombus Ravine, Scarborough, YO12 7QZ
Licensed family hotel. Colour TV, Tea/Coffee facilities, central heating all rooms, en-suite available. Choice of menu. Car parking. Non-smoking bedrooms and dining room. Reduction OAP/Children sharing. Special breaks. Open all year. Full Christmas itinerary.
Tel: 01723 372887

SCARBOROUGH. Family run private licensed hotel overlooking North Bay. All rooms colour television, tea and coffee making, most en-suite. Home cooking. Car park. Friendly Yorkshire welcome. Bed and breakfast from £16, dinner £6. Phone: (01723) 364834.

SCARBOROUGH. Plane Tree Cottage Farm. Enjoy peace and quiet on this small farm situated in open countryside in Stainton Dale. Sea views. 8 miles north of Scarborough. Good home cooking. Well recommended. AA, QQ listed - approved. Phone: (0723) 870796.

SCARBOROUGH. Northbay. 'Northcote'. 100% non-smoking. Well established, modern semi-detached, private hotel. Car park. En-suites, colour televisions, tea-making. Menu choice. OAP's specials. Families welcome. Child reductions under 18's. Terms from £100 weekly. Phone: (0723) 367758.

SCARBOROUGH. Rivelyn Hotel. 55 en-suite rooms with television, telephone etc. Renowned for good food, entertainment and hospitality. Lift, car parking. Our many regulars say we offer the best value you will find anywhere. Phone: (0723) 361248.

PLEASE MENTION
DALTONS
DIRECTORY
WHEN BOOKING
YOUR HOLIDAY

SETTLE. Homely bed and breakfast accommo- dation in beautiful setting, overlooking River Ribble. Television, hot and cold, tea and coffee facilities in rooms. One double, one twin/family. £14.50 per person sharing. Reduction three nights. Phone: (0729) 823988.

THIRSK. Comfortable farmhouse. En-suite heated rooms. Television, tea/coffee making facilities. Guests' lounge - log fire. Open 1-12. Good home cooking a speciality. Ideal base for exploring York, moors, dales and east coast. ETB 2 crown. Brochure Phone: (01845) 522103.

YORK. Clean, warm, comfortable, non-smoking guest house near centre. Rooms have television, tea, coffee making facilities. Some rooms en-suite. Excellent full English breakfast. On street parking. Reasonable rates. Phone: Mrs. Stothard (0904) 627803.

YORK. Alemar Guest House. Clean and comfortable with family atmosphere. Good value. Near to historic city centre. All rooms have tea and coffee facilities and colour televisions. Strictly non smoking. For details Phone: (01904) 652367.

YORK. Crossways. Family run Guest House. En-suite rooms, televisions, free tea, coffee facilities. Bed and breakfast from £15. Close park, bowling green. 10 minutes Minster city centre. 23 Wigginton Road, York YO3 7HJ. Phone: (0904) 637250.

YORK. Hillcrest Guest House. 10 minutes walk city centre. Enjoy good food, comfort. Exceptional value in our friendly spacious Victorian house, beside Rowantree Park. Bargain off-season breaks. Evening meals available. Private parking. Phone: (01904) 653160.

YORK. Kismet Guest House. All rooms colour televisions, tea, coffee making, some en-suite. Breakfast menus, central heating. Private parking. Own keys. Honeymooners welcome. 10 minutes walk city centre. From £14 per person. Phone: (01904) 621056.

YORK. Feversham Lodge Guest House. Converted 19th century manse situated ten minutes walk city centre, Minster and attractions. Nearby park, bowling greens. Most rooms en-suite, tea making, televisions. Car park. 2 crowns. Proprietor Mrs Peacock. Phone: (01904) 623882.

YORK. 5 miles north. A warm welcome at 18th century converted farmhouse. Comfortable accommodation. 3 double rooms, 2 with private shower, tea/coffee facilities. Hearty breakfast with homemade bread. Smith, Ivy Cottage, Shipton-by-Beningbrough. Phone: (0904) 470465.

YORKSHIRE DALES. Small guest House in the lovely Dales village of Ingleton. All bedrooms en-suite with river or mountain views. Three day special dinner, bed and breakfast £72 per person. Recommended for excellent food and comfort. Phone: (015242) 41401.

SELF-CATERING

ASKRIGG VILLAGE, Wensleydale. 3/4 bed- roomed cottage, sleeps 6/8. Well equipped and maintained. Full central heating. Colour television. Garden. Off-road parking for 2 cars. Central position for walking and touring. Please Phone: (01332) 780697 for brochure.

BEVERLEY, Driffield. Quiet hamlet. Cosy coun- try cottage (converted stables). Double glazed. Central heating. Sleeps six. Suitable partially disabled. Bathroom, shower-room, automatic washerdryer, well equipped, payphone, linen included. Dogs welcome. Ideal coast, moors, York. Phone: (01377) 270267.

BRIDLINGTON. Three bedroomed country cot- tage. Three miles inland. Sleeps six. Centrally heated. Peaceful and quiet. Set in the beautiful Yorkshire Wolds. Close to York, Moors and coast. Also winter breaks. No pets. Brochure Phone: (0262) 676649.

BRIDLINGTON, Sewerby village. Luxury self- contained holiday apartment overlooking the sea. Beautiful hall. Park and golf nearby. 5 minutes from town. Close to amenities. Suitable for disabled. Well behaved pets welcome. Sleeps 4. Phone: (0262) 676819.

BUCKDEN, Yorkshire Dales. Barn conversion cottages for 2-8 persons. Well equipped and heated. Private parking. Friendly village with cosy inns. In the heart of the dales. Long or short breaks. Phone: (0756) 760379.

CARLETON, near Skipton. comfortable two bedroomed first floor flat. Near village centre. Ideal for walking holidays in Yorkshire Dales or Pennine Way. Laundry room and payphone in the building. Phone: Mrs Walker (0756) 793381 or (0756) 793745.

CHAPEL LE DALE, Three Peaks area. Unwind in in cosy beamed cottage. Peaceful, magnificent views. Sleeps 3. Excellent walking. £100-£185. Weekend breaks £55. Television, central heating, fuel and linen included. Sorry no pets. Phone: (05242) 41149.

DALES/MOORS, LAKES. Superb selection of cottages. Yorkshire, Northumbria, Cumbria and throughout the North of England. Sleeping 2/20. Available all year. Brochure write Sykes Cottages, Knowles Barn, Gargrave, Skipton, North Yorkshire BD23 3RT or Phone: (0756) 749758.

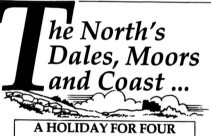

A HOLIDAY FOR FOUR
including fuel and linen
FROM ONLY £150 PER WEEK

Over 500 superb, personally inspected, self catering holiday properties from Yorkshire's 'Bronte', 'Herriot' and 'Heartbeat' country to Northumberland's Borders. Cosy cottages for 2, to country houses accommodating 12, many open all year. Contact Diane Ames.

Dales Holiday Cottages
Carleton Business Park, Skipton,
North Yorkshire BD23 2DG
ETB Registered Agency

Tel: 01756 • 799821 & 790919

FILEY. Listed refurbished 18th century cot- tage close to sea, Dales, Moors. 2 double bedrooms, fitted kitchen, bath, shower, lounge, dining room, coal fires. Bradshaw, Broadacres, Watson's Lane, Reighton, Near Filey, North Yorkshire YO14 9SD. Phone: (0723) 890735.

GARTON-ON-THE-WOLDS. Self-contained first- floor granary in non-working farm. Sleeps 2 to 4. Parking, garden. Convenient York, Beverley, North Yorkshire Moors and coast. From £140 per week, inclusive services, linen. Weekends available October to April. Walsh, Church Farm. Phone: (0377) 253988.

GLAISDALE. North York Moors. Cottage. Three bedrooms, sleeps six, plus modern facilities. Walkers' paradise, woodland within 200 yards. Large south facing garden, magnificent views. Near Whitby, Heartbeat country and North York Moors Railway. Details Phone: (0206) 577949.

GRASSINGTON, Wharfedale. 'Rooftops'. De- tached 3 bedroomed cottage. Sleeps 5/7. Superb views. Well equipped for owners' use. Garage, garden. Central heating, open fire. Available all year. ETB commended. Britton, 38 Meadlands, York. Phone: (01904) 416252.

HARDRAW. Cissy's Cottage. Delightful 18th Century Dales cottage. Open fire, beamed ceilings. Highest standards throughout. Sleeps four in comfort. Open all year. Fishing included. For brochure of this lovely warm cottage Phone: (0609) 881302.

HARROGATE HOLIDAY COTTAGES
Visit York and the Yorkshire Dales, Emmerdale, Last of the Summer Wine, Heartbeat and Herriot Country! Stay in one of our personally inspected cottages. Prices from £120 per week.
For FREE colour brochure, contact:
Harrogate Holiday Cottages, Essex House, Otley Road, Killinghall, Harrogate, N. Yorkshire. HG3 2DW.
Tel: 01423 520476

HAWORTH. Cottage on edge of famous Bronte village. Convenient for Yorkshire Dales, York, West Coast. Also excellent walking country. Sleeps 4. Phone: (0535) 645140 for brochure.

HAWORTH
BRONTE COUNTRY AND THE YORKSHIRE DALES
17th Century cottages in idyllic surroundings. Sleeps 4-5. Horse riding is available on premises.
Golf nearby. Also riding holidays or weekend breaks with full board.
Phone: (0535) 603292

HAWORTH. Yorkshire Dales. Rural sheep farm. 3 fully equipped cottages. Barn conversion. Secluded, peaceful, spectacular views. Close to Skipton and Bronte country. ETB 4 keys highly commended. No pets. For colour brochure Phone: (0535) 607720.

HAWORTH
Village in Bronte Country, close to the Keighley and Worth Valley railway.
MILL COTTAGE   COMMENDED
Cowhouse Bridge, Cullingworth, Bradford
Contact: Mrs. Y Chivers, Montrose,
Solomons Lane, Shirrell Heath,
Southampton SO32 2HU
Phone: Wickham (01329) 833345
Imaginatively modernised, yet a traditional stone cottage featuring a beamed ceiling, mullioned windows and a patio. 1 Self contained unit, sleeping maximum 6.

Price per week:	£min	£max
Low Season	£145	
High Season		£245

Prices inclusive of heating and bed linen

HELMSLEY, near, North Yorkshire Moors. Two bedroom cottage on family farm. Equipped to a very high standard. Central heating, bed linen and towels included. Excellent walking area. Central to Yorkshire Dales, coast and York. Phone: (01439) 798242.

INGLEBY GREENHOW. ETB 4 key highly com-mended cottage/apartments. Peace, space, beautiful views at 16th century Grade II* manor house in national park, on edge of moors. 50 acres gardens/woodland with trout stream. Brochure Phone: (01642) 722170.

KETTLEWELL, Yorkshire Dales. Barn conver-sion cottage for 2-6 persons. Well equipped and heated. Private parking. Touring, walking, cycling, fishing, horse riding or just relaxing. In the heart of the dales. Coach house. Phone: (0756) 760803.

MALTON. Luxury cottage, sleeps four in en-suite rooms. Midway York and coast. Ideal for shopping, walking, golf. Open all year for long and short breaks. Summer £140 per week. Phone: Mrs Heaton (0653) 693309.

NORTH YORK MOORS. Charming stone cottages. Comfortable cottage with many interesting features. Olde worlde furnishings with modern conveniences. Ideally based for touring and walking. Idyllic surroundings. York 30 minutes. For further details Phone: (01439) 798268.

POCKLINGTON. Near York. Two bedroomed detached bungalows overlooking lake in peaceful country setting. York 15 minutes, coast forty minutes. Free fishing. Choice of lakes, games room, and short breaks. For brochure Freephone: (0500) 657874.

RIPON. Delightful cottages, comfortable and well equipped. One in pretty village of Winksley, others in Kirkby, Malzeard. Central heating. 2 have garden. Bed linen provided. ETB registered. Brochure Phone: (01765) 658405. Bailey, Owster Hill, Galphay, Ripon.

RIPON, near Lightwater Valley, York, Knaresborough, Harrogate. Delightful Georgian cottage recently rebuilt. Fitted kitchen, washing machine, colour television. Quiet courtyard. Close Market Square. Gas central heating, constant hot water. Sleeps 7. £225 per week. Phone: (0113) 258 9254.

RYEDALE. Family run cottages in one acre. Pretty gardens and paddock in conservation village near Castle Howard. Easy access York, Moors and coast. Phone: (01653) 628656.

SCARBOROUGH. Farm cottage, sleeps 6. Ideal for East coast, York, Hull and North Yorkshire Moors. Pets and children very welcome. Phone: Mrs Byas (0377) 267318, 267646.

SCARBOROUGH 8 miles. Modernised cottage in picturesque village of Ganton. Sleeps 5/6. Hydra-spa bath. Garden, patio and off-street parking. Ideal for York, Bridlington, Filey and Moors. Family pub and golf nearby. No pets. Phone: (0115) 9607373.

SETTLE, Yorkshire Dales. Two bedroom cottage, sleeps four. Beautiful walking area. Five minutes shops, cafes, pubs and railway station. Excellent location for touring Yorkshire, Trough of Boland, visiting York or Lake District. Phone: 081 806 6361.

SKIPTON near. Yorkshire Dales National Park at Kirkby Malham, Comfortably furnished 2 bedroom cottage sleeps 5. Night store heaters, colour television, parking space 1 car, small garden. No pets. Beautiful area. Reasonable rates. Phone: (0729) 830274.

SKIPTON. Cottage in award winning village, on the Pennine Way. Handy for dales, lakes, Bronte Country. Sleeps 4. Parking. Pet. Colour television, microwave, auto washer, linen, towels, gas, electric inclusive. Phone: (0282) 843272.

SLINGSBY. Detached stone cottage in conser- vation village near Castle Howard. Beamed ceilings with open fire. Private garden. Ideal for couple. Shops and pub nearby. Excellent centre for touring. Easy reach York Moors and coast. Phone: (0653) 628384.

SLINGSBY. 'The Barn', olde worlde cottage with all modern conveniences. Near Castle Howard. Sleeps 4. All linen included. Situated on B1257, Helmsley to Malton. 20 minutes York, 30 minutes Scarborough. Hood, Banchory Cottage. Phone: (0653) 628409.

STAITHE. North Yorkshire. Attractive cottage to let in delightful seaside fishing village. Situated within the beautiful North Yorkshire Moors National Park. Sleeps four. Fully equipped. Linen included. Television and video. Phone: (0977) 554750.

STAITHES. Cosy fisherman's cottage over- looking the crashing waves of the wild North Sea in one of the most picturesque villages in England. Beaches, winding cobbled streets etc. South-facing sun terrace, sleeps 4/6. Brochure Phone: 071-254 5274.

STAITHES, near Whitby. Attractive fisher- man's cottage on the Cleveland Way, overlooking the village and sea. Perfect for walking, relaxing or touring North Yorkshire Moors. Modern facilities. Colour television. Sleeps six. Private parking. Phone: (0949) 838245.

THIRSK. Clean comfortable, well equipped cottages. Washing machine, central heating. Sleeping 2-8. Excellent bases for touring/exploring dales, moors, east coast, York. A pet and children welcome. Linen/towels provided, fuel included. Open 1-12. Brochure Phone: (01845) 522103.

THIRSK. Granary cottage on edge of North Yorkshire Moors National Park. Colour television, microwave. Outdoor table tennis, slide and paddling pool. All linen, towels, electric included in rent. Anderson, Cleaves Barn, Thirlby. Phone: (01845) 597462.

WENSLEYDALE. Traditional old Dales stone cottages with beamed ceilings. Open fires and Laura Ashley prints. Both peaceful locations with spectacular views. Well equipped, warm and comfortable. Free trout fishing on farm. Phone: (0969) 667481.

WHITBY. Riverside cottage, 3 cabins, sleep 6. Fishing, putting. Children welcome, dog okay. Beautiful garden, rare plant nursery, ample parking. 2 miles Whitby, great walking area. Mrs Perry, River Gardens, Sleights, Whitby, North Yorkshire. Phone: (0947) 810329.

WHITBY NATIONAL PARK. Self-catering 3 bedroomed period Warm, comfortable, well equipped. ETB 4 keys recommended. Convenient for coast, moors and steam railway. From £150 per week. Also farmhouse bed and breakfast. For brochure Phone: (0947) 895314.

WHITBY area. Port Mulgrave. Comfortable cot- tage, sleeps 6. Walking and touring centre. 3 minutes from Cleveland Way and cliffs. National Trust area. Open all year. Parking. Phone: (0535) 680901.

WHITBY. Near Sleights. Superior cottages. Ideal coast, country. Private parking. Supervised by owner living in village. Available all year. Please state numbers and dates required. Mrs Roberts, 5 Brook Park, Sleights, Near Whitby, Yorkshire YO21 1RT. Phone: (01947) 810763.

YORK area. Farm house, sleeps 6. Very com- fortable, linens and towels provided. Centrally heated. Good location for visits to moors, coast and Dales. Phone: (0904) 750075. Mrs Gillie Allison. Sorry no pets.

YORK, 14 miles. Two semi-detached, three bed-roomed houses, sleep 5/6. Fridge/freezer, colour television, enclosed garden, quiet rural surroundings. Children and pets welcome. Fishing, central for Yorkshire. Hall, The Haddocks, Myton-on-Swale, Helperby, York YO6 2RB. Phone: (0423) 360224.

YORK. Bootham Park View. Fully self-con-tained apartments. Close to city centre. Fully equipped. Bed linen provided. Colour television, payphone. Car parking. Contact Shelagh Wilson, 20 Grosvenor Terrace, Bootham, York YO3 7AG. Phone: (0904) 631011.

YORK, near. Two 4 berth farm holiday cot-tages. Peaceful views over open farmland towards the Wolds. Cottages tastefully decorated, new quality furniture making them very comfortable holiday homes. Peaceful but quick access coast, Dales and York. Phone: (0759) 368400.

YORK. The Coach House. Delightful 2 bedroom country cottage in a hamlet 8 miles east of York. Fishing, bird watching. Farming life all on your doorstep. ETB commended 3 keys. For brochure Phone: Theresa (01759) 318518.

YORK 8 miles. Tasteful granary conversion, ground floor. 2 bedrooms. Good touring base for North Yorkshire Moors, Yorkshire coast and Dales. Golf, fishing. Nature reserve 1 mile. Short breaks. Gas central heating. Well equipped. Private parking. Phone: (0904) 448575.

YORK. Five flats, two minutes walk from York Minster. Colour television, central heating, separate bathrooms. Sleeps two to four persons. Enquiries to Mrs H.C. Reed, Haverdell, Skates Lane, Sutton on Forest, York YO6 1HB. Phone: (0347) 810873.

YORK/HARROGATE. Charmingly converted comfortable village cottages, in pretty village. Ideally situated for exploring Historic towns, Abbeys and stately homes. Central for the North Yorkshire Moor and Dales. 4 keys, ETB commended. Owner supervised. Phone: (01423) 330153.

YORKSHIRE DALES/Bronte Country. 3 Fully equipped cottages on rural sheep farm. Peaceful location. Spectacular views. Barn conversion. Private parking. Short Winter breaks available. Sorry no pets. ETB highly commended. For colour brochure Phone: (0535) 607720.

YORKSHIRE DALES, near lakes. Self-catering well equipped holiday cottage to let. Also dinner, bed and breakfast in old worlde cottage. Washbasins in bedrooms, lounge with television, coal fire, dining room, home cooking. Phone: Mrs M. Williamson (0539) 625353.

YORKSHIRE WOLDS. Secluded four bedroomed farmhouse with lawns, woodland, garden furniture. Children's play area and games room. Situated on the Yorkshire Wolds. The ideal place for peace and quiet, yet only minutes away from Scarborough, Bridlington, Moors. Brochure available Phone: (01377) 267217.

YORKSHIRE DALES. Herriot country. 18th cen-tury cottage, overlooking green in delightful village. Ideally situated for touring the Dales and North Yorkshire Moors, National Parks. Visit ancient city of York, Harrogate or seaside resorts. Phone: (01609) 882396.

CARAVANS, CHALETS & HOLIDAY PARKS

FILEY. Primrose Valley Caravan Park. Luxury 34 foot caravan, sleeps 6. 2 twin, 1 double bedroom, shower. Colour television, video, microwave etc. Excellent entertainment, family clubs, swimming pool, boating, lake, golf, children's playground. Phone: Scott (0536) 403794.

HEBDEN BRIDGE, Howarth. Pennine country. Luxury caravan, sleeps 4 with comfort. Lounge, dining area. Separate shower, wc, double bedroom. Colour television. In secluded position. Good walks and pubs. Horse stable facilities. Modest rates. Phone: (0422) 842229.

HELMSLEY, near, North Yorkshire Moors. 6 berth static caravan, situated on family farm. All facilities included. Excellent walking area. Pony trekking and gliding nearby. Central to Yorkshire Dales, the coast and York. Phone: (01439) 798242.

KNARESBOROUGH. Scotton Holiday Park. Luxurious rose award caravans and chalets for hire. Quiet family run park. Service, cleanliness paramount. Licensed restaurant, shop, children's play area. Great centre for exploring Yorkshire and The Dales. Phone: (0423) 864413.

NAWTON, North Yorkshire. Close to Heartbeat country. 6 berth caravan on quiet farm. Gas, electric, flush toilet. Linen provided. Situated in unspoilt countryside. Phone: (0439) 771250.

RIPON near. Hussar Inn. Holiday caravan park, Markington, Harrogate. Holiday caravans with full services. Colour televisions. Near fountains. Abbey 2 miles, Herriot Country. Situated in village. Rear of inn. Motor caravans, tourers, tents welcome. Launderette, showers etc. Brochures Phone: (0765) 677327.

YORKSHIRE DALES, Ingleton. Langber End Farm. Three caravans, sleep 6. All modern conveniences. Two miles out of Ingleton. Good centre for lakes and Dales. £100 week. £90 over 65. Gas and electric included. Phone: Faraday (05242) 41776.

YORKSHIRE DALES, Bentham. 6 berth luxury caravan on farm with all amenities and beautiful panoramic views. Bed linen provided. Pets welcome. Reasonable rates, electricity extra. For a wonderful holiday please Phone: Mrs Isabel Carr on Bentham (015242) 61657.

YORKSHIRE DALES. Ingleton 4 miles. Fully equipped 4 berth static caravan on working farm. Panoramic views Ingleborough. Central for lakes, dales, coast. Good walking, fishing. Also cosy cottage for 4. Mason, Oxenforth Green, Tatham, Lancaster LA2 8PL. Phone: (05242) 61784.

For useful information to help you plan your holiday please turn to the back of this book.

WHERE TO GO

Sea Life Centre
Scarborough, North Yorkshire.
Tel: (0723) 376125

An opportunity to meet creatures that live in and around the oceans of the British Isles.

Yorkshire Dales Falconry and Conservation Centre
Crown Nest, Giggleswick, North Yorkshire.
Tel: (0729) 825164

Falconry centre with many species of birds of prey from around the world including vultures, eagles, hawks, falcons and owls. Free-flying displays, lecture room and avaries.

Yorkshire Mining Museum
Caphouse Colleriery, New Road, Overton, Wakefield West Yorkshire.
Tel: (0924) 848806

Exciting award-winning museum of the Yorkshire coalfield, including guided underground tour of authentic old workings.

Cannon Hall Country Park
Cawthorne, South Yorkshire.
Tel: (0226) 774500

18th Century landscaped parklands with lakes stocked with ornamental and indigenous waterfowl. Nearby Cannon Hall Museum and open farm.

North Yorkshire Moors Railway
Pickering Station, Pickering, North Yorkshire.
Tel: (0751) 72508

18-mile railway through the national park. Steam and diesel trains.

The Arc
St. Saviourgate, York, North Yorkshire.
Tel: (0904) 654324

Visitors can 'touch the past' handling ancient finds, pottery, bone and stitching. Roman sandals or picking a Viking padlock. Audio-visual display and exploration of dig by computer.

COVES AT FLAMBOROUGH
HUMBERSIDE
(photograph courtesy of
Yorkshire & Humberside Tourist Board)

CHANNEL ISLANDS

When I want a British holiday that's a little bit different, I'm never disappointed by the Channel Islands.

Jersey and Guernsey offer the best of both worlds. You can savour a distinct French flavour without worrying about passports and currency; you can enjoy the traditional pleasures of warm weather and sandy beaches without having to suffer all the usual tourist traps. Even experience the little adventure of travelling 'abroad' without actually leaving the British Isles!

Jersey, the largest of the islands, measures nine miles by five but still manages to boast fifty miles of picturesque coastline and soft beaches, as well as striking coves and caves sculpted by the waves. And how better to appreciate the view than from a stroll along one of the charming promenades? The one stretching from St. Helier to St. Aubin has long been a favourite of mine.

For those into more energetic pursuits, Jersey is the perfect place for watersports such as surfing and waterskiing; it also provides two 18-hole golf courses.

And, for such a small island, there are many places of interest to visit. The Val de la Mare Reservoir, the Les Mielles conservation area, and the Elizabeth Castle, which dates from the 1590s and which was named in honour of Elizabeth 1.

In fact, Jersey is steeped in interesting history. There are Neolithic monuments, Norman sites and the Towers around the coast were built to protect the island from French invasion during the Napoleonic Wars. More recent invaders were the Germans, and the German Underground Hospital is a fascinating location. Now a museum, this mile of underground corridors was originally hewn out of the rock in 1941, for use as an ammunition store and barracks.

For an insight into all this (and more!) visit the 'Story of Jersey' exhibition at the Jersey Museum, St. Helier. And to see some of the most beautiful and rare animals in the world, call in on the Jersey Wildlife Preservation Trust. It was founded by the well-known naturalist, Gerald Durrell, who actually lives on the island.

Equally attractive is the sister island, Guernsey. Its capital, St. Peter Port, is worth a visit in itself with its winding streets, waterside cafes and yacht-filled harbour. While on the south of the island, you can walk the cliff path that offers a 16 mile-long vision of changing seascapes and beguiling flowers.

And, of course, don't forget to treat yourself to a boat-trip to the three small islands Sark, Herm and Alderney.

On the subject of boats I have to admit I grew quite attached to the terra-firma of Guernsey to the stage where I never wanted to leave it! I have to confess, many though its attractions are they were not the influencing factor. As you will notice from your visit, there are quite a lot of yachts around and seven years ago I found myself on one learning to sail for a BBC Television programme together with fellow novices Annabel Croft who is more at home on a tennis court and singer, songwriter Peter Skellern. Suffice it to say Annabel and Peter found their sea-legs a lot quicker than I found mine!

CHANNEL ISLANDS

HOTELS & GUEST HOUSES

ALDERNEY

ALDERNEY

The best kept secret of the Channel Islands, offers peace and tranquillity in picturesque surroundings. Lots of absorbing history, birds, flowers and fortifications. Many different types of sports to challenge and try. Long and short breaks. Packages available.

Tel: 01481 823645

GUERNSEY

GUERNSEY. Woodvale. A unique totally non-smoking hotel. Situated within walking distance of town and leisure centre. Facilities include en-suite, colour television, radio, satellite, video channels, tea - coffee unit. Healthy options menu. 'Heartboat' award. Stanley Road. Phone: (01481) 722531.

Marine Hotel

GRADE ♛ ♛
LES ROUTIERS

♛ HIGHLY
RAC ACCLAIMED
AA Recommended QQQ

Well Road, St Peter Port, Guernsey
Telephone: (01481) 724978

Margaret and Arthur Clegg welcome you to their friendly and very comfortable hotel, which is quietly and conveniently situated approx. 30 yards from the sea. The main shopping centre, harbours, and bus station are only a few minutes' walk along the sea front. All bedrooms are en-suite and have tea/coffee making facilities, hair dryers, shaver points, and optional TV. We have central heating throughout, and full fire certificate. Full English breakfast with choice freshly cooked to order.

The Marine Hotel offers the following facilities:
– All 11 bedrooms are en-suite (bath or shower).
– Full central heating throughout.
– Full fire precautions.
– Tea and Coffee making facilities at no charge.
– Optional colour TV in every bedroom.
– Hair dryer and shaving points in all bedrooms.
– Lounge with colour TV and view over new Marina.
– Most bedrooms with sea view.
– Packed lunches to order.
– Car hire can be arranged.
– Mid-week bookings (cheaper travel costs!).
– No Service Charge or VAT.
– Sun Patio with views of Marina and nearby islands – Herm and Sark.
– 10 mins. walk from Leisure Centre
– Choice of breakfasts
– Vegetarians catered for
– Visa, Mastercard and Euro Access.
– Regret no Pets; no smoking in the dining room.

GUERNSEY. Small family hotel. Close to beach. Home cooking, en-suite, family rooms, television, tea - coffee. 3 miles St. Peter Port. Le Galaad Hotel, Castel, Guernsey. Brochure available on request. Phone: Yvonne or Richard (0481) 57233.

GUERNSEY WEST COAST
HARTON LODGE HOTEL

Three Crown Hotel and Restaurant. Renowned for its bar meals. Sunday roast and friendly welcome. Our family run hotel is on level ground within a short walk of the beaches, shops and indoor bowls. Bus stops outside for town and tour pick ups. All rooms en-suite with colour TV, phones and coffee, tea making facilities. Children are welcome. We would be pleased to arrange flight/ferry, car hire and holiday insurance inclusive with our daily rates. From £25 half board, £17 bed and breakfast. Discounts available.

Reservations call:

Viv or Tony (0481) 56341

HOTEL LES CARTERETS

Family run beach front hotel. All rooms en-suite, tea making facilities provided. Restaurant open all day including midday lunches and evening meals. B&B £16-£22.

The Cobo Coast Road, Cobo, Guernsey, Channel Islands. Tel: 0481 57352

JERSEY

JERSEY. Comfortable accommodation in private house on St. Aubins Bay. Seafront. Frequent bus service. Private parking. Tea making facilities in rooms. Phone: (0534) 31338.

SEACLIFF
Le Mont De Gouray, Gorey, Jersey.
Tel: 0534 853316.
2 diamond Guest House with magnificent views over Grouville Bay. Residents bar, restaurant, garden, secluded courtyard. Most rooms en-suite with tea and coffee facilities, heating and colour TV. 3 minutes walk to Gorey Harbour, village and beach. Tariff from £14 to £22 per night, according to room and season.
Phone: David or Hilary for further details.

JERSEY - Choice of quality hotels at affordable prices. All rooms private facilities, tea making, colour television. Centrally located. We can also organise flights by ATOL 1965. Call Destination Specialists. Phone: (0534) 617677. PO Box 791, St. Helier, Jersey.

PEBBLES
A FAMILY RUN GUEST HOUSE,
ST. AUBIN'S HARBOUR
Bed and breakfast, £16/£20.
Brochure on request.
Phone: 01534 43547. Fax: 01534 43547

BROMLEY GUEST HOUSE
7 WINCHESTER STREET
ST. HELIER, JERSEY JE2 4TH
Situated in town centre. Open all year. B.B., B.B.&E.M. Most rooms en-suite. Reduction for children under 15, if sharing parents room. Discount for O.A.P.'s.

PLEASE WRITE TO:

MRS. SCHILLACI, or
TEL: 01534/25045/23948.
FAX: 01534/69712

JERSEY
ANCHOR GUEST HOUSE
Quiet family run. 100 yards beach. 5 minutes walk through park, shops, St. Helier. All rooms hot and cold, colour TV, tea making. Own keys, access all times. Reductions children, low season.
PHONE: (01534) 21476

JERSEY. Roche De La Mer. Directly on the beach. Bed and breakfast. En-suite rooms, tea and coffee trays, television. Parking. Hire car arranged. Walking distance to town and all amenities. Phone: (0534) 608034 for reservations.

PARK VIEW VILLA
25 Peirson Road JE2 3PD.
Tel: 0534 22218
April-October • 5 rooms • £13-£16 BB • Evening meals optional • Short Breaks. Set overlooking park • 100 yards beach • Within walking distance to town centre.

JERSEY, St. Helier. Welcome to good homely accommodation. Bed and English breakfast £13.50. Drink making facilities, wash basins in rooms. 12 minute walk to beach. Car parking. Phone: Mrs Queree on (0534) 36806.

LA FRONTIERE FARM
Awarded 2 Diamonds.
RUE DE LA FRONTIERE, ST. MARY JE3 3EG
TEL: 0534 481475
January-December • 10 rooms (all en-suite, 3 singles) £15-£24 B&B • Short Breaks

ASHTON LODGE

SPRING	SUMMER	AUTUMN
1st Feb.	13th May	28th Sept.
to	to	to
12th May	27th Sept.	22nd Nov.

Prices Per Person Per night
From

£17.50	£24.50	£17.50

50% reductions for children under the age of 12 years
Single Supplement
Normal tariff rates plus 50%
Rates include:
All bedrooms have en-suite facilities. Colour TV, tea & coffee making tray. Buffet & Full English Breakfast is provided. Use of the garden, terrace and swimming pool. Car parking depending on availability. Extra beds and cots for children are available on request. Gratuities at the discretion of the client. Dogs are not accepted in the Guest House.
The propietor reserves the right to alter or amend the facilities or services without prior notice.

The Ashton Lodge is a family run Guest House registered for 19 guests situated in the heart of the beautiful countryside of the Island of Jersey. A short car or bus journey from the bustling shops of St. Helier and never more than

two or three miles from some of the most picturesque and clean beaches in the British Isles.
The Ashton Lodge has its own courtesy bus available to /from the airport/harbour.
For reservations Contact:
Mr. C. Guenier
St. Martin's Main Road
Maufant
St. Saviour
Jersey
Channel Islands.
Telephone:
0534 853537
Fax: 0534 851708

JERSEY, St. Clement. Playa D'Or Guest House. Comfortable, licensed with sea views. All rooms en-suite. Colour televisions and tea making facilities, hairdryers, central heating. Golf, tennis nearby. Tariff from £15 - £23 bed and breakfast. Phone: Angela Jeffery (01534) 22861 or Fax: (01534) 69668.

JERSEY. The Lyndhurst Hotel, St Brelade. Friendly comfortable licensed guest house overlooking the beach. All rooms with en-suite facilities and colour televisions. Excellent cuisine. Bed and breakfast, half board. Open all year. Phone: (0534) 20317

JERSEY. Olde-World Guest House, St Aubin. Close picturesque harbour sea front, safe beach. From £14.00 bed and breakfast, all en-suite. Beverage making facilities. Frequent bus service. Hire-cars arranged. Phone: (0534) 41788, Peter Cook, Les Burins, Rue-de-Croquet, St Aubin, Jersey, Channel Islands JE3 8BR.

JERSEY. Quiet family run guest house. 100 yards beach, 5 minutes walk through park, shops, restaurants. All rooms hot and cold, tea making, television. Full English breakfast. Iron/hairdryer available. Access all times. Reductions children. Phone: (0534) 21476.

JERSEY, St. Helier. Tynemouth Guest House. Family run guest house. Overlooks Howard Davis Park. Close to beach and town centre. Bed and breakfast £14.50 to £15.50. Children accepted at reduced rate. Anne Jones, St. Clement's Road. Phone: (0534) 32110.

JERSEY. Trafalgar Bay Hotel. Family run with a personal touch. All rooms en-suite, fully equipped. Fully licensed. Good food. Excellent location. By beach and harbour. Please contact Bob Pallot. Phone: (01534) 856643.

JERSEY, St. Aubin. Peterborough House. 17th Century guest house. En-suite, television, tea and coffee. Cobbled street. Quiet conservation area. 200 yards fishing harbour. Restaurants, crafts. Our sun lounge and floral sun terrace overlook sea. High Street, St. Aubin, Jersey. Phone: (01534) 41568.

ST. CLEMENT, Jersey. Rocqueberg View. Charming guest house. Quiet rural setting. 2 minutes from beach. Swimming pool. All rooms have facilities. Car park. Bed and breakfast from £14-£20. Travel arrangements made. Good rates. Phone: (0534) 852642.

ST. HELIER, La Bonne. Pleasant family run guest house. 10 minutes walk town centre/beach. By Howard Davis park. Lovely en-suite rooms, Sky television. Car/cycle hire. Coastal cruises. Beautiful garden. La Bonne, Georgetown Road, St. Saviour. Phone: (01534) 32747.

SARK

SELF-CATERING

GUERNSEY

GUERNSEY. 'Rose Cottage'. Self-catering. Grade A. In a peaceful lane, near L'ancresse Common with its golf course and beautiful beaches. Comfortably furnished. Well equipped. Car parking. No pets. Brochure from Jane Rowe. Phone: (01481) 46675.

LES MERRIENNES
FOREST

Old granite barn converted into well-designed, semi-detached single storey cottages, each with own garden and all mod cons. Each sleeps 2. Set in large private grounds. Tranquil rural setting off quiet south coast lane leading to beautiful cliff paths.

Travel inclusive bonded Holidays available with C.I. TRAVEL SERVICE ATOL 1965.

Mrs. S. Paine, Les Merriennes, Forest, Guernsey
Telephone: Guernsey (STD 0481) 63262

GUERNSEY, St. Peter Port. High quality holiday apartments. Centrally located, sleeping 2-4. Seaviews. Television, hairdryers, kitchen and all linen provided. From £155 per week. Grangeclare, 28 Les Canichers, St. Peter Port. Phone: (01481) 712803 or Fax: (01481) 712249.

GUERNSEY

Karma Flats, Route Des Coutures, Vale GY3 5QT
Situated short walk from St. Sampsons, shopping, restaurants, takeaways, within easy reach of Bordeaux and L'Ancresse Bays. Linen provided. Car park. Bus route. Central heating optional. Open all year.
Brochure Tel: 01481 45186
Ruth and John Mahy

GUERNSEY. Maisonettes and cottages. Situated on West Coast. Fully equipped. 2 bedrooms, lounge, kitchen, bathroom. From £140 per week. Phone: (01481) 64981.

 SWALLOW APARTMENTS
Les Clotures, L'Ancresse,
GUERNSEY, CHANNEL ISLANDS
10 fully equipped flats sleeping 2 to 8. Cot & high chair provided. Terms range from £105 to £470. Free car park. Close to sandy beaches, windsurfing, golf, marina. Tourist Board registered. Indicate numbers in parties and dates required.
Tel: 01481 49633

GUERNSEY. Cherry Tree Bungalow. Fully fur-nished modern bungalow. 2 bedrooms, lounge, kitchen, separate toilet, shower room. Sleeps 4/6 persons. Very peaceful yet few minutes walk St. Sampsons Harbour. Linen supplied. Parking. Brochure. Apply Mrs Rive. Phone: (01481) 55404.

JERSEY

JERSEY. Self-catering, peaceful country flat. 2 bedrooms, double, small bedroom with bunk beds. Lounge/diner, television. Kitchen, bathroom. Linen provided. Amenities close by. Reasonable rates. Mrs Bree, Les Vallees Cottage, St. Martin, Jersey. Phone: (0534) 854128.
JERSEY. De La Haye's Beuvelande Camp Site. Quiet, family run. In countryside. Flat, sheltered with all amenities. Heated pool, electric hook ups. Ideal for trailer tents. Fully equipped tents available. Phone: (01534) 852223.

JERSEY
SELF CATERING

Luxury privately owned ground-floor Apartment set in a country location on the North West of the island with distant views of race course and sea. The self-contained accommodation includes 2 fully fitted bedrooms, 1 double bed and 1 twin room. Sleeps 5. The ideal choice for a quiet relaxing holiday with cliff top walking nearby and 2 golf courses within easy reach. Children of all ages welcome.

SERVICES: ELECTRICITY INCLUDED IN RENT, ALL BED LINEN PROVIDED, COLOUR SATELLITE TV, FULLY FITTED SEPARATE KITCHEN, LOUNGE DINER, DOUBLE GLAZED AND CENTRAL HEATING. Separate entrance, parking, patio. Car recommended. Own telephone. Saturday-Saturday bookings only. Open all year. Prices per apartment per week from £250.

Tel: (01534) 482156

SARK

SARK. Relaxing, peaceful, self-catering bunga-low. Secluded, south facing. Overlooking quiet valley. Beaches and coastal walks easily reached. Comfortable accommodation. All amenities. Sleeps 4. Lower rates off season. Phone: (0481) 832002.

WHERE TO GO

Hanging Strawberry Farm
Les Issues, St Saviours
Tel: 64428
"Extraordinary" describes the hundreds of hanging baskets of growing strawberries. The indoor tea rooms make an ideal setting to enjoy a real feast complete with rich Guernsey cream. Then you can watch the Copper Smith making traditional Guernsey milk cans. Sample the adventure playground, crazy golf, holiday fashion shop and indoor tropical bird garden.

SCOTLAND

I have to confess a particular bias towards Scotland and all things Scottish. It's partly due to the strong historical, cultural and geographical similarities with my home of Northern Ireland, but also it's where I spent my honeymoon!

So, let's begin my love affair with Scotland in the capital – Edinburgh. From the dramatic splendour of its skyline, dominated by the great Castle, to the modern sophistication of Princes Street and the cosmopolitan delights of the Royal Mile, this is truly a Capital of Capitals. But a word of warning! If you can't cope with entertainers on every street corner then don't visit during the Edinburgh International Festival. Because that's when every performer in the world comes along – or perhaps it just seems like it!

Glasgow is also home to a major arts festival, the Mayfest; but all year round affords the splendid sight of Charles Rennie Mackintosh architecture, as well as theatres and galleries galore.

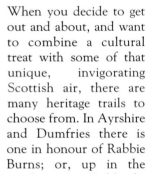

When you decide to get out and about, and want to combine a cultural treat with some of that unique, invigorating Scottish air, there are many heritage trails to choose from. In Ayrshire and Dumfries there is one in honour of Rabbie Burns; or, up in the Grampian Highlands, follow the fine Castle Trail in the Gordon District. The same region also offers a Malt Whisky Trail – a tour taking in eight distilleries.

In fact, the Grampian area should keep you entranced for days, and it's easy to see why: Aberdeen, the great 'granite city' itself; the bracing coastline; and Royal Deeside, site of Balmoral.

Venture south and – from Dunfermline to Dumfries – there are attractions to please even the most jaded palette. Galloway Forest Park; championship golf courses; and, the River Tweed – home of the textile industry.

Go northwards again (who said a holiday in Scotland had to follow the logic of a map?) and savour even more delights. The area is dominated by the big towns of Stirling, Perth and Dundee, but it's also laced with lovely lochs – none more celebrated than Loch Lomond.

Indeed, perhaps the further north you travel, the more in tune you become with the romantic, mystical flavour of Scotland. Orkney has an atmosphere of brooding remoteness but is actually just six miles from the mainland. So just imagine – or better still, experience for yourself – how much more moodily majestic is Shetland, sixty miles further north.

One of the early films I shot for the Holiday Programme gave me the best cross-section of Scotland it's probably possible to get – and it may be a novel way to see as much as you can at a leisurely pace. It was a trip by cruiser along the Caledonian Canal. The Canal is a series of 28 locks stretching along 22 miles of the Great Glen, linking 45 miles of locks to create a magnificent passageway between Fort William on the West Coast, to Inverness on the East, through some of the most spectacular mountains and glens Scotland has to offer. Right in the middle – Loch Ness, and you never know who you might bump into there! Boats are easy to hire, superbly fitted out, and you're taught everything you need to know before setting out on your passage.

Oh, and by the way...If you don't believe in the Loch Ness Monster, all I can say is – you have no soul and you don't deserve Scotland!

SCOTLAND

HOTELS & GUEST HOUSES

AUCHTERMUCHTY, Fife. Ardchoille Farmhouse. Wonderful 'taste of Scotland' meals. 3 en-suite twin bedrooms. Golf at St. Andrews. AA premier selected 5 Q's. Scottish Tourist Board highly commended 3 crowns. RAC highly acclaimed. Excellent cuisine. Phone/Fax: Donald and Isobel Steven (01337) 828414.

AULTBEA. Comfortable guest house, home made meals, en-suite bedrooms with television, central heating. Inverewe Gardens 9 miles. Scottish Tourist Board highly commended 3 crowns. Sae Mrs A. Macrae, 47 Mellow Charles, Aultbea, Ross-shire. Phone: (0445) 731326.

AYR. Parson's Lodge licensed bed and break- fast establishment with restaurant and craft shop. All rooms with colour television and tea making facilities. Available en-suite or private bathroom. Salmon fishing, golf, walking in the village. Phone: (0292) 531306.

Rockhill Guest House
& Self Catering Cottages
Lochawe, Argyll

Waterside secluded magnificent mountain view

One mile free private trout fishing

170 Acre estate

Breeding Hanoverian Competition Horses

For Brochure Please Phone
01866 833218

BALQUHIDDER, Perthshire. Monachyle Mhor. Fully licensed farmhouse/courtyard, in own 2,000 acres. All en-suite bedrooms. Antiques, country fabrics. Magnificent views over 2 lochs. Award winning renowned restaurant. Rob, Jean Lewis, Monachyle Mhor, Balquhidder, Perthshire. Phone: (01877) 384622. Fax: (01877) 384305.

BIGGAR. Walston Mansions Farmhouse. Situa- ted between Edinburgh, Glasgow. Relaxing homely farmhouse. Good home cooking with home produced products. Log fires. Pets welcome. Bed and breakfast £12.50, en-suite £14.50, evening meal £7.00. 3 crowns commended. Phone: Margaret Kirby (0189981) 338.

BRECHIN, Angus. Wood of Auldbar. Farmhouse, comfortable well appointed accommodation. Peaceful setting. Excellent food. Ideal touring area. Food hygiene certificate. Smoke alarms. Nature walks, fishing, golf, leisure centre all nearby. Many castles, Edinburgh, Aberdeen, Royal Deeside 1 1/2 hours. Phone: (0307) 830218.

BY PITLOCHRY. Pitnacree Guest House. Beautifully situated 9 bedroomed magnificent house.Overlooking the river in an area which has everything to offer the tourist. Television, tea making facilities all rooms. Phone: Mr and Mrs Campbell (0887) 840271 or send for brochure.

BY KEITH, Banffshire. Chapelhill Croft. Rural accommodation on working croft where guests are welcome to help with farm activities. Excellent home cooking using local produce. Bed and breakfast £12.50 to £15.50, evening meal £8.00. Phone: (0542) 870302.

CASTLE DOUGLAS, Auchencairn, Collinhill. Tastefully furnished bed and breakfast with panoramic sea views over Solway. En-suite bedrooms, tea/coffee facilities. Scottish Tourist Board, highly commended. Village and sea 1/2 mile. Sae for brochure. Phone: (0556) 640242.

FORFAR. Wemyss Farm. Situated on the B9113. Family run farm, lots of animals. Ideal base touring, Edinburgh, St. Andrews, Glens, East coast resorts. Tourist Board commended, listed. Home cooking. Children welcomed. Peaceful location. Phone: (0307) 462887.

FORT WILLIAM, Torlundy. Thistle Cottage. Set in beautiful valley, 3 miles north of Fort William town. Nearest to Nevis Range ski centre. Some en-suite. Warm and friendly. Reduction for children. Pets welcome. Tea on arrival. Matheson, Thistle Cottage. Phone: (01397) 702428.

GIRVAN, Ayrshire. Victorian Shooting Lodge, now farmhouse offers en-suite bed and breakfast. Also self-catering. 2 crowns commended Scottish Tourist Board. Lovely views Culzean Castle. Burns country nearby. Phone: 046 5861220.

HAWICK. Wiltonburn Farm. Friendly, Comfort-able farmhouse bed and breakfast in beautiful location on working farm. 2 miles form Hawick. Cashmere designer knitwear shop on site. Self-catering cottages also available. Phone: Shell (0450) 372414 or (0374) 192551.

INVERGARRY, Inverness-shire. Country cot-tage. Search for Nessie, climb Ben-Nevis, tour our beautiful countryside. Come home to a friendly welcome and relax in comfortable accommodation. Scottish Tourist Board listed commended. Lilac Cottage, South Laggan, Spean Bridge, Inverness-shire. Phone: (01809) 501410.

INVERNESS. Spacious bedsitting room en-suite (twin); well appointed accommodation converts to family bedroom. Panoramic views. Bed and breakfast from £15. Longer stays/family rates on application. Non-smokers. Balvonie Cottage, (Near Drumossie Hotel). Brochure Phone/Fax: (01463) 230677.

ISLE OF RAASAY. Unspoilt Hebridean island, 20 minute sail from Skye. Family run hotel. En-suite, colour television. Loch and sea, fishing, hill walking, bird watching. Group discount. Up to 22 outdoor activities arranged. Phone: (0478) 660222.

MOFFAT, Dumfreisshire, Scotland. Hartfell House is a comfortable licensed Guest House in a quiet rural setting overlooking the Lowther Hills. En-suite rooms. Guest lounge. Evening dinner. An ideal base to explore the Southern Uplands. Phone: (0683) 20153.

NEW GALLOWAY. High Park is a traditional Galloway farmhouse built in 1838. The farm is family run with dairy beef and sheep. It is situated by Loch Ken amidst beautiful unspoilt scenery. For brochure Phone: (0644) 420298.

NEWTON STEWART. Situated within Glentrool National Park. Forest walking, hill climbing, cycling. Clean, comfortable. Original hunting lodge. Lounge with telextext television. All rooms private bathrooms, tea trays with home baking. Auchenlock Farm, Wigtownshire, South West Scotland DG8 7AA. Phone: (0671) 402035.

NEWTON STEWART. Comfortable dining room, lounge, 2 bedrooms on ground floor next bathroom. Hill walking. Golf nearby. Also 2 self-catering flats, furnished to high standard, sleeps 2/3 persons. Adams, Clugston Farm, Newton Stewart DG8 9BH. Phone: (0671) 830338.

NEWTON STEWART, Galloway. Villa Cree. Riverside guest house. Most rooms en-suite. Television lounge, tea making facilities, games room. Golf, shooting, walking, fishing. Central but rural. Restaurant 2 minutes, pub 1 minute. Swimming. Beaches nearby. Phone: Rankin (0671) 403914.

SELF-CATERING

APPIN, Argyll. 2 cottages in scenic, rural surroundings. 200 yards from Loch Linnhe. Close to famous climbing, hill-walking area. Horse riding, boat hire available locally. Spacious accommodation. All facilities. Pets welcome. Pery, Ardtur, Appin, Argyll PA38 4DD. Phone: (063173) 223.

ARDRISHAIG. Luxury 3 bedroomed self-cater-ing cottages, tastefully designed and beautifully set on the shores of Lochfyne. Fully equipped with large garden. Mountain bikes, fishing tackle available. Suitable for disabled. Scottish Tourist Board 4 crown highly commended. Phone/Fax: (0546) 603284.

ARGYLL. Appin Holiday Homes, Appin, Argyll. Lodges, cottages, caravans on Lochside Farm. Scottish Tourist Board. 4-crown commended. Magnificent situation. Midway Oban - Fort William. Ideal touring centre. Licensed inn nearby. Free fishing boats available. Resident proprietors. Colour brochure Phone: (0631) 730287.

ARISAIG, Inverness-shire. 'Derryfad Holiday Homes'. On the road to the Isles, looking towards Isle of Skye. Colour television, microwave, washing machine. Golfing, fishing, shop and hotel nearby. Post code, PH39 4NS. Phone: (0687) 450667.

AUCHTERARDER, Perthshire. The old dairy cottage has been totally renovated to form two luxury apartments. Non-smoking. Sleeps 4-6. Golf, fishing, walking. Edinburgh, Glasgow 55 minutes. Phone: Hazel Morrison (0764) 662369.

AULTBEA, Wester-Ross, Scotland. Self-catering cottage. Sleep 6. Overlooking private stocked loch. View of Torridon Mountains. Scottish Tourist Board 4 crown commended. Terms include linen. Ideal hill walking, fishing, bird watching, swimming, sandy beaches. Phone: (0445) 731349.

AULTBEA. Luxurious bungalows situated in beautiful scenery overlooking Lochewe. Sleeps 4, en-suite bedrooms, Inverewe Gardens 9 miles. Scottish Tourist Board highly commended 5 crowns. Sae Mrs Macrae, 47 Mellow Charles, Aultbea, Ross-shire. Phone: (0445) 731326.

AVIEMORE. Comfortable end terrace stone railway cottage, sleeps six. Three bedrooms. Open views to Cairngorms. Five minutes walk shops, restaurants. No pets. Scottish Tourist Board 3 crowns approved. From £140 to £250 per week. Phone: Clark (0865) 516414.

AVIEMORE - Pine Bank Chalets. Quality log cabins/holiday homes in Highlands, by Spey river, near mountains. Ideal family/touring holiday. Near all amenities. (Children's activities). Inn, pool adjacent, mountain bikes, Sky television, barbeques. Brochure Phone: (0479) 810000.

AYRSHIRE/GALLOWAY. Three bedroomed cot- tages in river/woodland setting. Modern facilities. Each with lounge, kitchen, shower, bath. Central heating. Convenient south/west coasts, Turnberry, Girvan, Ayr, Galloway Hills. STB 3 crowns. Phone or Fax: (0465) 82288.

BOAT OF GARTEN. Spey Valley. Five quality lodges on a working farm, set amidst the scenic splendour of Strathspey. Well equipped, clean, comfortable, sleeping 6. Ideal touring, fishing, golf, relaxing, bird watching. Phone: (0479) 831551.

CASTLE-DOUGLAS. Warm comfortable accom- modation on working farm for relaxing breaks. Houses and flats sleep 2-8. Easy access hills, coast, forest. All linen and towels, colour television. For brochure Phone: (0155) 668216, Barncrosh, Castle-Douglas DE7 1TX.

CREETOWN, South West Scotland. Comfortable 3 bedroom cottage in quiet village, near the coast, sleeps 5. Ideally situated for exploring the Galloway Hills. Walking, golfing, fishing etc. or for just relaxing. Phone: (0671) 403704 evenings.

CROACHY. Inverness-shire. Four Comfortable stone cottages providing excellent self-catering accommodation for 2/6 people. Delightfully situated in magnificent countryside overlooking Loch Ruthven. Splendid walks, bird watching, wildlife, fishing. Brochure Kay Humfrey, Balvoulin, Croachy, Inverness IV1 2UA. Phone: (0808) 521283.

DANDRENNAN, near Kirkcudbright. Overlook- ing abbey. Two miles sea. Fishing, forest walks. Comfortable well equipped cottage, sleeps 4/6. £100 to £155 weekly. Descriptive leaflet Phone: (0772) 784623.

EASDALE, Oban. Warm comfortable stone cot- tage with extensive sea views. All on ground level. Colour television, bathroom with bath and shower. Parking. Walking, fishing, cruises. Linen, duvets. Sleeps 2/4. No pets. Simcox Seaview. Phone: (0852) 300222.

EASDALE. Oban 16 miles. Cottage and chalet to let. Sleeps 4/2. Central for touring West Scotland and the Isles. Fully furnished including linen. All electric. Mrs Nathan, Caolas, Ellenabeich, Easdale, by Oban, Argyll. Phone: (0852) 300209.

EASDALE, Oban. Cosy stone cottage by the sea. Sleeps 2/4. All modern conveniences. Parking for 2 cars. Fishing, bird watching, walking. Friendly pubs. No pets. Glorious sunsets. Sae for brochure. Simcox, Seaview Easdale. Phone: (0852) 300222.

EAST INVERNESS, Easter Dalziel Farm, Dal- cross. Three cosy cottages, fully equipped, including linen, towels. Superb central location, scenic views, nearby tourist sites. Woodland, coastal walks. Between A96/B9039. Open all year. Phone/Fax: (01667) 462213.

EDINBURGH. Glen House apartments. Central, well appointed self-catering for all business and vacation needs. Open all year. Sleep 2-7. Linen, telephone, television, housekeeping service. Three nights minimum. Scottish Tourist Board commended. 22 Glen Street, EH3 9JE. Phone: 031 228 4043.

ELGIN, Morayshire. Furnished cottages on private estate in magnificent woodland garden setting. Central heating, linen, open fires. Tennis court. High season prices £180 to £260. Blackhills Estate by Elgin IV30 3QU. Fax and Phone: (0134) 3842223.

ENOCHDHU, Highland, Perthshire in glorious country setting. Private annexe to converted church. Comfortable with all amenities. Sleeps two. En-suite shower. Ideal for touring, golf, walking and other outdoor pursuits. Bed and breakfast also available. Phone: (0250) 881300.

FORT WILLIAM (12 miles). Near Tighean Beaga. Bungalows, sleeping 2/6 and chalets, sleeping 6/8. Set amid heath and birch in Glen Spean. Pets welcome. Discounts for couples and OAP's. Colour brochure available. Phone: Ian Matheson (01397) 712370.

FORT WILLIAM. 4 crown cottages with mag- nificent elevated views of the Nevis Mountains. 3/4 bedrooms, central heating. All modern conveniences plus linen. No extra cost. Skiing, rambling, biking, golfing all near. From £150. Phone: Heidi (0983) 866286, (0983) 406716.

FORT WILLIAM. Bunree holiday cottages, Onich, 8 miles south Fort William. Glencoe 6 miles. Situated on croft by Loch Linnhe at Corran Narrows. Phone/write Mary MacLean, Janika, Bunree, Onich, Fort William PH33 6SE. Phone:/Fax: (0855) 821359.

FORT WILLIAM. Spean Bridge. 2 self-catering cottages on working croft. Each cottage sleeps 4. Cot available. Central heating and double glazing. Cosy and comfortable. Beautiful locations and friendly welcome. Sorry no pets. Phone: (0397) 712612 or (0397) 703009.

GAIRLOCH, Ross-shire. Cottage to let, 25 metres from beach. Sleeps two. Off-road parking. Beautiful view. Amenities near. Fishing, walking, sailing, water sports. 6 miles Inverene Gardens. £90 to £140 per week. Phone: (0445) 712369.

GAIRLOCH, Ross-shire. Character houses. Panoramic views. Scottish Tourist Board commended - approved four crowns. One completely alone. Hillside, set in acres fenced ground. Another has hens collect eggs. Sleeping four to ten. Golf, sea, taxi. Grigor Duvill, Gairloch IV21 2AB. Phone: (0445) 741317.

GAIRLOCH, North West Highlands. Self-cater- ing accommodation, sleeps 2. £160 per week. Beautiful mountains and seascape views. Good garden, off street parking. Fully equipped, comfortable. Local attractions, water sports, nature reserve, golf, fishing. Phone: (01445) 712128.

GALASHIELS (8 miles). Comfortable first floor/attic flat beside River Tweed in Walkerburn village. Lovely hill views. Scottish Tourist Board commended. Sleeps five. Touring, fishing, walking, golf. Edinburgh 30 miles. Bed linen, towels included. Reasonable prices. Phone: anytime (0968) 674821.

GLENCOE, Argyllshire. Bungalow, sleeps 6. Fully equipped. Situated in centre of village. Private parking. Central for hill walking, ski-ing. 13 miles from Fort William, 40 miles from Oban. Available all year round. Phone: (0631) 62789.

S.T.B.
COMMENDED

Modern, purpose-built cottages in the midst of the best of Highland scenery in famous Glen Nevis, close to mighty Ben Nevis. Enjoy peaceful surroundings, with lots to see and do nearby. Our own spacious restaurant and lounge bar is only a short walk away and the historic town of Fort William only 2½ miles distant. Well equipped, insulated and heated, colour television, laundry facility etc. Ideal for holidays at any time of the year.

Brochure: Glen Nevis Holiday Cottages, Glen Nevis, Fort William, Inverness-shire. PH33 6SX.
Tel: 01397 702191   B4

BLUEFOLDS COTTAGES
HILLHEAD OF MORNISH, BALLINDALLOCH, SCOTLAND

ABERLOUR
SLEEPS 5 + COT

Bluefolds Cottages are newly converted farm buildings of great character in a courtyard setting. Surrounded by wide open countryside and grouse moors with panoramic views of the Hills of Cromdale and the Cairngorm Mountains. An undeveloped and unspoilt area, magnificent walking country, and an excellent touring base. Peaceful and secluded but not isolated. Inn and restaurant approx. 2 miles. Trout and salmon fishing on the rivers Spey and Livet approx 2 miles. Tamnavoulin village 5 miles. Whisky and Castle Trails approx. 5 miles. Several golf courses within a 20 miles radius. Each cottage is double glazed, furnished to a high standard with beamed ceilings and multi-fuel stoves. Patio doors lead on to a paved area with garden furniture. All cottages share the immense landscaped garden area, which leads directly on to the moors. A car is essential.

For information pack please contact Clare or Anton Dikken on
0903 763517
32 Firle Road, North Lancing West Sussex BN15 0NZ

GLENLIVET
SLEEPS 8 + COT

PLEASE MENTION

DALTONS
DIRECTORY

WHEN BOOKING
YOUR HOLIDAY

SMA GLEN, CRIEFF
(photograph courtesy of Perthshire Tourist Board)

GLENLIVET. Traditional stone cottages in different locations amidst beautiful surroundings on the Glenlivet Estate. Centrally located for whisky and castle trails, skiing, Speyside Way. Fishing available. Inverness one hour's drive away. Phone: Jaqui White (0807) 590220.

GLENLIVET. Self-catering cottage and chalet. Sleeps 2-8. Lovely countryside, walking, pony trekking, whisky and castle trails. Fishing, skiing nearby. Babysitter available. Phone: (0229) 822500.

GOUROCK. Gateway highlands. Loch Lomond. Visit Edinburgh, Ayrshire. Private terraced cottage. Pretty Clydeside resort. Home from home. Sailing, fishing, 20 minutes car ferry Argyle. Pets welcome. Central. Fully equipped. Bookings all year. Cleanliness assured. £95 - £135 per week. Phone: 041 429 5459.

INVERGARRY in the heart of the Great Glen. 3 self-catering properties, sleeping 2 - 3 - 12. Panoramic views of Loch Oich. Hill walking, salmon fishing available. Horse riding, golf and water sports nearby. Phone: (0809) 501287.

INVERGARRY. West Highlands of Scotland. Modern cottage to let. Sleeps 4. Peaceful surroundings on small farm near Loch Lochy. Loch Ness 9 miles. STB. 4 crowns. £150 to £320 per week. Sorry no pets. Phone: (0809) 501311.

ISLAY. Beautiful Hebredean island. Comfort-able family house, sea view, sleeps 12. Basins in bedrooms, 3 wc's, 2 baths, 1 shower. Full central heating. Washing machine, tumble dryer, dishwasher. Shops, hotel 1 mile. Phone: Covell (0496) 810563.

ISLE-OF-SKYE. Cottage, house and chalets in idyllic locations near sea and mountains. Reasonable weekly rates from £100. Linen supplied. Scottish Tourist Board inspected. Write or phone for brochure: J. Cox, Varkasaig, Orbost, Dunvegan, Isle of Skye IV55 8ZB. (01470) 521231.

ISLE OF SKYE, Portree. Modern 4 bedroom bungalow on private ground. Panoramic views. Available all year. Linen provided. Large garden, patio. Ideal base for touring, climbing and hill walking. Enquiries to Mrs MacDonald. Phone: (0470) 562217.

ISLE OF WHITHORN, South West Scotland. Harbour- side cottage. Attractive fishing village. 2 double bedrooms, fully fitted kitchen, bathroom and shower. Lounge, colour television. £150 - £200 per week. Sorry no pets. Golf, bowling, fishing. Phone: 071-244 7562.

KILBERRY, near Tarbert, Loch Fyne. Tastefully renovated house on working farm, sleeps two and cot. Own beach, sea fishing. Access to golf. Ferries to Islay, Gigha, Arran. No pets, no smoking. Open all year. Phone: (08803) 256.

KINLOCHEWE, west coast. Modern detached bungalow set in magnificent mountain scenery. Fully equipped and furnished to high standard. 4 crowns commended. Sleeps four. Ideal for walking, birdwatching, touring. Open all year. For brochure Phone: 051-608 2663.

KIRKMICHAEL. Village cottages. Quality cot-tages, situated in picturesque highland village. STB 4-crown commended. Equipped and maintained to highest standard. Sleep 2-6. Ideal location for touring Scotland. Activity holiday or relaxing. For details Phone: (0250) 881385.

KIRRIEMUIR, Angus. Swedish Log House, on farm, in an Angus Glen. Very peaceful with lovely views. Fishing, pony-trekking nearby. Glamis Castle, Barrie's Birthplace 7 miles. Scottish Tourist Board 5 crowns highly commended. Purgavie Farm, Lintrathew, Kirriemuir. Phone/Fax: (0575) 560213.

LOCH RANNOCH, Perthshire. Cottages flat on Loch shore. Fully furnished. Children, dogs welcome. McNaughton, Torvan, Church Lane, Oxted, Surrey RH8 9LH. Phone: (0883) 714395.

LOCH SHIELDAIG, Torridon, West Highlands. Well equipped comfortable heated cottage. Television, telephone, washing machine, freezer. Magnificent coastal, mountain scenery. Fishing, boating, wildlife - pine martens. Also cottages, Loch Kishorn and Loch Carron. Both well equipped, heated, telephone, television. Phone: (0536) 513077.

LOCHINVER. To let, bungalow and caravan, both fully equipped. Private site. Car parking. Near shops, hotels and cafes. Excellent base for hill walking. Fishing on angling club lochs. Enquiries Macleod, 37 Strathan, Lochinver. Phone: (0571) 844631.

LOCHNESS. In picturesque highland village. Quality modern bungalow fully equipped and tastefully furnished. Sleeps 6. Ideal location to explore the Highlands. Central for fishing, golf, forest walks, pleasure cruising, horse riding, mountain biking. Phone: (0463) 237379.

LOCHNESS, Inverness. Cottage, sleeps 4/5. Ideal touring base. Forest walks, fishing - trout and salmon nearby. Golf and boating. Television, log fire. Phone: (0320) 351251.

MOIDART. Roshven Farm. Lochside chalets. 30 miles west of Fort William. Small working sheep farm. Open all year. Children and dogs welcome. Ideal location for touring, walking etc. Scottish Tourist Board approved. 4 crowns. Blackburn, Lochailort. Phone: (0687) 470221.

MORAY FIRTH, Portsoy. 2 beautifully restored houses. Sleep 2 and 6. By picturesque harbour. Off-peak heating, colour television. Phone: (0261) 842220 evening, (0261) 842404 day.

NETHY-BRIDGE, near Grantown-on-Spey. New bungalow, sleeps 5. Four crowns and commended. Ideal area for walking, fishing, bird-watching, golf. It sits 50 yards off the main road and is looking over to hills. Phone: (0479) 821663.

NEW GALLOWAY, South West Scotland. Cosy cottage, sleeps 6/8. Coal fire, sunbed, colour television. Scenic area. Village pub. Golf, fishing, Loch Ken, walking, touring base. Phone: (0942) 894044 evenings.

NEWCASTLETON near. Courtyard apartments and trekking centre. Set amid forests on beautiful Scottish borders. Ideal touring centre or relax here in home from home atmosphere. Meal service. Fishing. Laundry, solarium, sauna, multi-gym, games room and bar on site. Phone: (0697) 748617.

OBAN, near. (Argyll). New Scandinavian style chalet for two situated at waters edge. Wonderful views over West Highland sea loch. Adjacent moorings and slipway. Secluded but not remote. Open all year. For brochure Phone: (01631) 720265.

ONICH, Fort William. 'Springwell Holiday Homes'. Cottages on a secluded, elevated 17 acres with panoramic Loch views. Fully equipped. Baths, linen. Colour televisions. Sleeps 4 to 6. Ideal Highland historical and sporting area. Phone: Murray (08553) 257.

ORKNEY, Hoy. Cantickhead Lighthouse, two or three bedroom ex-keepers cottages. Stunning views over Pentland Firth and Scapa Flow. Ideal for families, fishing, bird-watching, walks or just recharging your batteries. Pets welcome. Phone: (0856) 701255.

POOLEWE, Ross-shire. Crofters cottages. Scottish Tourist Board 4 crown commended. In very secluded tranquil spot by river and loch. Good base to tour Highlands. Walking, climbing, golf, fishing, bird life, beaches plus Inverewe Gardens close by. Cottages, sleep 4, 6, and 9. Phone: (0445) 781268.

ROSS-SHIRE, Poolewe. Croft-house, sleeping 8. Commended 4 crowns. Escape, go back in time. Peaceful, relaxing holidays overlooking mountains and sea. Fishing, walking, bird watching, beaches. Regret no pets. Mrs A.E. Ella, 'Sonas', Cove, Poolewe, Ross-shire 1V22 2LT. Phone: (0445) 781203.

ROY BRIDGE, Inverness-shire. Bunroy Holiday Park. Quality self-catering, sleeps four. Linen and colour television. Seven acres woodland and river. 12 miles Fort William and Ben Nevis. Quiet, no through traffic. Pets welcome. Credit cards. Phone: (01037) 712332.

ST. ANDREWS near. Comfortable self-catering house, sleeps 8/10. 4 bedrooms, large lounge, 2 bathrooms, fully equipped kitchen. Linen available. Safe parking. Secluded garden. Children welcome. Brochure Phone: Steven (01337) 828414.

ST. ANDREWS. Elegant town houses, cottages, farmhouses and flats. In idyllic countryside nearby. Available all year. Sleeping up to 12. Magic for golf or families. Scottish Tourist Board 4/5 crowns commended to Deluxe. Mountquhanie Holiday Homes, Cupar. Phone: (01382) 330252.

STRATHPEFFER, Ross-shire. Scottish Tourist Board 4 crown commended house in picturesque Victorian spa village. 3 bedrooms, en-suite. Large enclosed garden. Close to shops, hotels. Central for touring, hill-walking, fishing, golf 5 minutes. Phone: (0349) 861561.

ULLAPOOL. Scottish Tourist Board highly commended 5 crowns self-catering houses. Peacefully situated overlooking Lochbroom. 3 rooms, sleeping 6. Linen provided. Open fires. Excellent centre for climbers. £180 to £350 weekly. No Sunday enquiries. Phone: Mrs Renwick (0854) 655209.

WESTER ROSS, near Ullapool, Ross-shire. Comfortable and well equipped accommodation with all modern conveniences. Set in peaceful and picturesque surroundings. Overlooking Loch Broom. Ideal for family holidays. Scottish Tourist Board highly commended. Further details Phone: Mrs Renwick (01854) 633269.

CARAVANS, CHALETS & HOLIDAY PARKS

AVIEMORE - Pine Bank Chalets. Quality log cabins/holiday homes in Highlands, by Spey river, near mountains. Ideal family/touring holiday. Near all amenities (Children's activities). Inn, pool adjacent, mountain bikes, Sky television, barbeques. Brochure Phone: (0479) 810000.

FORT WILLIAM. 6 berth caravan with mag- nificent elevated views of the Neviss Mountains. Laundry, linen, heating no extra cost. Quiet, rural setting. Skiing, rambling, biking, golfing all near. From £90 weekly. Phone: Heidi (0983) 866286/(0983) 406716.

FORT WILLIAM. Small caravan site of just 8 units with modern facilities. Children and their pets welcome. Ideal centre for touring the scenic West Highlands. Good walks and fishing. Fraser, 19 North Ballachulish. Phone: (08553) 335.

INVERNESS. At Auchnahillin. Caravan and Camping centre. One of the best holiday parks in the Highlands. Superb caravans in scenic location. 4/6 berth. Tourers and campers welcome. Please Phone: (01463) 772286. Fax: (01463) 772286.

ONICH, Fort William. Chalet, double bedroom en-suite. Fitted kitchen. Marvellous views. Colour television. Central for touring. No pets. From £120-£150. Phone: (01855) 821.

ORKNEY ISLANDS. 3 caravans for let from 1 night onwards. Caravans overlooking Pierowall Bay. Superb view. Relax on this beautiful island. Five minutes' walk to the village, indoor swimming pool, and golf course. Phone: 0857 7229.

ORKNEY ISLANDS. Island of Westray. Caravans for let on this beautiful and peaceful island. Ideal for Canadians who want to retrace their ancestors history. For more details write to Mrs Seatter, Mount Pleasant, Westray, Orkney KW17 2DH.

ROSS-SHIRE, Poolewe. 6 berth caravans. Small homely site. Escape, go back in time. Peaceful, relaxing holidays overlooking mountains and sea. Fishing, walking, bird watching, beaches. Regret no pets. Mrs A.E. Ella, 'Sonas', Cove, Poolewe, Ross-shire 1V22 2LT. Phone: (0445) 781203.

WHERE TO GO

Edinburgh Castle
Castle Rock, top of the Royal Mile.
Tel: (031) 2443101
One of the most famous castles in the world. Military Tattoo staged each year, late August to early September.

Edinburgh Zoo
Corstorphine Road, Murrayfield, Edinburgh.
Tel: (031) 3347730
Scotland's largest animal attraction, over 1,000 rare and endangered animals, daily penguin parade, licensed self-service cafeteria, shops and play areas, picnic area.

Wonderwest World (Butlin's)
Dunure Road, Ayr.
Tel: (0292) 265141
Scotland's largest theme park featuring Wondersplash sub-tropical waterworld, over 25 funfair rides and a host of family entertainment.

ABOVE LOCH TAY
(photograph courtesy of Perthshire Tourist Board)

EDINBURGH CASTLE
(photograph courtesy of Edinburgh Tourist Board)

WALES

"There'll be a welcome in the hillsides" goes the song. But – knowing what I know about the spirited souls of the Welsh – I wasn't surprised to learn that they have a special, much more resonant word for it. "Croeso" is the traditional greeting of friendship in Wales.

But, of course, it isn't just a word. The people of Wales are more than happy to extend a warm welcome to the holidaymaker, in whatever way they can. And I'm not just saying that as a fellow Celt!

No, the fact is that the Welsh believe in promoting holidays that are as hassle-free and relaxing as they come. In what other country can you still drive from the South to the North without coming across a single traffic light?

And – as well as feeling that you're driving in more measured, relaxed times past – the views that you can enjoy along the way afford a real insight into the past, from prehistoric monuments to Roman remains and beyond.

You'll witness proud castles, many with pageants held within their walls; and a host of historic houses and gardens. There are reminders, too, of Wales' industrial past, in such commodities as coal, slate, iron, steel and even gold. Indeed, many of yesterday's workshops and mills are today's heritage centres and galleries. Not to mention five official Areas of Outstanding Natural Beauty and three National Parks.

Perhaps the most celebrated of these is Snowdonia in North Wales – which, of course, takes its name from Snowdon, the highest mountain in England and Wales. But the north has much else to offer, including Anglesey Sea Zoo and Rhyl's Sea Life Centre (for a beguiling insight to marine life) and Llangollen, site of the annual International Music Eisteddfod.

Then there's the scenery itself: rugged slopes and gentle woodlands and moorlands, vibrant vales and sandy beaches.

Travel down to mid-Wales and the landscape is equally holiday-friendly (which, don't worry, is the sort of unromantic language you'll never hear in Wales!). The most notable natural feature is probably the Cardigan Bay coastline with its sandy dunes and timeless harbours. Equally timeless are the narrow-gauge "Great Little Trains" which run through the region like a series of arteries beating into the heart of the great Welsh past; as well as the attractions of Aberystwyth which are still in tune with its Victorian past – the Cliff Railway, the Camera Obscura and music hall museum.

Interestingly, mid-Wales also stretches into uncharted time zones. The Centre of Alternative Technology near Machynlleth is an environmental "village of the future", while nearby Portmeirion is perhaps the "village of the future", having been the setting for the cult TV series, "The Prisoner".

Not to be outdone, the south can also stake its share of that traditional warm Welsh welcome – sorry, "Croeso"! It is, after all, dominated by the Brecon Beacons National Park – a rich, expansive spread of countryside and riverland. And the popular Pembrokeshire Coast is Britain's only shore-based National Park. But perhaps the one the wildlife appreciate most is Penscynor Wildlife Park, home to many exotic animals and birds. (Oh, and humans get a kick from it too).

Then there beckon the bright lights of the two great cities, Cardiff and Swansea...

In fact – from the land that inspired everyone from Merlin the wizard to Dylan Thomas the poet – the Welsh extend a great big "Croeso" to one and all.

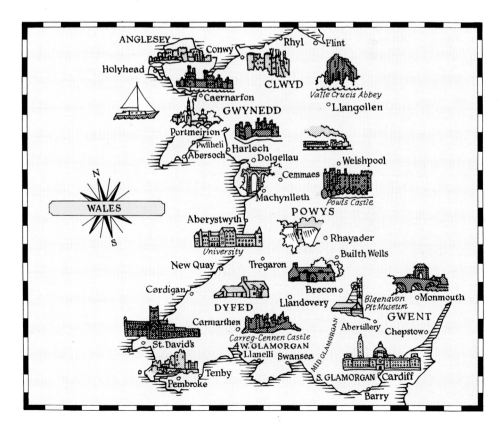

WALES

HOTELS & GUEST HOUSES

AMROTH, Pembrokeshire. Ashdale Guest House. Licensed family accommodation, providing all amenities with comfort, friendliness and notorious home cooking. Beach, shops and pubs in a village atmosphere, all within 100 yards. Private parking. Reasonable rates. Brochure Phone: (0834) 813853.

ARTHOG, Gwynedd. Situated in 42 acres woodland and pasture overlooking mountains and spectacular Mawddach Estuary. Ideal for walkers, mountain climbers, cyclists, bird watchers. En-suite, family and disabled bedrooms available. Also self-catering. Choice of breakfast. Phone: (0341) 250482.

BEAUMARIS. Mor-Awel is a friendly guest house from which there is scenic walks, fishing, riding, bird-watching, beaches nearby. Evening meal by arrangement. Welsh Tourist Board 2 crowns. From £12.50 per person weekly rates. Thomas, Mor-Awel, Llangoed. Phone: (0248) 490826.

BETWS-Y-COED. Cross Keys Hotel. A charming 14th century hotel of real character. We are a very comfortable and friendly run hotel. Serving excellent food and wines. Rooms en-suite, colour television and tea making facilities. Gwynedd, North Wales. Phone: (0690) 710334.

BETWS-Y-COED near. Bed and breakfast, en-suite. Colour television, tea making facilities. Semi rural position, beautiful views. Convenient for coast and Snowdonia National Park, golf course. Ideal position for hill-walking. £14 each nightly. Phone: (0492) 640614.

BETWS GARMON, Gwynedd. Plas-Y-Coed Hotel. Mountain-side, fully licensed hotel in wooded grounds. Superb views. Spacious family and en-suite rooms. Bed and breakfast from £15. Also self-catering garden flat. Sleeps 5. Pets welcome. Phone: (0286) 650284.

BRECON BEACONS

Two miles from Brecon in quiet location with views to Pen-Y-Fan. Two ground floor double rooms with private bathroom, TV lounge. £13 per person per night. Ideal for fishing, walking, touring.
Mrs. Jones "Arosfa," Groesfordd, Brecon, Powys LD3 7SN
Phone: 0874 665495

BRECON BEACONS NATIONAL PARK. Guest House. Peaceful setting, panoramic views. En-suite bathrooms. Colour television, tea/coffee making. Licensed. Bed and breakfast or dinner, bed and breakfast. Ample parking. Trewalter House, Llangorse, Brecon, Powys LD3 OPS. Brochure Phone: (0874) 84442.

CAERNARFON. Snowdonia Farmhouse Guesthouse. Bed and breakfast on working sheep farm. Double, twin, single rooms, tea making facilities. Lounge, television. Pets welcome. Horse riding and beach within four miles. Williams, Llwyndu Mawr. Phone: (0286) 880419 evenings.

CARDIGAN. Welsh cottage bed and breakfast set in 5 acres. Quiet village 7 miles from lovely beaches. £12 per night. We have special children's and weekly rates. Also large secluded caravan from £100. Phone: (0239) 710681.

CARMARTHEN, Dyfed. A484 road. Gwili and Tivy Valley. Must for railway, fishing, walking, golfing enthusiasts. En-suite, excellent cuisine. Real ales, 18th century inn. Welsh welcome. Yr Afon Duad, Cwmduad, Carmarthen. Beaches, pleasure parks close by. Phone: (0267) 281357.

CONWY, GWYNEDD. Edge of Snowdonia. Bed and breakfast in large dormer bungalow. All facilities, use of lounge with television. Ample parking. Llandudno 3 miles. Anglesey 16 miles. Adults £12. Children half price. Phone: Aberconwy (0492) 592626.

CRICCIETH. Glyn-y-coed Hotel. AA/RAC family hotel, facing sea, mountains, castle. En-suite bedrooms. Highly recommended. Home cooking, cosy bar, parking. Children's rates. Also bungalow sleeping 2-8 available. Reynolds, Portmadoc Road. Phone: (01766) 522870. Fax: (01766) 523341.

CRICCIETH. 'Bryn Derwen' Victorian guest house offering bed and breakfast in very popular coastal resort. Colour televisions, hospitality trays, some rooms with superb panoramic views of Cardigan Bay. For further details Phone: Mrs Wood (01766) 522887.

CRICCIETH – NORTH WALES
MIN Y GAER HOTEL
PORTHMADOG ROAD, CRICCIETH, GWYNEDD LL52 0HP
TEL: 01766 522151 FAX: 01766 522151

A pleasant licensed hotel, conveniently situated near the beach with delightful views of Criccieth Castle and the Cardigan Bay coastline.
Ten comfortable, centrally heated rooms (9 en-suite). All with colour TV and tea/coffee facilities. An ideal base for touring Snowdonia. Reduced rates for children. Car parking on premises.

RAC
ACCLAIMED

AA
RECOMMENDED

BWRDD CROESO CYMRU
WALES TOURIST BOARD
COMMENDED

CRICCIETH, Glyn-Y-Coed Hotel. Lovely Vic-torian family hotel. Facing sea, mountains Criccieth and Harlech Castles. En-suite bedrooms with tea making facilities, colour television. Parking. Cosy bar. Sports facilities available nearby. Highly recommended. Home cooking, self-catering also available. Phone: (01766) 522870.

CROSSHANDS near Swansea. Deangate Lodge. Beautiful house set within five acres. En-suite rooms, colour television, separate television lounge area. 8 miles from Gower/Pembray Country Park. Full cooked breakfast. Mrs B. Thomas, Deangate Lodge, Black Lion Road, Crosshands, Llanelli, Dyfed SA14 6RU Phone: (0269) 831900.

FFESTINIOG. Guesthouse with spectacular mountain views. Ideal base for touring Snowdonia, outdoor pursuits, tourist attractions including Ffestiniog railway. We offer en-suites, log fires, home cooked food including vegetarian. Group rates. Non smoking. Traditional Christmas breaks. Phone: (0766) 762734.

GLANCLEDDAU. Farmsite. Looking for a peace-ful countryside holiday. Private fishing on River Cleddau, salmon, sea trout. Modern comfortable farmhouse sleeps 6. 2 & 6 berth caravans with all modern conveniences on dairy farm. Beaches nearby. Llewellin, Glancleddau, Clynderwen, Pembrokeshire. Sae Phone: (01437) 563368.

GOWER COAST, near. Swansea. Idyllic 17th Century farm guest house. In 200 beautiful acres with magnificent views. 5 en-suite bedrooms with television, video, tea making. Riding, fishing, licensed bar. 3 crowns. 'Which?' Best bed and breakfast. AA/RAC. Brochure Phone: (0269) 595640.

LETTERSTON, near Fishguard, Pembrokeshire. Exclusive Georgian country house in tranquil setting. Ideally situated for coastal path, beaches, golf, horse riding. Comfortable rooms, en-suite, good food and wine. £18 person night maximum. 3 crowns Welsh Tourist Board. Phone: (0348) 840263.

BRON CELYN

WTB ☗ ☗ ☗ Highly Commended
Beautiful situation in Snowdonia National Park overlooking the village of Betws-Y-Coed and Conwy/Llugwy Valleys. Most rooms en-suite, all with colour TV and beverage trays, etc.
Ample car parking. Full cooked hearty breakfasts, packed lunches, snacks and evening meals. Open all year. Special Christmas/New Year and out of season breaks.
We also have a delightful converted coach house to let, accommodating up to 4-5 persons. Bed and Breakfast or self-catering terms.
Jim and Lilian Boughton, Bron Celyn Guest House, Llanrwst Road, Betws-Y-Coed, Gwynedd, N. Wales LL24 0HD. Phone: 01690 710333.

LLANDUDNO. Westbourne Private Hotel, Arvon Avenue. Phone: (0492) 877450. Licensed, very central, first class food and service. Bedrooms contain colour television, tea making, en-suite, including ground floor. Pensioner reductions. Details and colour brochure ring Doris or write, sae.

SOUTHCLIFF HOTEL
2 STAR LLANDUDNO AA RAC

32 bedrooms, all en-suite. Ultimate views.
Excellent cuisine. 3 minutes all amenities.
Busy happy hotel.
Phone: (0492) 876277

LLANDUDNO. Belvedere Hotel. All rooms colour television, welcome tray, centrally heated. Families welcome. Vegetarians catered for. Non smoking. Lounge overlooking sea. Close all amenities. Reasonable prices. Single, double, family rooms. Central promenade. Phone: Llandudno 876388.

LLANDUDNO – NORTH WALES

Elegant Edwardian guest house. Close to all facilities, with golden beaches and spectacular mountain scenery minutes away. Warm welcome assured in tasteful, well appointed no smoking accommodation.

WTB HIGHLY COMMENDED
B&B £14 per night, £85 per week. Open all year.
Pets by arrangement
Tel: 01492 871802 Mrs. C. Beesley

LLANDUDNO. Whitefriars Hotel, 10 Abbey Road. Highly recommended family run hotel. All rooms en-suite with tea - coffee facilities and satellite television. Conveniently situated but quiet. Licensed. Good and plentiful food, home cooking. Parties welcome. Phone: (0492) 876287.

NANT-Y-GLYN
59 CHURCH WALKS, LLANDUDNO, LL30 1HL

A family run hotel. Situated at the foot of the Orme but being in walking distance of local entertainments and amenities. Large comfortable lounge, sun terrace enjoying panoramic views of Snowdonia and Conwy Estuary. Full central heating, full en-suite rooms available. 4 course evening meal (choice of menu). OAP's and children special rates. Open all year.
Tel: 01492 875915

TAN-Y-MARIAN HOTEL
WEST SHORE, LLANDUDNO, NORTH WALES LL30 2AS
This charming small hotel is ideally situated on the peaceful west shore. All the centrally heated bedrooms (most en-suite) are on the first floor with sea or mountain views. Excellent and varied meals with special diets catered for. Licensed. Parking.
AA ★
WTB ☗☗☗ Highly Commended
01492 877727

CRAIGLANDS
7 CARMEN SYLVA ROAD, LLANDUDNO, GWYNEDD

A small select private Hotel. Where every effort has been made to restore the original charm and elegance of this Victorian house.
The best of modern amenities have been introduced to give a high degree of comfort and service. All bedrooms have bath/shower en-suite, central heating and tea/coffee making facilities.
The promenade and beach are just yards away and the conference centre within walking distance.
AA Special Merit Award for the 8th consecutive year.
TELEPHONE FOR BROCHURE:
01492 875090

  W.T.B.
AA SELECTED

LLANDUDNO. West Shore. Modern, very clean, well equipped, select flats. 4 rooms, own services. Ideal quiet or touring holidays. Phone: (0492) 860373 or write 1 Morfa Road, West Shore, Llandudno, Gwynedd LL30 2BS.

ORME VIEW
5 VAUGHAN STREET, LLANDUDNO, GWYNEDD LL30 1AB
Family run guest house. Close to rail/coach stations, shops and promenade. All rooms central heated, TV, tea/coffee facilities. Home cooking, varied menu. Reductions for weekly booking and for OAP's and under 16's. Special low season rate. B&B £11.50, with evening meal £16.50. S.A.E. for brochure.
For further details please call:
Susan Watkins 01492 870840

LLANDUDNO. Stratford Hotel promenade. Welsh Tourist Board 3 crown. Highly commended. Refurbished. Licensed hotel. En-suite rooms, one with spa bath. Satellite television, tea making facilities, hairdryers. Excellent cuisine. 6 golf courses nearby. 8 Craig-Y-Don Parade. Phone: (0492) 877962.

LLANDUDNO. Mayville Hotel. 3 crown. Family run. Most rooms en-suite. Close to shops, railway station and promenade. Licensed. Car parking. Golf courses, ski-slope, cable cars and many other attractions nearby. 4 St. Davids Road. Phone: (0492) 875406.

LLANDUDNO. White Lodge Hotel. Situated on the promenade, facing the sea. This Victorian hotel offers charming, comfortable accommodation. All interior decorated bedrooms have colour television and tea/coffee facilities. There is a small bar and large car park. Phone: (01492) 877713.

LLANDUDNO, North Wales. Carmel Private Hotel. Seafront location with uninterrupted sea views. Ideally situated for exploring Snowdonia and North Wales. Moderate terms. From £13.50. L.P. Lesiter, 17 Craig-y-Don Parade, Promenade, Llandudno, Gwynedd LL30 1BG. Phone: (0492) 877643.

LLANDUDNO. Hotel Carmen. Licensed AA. WTB 3 crown. All rooms en-suite. Golf, bowling and new theatre close by. Choice menu. OAP specials. May, June, July accommodation free for organiser on group bookings. Entertainment available. Phone: (0492) 876361.

LLANERFYL, Mid Wales. 5-8 berth caravan holiday situated on family farm. Colour television. Shower, electric, gas etc. Only 35 minutes from the delightful Welsh coastline. £80-£120 per week. Horse riding, fishing, golf nearby. Phone: (0938) 820453.

LLANFYLLIN. Victorian farmhouse in elevated position commanding spectacular views of peaceful valley. Close to lakes, Vyrnwy, Bala and Pistyll, Rhaeadr Falls. Quality accommodation. 3 crowns highly commended WTB. Emberton, Cwm Alan Farm, Llanfyllin, Montgomeryshire. Phone: (0691) 648301.

LLANGOLLEN. Hendy Isa. Attractive country house, with abundant wildlife and friendly horses. 2 miles from town. Steam trains, canal trips and many local attractions. Spacious, tastefully furnished en-suites. Wholesome breakfasts. Highest standards. Keen terms. Phone: (01978) 861232.

LLANGRANOG. Seaside village. Magnificent Cardigan Bay coast guest house, fully appointed or self-catering cottages, sleep four. Excellent walking, bathing, surfing, fishing, bird-watching, golfing, ski-ing or just relaxation. Hostelry. Good eating. Leyshon, Frondolau Fach, Llangranog. Phone: (0239) 654748.

LLANIDLOES, Dyffryn, Glyn. Comfortable bed and breakfast. Displaying maginificent views of the tranquil Mid-Wales countryside. En-suite room available. Tea making facilities in rooms. Full English breakfast. Sailing, fishing and numerous walks nearby. Phone: Evans (0686) 412129.

NEWPORT, Gwent. Converted lighthouse, grade II listed, now guest house, with flotation tank. Offers super bed and breakfast accommodation. Including waterbed and four poster bed in wedge shaped rooms, en-suite. Peaceful and relaxing and quite different. Phone: (0633) 810126.

PRESTATYN. Roughsedge Guest House. Friendly establishment. Some en-suite rooms. 1 ground floor. All with colour television, tea/coffee facilities and clock radios. Perfect for touring North Wales. Home cooked meals. AA. Welsh Tourist Board. Credit cards accepted. Phone: (01745) 887359.

RHYL. Angharad. Licensed Guest House. Off promenade. Close to all amenities. Colour television, complimentary tea, coffee. Good home cooking. Bed and breakfast from £11, weekly £67. Optional evening meal. Kay, 12 Bath Street, Clwyd. Phone: (0745) 350860.

RHYL. Medeor Hotel. All rooms en-suite. Colour televisions, tea - coffee making facilities. Car park. 5 golf courses. WTB 3 crowns. Savory, 3. Elwy Street, Clwyd, North Wales LL18 1BS. Phone: (0745) 354489.

SAUNDERSFOOT. Small countryside hotel in own grounds. 2 crowns, highly commended. Heated swimming pool. 500 yards Wisemans Bridge beach, 30 minutes stroll Saundersfoot. Tenby 5 miles. Parking within grounds. Licensed. Tea making. £91-£140 weekly. Phone: (0834) 813607.

SAUNDERSFOOT, Tenby area. Award winning accommodation. En-suite bedrooms with colour television, refreshment tray. Excellent food, wide choice. Parking. Licensed. Snooker, table tennis. Reductions OAP's, children. Dnner, bed and breakfast £155 - £165 weekly. Pleasant View. Phone: Kilgetty (01834) 814040.

SNOWDONIA. Old Rectory Hotel, Maentwrog. Amidst three acre riverside garden. Main house or budget annexe, all en-suite. Ideal for walking. Near Portmeirion, Harlech. Discount for three plus nights. Italian, English and vegetarian menus. Informal atmosphere. Phone: (0766) 85305.

SNOWDONIA. Old Rectory Hotel, Maentwrog, Phone: (0766) 85305. Amidst three acres, riverside garden. Main house or budget annexe accommodation. All en-suite. Italian, English or vegetarian/vegan menus. Special rates families or weekly stays. Near Portmeirion & Harlech.

SNOWDONIA. Craig-Y-Dderwen Hotel. Riverside hotel set in 16 acres of grounds in Betws-Y-Coed. En-suite rooms. Excellent cuisine. Log fire. Friendly service plus lots more. Seasonal packages throughout the year. Christmas, conference parties, coach parties. Phone: (0690) 710293.

TENBY, near. Manian Lodge Hotel. Well appointed, friendly, country hotel. All rooms en-suite, television, tea, coffee. Licensed bar, pool room. On small holding with children's riding pony etc. From £90 per week per person. Phone: (0834) 813273.

TENBY. Non smoking, three crown com- mended, refurbished small family run hotel. Excellent cooking. Evening meal optional. Spacious family rooms with colour televisions. En-suites available. Central heating. Full fire certificate. Car parking. Children welcome. Phone: (01834) 844148.

TENBY. Lynmaure Hotel. Beautiful award win- ning beaches. Two minutes town centre and all amenities. Prices from £78.50 a week. Special rates OAP's and unemployed groups welcome. All rooms television, tea, coffee facilities. Licensed. Brochure Phone: (0834) 842844.

TENBY. Dinner, bed and breakfast. Bungalow homely accommodation. Coastal views. Ample private parking. Central for lovely sandy beaches. Television lounge. Hot and cold all rooms. Mrs. Green, 'Morawel', Rowston Drive, New Hedges, Tenby, Dyfed. Phone: (0834) 842057

TENBY. Lynmaure. Licensed hotel. 3 crowns. Weekly dinner, bed and breakfast from £110. Bed and breakfast from £68. Colour televisions, tea and coffee all rooms. Some en-suites. Special short breaks available throughout year. Phone: (0834) 842844.

SELF-CATERING

ABERAERON, Dyfed. Stay on Welsh estate farm. Two superb cottages in pretty surroundings. Both sleep six. Centrally located. Games room, play area. Barbecue, pony rides, mountain walks, beautiful beaches. Welsh Tourist Board highest award. Brochure Phone: (0974) 272234.

ABERDOVEY. Four bedroomed cottage. Cots, highchair. Boathouse-playroom. Sun balcony. 2 minutes harbour, shops, beach. Free parking. Television. Water skiing, golf, riding. Off season weekends £45. Weeks from £65 - £300. Night storage heaters. Phone: 021 458 2673/1984.

ABERDOVEY. Well-equipped pine bungalow, sleeps 8. Overlooking sea. Superb view. Sandy beach, sailing, golf, walking. Dogs permitted. Available March to October and weekends at short notice. Phone: Wood 021 454 4913.

ABERDOVEY. Large (sleeps 11) warm comfort-able Victorian terrace house, facing superb beach, dunes, golf course. Very well equipped with dishwasher, washing machine, freezer, microwave etc. £200 - £380 per week. Short breaks £40 per night. Phone: (0342) 832151.

ABERDOVEY. Hillside village. A cluster of cottages and apartments nestled on the hill, overlooking the Dovey estuary with superb views and individual south facing terraces. 300 yards from village and superb sandy beaches. Phone: (01654) 767522.

ABERDOVEY 5 miles, sea 2 miles. Bungalow with 3 bedrooms. Gardens, garage. Views, with river (fenced) at bottom of garden. In a quiet and picturesque position. Available weekly and for long weekends. Phone: (0121) 707 0635.

ABERGAVENNY. Set in the tranquillity of the Black Mountains. Spacious house comprising of sitting - dining room. Colour television, oil central heating, kitchen, microwave, fridge freezer, dishwasher, washing machine. 3 bedrooms, cot, bathroom, wc, shower room wc, linen provided. No pets. Phone: (0873) 890228.

ABERPORTH. Comfortable fully furnished self-contained bungalows and flats, in village next to lovely beaches and clean bathing waters. Tourist board graded. Ample parking. Dogs by arrangement. Attractions include Cardigan Bay Dolphins. Tucker, Phone: (0239) 810387.

ABERSOCH, Aberdaron. Peaceful three bed-roomed farmhouse. Centrally situated. Open inglenook fireplace in lounge with colour television. Automatic washing machine/tumble dryer, fridge freezer. Open all year. Central heating. One pet welcome. Linen supplied. Garden. Parking. Phone: (0758) 83670.

ABERYSTWYTH. Self-catering farmhouse on working farm in beautiful Ystwyth Valley. Sleep 7/9 plus cot. Forest walks, fishing and pony trekking nearby. Reasonable rates. Further information Phone: (0974) 261313.

ABERYSTWYTH, Clarach. 4 bedroomed house, sleeps 6. 2 miles town, 1 mile sea. Convenient base for walking and outdoor pursuits. Central heating. Available July to September. Phone: (0970) 828819 evenings/weekends.

ANGLESEY. Well equipped Dormer bungalow in quiet village. Sleeps 6 in comfort. Colour television. Garden, off road parking. Welsh Tourist Board grade 3. Conveniently situated for excellent beaches, forest walks. Many other attractions. Further details Phone: Gundry (0407) 840977.

ANGLESEY, Snowdonia. Excellent selection of self-catering houses, sleeping 2 to 20. Open all year. Short breaks. Best possible value. Brochure. Menai Holidays, 1 Hill Street, Menai Bridge, Anglesey LL59 5AY. Phone: (01248) 717135.

BALA near. Recommended, well equipped com-fortable spacious cottage. Garden and grounds almost an acre. Splendid position, secluded and quiet. Walking, fishing, boating and riding nearby. Sleeps 6. Reasonable terms. For photo and details, Phone: (0735) 580081.

BALA, North Wales. Cottage. Television, double glazing, central heating. Private parking. Minutes' walk shops, lake. Please write Mrs M.H. Roberts, Gelli, 46 Tegid Street. Phone: (0678) 520402.

BALA, Godre'r Aran, Llanuwchllyn. Luxury riverside apartment, near Bala lake. Scenic mountain views. Private detached residence without remoteness. Parking in forecourt. 2 bedrooms, 1 en-suite. Colour television, microwave. Free fishing. Ideal touring centre. Phone: (06784) 687.

BALA. Snowdonia National Park. Beautiful 18th century secluded, detached cottage, sleeps 2-7. Oak beams, 2 bathrooms, luxury kitchen. Stream. Large gardens. Bala lake and many other attractions nearby. Pet welcome. Phone: (01785) 780253.

BARMOUTH, Gwynedd. Beautiful detached 4 bedroom house. Situated hillside behind town. Sleeps 6. Magnificent views of coastline. Available reasonable rates during year. Write Gwyndy, Gellfachen Road, Barmouth, Gwynedd. Phone: (0341) 281351.

BEDDGELERT, Gwynedd. Terraced cottage. Nearby village. Sleeps 5. Fully equipped and modernised. Ideal for walking and easy reach North Wales, beaches. For further details, prices and availability for weeks and weekend bookings, Phone: (0778) 348370.

BEDDGELERT near, 160 year old cottage in a pretty village at foot of Snowdon. Sleeps 8 in 3 bedrooms. Colour television, shower, storage heaters. Near pub. £100 - £270 per week. Phone: Mr and Mrs Vernon 081 693 3971.

BEGELLY, Tenby. Very large, luxury, clean 3 bedroom bungalow with 2 toilets and 2 acres land with riding, pony, pigs. Overlooking magnificent countryside. Parking. From £200 to £350 per week. Phone: (0834) 813273.

BETWS-Y-COED. Cottage in forest, above a picturesque village. White stone cottage set in idyllic scenery in the heart of Snowdonian National Park. Guydir Forest, Oldie World. Cosy furnishing, wooden beams, log fire, television. Sleeps 6. Phone: (0690) 710617.

BETWS-Y-COED. Artist's cosy cottage. Superb views Snowdonia. Ideal centre for mountains and coast, rivers and lakes. Sleeps 4/5. Short and long breaks available. Phone: (0690) 710280.

BETWS-Y-COED area. Cosy riverside cottage, sleeps 5. Oak beams, central heating. Colour television. 2 bedrooms, kitchen, bathroom. Parking. Central for North Wales, mountains, lakes, beaches and attractions. Local leisure centre. Swimming pool, golf, walking, pony trekking. Phone: (0492) 640248.

BODORGAN, Anglesey. Rural location with panoramic views. Near beaches. Luxury modern holiday bungalow, fully equipped. Two double bedrooms, cot, colour television, microwave, washing machine. Patio, garden furniture. Sailing, bird watching, golf, walks. Ample parking. Phone: (0407) 840354.

BRECON. Peaceful comfortable modernised cottage in lovely countryside with mountain views, lawns, stream and ample parking. Near Brecon Beacons, Black Mountains and Llangors Lake. Sleeps 6. No pets. Ideal centre for walking and touring. Phone: (0873) 857866.

BRECON BEACONS, Pontsticill. Cottage, con-verted chapel. Fully equipped, luxury accommodation, sleeps 6. Central heating plus woodburner, linen, cot. Pets. Peaceful village. Pubs, restaurants. Spectacular views, walking, fishing, steam railway, pony trekking, waterfalls, canal, reservoirs. Phone: (0685) 374746.

BRECON BEACONS. Luxury converted granary, sleeps 5. Bathrooms, en-suite, gas central heating. Situated on farmyard in National Park. Also available secluded, picturesque bungalow, sleeps 6. Gas central heating. Good walking and views of Black Mountains. Phone: (0874) 636401.

BRECON BEACONS. Isolated wooden cottage. Sleeps 4. Wind powered electricity. Superb walking from door. Beautiful situation. From £85 per week. £55 weekends. Phone: (0558) 822288.

BRECON BEACONS National Park. Small family business, offering selection self-catering accommodation cottages/flats. Personally inspected. Ideal walking, touring area. Hills and vales. Quality Holidays, Trewalter House, Llangorse Brecon, Powys LD3 OPS. Phone: (0874) 84442.

BRECON BEACONS. Fully equipped self-cater-ing cottage, sleeps 4. Linen, towels, heating included. Pets welcome. Use of washing machine. Beautiful scenery. Ideal base for touring, fishing, walking, canal, pony trekking. April prices from £115. Phone: (0873) 830219.

BRECON 2.5 miles. Large farmhouse, divided into 2 units. Each apartment has 2 double bedrooms, shower room with toilet and washbasin. Fitted electric kitchens, oil central heating. Ample parking, large garden. Phone: (0874) 624358 evenings.

BROADHAVEN. Self-catering holidays' cara-vans (sleeping up to eight - no pets), and bungalow (four plus cot), are ideally located in and around Broadhaven. Excellent facilities and high standards at competitive rates. Details and brochure Phone: (01203) 348672.

BUILTH WELLS. Farm cottage in peaceful sur-roundings adjoining open moorland. Ideal walking holiday. 4 miles Erwood Village, 10 miles Builth Wells. 4 bedrooms, sleeps 7/8 persons. Reasonable rates. Details from Mrs Lloyd, Skreen Farm, Erwood, Builth Wells, Powys. Phone: (0982) 560673.

CAERNARFON. Detached house overlooking valley at Betws Garmon in Snowdonia National Park, sleeps 8. 3 bedrooms, upstairs lounge, bathroom, shower room, large modern kitchen, and dining room, fully inclusive shop and pub nearby. Phone: (0286) 650537.

CAERNARFON. Bungalow on quiet beach. 10 miles south of Caernarfon. Sleeps 5 in 2 bedrooms. Clean and comfortable. Colour television, washing machine, freezer. Parking. Sea, mountains, castles, lakes. Roberts, Llandegai Vicarage, near Bangor, Gwynedd. Phone: (0248) 353711.

CAERNARFON BAY. Character cottage with adjoining self-contained flat. Sleep six/four. Tiny village. Sea 100 yards. Seven miles South Caernarfon. Available all year. Central heating, open fire. Phone: Ward 051 734 3550.

CAERNARFON, Snowdonia. Dormer flat for two. Mountain village situation. Kitchen, lounge/diner with colour television, bathroom, bedroom. All electric. Parking space. Easy access to wide range of interests. £110 - £130 per week. Phone: Trottier (0286) 880718.

CAERNARFON. Historic harbour town, 3 miles. A delightful traditional farmhouse, sleeping 12. Set between Snowdon and the sea. Provides all you require for a perfect family/friends re-union. Children most welcome. Much acclaimed playbarn. Brochure Phone: (0286) 830327.

CAERNARFON. Bungalow accommodation, sleeps seven. Seaside. River for salmon and trout fishing. Snowdon range walking, climbing. Convenient buses, towns, villages, beaches. Apply: Hughes, St. Ives, Pontllyfni, Caernarfon. Phone: (0286) 660347.

CAERNARFON. Traditional cottage, set in peaceful countryside with sea view. Situated 5 miles from the coast and Snowdonia mountains. 2 bedrooms, sleeps 6. Fully equipped, colour television, washing machine. Phone: (0286) 650711.

CARDIGAN coast 5 miles. Modern, spacious split-level barn conversion on small working farm, set in peaceful rural hillside location. Outstanding views. Private courtyard garden. Ample parking. Fully equipped to sleep 6. Phone: (0239) 851419 (evenings).

CARDIGAN one mile. Charming furnished holi-day house. Sleeps five. Mini breaks. Central for touring, beaches, fishing. Well equipped. Lawn front and rear, ample parking space. Terms from £100 per week inclusive. Mrs Evans, Rhydfuwch, Cardigan. Phone: (0239) 612064.

CARDIGAN BAY. Period cottage, sleeps six
Fully equipped, two bathrooms. Garden, paddock. Children, pets welcome. Television, video. Beautiful countryside near sea. Smaller property also available, suit four. Fishing sea and coarse, golf, dry ski slope, pony trekking. Phone: (0239) 851531.

CARDIGAN 9 miles. Cosy cottage for two on peaceful smallholding near A478. Kitchenette, cooker, fridge, storage units, colour television, shower. Also spacious six berth caravan. From £95. Ideal for touring West Wales. Phone: (0239) 831265.

CARDIGAN area. Detached bungalow, sleeps 4/5. Part of secluded smallholding. Owned by wildlife photographer. Beautiful cliffs and cove at Cwmtydu are only 8 miles away and surroundings excellent for walking, birdwatching, exploring. Steeped in History. Phone: (0239) 858910.

CARDIGAN, Dyfed. Converted 2 storey barn.
Private position, surrounded by lawns - trees. 3 bedrooms, sleeps 4/5 on quiet 30 acre smallholding. Near sea. Fitted kitchen, microwave, cooker. Comfortable lounge with colour television. Phone: (0239) 811286.

CARDIGAN BAY. Lovely self-contained flat
Sleeps 2/4. Situated 2 miles Llangrannog, on A487 coast road. Convenient. Many sandy beaches including New Quay and Aberporth. Golf, tennis, pony-trekking, scenic walks, village pub. Reasonable terms. Brochure: Phone: (0239) 654371.

CARDIGAN. Designed for 2, beautiful slate cot-
tage, stone and oak interior. Cosy underfloor heating, open fire for atmosphere. Set on small farm by quiet back road. Table tennis, undercover badminton. Sleeps 2-4. £100-£200. Phone: (0239) 614903.

CENARTH, Dyfed. Ideally situated, secluded,
2 bedroom cottage on River Teifi with private fishing. Sleeps 4. Within easy reach of the Pembrokeshire Coast and Preseli Mountains. Includes colour television, video, hi-fi. For details Phone: (0239) 711032.

CONWAY VALLEY. Attractive detached house.
Own garden, orchard. Parking. Three double bedrooms. Ideal for touring, beaches, mountains. Restful holiday. Peaceful setting in quiet surroundings. An ideal family holiday base. Personal supervision. Phone: Williams (0492) 548268.

CONWY. Delightful two bedroomed cottage on farm with gas central heating, colour television, microwave and shower. Linen and heating included. All round the year holidays. Static caravan with all amenities also available. Phone: (0492) 596172.

CRICCIETH, North Wales. Attractive cottage with garden. Television, microwave etc. Open fire. if desired. Suitable for Snowdonia holiday. Beach, castle, shops, horse riding, golf nearby. E. Parry, 28 Llys Gwyn, Caernarfon, Gwynedd LL55 1EN. Phone: (0286) 674642.

CRICCIETH. Homely, quiet, 1st floor flat,
overlooking castle. Sleeps 4. Modern facilities. Conveniently situated for beaches, miniature golf, bowling green, children's playground. Has pleasant views of Snowdon Garden. Private parking. Smith, Bryn Gwalia. Phone: (0766) 522102.

CRICCIETH. Holiday flat, seafront. All modern conveniences. Linen optional. Central for Snowdonia, Lleyn Peninsula. Owner living on premises. Pets by request. Colour television, electrical fire £1 coin meter. Friendly atmosphere. Terms on request. Phone: (0766) 522148.

DINAS CROSS. Cottage, sleeps 5. Double glazed. Gas central heating. Children and pets welcome. The village is a good base to explore the unspoilt Pembrokeshire coast. Contact Mr B. Lewis, Dinas Cross. Phone: (03486) 277.

DOLGELLAU, Snowdonia. Comfortable pretty period stone terraced cottage on edge town. Delightful small garden, beams, log stove. Television. Sleeps 4. Linen, electricity inclusive. Close mountains, coast, lakes. Glorious walking in magnificent countryside. Phone: (0743) 232774.

FISHGUARD near, Pembrokeshire. A 2 bedroom chalet situated in a West Wales coastal village. Comfortable accommodation with superb sea and countryside views. Shops and pubs. £90 to £225. Welsh Tourist Board grading 4 dragons. Phone: (0222) 883436.

GARNDOLBENMAEN, Gwynedd. Luxury cara-
van situated in a quiet garden. Ideally located for exploring Snowdonia and Lleyn Peninsula. Superbly equipped. Bed linen supplied. Sleeps 4. Open all year. Terms from £85 per week. Evans, Melin Llecheiddior, Phone: (0766) 530635.

GOWER COAST, Caswell. A choice of self-cater-
ing chalets in a quiet select site. Fully equipped. Sleeping 2/6. 300 yards from Caswell Bay's beautiful beach, 3 miles from Swansea, the Maritime City. Phone: (0554) 758091.

GOWER, Mumbles. Two bedroomed comfort-
able holiday bungalow situated at Limeslade. Colour television. Five minute walk to nearest beach. Glorious scenery, sandy beaches. Leisure centre in Swansea. Shops and restaurants nearby. Phone: (0926) 334567 or 338774.

GOWER COAST (Swansea). Various small to large modern bungalows and houses to suit from 2 persons to 9 persons. Mostly near small sheltered beach. Personally supervised. Lewis, 11 Valley View, Derwenfawr, Swansea SA2 8BG Phone: (01792) 201605.

HARLECH near, Llanbedr, Merioneth. Welsh stone cottage. 3 bedrooms, bathroom, wc, kitchen - diner. Electric cooker, lounge, open fire, colour television. Parking, garden. Meter. Ellen Owen, Yfedw, Llanbedr, Gwynedd LL45 2LE. Phone: (0341) 23408.

HARLECH. A warm welcome awaits you in the heart of Snowdonia. Self-catering properties. Close to mountains and sea. Good walking country, sailing, golf etc. Phone: Jill (0341) 23475.

HARLECH. Modern detached house, with large garden. Sleep 6. Sorry no dogs. Shops and restaurants nearby. Golf and beach .5 mile. Garage. Ideal centre for touring. Welsh Tourist Board 4 Dragon Award. Phone: (01639) 813302.

HARLECH, Llanbedr. In beautiful Snowdonia National Park. Between mountains and sea. Comfortable two bedroom bungalow, sleeps four. Colour television, bath, shower, central heating. 200 metres from quiet village centre. 2.5 miles from golden beaches. Phone: (0766) 780013.

KNIGHTON, near, Welsh border. Relax 'off the beaten track' in the peaceful seclusion of our luxury farm cottage. The spacious accommodation, sleeps seven plus two cots. ETB five keys, highly commended. Short breaks. Phone: (0544) 260237.

LAUGHARNE. Panoramic clifftop location. Lovely cottage on traditional style working farm. Lots of animals. Ponys for children to ride, goats, ducks, rabbits and many more. Children's paradise. For a real farm holiday. Brochure Phone: (0994) 427667, 071 584 6986.

LLANBEDR, Harlech. Comfortable farmhouse sleeping 12 and cosy stone cottages (charming barn conversion) with central heating, sleeping 6. Ideal family holiday. Safe sandy beaches, mountains, plenty to do. Reasonable prices. Weekends, minibreaks. Phone: (0509) 853975 evenings.

LLANBEDROG, Pwllheli. Self-catering farm- house accommodation. Welsh Tourist Board 4 tick. Sleeping 6. Superb coastal/mountain views. Sandy sheltered beach 1.5 miles. Colour television, microwave. Cot, free babysitting. Rough shooting. Terms £110 - £250 weekly. Bed linen, electricity included. Phone: (01758) 740341.

LLANBERIS. Cosy cottages. For quality, self- catering accommodation at the foot of Snowdon, North Wales. Open all year. Easy access via new A55 dual carriageway. Phone: (0286) 674481.

LLANBERIS (5 miles). Character cottage/cara- van. Attractive secluded location. Set in own grounds overlooking Snowdonia. Colour television, log fire, parking. Short breaks from £65-£95. Full weeks from £85-£210. Phone: (0248) 670629, (0286) 672063.

LLANDDEUSANT. Large comfortable self- catering cottage on working Welsh farm. Heart of the Brecon Beacons National Park. Excellent for walking, fishing, birdwatching. Safe for children. Sleeps 6. Linen provided. Wales Tourist Board approved Grade 5. Phone: (05504) 242.

LLANDUDNO. West Shore Holiday House. Very comfortable and clean, nicely furnished and decorated. Tourist Board Dragon Award. Private parking. Near beach, short walk to main town centre. Sleeps two to four adults only. Phone: (0492) 877450.

LLANDUDNO. Ffraid Villa, 27 Caroline Road. Holiday flatlets, central position. Near shops, beach and pier. Highly recommended. Bed linen provided. Phone: Mrs Wood (0492) 877820, Gwynedd, North Wales.

LLANDUDNO. Sandown Cottage, 3 Rectory Lane. 2 bedrooms, sleeps 4/5. Fitted kitchen with cooker, fridge, washer and microwave. Central but quiet. Parking at door. Price £150-£225, includes bedding, gas and electric. Central heating. Phone: (0492) 876287.

LLANDUDNO. Balmoral Holiday Flats. One, two or three bedrooms, fully self-contained. Open all year. Five minutes from theatre, promenade, shops. Phone: (0492) 544830 or 877131 or write to 6 Trinity Square, Llandudno, Gwynedd LL30 2RD.

LLANDUDNO. Central. 'Highlands', No. 6 Caroline Road. First floor, front, one room flatlet with twin beds, electric cooker, fridge - freezer, gas fire. Shower and toilet shared by one other person only. Phone: (0492) 877810.

LLANDUDNO. Fully equipped self-contained 3 bedroomed holiday flat to sleep 6. With panoramic views over Conwy estuary. Approximately one mile from town centre. For further details Phone: (0705) 736961.

LLANEGRYN, near Aberdovey. Attractive farm- house with beautiful views. Peaceful, lovely gardens. Bird and badger watching. Bikes available. Sorry, no pets or smokers. Tallylyn railway, sandy and rocky beaches nearby. Sleeps five. Phone: White (0654) 710959.

LLANGOLLEN, North Wales - Character cot- tage. Situated in the town and sleeping 5 plus cot. Well equipped, microwave, washer/dryer. Steam trains, canal boats, golf, horse riding, canoeing and mountain biking all nearby. Welsh Tourist Board approved. Phone: 081 422 4768.

LLANGRANOG. Seaside village, magnificent Cardigan Bay, coast. Self-catering cottages, sleep 4 or guest house. Fully appointed. Excellent walking, bathing, surfing, fishing, bird-watching, golfing, ski-ing or just relaxation. Hostelry good eating. Leyshon, Frondolau Fach, Llangranog. Phone: (0239) 654748.

LLANNEFYDD. Charming character cottage in quiet village between sea/mountains. Superbly equipped. Woodburning stoves, central heating. Pretty garden with patio. Ideal for walking, touring, relaxing. All linen provided. Warm welcome. Sleeps 6/8. WTB 5 dragons. Phone: (01745) 79345.

LLANRWST, "Bron Derw". Comfortable self- contained part of farmhouse, sleeps 6. Cleanliness assured, sorry no pets. Within easy reach of the Snowdonia range as well as the popular seaside resorts. Details Edwards, "Bron Derw", Llanrwst, Gywnedd. Phone: (0492) 640494.

BARAFUNDLE BAY
SOUTH PEMBS. COAST
(photo courtesy of Wales Tourist Board)

LLEYN PENINSULA. Furnished farmhouse, sleeps 7. Colour television, microwave, bed linen. Pets welcome. May to September. Brochures available. Chidley, Trygarn, Sarn, Pwllheli, Gwynedd. Phone: (0758) 730227.

LLEYN PENINSULA, North Wales. Fisherman's cottage, sleeps 6 plus cot. Microwave, fridge, freezer. Pets welcome. Near sandy beaches. 3 miles from shops. Dates available from Easter onwards. Phone: Mrs Griffith (0341) 23516.

LLEYN PENINSULA. Ideal for family holidays. Sleeps 8. Enjoys views of surrounding countryside. Several beaches are within easy reach by car. Spacious house, comprises 4 bedrooms, bathroom, lounge, din-ing room, kitchen. Garden. Phone: (01758) 730202.

LLEYN PENINSULA, Gwynedd. Quiet farm- house sleeps 7 or cottage sleeps 5. Near Llanbedrog. Views of sea and Snowdonia. Each dwelling has own lawn and ample parking space. Illustrated brochure Phone: (0758) 740284.

MACHYNLLETH, Eglwys-fach. Farm cottage in secluded valley off the Aberystwyth/Machynlleth coast road. Sleeps 5. Beams, log fire, storage heaters, modern kitchen. Easy reach of Snowdonia, beaches, bird reserve, Centre of Alternative Technology. Phone: (0654) 781335.

MACHYNLLETH, Montgomeryshire. Comfort- able Welsh Tourist Board 4 star inglenook cottage in quiet hill village. Colour television. Sheltered garden. Ideally situated for beaches and mountains. Sleeps 4 or 5. Sights and new Celtica exhibition nearby. Reasonable prices. Brochure Phone: (0650) 511681.

MALLTPAETH, Anglesey. Luxury Bungalow, sleeps 6. Large lounge, sunroom, bath, shower, central heating by Estuary. Glorious views Snowdon range. Private garden. Ample parking. Golf, riding nearby. Ideal walkers, bird watchers. Phone: (0766) 512914 evenings.

MANORBIER. Absolutely no smoking! Cottage sleeps 4, in 1 king-sized double and 1 twin room. Linen, electricity, central heating included. No pets. Beaches .5 mile. McHugh, The Old Vicarage, Manorbier, South Pembrokeshire SA70 7TN. Phone: (01834) 871452.

NARBERTH, PEMBROKESHIRE

Spacious cottage adjoining country house in beauti-ful countryside, 15 minutes from seaside and Preseli Hills. Cobbled courtyard and extensive grounds. 3 bedrooms sleeping 5 adults and 2 children. Colour TV, Telephone, Microwave.
Phone: 01834 860925

NEW QUAY 1 mile. Large 18th century farm- house (sleeps 12). 5 bedrooms, 2 bathrooms. Olde-worlde charm. Log fire plus all modern conveniences. Panoramic sea-cliff views. Near deserted beach and woods. Superb secluded location - the best in the area. Phone: (0545) 560164 10 am - 10 pm.

NEW QUAY, West Wales. Eleven miles inland. Secluded old weavers cottage, beside stream, wood-lands. Overlooking valley in sunny, sheltered position. Sleeps 6/8. Available all year. Riding, fishing, dri-ski nearby. Leaflet Phone: (0684) 294008/294629/850571.

NEW QUAY, West Wales. Bungalow. Quiet area overlooking woods, fields. Five minutes from beach. Short walk into village. Horse riding, golf, fishing near-by. Television, gas, electricity inclusive. Payphone. Pets allowed. Phone: for brochure. Davies, Cwmhalen. (0545) 560575, mobile (0831) 420867.

NEWCASTLE-EMLYN. Bronest Beulah. Pleasant 3 bedroom bungalow, sleeps 7-9. All moderate conveniences suitable for disabled. Duvets on all beds, no linen supplied. Central heating inclusive. Phone: Elias, Aberporth (0239) 810899.

NEWTOWN, Powys. Large farmhouse, four bedrooms, sleeps eight plus cot. WTB three dragon rating. Quiet location. Good walking. No pets. Marilyn Price, Clomearl, Sarn, Newtown. Phone: (0686) 670237.

NOLTON HAVEN, Pembrokeshire. Small selec- tion of holiday bungalows, only 7 minutes walk from the beach. Ideally situated for spectacular coastal walks and stunning countryside. All Welsh Tourist Board graded. Pets welcome. Phone for colour brochure, Ceri, Price (01437) 720027.

OLD COLWYN. Self-contained flat. Quiet ele- vated rural setting. Sea and country views. Ideal for two but accommodates four. Combined living room, kitchen, double bedroom, bathroom en-suite, colour television. Non smokers preferred. £70 - £90. Phone: (01492) 516388.

PEMBROKESHIRE

Large 5 bedroom house, executive accommodation, sleeps 10. Situated in small idyllic village, close to Marina's, National Parks and lovely beaches. In reach of all amenities, pubs, restaurants, etc. Golf, horse riding nearby. All facilities for babies. Pets allowed.

PHONE: MRS. S. A. JOHN
0437 891441

PEMBROKE COAST. Cottages, sleep 2-12. Beach 200 yards. Well equipped. Linen included. Laundry room. Pets welcome. On coastal path. Ideal windsurfing, fishing, golf, walking or family beach holiday. Haven Cottages, Little Haven, Haverfordwest, Dyfed. Phone: (0437) 781552.

ROSEMOOR
COTTAGES
& NATURE RESERVE
PEMBROKESHIRE COAST
NATIONAL PARK

Comfortable well-equipped red sandstone cottages 3 miles from safe sandy beaches. Free linen, baby equipment. Pets welcome. Home cooked meals available. Brochure, price & availability list – compare our prices! – from Mrs Barbara Lloyd, Rosemoor, Walwyn's Castle, Pembrokeshire, SA62 3ED.

01437·781326
FAX: 01437·781080

PEMBROKESHIRE

Award winning cottages and apartments in heart of National Park.

Perfect for family holidays, honeymoons and short breaks.

Managed and supervised by owners who care.

Colour brochure from:

Eric & Helen Mock, Millmoor Cottages, Broad Haven, Haverfordwest SA62 3GB.

Tel: 01437 781507.   Fax: 0437 78002.

PEMBROKESHIRE NATIONAL PARK, Strumble Head, Fishguard. 2 comfortable bungalows. Peaceful unspoilt area. Panoramic sea, hill views. Walks coastal path, sandy beaches. Phone: (03485) 252.

ROMANTIC RETREATS
PEMBROKESHIRE COAST NATIONAL PARK
Panoramic views of unspoilt coastline where Preseli Mountains meet the sea at Newport. Architects outstanding quality historic cottage, sleeps 4-8, lovingly restored Georgian house, sleeps 8-12. Huge, walled garden. Every comfort. Long sandy beach 5 minutes. Short breaks. Good rates.
COLOUR BROCHURE
PHONE 0239 820277 FAX: 0239 820779

COUNTRY COTTAGES on a
PEMBROKESHIRE FARM!

Tenby 6 miles, Saundersfoot 3 miles. A family holiday with all modern comforts in a real farm atmosphere. Enjoy fresh milk, free range eggs. Freshly baked bread and the company of the farm animals.
Free brochure: Mrs. Rickaby, Upper Broom Farm, Begelly, South Pembrokeshire SA68 0XG
Phone Saundersfoot: (0834) 813530

PENMAENMAWR, North Wales. House also self-contained flats. Magnificent sea views. Edge Snowdonia National Park. Detached 1 acre. Parking. Colour television, fitted carpets. Large cooker/fridge. Noorbrit, Fernbrook Road, Penmaenmawr, Gwynedd LL34 6DE. Phone: (0492) 622248.

PENMAENMAWR, Glan-y-coed Lodge, Glan-yr- Afon Road, Dwygyfylchi. Chalet, sleeps 4/6 or caravan, sleeps 4 in garden. Colour television. Private parking in Snowdonia National Park, North Wales coast. Between mountains and sea. Phone: (0492) 622568.

PENMAENMAWR, North Wales Coast. Self-con- tained flats. Well equipped. 96 acres parkland/woodlands. Licensed club, laundrette. Short walk to beach. Central for touring Snowdonia. Also camping park for tourers, tents, motorhomes. Penddyffryn Hall, Penmaenmawr, Gwynedd. Phone: (01492) 623219.

PENRHYNDEUDRAETH. (3 miles Porthmadog). Comfortable detached bungalow in quiet corner. Sleeps 5/6, cot. Mountain views. Open fire in winter. Parking - 2 cars. Reasonable rates. Steam train enthusiasts will love it! Phone: (0579) 50447 (after 1st May (0579) 350447).

PENRHYNDEVORAETH. Harlech - Portmeirion coast. Stationmaster's house, sleeps 6 plus cot. 3 bedrooms. Daytime trains. Close beaches, mountains, shops. Festiniog railway. Sunny patio. Glorious views across estuary to mountains, Harlech Castle. Car-parking. Ideal holiday with/without a car. Phone: (0272) 730024.

PITLOCHRY, Dalshian. Self-catering. 3 cottages and 7 residential caravans in 6 acres of private wooded grounds. Brochures from Telford, Dalshian, Pitlochry PH16 5JS. Phone: (0796) 472173.

POPPIT SANDS. Pembrokeshire. 3 apartments for couples/families. Situated on quiet smallholding, overlooking Poppit Sands and Cardigan Island. Each sleeps 4, plus cot. Prices from £69 - £220 per week. Open all year. Pets welcome. Phone: (0239) 615279.

PORTHMADOG. Modern bungalow, sleeps 6. Detached. Cleanliness guaranteed. Close to beach, shop, mountains, golf, fishing, Snowdonia, Porth Meirion. Fully equipped kitchen. Suitable for both young and not so young! Phone: (0949) 842736 now for details.

PORTHMADOG, Aberglaslyn Estuary. Idyllic riverside millhouse and cottage. Sleeps 2/12. Private waterfall valley with parking. Character accommodation, open fires, modernised kitchens and bathrooms, colour television. Superb scenery. Snowdon, Portmeirion nearby. Details Phone: Williams - Ellis (0181) 6533118.

POWYS. Quiet, comfortable family cottage in Vyrnwy Valley. Sleeps 4/5. Open fire. Well-behaved pets welcome. Lovely views, fishing locally, walks, riding and castles nearby. For details Phone: Bowden 081 741 0630 or write 5 Merthyr Terrace, London SW13 9DL.

BARN-VIEW COTTAGES

Stone and timber clad barn, newly converted, self contained character cottages. Idyllic hillside position overlooking magnificent views. A perfect setting for a relaxing peaceful holiday.

Mrs. W. M. Knight, The Old Farm House, Drainbyrion, Llanidloes, Powys SY18 6PW Tel: 01686 413527

PRESELI HILLS, Pembrokeshire. Character stone cottage on 400 acre estate in wooded river valley. Fishing, walking, near beaches. Heated, fully equipped & comfortable. No smokers! Phone: Office (0923) 224445, farm (0437) 563260.

PWLLHELI, North Wales. Town houses. Balcony overlooking marina and Snowdonia. One minute from beach. Sleeps six. All modern conveniences. Welsh Tourist Board high grading four dragons. Phone: (0758) 612741 and (0758) 701257.

PWLLHELI, near Aberdaron. Farmhouse, sleeps 6. Children and pet welcome. Linen, microwave, cot and high chair. Colour television included. Vacant Easter to October. Ring for brochure. Mrs Evans (0175) 8780284 or (0175) 8740961.

RHAYADER area (mid Wales). Picturesque keeper's cottage in own peaceful grounds with stream and deciduous woodland nearby. Colour television. Fully modernised. Couples especially welcome but sleeps 4 in comfort. Williams, 59 Marine Terrace, Aberystwyth. Phone: (0970) 617549.

RHYL. Self-contained ground floor flat with en-suite shower room. Also self-contained 4 roomed first floor flat. Both fully equipped. Colour television, fridge. No meters, inclusive terms. Suter, Holmlea, 14 Sandringham Avenue, Rhyl. Phone: (0745) 334416.

SAINT DAVID'S, Pembrokeshire. House, sleeps 6. Private garden, lovely views. Close to amenities, shops, cathedral, cliff walks, beaches, golf. Linen supplied. Phone: Mrs Pam Wilcox (0437) 720511.

SAUNDERSFOOT. Luxury annexe flat, very private. Sleeps 2. Modern amenities. Lounge, bedroom, kitchenette, shower, toilet, heating. Parking. Beach, shops 10 minutes. Married couples only. Sorry no smoking, no pets. From £90 per week. Phone: (0834) 811119.

SAUNDERSFOOT, Pembrokeshire. Attractively furnished ground floor flat, 2 bedrooms, sleeps 6. Colour television. Fully equipped kitchen. Parking. From £80 per week. Also available for weekend breaks. Out of season details Phone: (0203) 403491 or 225079.

SNOWDONIA. Comfortable country house in beautiful hamlet of Betws Garmon. Ideal for walking, climbing, fishing, beaches, relaxing. Outstanding views of mountains, valley and river. Well equipped, washing machine, freezer, sleeps 8. Pets welcome. Phone: (0286) 650682.

SNOWDONIA, Betws-Y-Coed. Cottage, sleeps 6. Central heating. Excellent walking, climbing, canoeing, skiing, wildlife, horse riding, fishing, golfing. Scenic area. Weekend rates, Autumn, Spring. Highly recommended. Phone: (0690) 710289.

SNOWDONIA, Bala. Self-catering country farmhouse cottages. Beams and log fires. Sleeps 2/6. Beautiful tranquil location. Ideal for all outdoor activities and exploring North Wales. Pets welcome. Phone: (0490) 81448.

SNOWDONIA. Lakeside two bedroomed centrally heated cottage. Sleeps four. Very comfortable. Excellent base for trout fishing, hill walking, bird watching. Beautiful scenery. Welsh Tourist Board grade five. Collins, Cynllwyd Mawr, Llyn Crafnant, Trefriw, Gwynedd LL27 0JZ. Phone: (0492) 640818.

SNOWDONIA. Comfortable semi-detached traditional stone cottage with own land. Outskirts village. Superb mountain views. Sleeps 4. Ample parking. Fully equipped, colour television, microwave, full central heating. Moderate inclusive terms. Short breaks possible. Brochure Phone: (0869) 345403.

SNOWDONIA, Harlech. Farm cottage, sleeps 5 plus cot. Ample parking, large garden. All modern conveniences. 5 minutes from shop, beach, pool, castle, golf. Tourist Board approved. Available from May to September. Sorry no pets. Phone: (0766) 780709.

SNOWDONIA. Holiday cottage privately owned in peaceful wooded valley. Ample parking. Convenient. Many sandy beaches. 3 miles Caernarfon and Castle, five miles Snowdon. Phone: (01286) 650271.

SNOWDONIA near. Caernarfon. Comfortable centrally heated cottage in mountain village. Sleeps 5. Panoramic views. Children and dogs welcome. Ideal walkers or climbers. Craft centres, beaches, tourist attractions quite close. £115 - £195 week. Breaks from £85. Phone: (01692) 650775.

SNOWDONIA. Cottage on smallholding. Comfortable, warm, sleeps 6. Beautiful accessible area at foot of hills. Near beaches. Perfect for walking, touring. Gorgeous views. Also caravan sleeps 4. Phone: (0286) 881604 (long ring).

SNOWDONIA. Traditional stone built detached cottage at Nebo. Midway Between Caernarfon and Port Madoc. Completely secluded. Ideal honeymoon retreat. Contact Mrs Woolcott, 26 Kings Road, Clacton CO15 1AZ or Phone: (0255) 423861.

SNOWDONIA. 2 beautifully renovated, comfortable stone cottages with woodburning stoves. Both in peaceful locations close to mountains and quiet beaches, 6 miles from Caernarfon. Sleeps 5. Pets welcome in one cottage. Phone: (0286) 880143/(0286) 881868.

SOLVA. Pembrokeshire. Comfortable part farmhouse, self-catering, quiet location, close to sea. Available from Whitsun onwards. Sleeps 6. Details Phone: St. Davids (0437) 721246.

SOLVA. Walking distance coastal path. Half mile Solva harbour, 1 1/2 miles St. Davids. In own grounds. Well equipped old farmhouse. Central heating, AGA cooker, log fires. Sleeps 8-10. Ample parking. Play area for children. No pets. Phone: (0437) 532318.

ST DAVIDS, Pembroke Coast. Five bedrooms, sleeps 8-12. Private gardens, sandy beaches nearby. Very safe for children. EEC standard. Panoramic views. Central heating, washing machine, colour television, cot, highchair. Welsh Tourist Board graded. Phone: (0734) 266094.

SWANSEA, Caswell Bay, Gower. Holiday chalets WTB approved. Sleeps five. Two bedroomed, fully equipped, kitchen, everything provided except linen. Colour television. 300 yards from glorious beach. Scrupulously cleaned between visits. Pets welcome. Brochure Phone: (01558) 668637.

SWANSEA. Superbly furnished and equipped bungalows on quiet park overlooking Port Eynon Bay on the beautiful Gower Peninsula. Sleep four. Welsh Tourist Board four star rating. Baxter, Pennard Hill Cottage, Parkmill, Swansea SA3 2EH. Phone: (0792) 371301.

TAL-Y-BONT, near Conwy. Sleeps four. Pets taken. Comfortable two bedroom, character cottage on edge of National Park. Secluded garden with views. Parking. Ideal for walking, mountains, river, coast, castle, Bodnant gardens. Winter breaks. Phone: (0492) 650233.

TEIFY VALLEY. Farm holiday cottage. Sleeps six. Children enjoy the animals and space. Beach, golf, horse riding, dry ski slope nearby. From £177 per week, includes bed linen. Dogs, horse welcome. Phone: (0239) 851606 Dyfed.

TENBY. Penally Manor. Character self-contained apartments in glorious setting overlooking sea, golf course and beach. Colour television, central heating. Private parking, heated swimming pool. Most apartments have two bathrooms, launderette. For brochure Phone: (0834) 842958.

TENBY
3 BELLE VUE, CRACKWELL STREET
Prime situation flats overlooking harbour and north beach. Sleeps 2-8. Immediate vicinity of shops and beaches. WTB approved. S.A.E. for details:
Mr. H. W. Davies
Phone: (01834) 844888 or (01269) 841302

TENBY, near. Pembrokeshire Coast. Privately owned beach house. Situated 300 yards from beautiful unspoilt safe sand duned beaches. Also 3 bedroom cottage close to The National Parks and Pembroke Castle. Colour television. Sensible prices. Brochure Phone: (0344) 57339 (24 hours).

TENBY five miles. Luxury apartment, sleeps five. Spacious lounge, colour television, kitchen, dining area, bathroom. Parking. Games room, indoor heated pool. June - August. Bed linen provided. Phone: (0646) 651424 after 4 p.m. Ideally located for all attractions.

TENBY. Luxury detached house in the country with large garden, patio and furniture, sleeps 6 plus cot. 5 miles from Tenby/Saundersfoot. Modern facilities include microwave, corner bath and shower. 4 poster bed etc. Phone: Thomas (0646) 651881.

TREFOR, GWYNEDD. Quarryman's cottage on seaward slope of Yr Eifl on magnificent mountains of North Llyn coast. Excellent accommodation for six adults at reasonable rates. Superb base for Snowdonia, angling, walking etc. For brochure Phone: (0503) 72810.

TRENENTH HOLIDAY FLATLETS
32 BATH STREET, RHYL. TEL: 01745 343566
ADJACENT TO SEA LIFE CENTRE AND PROMENADE
Mrs. D. J. Williams (Proprietress)
Own flatlet and front door key. Forefront parking.
Electricity on slot meters. Electric cooker, fridges, colour TV.
Only 5 minutes from town centre, Buses and trains.
TEL: 01745 343566

TY-NEWYDD, Tremadog, Gwynedd. Two holiday flats, sleep three and four people. Central to all parts, Ffestiniog and Snowdon railways, beaches. Private car park. Welsh Tourist Board listed. Sae or Phone: Portmadog (0766) 512553 for enquiries.

TYWYN, near Aberdovey. Comfortably furnished first floor 2 bedroomed flat, sleeps 4, facing sea. Parking close to British Rail station and Talyllyn Steam Railway. Regret no pets. £130 to £160 per week. Phone: (0654) 711297.

USK VALE and Wye Valley. Spacious Converted stone farm buildings on site of ancient hilltop fort, set in 20 peaceful acres. Wonderful scenery, wildlife, walking, disabled facilities. WTB. Sleeps 2/4. Dogs really welcome. Brochure Llewellyn Phone: (0291) 650700.

USK, Gwent. Luxuriously converted 17th century cyder-mill situated on a small farm set amidst the beautiful countryside of the Usk Valley. Sleeps 4. Spacious lounge with beamed ceiling and stoned fireplace, colour television, video, linen provided. Phone: (0291) 672260.

QUALITY COTTAGES
AROUND THE MAGNIFICENT WELSH COAST
Away from the madding crowd near safe sandy beaches
A small specialist agency with over 30 years experience of providing quality self-catering, offer privacy, peace and unashamed luxury.
The first WTB self-catering award winners.
Highest residential standards. Dishwashers, microwaves, washing machines, central heating. No slot meters. Log fires. Linen provided.
PETS WELCOME FREE
All in coastal areas famed for scenery, walks, wild flowers and badgers.
Free colour brochure: D. A. REES
"QUALITY COTTAGES", CERBID, SOLVA, HAVERFORDWEST, PEMBROKESHIRE SA62 6YE. Tel: (01348) 837871

CARAVANS, CHALETS & HOLIDAY PARKS

ABERGELLY near. Haven Holiday Park. 6 berth luxury caravan. Television, shower. Lovely views. Indoor heated pool. Night club, children's club, shops, launderette, sauna, solarium. Phone: (0745) 886674, (0745) 886936.

BARMOUTH, Gwynedd. Sunnysands Caravan Park. 12 foot wide, 3 bedroomed caravans available. Park on seashore. Family club with entertainment. Outdoor heated pool. Supermarket, launderette, amusements, cafe, takeaway. Playground. Serviced. Touring pitches available. 24 hour brochure hotline Phone: (0341) 247301.

BARMOUTH, Gwynedd, Wales. 6 berth caravan with shower, flush toilet, television, fridge. Site offers club, shops, swimming pool, children's playground, boat ramp, sandy beach. No pets. Stamp required for leaflet. 38 Central Avenue, Nuneaton CV11 5BB. Phone: (0203) 384323.

BARMOUTH. Clean, comfortable, spacious caravans, on park adjacent to sandy beach. Personally supervised. All amenities (shop, launderette, indoor pool, amusements, takeaway, bar). Pets welcome. Mrs Evans, Y Dderwen, Talybont, Barmouth, Gwynedd LL43 2AE. Phone: (0341) 247474.

BARMOUTH near, Gwynedd. Six berth caravan on smallholding, within Snowdonia National Park. Colour television and shower. Near beaches and shops. Private parking. Quiet location. Phone: (0341) 242604.

BORTH, near Aberystwyth. 8 berth 3 bedroom luxury caravan. In central Wales, on Haven premier park with heated indoor pool, nightly cabaret and amusements with panoramic views across Cardigan Bay/Cambrian mountains. Phone: (0527) 591159.

BORTH. Luxury caravan on haven site. Overlooking beach with splendid sea views. Private patio and parking. Indoor heated pool, adventure playground, kiddies club, full entertainment programme. Phone: (0384) 279881 between 6 & 8 p.m.

BROAD HAVEN. Beach 3 miles. Modern 30 foot caravan, 2 bedrooms. Sleeps 4. Shower, toilet, colour television. Rural quiet location in own grounds. No pets. Mrs Rees, Moor Farm, Walwyn's Castle, Haverfordwest, Pembrokeshire SA62 3EE. Phone: (0437) 890288.

BRONABER. In the heart of the unspoilt scenic splendour of the Snowdonia National Park. 2 bedroom log cabin. All modern conveniences, colour television. Near forests, sandy beaches, lakes, dry slope skiing. Reasonable rates. Phone: 081 868 5650.

BURTON, Pembrokeshire. Luxury five berth caravan. Picturesque waterside rural location, adjacent village pub and restaurant. Mains water and electricity, fridge, shower, toilet, television, bed linen provided. Private boat mooring and jetty. Dogs welcome. Phone: (0646) 600378.

CAERNARFON. Self-contained comfortable six berth caravan, near Snowdonia National Park and the Lleyn Peninsula, fifteen minutes from the beach. Ideal for horse riding, mountain climbing, canoeing and fishing. Pets welcome. Phone: (0286) 880791 evenings only.

**CARMARTHEN BAY, Llansteffan. Beautiful valley setting. Clubhouse, restaurant, heated pool, children's playground, local leisure centre, golf, fishing, beaches. Personal welcome. Private owners. Pets welcome. Chalet £65.00 to £185.00 per week. Winter breaks from £50.00. Phone: (0792) 201873.

CASWELL BAY. Chalet, sleeps 6. Clean and comfortable with bath, w.c., colour television etc. Beach 250 yards. Also available 7 berth caravan at Pendine Sands, Dyfed. For details Phone: Mr or Mrs Lewis (01495) 723003. OAP discounts.

CENARTH FALLS, near Cardigan. 5/6 berth caravan, or holiday home, sleeps four. Private site in the beautiful Teifi Valley. Ideal for exploring West Wales. Well equipped facilities including linen. From £85 per week. Phone: (0239) 710067.

CENARTH FALLS, West Wales. 4/6 berth, well appointed caravan on Dragon Award site. Near River Teifi in beautiful countryside. Ideal for fishing and walking. Numerous sandy beaches. £160 per week. For further details Phone: (0702) 230097.

CRICCIETH, near. Spacious modern caravan on small highly graded park. Quiet countryside setting, choice good beaches. Edge Snowdonia. Pets farm, fishing rivers. Porthmadog steam trains. Beautiful 6 miles tree lined walks through this farmland. Phone: (0766) 810441.

FERRYSIDE, Dyfed, detached beach chalet. 20 yards from beach. Beautiful sea and country views. Double glazed, patio. Comfortable lounge, colour television. Well equipped kitchen, microwave. Indoor heated pool. Adult and children's entertainments are available. Phone: (01792) 891134.

FISHGUARD near. Beautiful views/walks available from this secluded park on the Pembrokeshire National Park coast. Modern holiday caravans, equipped to high standard. Also available tourers, tents, motorcaravans welcome. Shop, launderette, games room. Phone: (013486) 415. (From May (01348) 811415).

FISHGUARD. 6 berth caravan in garden of small farm near Preselly Hills. Fully equipped. Outside toilet, bathroom and shower in farmhouse. Bed linen not provided. Ideal beaches, walking etc. From £65 per week. Phone: (0348) 881376.

BWLCHGWYN FARM CARAVAN PARK
AND TREKKING CENTRE, FAIRBOURNE, GWYNEDD
Luxury self-catering static caravans. Superb unique view over Mawddach-Estuary, sea, mountains. Sleeps 6. All facilities, heated, colour TV, close shops and long sandy beach. Children and pets welcome. Pony trekking available for all. Livery by arrangement.
Phone: (0341) 250107 or (0341) 280872
Short breaks out of season

GOWER, Caswell Bay. Well-appointed chalet in area of outstanding natural beauty. 300 yards beach. Sleeps 4-6. Sitting room with colour television and hi-fi, kitchen area, 2 bedrooms, bathroom. Terrace and secluded patio. Parking. Phone: (0181) 2891225.

GOWER PENINSULA. Modern 2 bedroom chalet on small private site. Personally supervised. 25 Bridle Mews, Mumbles, Swansea, West Glamorgan SA3 4JP. Phone: (0792) 369857.

GOWER, Oxwich. 6 berth caravans. Private farm site, fully equipped. No linen. Shop in village, 20 minutes from sea. No television. Phone: (0792) 774177.

HARLECH. Small quiet park. Caravans have colour television, fridge, shower. Near town, sandy beach, castles, golf course, fishing, Snowdonia. Prices from £70 weekly. For brochure Sae Steward, Pant Mawr, Harlech, Gwynedd. Phone: (0766) 780 226 or (0766) 780 617.

LAMPETER, near. Mobile three bedroomed home. All services. Alone in three acres paddock and woodland. Panoramic views of beautiful Teifi Valley and thirty minutes south of fine beaches and coastal scenery. Phone: (0559) 35336.

LLANBEDROG, Pwllheli. 32 feet 6 berth Galaxy caravan - private farm paddock. Superb coastal views. Concreted parking. Free babysitting. Rough shooting. Shower, flush toilet, fridge, microwave, colour television, gas/electric fires. £95 - £140 Weekly. (Fuel included). Phone: (01758) 740341.

LLANGYBI, Dyfed. Luxury holiday caravan. All mains services plus shower and colour television. On site shop, licensed club, swimming pool, recreation and play areas. Laundry facilities. Nearby golf club, fishing, trekking, walks, seaside, ornithology. Phone: (0280) 702703.

LLANMADOC, North Gower. Well equipped caravan. 2 bedrooms, shower, toilet, fridge, microwave oven, freezer, television. Phone: Abercraf (0639) 730935.

LLANSTEPHAN. Detached chalet, sleeps 4/6, electric heater, full-size cooker and fridge, colour television. Linen provided, electricity free. Licensed club. Heated pool, play area. Beaches, picturesque village and ideal touring. Quote Chalet 82. Phone: (0267) 83457.

LLANTEG, near Amroth Beach. Exclusive site. Self-catering pine chalet, sleeps 6 plus cot. Linen supplied, electric meter. Clubhouse, shop. Reasonable rates. Phone: (0994) 448388

LYDSTEP BEACH, near Tenby. Six berth, two bedroom, luxury caravan, shower room, toilet, colour television, fridge, mains, gas, electricity inclusive. Award winning site, private beach, clubhouse, swimming pool. Family groups only. Phone: (0443) 205030.

NEW QUAY near. Luxury 6 berth caravan on farm. Sea views. Colour television, shower. Equipped to high standard. Quiet location. Riding, golf, dry ski slope, all nearby. 2 miles beach and National Trust coastline. Phone: (0239) 654970.

NEW QUAY, West Wales. Luxury caravan to let. Quay West Holiday Park. Quiet area, five minutes from beach. Facilities of club. All amenities. Phone for brochure. Davies, 33 Cwm-halen. Phone: (0545) 560575, Mobile (0831) 420867.

OXWICH VILLAGE, Gower Coast. Luxury holi-
day bungalow, sleeps 4-6. All modern conveniences.
Microwave, colour television. Sunny position. Quiet well
kept site. Short walk through pretty village to lovely
beaches, woods and nature reserve. Phone: (0905)
422819.

PEMBROKESHIRE
Caravan to let 7 miles inland, between Fishguard
and Haverfordwest. 6 berth caravan with shower,
flush toilet, end bedroom, fridge, colour TV,
beaches approx 6 miles. Reservoir fishing 5 miles.
Mountain views. Very peaceful. Pets welcome.

Phone: 0437 741265

PENMAENMAWR, near Conwy. Luxury six
berth caravans. Small farm site. Full services. Colour televisions, superb sea views. Ideal for touring Snowdonia.
Short breaks. Pensioners' discounts. Watson - Jones,
Tyddyn Du Farm, Penmaenmawr, Gwynedd LL34 6RE.
Phone: (0492) 622300, (0492) 623830.
PORTHMADOG. Spacious six berth leisure
home on farm with magnificent coastal and mountain
scenery. Near tourist attractions - 'little trains' etc. Three
separate bedrooms. All modern amenities. Colour television. Williams, Tyddyn Deucwm Isaf, Penmorfa LL49
9SD. Phone: (0766) 513683.
PORTHMADOG. Black Rock Sands. 150 yards
beautiful beach. Small private site, 14 caravans only.
Modern, well equipped 6 berth caravans. Own showers,
toilets, colour television. Pets welcome, no extra
charges. Phone: Mavis Humphries (0543) 279583.
PRESELI HILLS, Crymych. 32 feet caravan,
sleeps 4. Cooker, fridge, water heater, bath, flush toilet.
All linen, duvets supplied. Tenby 30 minutes, Oakwood
30 minutes, Cardigan town 9 miles. Phone: (0239)
831358.
PRESELI MOUNTAINS, Pembrokeshire. Farm-
house luxury caravan, sleeps 6. Private lawned areas,
panoramic views. Central to towns, beaches, fishing
nearby, lovely walking area. Pets welcome. For a relaxing holiday Phone: Helena on (0437) 532336.

SNOWDONIA
LLYNNAU CREGENNEN
(photograph courtesy of Wales Tourist Board)

RHAYADER, POWYS. 30 feet well equipped
4-6 berth static holiday caravan on small family hill
farm. Private, secluded position with views. Ideal for
touring, walking etc. Pony trekking and golf nearby.
Colour television. Pets welcome. Phone: (0597) 810467.

RHYL. To let, 8 berth, 3 bedroom caravan.
Colour television, fridge, shower, microwave. Indoor
pool, clubhouses, arcade, supermarket. Beautiful site.
Most dates. Sheward. Phone: (0203) 610884.

SAUNDERSFOOT. Tenby area, on peaceful
smallholding, six berth caravans. Also cottage sleeps
four. Sae to Little Masterland, Jeffreston, Kilgetty,
Pembrokeshire, Dyfed SA68 ORH. Phone: (0834) 813893.

SAUNDERSFOOT. 6 berth luxury caravan to
let. Fully equipped, quiet family site. Laundry, children's
play area. Use of club, shop, swimming pool. Beautiful
area, edge of Pembrokeshire coast. National Park, sandy
beaches. Phone: (0834) 812069.

SNOWDONIA, Caernarfon 6 miles. Modern caravan. Sleeps 6. Situated secluded field, panoramic views, mountains, sea. Shower, television, mains services. Also available self-catering cottage, sleeps five. Similar panoramic views. Full amenities. Phone: Williams (0286) 880419 evenings.

ST. DAVIDS, near. Pembrokeshire Coast. Spend relaxing holiday in luxury caravans with colour television. On quiet family park near beach and coastal path. Tourers and tents welcome. Prendergast Holiday Park, Trefin, Haverfordwest. Phone: (0348) 831368.

TENBY. Touring caravan and tent park. Small, friendly site. 2 miles Saundersfoot, 4 miles Tenby. Modern facilities, including washing-up, baby bathroom, electric hook-ups. 6 berth caravan available. Brochure available. Davies, Masterland Farm, Broadmoor, Kilgetty, Pembrokeshire SA68 0RH. Phone: (01834) 813298.

TENBY. Caravans, apartments. Low terms. Heated pool, shop, off-licence, play area. Club with entertainment few minutes. All conveniences, picturesque scenery, beautiful beaches. Nearest beach minutes. Peaceful site, horses and sheep on farm. Brochure Phone: (0834) 891695, (0834) 812428.

TENBY CARAVAN PARK. Award winning holi-day park with excellent leisure facilities - clubhouse with nightly entertainment for adults and children. Heated swimming pool. Shop, restaurant - takeaway. Games room. Cross Park. Broadmoor, Kilgetty, Dyfed. Phone: (0834) 813205.

TENBY five miles. Six berth caravan, double bedroom, single with bunks, lounge, dining area, colour television, fitted kitchen, shower room, water closet. Electric slot meter, gas inclusive. Ideally located for all attractions. Phone: (0646) 651424 after 4 p.m.

TENBY. Penally Court Holiday Centre. Six berth caravan. Mains. Colour television. Small site with shop, swimming pool and children's play area. Horse riding and golf nearby. Sorry no pets. Phone: (0562) 67445.

TENBY, near. Manian Lodge. Self-catering 2 bedroom chalets. Friendly, licensed bar, pool room, children's corner. On small holding. Riding, pony, pigs etc. Parking. £150 to £195 inclusive. Phone: (0834) 813273.

TOWYN, near Rhyl. Comfortable six berth cara- van to let, close to beach. Shower, colour television, fridge etc. Ideal touring Colwyn Bay, Anglesey, Snowdonia. Very reasonable rates. Phone: 081 202 9346.

TOWYN. 1994 8 berth caravan for hire. Shower, wc. Colour television, microwave, video, satellite. 3 bedrooms. Reasonable rates. Available Easter to end of September. Phone: 061 220 8978.

WALWYNS CASTLE. 4 berth caravan situated in peaceful countryside. Ideal base for walking, bird islands, relaxing on sandy beaches or touring Pembrokeshire. All mains services, shower, television. 2 bedrooms. Linen provided. Phone: Sandra Davies (01437) 781254.

WHERE TO GO

Oakwood Adventure Park
Canaston Bridge Narbeth.
Tel: (08347) 891373

A family leisure complex. Main park; miniature train, mini golf, bob sleigh ride, skyleap, junior and senior go-karts, water fall ride, boating lake, assault courses, treetop roller coaster. Play area with aeroplane ride, trucking ride, Will Digut's Quarry, carousel, ferris wheel and Playland, an undercover play area packed with ball pools, bouncers, slides, spider's web and climbing equipment. Restaurant and cafeteria. Disabled visitors welcome.

Welsh Highland Railway
Porthmadog, Gwyned.
Tel: (051) 6081950

Narrow-gauge railway steam every weekend and most of Summer, platform-located cafe, shop, railway bookshop and shed tours.

Welsh Mountain Zoo and Flagstaff Gardens
Old Highway, Colwyn Bay, Clwyd.
Tel: (0492) 532938

A well stocked zoo presented in a natural setting surrounded by gardens and woodland with tropical houses and Jungle Adventure Land. Restaurant and cafeteria. Disabled visitors welcome.

Alice in Wonderland Visitor Centre
The Rabbit Hole (Llandudno) Ltd, 3-4 Trinity Square, Llandudno, Gwynedd.
Tel: (0492) 860082

Retail shop setting 'alice' related items. Walk-through grotto with life-sized animated tableaux. Professionally recorded narration with sound effects

Anglesey Sea Zoo
The Oyster Hatchery, Brynsiencyn, Anglesey.
Tel: (0248) 430411

A large array of fish and sea animals on display. Fish farming tide tank. Shop and cafeteria. Disabled visitors welcome.

National Museum of Wales
Cathays Park, Cardiff.
Tel: (0222) 397951

Collections on display include silver, ceramics, coins and medals, fossils, art, minerals, shells, archaeological, botanical. Restaurant.

Caernarfon Castle
Castle Ditch, Caernarfon, Gwynedd LL55 2AY
Tel: (0286) 677617

Begun in 1283 by Edward I, it is one of Europe's great mediaeval fortresses. Scene of recent royal pageantry including the 1969 investiture of the Prince of Wales. World Heritage Site and Regimental Museum.

Dinosaur World
Eirias Park, Colwyn Bay, Clwyd
Tel: (0492) 518111

The Dinosaur World has the largest collection of dinosaurs in the UK, which is set in a woodland area giving the natural habitat effect

CARREG CENNEN CASTLE
(photograph courtsey of Wales Tourist Board)

USEFUL INFORMATION

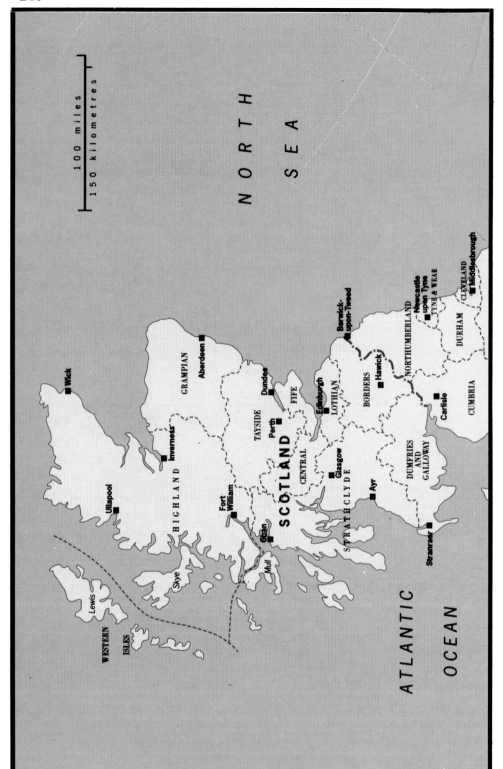

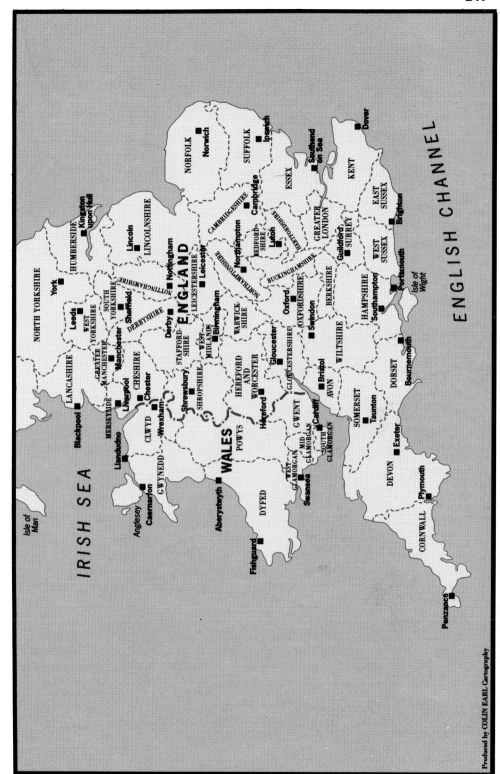

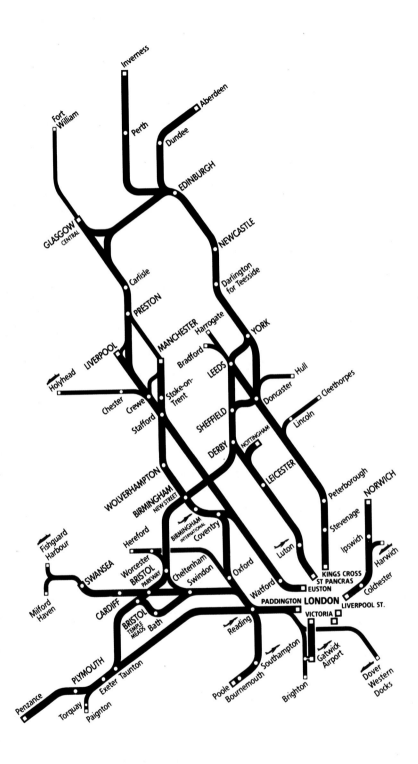

TRAVEL

BRITISH RAIL

Kings Cross Station
East coast of Scotland, Midlands,
North East   0171-278 2477

Paddington Station
South West, Wales   0171-262 6767

St. Pancras Station
Midlands   0171-387 7070

Victoria Station
Sussex, Kent, Surrey 0171-928 5100

Euston Station
West Coast, West Coast of
Scotland   0171-387 7070

Liverpool Street Station
East Anglia, Essex   0171-928 5100

Waterloo Station
Dorset, Hampshire   0171-928 5100

Charing Cross Station
Kent, Essex   0171-928 5100

London Bridge Station
                    0171-928 5100

COACH SERVICES

NATIONAL EXPRESS COACHES

Aberdeen	(01224) 580275
Birmingham	(0121) 622 4373
	(0121) 622 4225
	(0121) 6266226
Bournemouth	(01202) 551481
Bristol	(01272) 541022
Cambridge	(01223) 460711
Cardiff	(01222) 344751
Cheltenham	(01242) 584111
Darlington	(01325) 481447
Edinburgh	(0131) 4528777
Exeter	(01392) 215454
Fareham	(01329) 230023
Glasgow	(0141) 3324100
Horsham	(01403) 241757
Hull	(01482) 212644
Leeds	(01532) 460011
Leicester	(01533) 516696
Liverpool	(0151) 709 6481
London	(0171) 730 0202
Manchester	(0161) 228 3881
Newcastle	(0191) 261 6077
Nottingham	(01602) 585317
Oxford	(01865) 791579
Penzance	(01736) 69469
Perth	(01738) 33481
Peterborough	(01733) 237141
Plymouth	(01752) 671121
Preston	(01772) 885600
Sheffield	(01742) 754905
Stoke-on-Trent	(01782) 747000
Swansea	(01792) 470820
Thanet	(01843) 581333
Truro	(01872) 40404

MILEAGE CHART
BRITAIN

Map of Britain with the following city labels: Inverness, Aberdeen, Fort William, Perth, Glasgow, Edinburgh, Stranraer, Newcastle, Carlisle, Middlesbrough, Kendal, Preston, York, Hull, Liverpool, Leeds, Holyhead, Manchester, Sheffield, Stoke-on-Trent, Lincoln, Shrewsbury, Nottingham, Aberystwyth, Birmingham, Norwich, Peterborough, Hereford, Northampton, Carmarthen, Cambridge, Gloucester, Colchester, Cardiff, Oxford, Bristol, LONDON, Guildford, Barnstaple, Taunton, Salisbury, Maidstone, Southampton, Dover, Exeter, Brighton, Dorchester, Portsmouth, Plymouth, Penzance.

Mileage chart (distances in miles). Diagonal labels in order: Aberdeen, Aberystwyth, Barnstaple, Birmingham, Brighton, Bristol, Cambridge, Cardiff, Carlisle, Carmarthen, Colchester, Dorchester, Dover, Edinburgh, Exeter, Fort William, Glasgow, Gloucester, Guildford, Hereford, Holyhead, Hull, Inverness, Kendal, Leeds, Lincoln, Liverpool, Maidstone, Manchester, Middlesbrough, Newcastle, Northampton, Norwich, Nottingham, Oxford, Penzance, Perth, Peterborough, Plymouth, Portsmouth, Preston, Salisbury, Sheffield, Shrewsbury, Southampton, Stoke-on-Trent, Stranraer, Taunton, York, LONDON.

```
471  (Aberystwyth)
607 222  (Barnstaple)
434 123 178  (Birmingham)
609 290 205 171  (Brighton)
517 132 100 88 170  (Bristol)
465 231 267 113 121 171  (Cambridge)
537 118 137 108 205 47 206  (Cardiff)
234 236 372 198 374 282 258 302  (Carlisle)
521 50 199 157 267 110 269 68 285  (Carmarthen)
518 289 292 171 112 196 48 231 311 293  (Colchester)
599 214 94 170 117 62 181 129 364 191 208  (Dorchester)
587 323 275 205 81 209 121 244 397 307 113 204  (Dover)
126 336 471 298 474 381 336 402 99 385 389 463 458  (Edinburgh)
591 206 55 161 172 83 251 121 355 183 275 54 247 455  (Exeter)
157 446 582 408 585 492 469 512 209 496 522 574 608 133 566  (Fort William)
149 336 472 298 474 382 359 402 99 386 412 464 498 46 456 102  (Glasgow)
483 111 126 54 156 36 123 65 247 127 171 118 195 347 110 458 347  (Gloucester)
566 227 174 124 44 106 91 142 331 204 104 97 100 430 146 542 431 101  (Guildford)
486 80 143 57 188 54 170 58 250 85 203 135 227 350 128 461 350 31 133  (Hereford)
463 105 341 168 344 251 276 205 228 155 334 333 367 327 326 439 328 217 301 157  (Holyhead)
361 229 322 141 283 232 140 252 171 301 193 314 262 232 306 382 271 197 241 200 220  (Hull)
106 496 632 458 634 542 519 562 259 546 572 624 658 157 616 65 174 507 592 510 487 431  (Inverness)
286 191 326 153 329 237 253 257 51 241 319 318 352 150 311 262 151 205 182 165 311  (Kendal)
328 174 310 120 263 220 148 240 122 224 201 302 269 199 294 333 222 185 220 189 166 60 382 71  (Leeds)
390 200 274 88 215 184 94 204 183 253 148 262 216 261 259 394 283 150 173 153 205 48 443 177 73  (Lincoln)
360 111 274 101 277 184 215 205 125 168 267 266 300 225 259 336 225 150 234 119 102 127 385 80 72 139  (Liverpool)
550 286 232 168 49 166 84 202 361 264 76 161 44 421 205 527 461 152 57 184 329 225 621 315 233 179 263  (Maidstone)
355 131 262 88 265 172 161 192 120 181 214 254 288 219 246 331 220 138 222 141 122 99 380 75 44 85 35 251  (Manchester)
276 245 359 178 321 269 200 289 94 294 253 351 322 147 343 279 194 235 278 238 236 89 306 83 64 125 145 285 115  (Middlesbrough)
237 277 391 211 353 302 233 322 59 327 286 383 354 108 376 240 155 267 311 270 268 145 267 101 96 157 177 317 147 40  (Newcastle)
483 173 211 55 133 115 54 162 248 211 119 159 152 347 195 459 348 79 90 110 216 153 508 203 134 91 150 115 138 190 223  (Northampton)
490 294 329 176 286 233 63 268 283 331 59 242 170 361 314 494 383 186 161 231 314 104 381 173 104 136 185 225 257 117  (Norwich)
395 161 234 54 196 145 87 165 189 213 140 226 216 266 219 400 289 110 153 113 174 93 449 149 74 36 108 179 70 131 163 66 119  (Nottingham)
506 160 170 68 110 74 100 109 270 171 125 115 149 370 154 481 370 48 67 80 239 191 531 225 171 128 173 106 161 228 261 43 162 103  (Oxford)
701 317 109 277 284 194 362 232 466 294 386 166 359 566 110 677 566 220 258 435 416 726 421 404 369 317 356 453 486 305 423 328 264  (Penzance)
87 384 520 346 522 430 381 450 147 434 434 512 546 42 504 103 62 395 480 398 375 277 114 199 244 306 273 509 268 192 153 396 406 311 419 614  (Perth)
436 206 254 88 159 158 38 195 229 244 91 206 159 307 238 440 330 140 116 144 275 111 490 224 120 51 188 123 132 171 204 43 77 58 86 348 352  (Peterborough)
632 248 61 203 215 125 293 163 397 225 317 97 290 497 45 608 497 151 189 169 366 347 657 352 335 300 248 287 384 417 236 354 259 195 77 545 279  (Plymouth)
591 245 162 153 50 99 136 350 396 222 148 75 145 455 15 567 456 119 47 151 324 285 616 310 266 217 258 102 246 323 355 135 206 198 85 246 504 161 178  (Portsmouth)
324 148 283 110 286 193 211 213 89 197 276 275 309 188 268 300 189 159 244 62 139 123 349 44 68 135 36 272 32 107 139 159 235 107 183 317 237 182 308 268  (Preston)
552 186 118 123 87 54 139 101 317 163 166 40 162 416 90 528 417 74 61 106 285 575 277 173 104 241 134 185 225 257 117 90 207 324 107 201 167 63 202 465 164 133  (Salisbury)
369 166 272 92 234 183 123 203 162 252 177 264 254 240 257 373 262 148 192 151 157 67 423 121 36 48 78 217 37 104 137 104 148 44 142 367 285 94 298 236 78 205  (Sheffield)
416 74 222 48 224 132 156 110 180 112 214 214 247 280 206 391 280 97 182 5 105 163 440 135 118 125 66 211 70 188 86 121 316 328 130 247 206 92 167 114  (Shrewsbury)
572 226 141 134 64 78 131 141 336 203 158 54 155 416 114 547 437 107 48 132 305 257 591 238 213 239 112 247 254 186 305 163 78 130 186 43 92 57 41 45 163 195 98 175  (Southampton)
390 114 222 48 224 132 156 110 180 112 214 214 248 254 206 366 255 97 182 100 133 130 415 109 43 92 57 21 45 163 195 98 175 52 121 316 303 102 247 207 66 167 51 38 187  (Stoke-on-Trent)
241 344 480 306 482 390 367 410 107 394 420 472 506 132 464 187 85 355 440 358 335 279 266 159 230 231 243 469 228 202 163 356 391 379 374 154 338 505 465 197 425 270 288 445 263  (Stranraer)
559 174 50 130 156 51 219 89 323 151 244 45 227 423 35 534 423 77 126 95 292 273 584 278 261 226 226 184 214 310 343 163 281 186 122 144 472 205 75 114 235 69 224 173 93 173 41  (Taunton)
322 201 315 134 277 225 157 245 115 251 210 307 278 193 300 326 216 191 234 194 192 38 376 90 24 81 101 241 71 50 90 147 181 87 184 409 238 127 340 279 95 248 60 145 250 119 224 267  (York)
549 238 216 120 60 120 60 155 313 217 62 129 78 413 200 524 413 103 30 135 282 188 573 268 199 142 216 38 203 256 288 68 115 131 57 310 461 86 241 75 225 88 169 163 80 163 421 167 212  (LONDON)
```

REGIONAL TOURIST BOARDS

Cumbria Tourist Board
Ashleigh
Holly Road
Windermere
Cumbria LA23 2AQ
Tel: 015394 44444
Fax: 015394 44041

**East Anglia
Tourist Board**
Toppesfield Hall
Hadleigh
Suffolk IP7 5DN
Tel: 01473 822922
Telex: 987447 EATB
Fax: 01473 823063

**East Midlands
Tourist Board**
Exchequergate
Lincoln LN2 1PZ
Tel: 01522 531521
Fax: 01522 532501

**Heart of England
Tourist Board**
Woodside
Larkhill Road
Worcester WR5 2EF
Tel: 01905 763436
Fax: 01905 763450

London Tourist Board
26 Grosvenor Gardens
London SW1W 0DU
Tel: 0171-730 3450
Telex: 919041
Fax: 0171-730 9367

**North West
Tourist Board**
Swan House
Swan Meadow Road
Wigan Pier
Wigan WN3 5BB
Tel: 01942 821222
Fax: 01942 820002

**Northumbria
Tourist Board**
Aykley Heads
Durham DH1 5UX
Tel: 0191-384 6905
Telex: 53281
Fax: 0191-386 0899

**South East England
Tourist Board**
The Old Brew House
Warwick Park
Tunbridge Wells
Kent TN2 5TU
Tel: 01892 540766
Telex: 95523
Fax: 01892 511008

Southern Tourist Board
40 Chamberlayne Road
Eastleigh
Hampshire SO5 5JH
Tel: 01703 620006
Fax: 01703 620010

**West Country
Tourist Board**
60 St. David's Hill
Exeter EX4 4SY
Tel: 01392 76351
Fax: 01392 420891

**Yorkshire & Humberside
Tourist Board**
312 Tadcaster Road
York YO2 2HF
Tel: 01904 707961
Telex: 57715
Fax: 01904 701414

NATIONAL TOURIST BOARDS

**British Tourist
Authority**
Thames Tower
Black's Road
Hammersmith
London
W6 9EL
(written enquiries only)

British Travel Centre
12 Regent Street
Piccadilly Circus
London SW1Y 4PQ
(personal callers only)

English Tourist Board
Thames Tower
Black's Road
Hammersmith
London
W6 9EL
(written enquiries only)

**Edinburgh and Scottish
Travel Centre**
3 Princes Street
Edinburgh EH2 2QP
(personal callers only)

**Guernsey Tourist
Information Centre**
North Esplanade
St. Peter Port
Guernsey GY1 3AN
Tel: 01481 723552
Fax: 01481 714951

**Isle of Man
Dept. of Tourism,
Transport & Leisure**
Sea Terminal Building
Douglas
Isle of Man
Tel: 01624 686801
Fax: 01624 686800

Jersey Tourism
Liberation Square
St. Helier
Jersey JE1 1BB
Channel Islands
Tel: 01534 500700
Fax: 01534 500899

Scottish Tourist Board
23 Ravelston Terrace
Edinburgh EH4 3EU
Tel: 0131-332 2433

Scottish Tourist Board
19 Cockspur Street
London
SW1Y 5BL
Tel: 0171-930 8661
Fax: 0171-930 1817

Wales Tourist Board
Brunel House
2 Fitzalan Road
Cardiff CF2 1UY
Tel: 01222 499909
Fax: 01222 485031

SUMMARY PLANNER
1995

JANUARY
S	1	8	15	22	29
M	2	9	16	23	30
Tu	3	10	17	24	31
W	4	11	18	25	
Th	5	12	19	26	
F	6	13	20	27	
S	7	14	21	28	

FEBRUARY
S		5	12	19	26
M		6	13	20	27
Tu		7	14	21	28
W	1	8	15	22	
Th	2	9	16	23	
F	3	10	17	24	
S	4	11	18	25	

MARCH
S		5	12	19	26
M		6	13	20	27
Tu		7	14	21	28
W	1	8	15	22	29
Th	2	9	16	23	30
F	3	10	17	24	31
S	4	11	18	25	

APRIL
S		2	9	16	23	30
M		3	10	17	24	
Tu		4	11	18	25	
W		5	12	19	26	
Th		6	13	20	27	
F		7	14	21	28	
S	1	8	15	22	29	

MAY
S		7	14	21	28
M	1	8	15	22	29
Tu	2	9	16	23	30
W	3	10	17	24	31
Th	4	11	18	25	
F	5	12	19	26	
S	6	13	20	27	

JUNE
S		4	11	18	25
M		5	12	19	26
Tu		6	13	20	27
W		7	14	21	28
Th	1	8	15	22	29
F	2	9	16	23	30
S	3	10	17	24	

JULY
S		2	9	16	23	30
M		3	10	17	24	31
Tu		4	11	18	25	
W		5	12	19	26	
Th		6	13	20	27	
F		7	14	21	28	
S	1	8	15	22	29	

AUGUST
S		6	13	20	27
M		7	14	21	28
Tu	1	8	15	22	29
W	2	9	16	23	30
Th	3	10	17	24	31
F	4	11	18	25	
S	5	12	19	26	

SEPTEMBER
S		3	10	17	24
M		4	11	18	25
Tu		5	12	19	26
W		6	13	20	27
Th		7	14	21	28
F	1	8	15	22	29
S	2	9	16	23	30

OCTOBER
S	1	8	15	22	29
M	2	9	16	23	30
Tu	3	10	17	24	31
W	4	11	18	25	
Th	5	12	19	26	
F	6	13	20	27	
S	7	14	21	28	

NOVEMBER
S		5	12	19	26
M		6	13	20	27
Tu		7	14	21	28
W	1	8	15	22	29
Th	2	0	16	23	30
F	3	10	17	24	
S	4	11	18	25	

DECEMBER
S		3	10	17	24	31
M		4	11	18	25	
Tu		5	12	19	26	
W		6	13	20	27	
Th		7	14	21	28	
F	1	8	15	22	29	
S	2	9	16	23	30	

New Year – 1 January
Good Friday – 14 April
Easter Monday – 17 April
May Bank Holiday – 8 May

Spring Bank Holiday –29 May
Summer Bank Holiday – 28 August
Christmas Day – 25 December
Boxing Day – 26 December

WIN A FREE PERSONAL CD PLAYER

By completing our simple readers' questionnaire

Thank you for purchasing this copy of **Daltons Directory of British Holidays** and we would very much appreciate your comments on the guide so that we can make any necessary improvements to future editions. In return for your time we will enter your name into our free prize draw. The three lucky winners will each receive a personal CD player.

Any information you give us will be strictly confidential and will only be used by us to help make **Daltons Directory** an even better guide book.

1   How did you hear about **Daltons Directory?**
. . . .

2   Where did you buy it?
. . . .

3   In which month did you buy it?
. . . .

4   How easy was it to find?
. . . .

5   How do you rate it for value?
. . . .

6   How easy is the book to use?
. . . .

7   How likely are you to buy **Daltons Directory** again?
. . . .

8   How likely are you to book holiday accommodation through **Daltons Directory?**
. . . .

9   What area are you likely to choose?
. . . .

10 What type of accommodation are you likely to book?
. . . .

11 Will you be using **Daltons Directory** for your main holiday, short break or both?
. . . .

12 In what ways can **Daltons Directory** be improved? (additional information required etc.)

. . . .

. . . .

13 What other sources have you used to find holiday accommodation?
This year . . . .

. . . .

Previous years . . . .

. . . .

ABOUT YOU

14 Into which age group do you fall?
16-24 ☐   45-54 ☐
25-34 ☐   55-64 ☐
35-44 ☐   65 or over ☐

15 What is your occupation?
Industry . . . .
Profession . . . .
Job Title/Position . . . .

16 If you are not the chief wage earner in the household what is the occupation of the chief wage earner?
Industry . . . .
Profession . . . .
Job Title/Position . . . .

To enter the prize draw please complete the following details:
Name . . . .
Address . . . .

. . . .

. . . .

Tel No. . . . .

And in no more than 10 words please complete the following sentence:
I like **Daltons Directory of British Holidays** because . . . .

. . . .

. . . .

Please cut out page and return to: Daltons Weekly, FREEPOST SW2890, C.I. Tower, St. Georges Square, New Malden, Surrey, KT3 4BR. (No stamp required).

Closing date for entries is April 21st. 1995.

The Publisher's decision is final and no correspondence will be entered into.